Organizational Communication

Behavioral Perspectives

Second Edition

Jerry W. Koehler
University of South Florida, Tampa

Karl W. E. Anatol
California State University, Long Beach

Ronald L. Applbaum
California State University, Long Beach

Holt, Rinehart and Winston
New York   Chicago   San Francisco   Dallas
Montreal   Toronto   London   Sydney

Library of Congress Cataloging in Publication Data

Koehler, Jerry W.
  Organizational communication

  Bibliography: p. 349
  Includes index.
  1. Communication in organizations.   2. Communication in management.   3. Organization.   I. Anatol,
Karl W. E., joint author.   II. Applbaum, Ronald L.,
joint author.   III. Title.
HD30.3.K63   1981   658.4'5   80-18239

ISBN 0-03-049376-5

Preface

To study the behavior of human organizations it is necessary to stress the importance of defining organizational goals. Without clear objectives an institution cannot evaluate how well it is performing, decide how to allocate its resources wisely, plan for future growth, motivate its members, or justify its existence to the larger public.

In preparing to write the second edition of *Organizational Communication: Behavioral Perspectives*, we began by defining our goals. Like the first edition, we wanted a book which would examine the processes of human behavior and communication within the organizational context; one that would reflect the dynamic, all-encompassing role of communication in the operation of organizations. We wanted to provide readers with major theoretical and conceptual issues, assumptions, and positions operating within the organization. Although the book would be basically descriptive in nature, there would be points at which suggestions were made for improving communicative behaviors to produce a more efficient organizational unit. However, the book was not to be designed as a training manual for organizational employees or as a definitive set of prescriptive practices for readers and students.

In preparing this new edition, we were also privileged to have a number of insightful reviewers and editors who proposed constructive suggestions based on the use of the original text. We incorporated their suggestions into the manuscript. Based on their recommendations we increased our use of hypothetical and real examples in order to motivate reader interest and provide concrete bases for the abstract conceptual and theoretical issues that had to be dealt with in order to properly study behavior and communication in the organization. In addition, we developed short case studies for reader analysis after each chapter. Since the terms used in organizational communication are unfamiliar to some readers, we added a glossary at the end of the text. To provide readers with more guidance and structure as they internalized the materials, we posited a set of objectives, review questions, and a list of major terms and concepts in each chapter.

Our reviewers also recommended that we restructure our text to more adequately present the primary function of communication in the operation of all organizations. In response, we have divided the book into four parts.

The first, an introductory/theoretical section, is composed of two chapters. The three remaining parts are organized under the three most crucial elements of the human communication process, message, communicators, and environment, operating in an organization.

Chapter 1 begins with a behavioral definition of communication in organizations. Then we describe the primary variables in a model of human communication. We examine the four functions of communication in organizations and, finally, explore the coordinating role of communication in organizations.

Chapter 2 focuses on five theoretical approaches to the study of organizations—scientific, humanistic, systems, decision-making, and communication. This overview of the different perspectives highlights the contributions of significant researchers and provides the basic assumptions that underlie these approaches.

Chapter 3 discusses the various features that constitute the content and form of messages, both verbal and nonverbal. First, we define communication style and identify six basic styles in organizations. Second, we describe six areas from which nonverbal messages are emitted—proxemics, kinesics, facial expressions, visual interaction, vocalizations, and chronomics. And finally, we explore six message barriers found in organizational environments.

Chapter 4 examines the directional impact of messages in organizations. We explore upward, downward, and horizontal communication. Each direction is discussed by first presenting the message channels utilized, and second, by presenting message problems and appropriate corrective actions.

Chapter 5 presents key elements that have an impact on the effectiveness of messages in organizational environments. First, we deal with feedback and listening. Second, we explore the actual role of the organizational grapevine and rumor in communication. Third, we look at how communication networks affect our messages. And, fourth, we explain the impact of organizational climates upon organizational communication.

Chapter 6 provides a brief overview of six theories of models that are descriptive of management's orientation toward employees. Each theory constitutes a set of assumptions concerning the nature of an individual's behavior under the impress of organizational roles, goals, and expectations. We examine Maslow's Need-Hierarchy Theory, McGregor's Theory X and Theory Y, Herzberg's Motivator-Hygiene Theory, Likert's Participative Management Theory, Blake and Mouton's Managerial Grid Theory, and Fielder's Situational Contingency Theory.

Chapter 7 examines the communicator's personality variables. First, we discuss the nature and general characteristics of personality. Second, we explore the various types of personalities encountered in organizational environments. Third, we deal with the relationship between personality and defense reactions. And, fourth, we discuss the association between personality and occupation.

Chapter 8 investigates the nature and effects of power, status, and roles, and demonstrates the degree of cooperation necessary between individuals for the exercise of these major variables in the organizational system. The relationship of communication to roles, status, and power is also explored.

Chapter 9 deals with leadership effectiveness. First, we explore communication and leadership; the traits of leadership; leader as motivator in the organizational situation; and leadership skills necessary for effective group performance at different levels of management. Second, we investigate a wide range of factors influencing the effectiveness of leaders. We discuss leadership styles, attitudes, and behaviors, and the communication elements influencing leadership. Third, we provide a verbal-pictorial model of leadership effectiveness drawn from our examination of the elements of effective leadership and our knowledge of the organizational setting.

Chapter 10 deals with the impact of group formation on organizational communication. First, we examine the nature of groups and their systematic characteristics. Second, we explore the motives that underlie the formation of groups. Third, we identify the roles that members play or fulfill in the organization. And, fourth, we discuss the key factors that affect group performance.

Chapter 11 explores decision-making processes and strategies in organizations. We begin by focusing upon the decision-making process. Next, we examine seven decision-making models including behavioral, information, problem-identification, normative, and PERT.

Chapter 12 examines conflict and communication in organizational settings. We discuss the various phases through which conflict, the effects of conflict, factors inducing conflict in organizations, and strategies for resolving conflict.

Chapter 13 explains how some organizations deal with their everchanging environment. First, we define and examine the concept of organizational development. Second, we define intervention and discuss a number of intervention strategies, including survey feedback, T Groups, Managerial Grid, Transactional Analysis, Planning and Goal Setting, Organizational Mirroring, and process consultation. We conclude the chapter by identifying externally based programs or personnel for improving communication in organizations.

On the title page of this edition, three authors are given credit for the text. In reality, the publication of a text is the product of the efforts of authors, editors, reviewers, copy editors, researchers, former instructors, teachers, secretaries, friends, and family. While space will not permit us to acknowledge that assistance and encouragement of all, we would like to give special thanks to Roth Wilkofsky and Marjorie Marks of Holt, Rinehart and Winston for their constructive advice and criticism, to Gretchen Icenogle and Bert Potter for their outstanding secretarial services, to David Taugher and Thom Dupper, and, of course our wives—Noreen, Peggy, and Sue.

Tampa, Florida   J. W. K.
Long Beach, California   K. W. E. A.
                                                                  R. L. A.

January 1980

Contents

PART FOUR

The Organizational Environment   249

PART ONE

Communication:
Process and
Behavior
in Organizations

1 | The Role of Communication in Organizations

After reading this chapter, you should be able to
1. Diagram a model of the human communication process.
2. Define the following terms: source, receiver, feedback, messages, ideation, encoding, decoding, and channel.
3. Explain the coordinating role of communication.
4. Identify and explain the four functions of communication in organizations.
5. Explain the behavioral definition of communication.

A clerk in Bloomingdale's feels that his supervisor is mistreating him. He picks up the telephone and talks with the personnel officer who readily listens to his complaints.

Across the continent, in Los Angeles, the Standard Company sponsors meetings between management and workers in the cafeteria. In the informal atmosphere at these meetings both sides are more open to frank discussions.

At a university in Long Beach, California, administrators meet weekly to thrash out topics of particular concern.

In Amarillo, Texas, Bob Jenkins attempts to convince his secretary that a pay raise for her is not justified at this time.

Each month Max Colodzin sends out the *Weight Watchers* magazine to members in the San Francisco Bay area to notify each member of upcoming activities of the organization.

Communication is the prime ingredient of human behavior in each of these examples. The ability to think and transmit ideas through the process of communication provides the binding element of all social interaction. Employees of all organizations—large or small—devote most of their time to communicating (discussing problems, studying or preparing reports, giving or receiving instructions, reading or dictating correspondence, talking or listening on the telephone, interviewing, giving speeches, interacting interpersonally, and observing human behavior). Everybody talks about communication and about the problems that arise from ineffective communication in organizations.

There is, perhaps, no feature in which contemporary and traditional views contrast more sharply than in the assessment of the role and significance of communication in determining organizational behavior, structure, and effectiveness. Early studies of organizations treated communication merely as a tool of management. Today, however, there is a recognition of the dynamic role of communication within the life of an organization.

A survey of industrial research personnel indicated that first-level supervisors spent 74 percent of their time communicating, second-level managers spent 81 percent, and third-level managers spent 87 percent. The survey also showed that two groups of nonmanagement technical employees spent 57 and 60 percent of their time communicating.[1]

A study of over 3,000 employees in a research and development activity indicated that they spent 69 percent of their time communicating, and, a second survey of 120 companies in Iowa noted that workers on the average spend 48 percent of their time on the job in oral communication.[2]

Research has shown that managers have great difficulty with communication in organizations. When asked, "What causes you trouble in your job?", over 80 percent of the managers identified communication.[3] In another study, managers expressed the need for communication training; almost 75 percent wanted training in communication.[4]

A recent computer search of the business/organizational data base by one of the text authors uncovered over 4,000 articles on communication in organizations that were published between 1972 and 1979.

One recurrent theme in recent literature of management and organizations is the need for effective organizational communication. Despite the obvious importance of communication, it remains one of the least understood subjects in organizations, and it is the area needing the most improvement by organizational personnel. Peter Drucker in *The Effective Executive* remarked:

> Communications have been in the center of managerial attention these last twenty years or more. In business, in public administration, in armed services, in hospitals, in all major institutions of modern society, there has been great concern with communications. Results to date have been meager. Communications are by and large just as poor today as they were twenty or thirty years ago when we first became aware of the need for, and lack of adequate communications in modern organizations.[5]

It should be obvious that effective communication is essential in all organizations. Employees, managers, executives, and all organizational communicators need to understand and improve their communicative abilities. According to Ray Killian:

> Large corporations in particular, because of their complex multidivisional setup and the trend toward decentralized operations in recent years, would be helpless without their communication networks for cooperation, coordination, and overall utilization of resources. Such networks may employ computer systems, teletype, telephones, visits, meetings, written messages, and a variety of other means of dispersing information and influence. Efficiency and results, both for individual units and for the organization as a whole, depend on communication.[6]

Because human communication and a knowledge of how communication functions is so important in organizations, we begin our text by examining the basic human communication process.

The Communication Process

Trying to define a concept such as "communication" is a most difficult, if not impossible, task. As Fisher pointed out, "If communication is ubiquitous, it is equally equivocal. Go to any convention of the International Communication Association or the Speech Communication Association—communication specialists all—and trip ten persons in the hall at random. Ask each of them to define his or her specialty, that is, communication. The chances are excellent that you will receive ten differing definitions."[7]

Although a variety of definitions of communication exist depending on the perspective of the definer, we consider two viewpoints here. Colin Cherry focuses on a cognitive perspective: Communication is the use of words, letters, symbols, or similar means to achieve common or shared information about an object or occurrence.[8] Information is something (facts, opinions, ideas) passed from one individual to another by words or other symbols. If the message transmitted is received accurately, the receiver has the same information as the reader and communication has occurred. B. F. Skinner, on the other hand, takes the behavioral perspective: Communication is the verbal or symbolic behavior by which the sender achieves an intended effect on the receiver.[9] Similarly, F. E. X. Dance suggests that communication is "the eliciting of a response through verbal symbols" in which "verbal symbols" act as the stimuli for the elicited response.[10] The last two definitions avoid the question of shared information and focus on a stimulus-response relationship between sender and receiver.

From the perspective of an organization, the behavioral conceptualization of communication appears to be the most practical. Communication in the organization is intended to influence the receiver. A specific response is desired by the source of any message in an organization. When a message has the intended effect, it does not matter whether information is shared or not.

Let us turn our attention to an examination of the basic human communication process. A simple model of this process is presented in Figure 1-1. The communication between two individuals includes several elemental steps and elements, whether they talk, use hand signals, or exchange memorandums.

The process begins with a *source*, the individual or group, attempting to communicate with some other individual or group. The first step by the source is *ideation*, that is, creating an idea or choosing a piece of information to communicate. Ideation provides the basis of a message. The second step in the creation of a message is *encoding*. That is, the source translates the information or idea into words, signs, or symbols which are intended to convey information

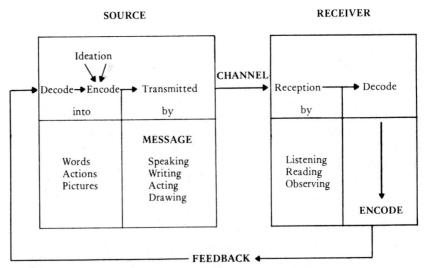

Figure 1-1. Human Communication Model

and have an effect upon the other person. The ideas are organized into a specific series of symbols that the sender feels will communicate to the receiver. The specific symbols selected and their organization will be related to the channels used to communicate the message. An idea presented in a memorandum, for example, is worded differently than in a face-to-face conversation.

The *message* is the means by which the source expresses the ideas. It may be spoken words, written words or symbols, nonverbal behavior such as gestures, facial expressions, pictures, or other forms of communication, limited only by the capabilities of the source.

The third step in the communication process is the transmission of the message as encoded. The source transmits the message to the receivers by speaking, writing, drawing, or acting.

The *channel* is the means by which the message is transmitted. The channels for oral communication include face-to-face communication, radio, telephone, and tapes. Channels for written communication include any material that is written or a medium that can reproduce the written word, such as television, video cassettes, or overhead projector. The source attempts to free the communication channel from interference or barriers, so that the message reaches the receiver as intended. An interviewer, for example, will attempt to remove all distractions during the interview.

In the fourth step, attention is transferred to the receiver who receives the message. If the message is oral, the receiver needs to be a good listener; if receivers do not listen, the message is lost. The receiver takes the message and *decodes* it. Decoding means the interpretation of the message by the receiver. The receiver must go through the process of translating the message into some form that he or she can understand. Understanding is the key to decoding. If the source transmits an idea that a change in job performance must occur, but the receiver does not perceive the request for change, then the communication is ineffective. Although some receivers may not want to understand the message, receivers normally attempt to understand the intended message. Generally, a realistic goal in communication situations is that understanding is close enough to the intended meaning that the response is as intended. Understanding occurs only in the receiver's mind. The receiver and not the source determines what to receive and understand and how to respond.

The encoding-decoding sequence is somewhat like moving a stereo system from one home to another. The source has an idea and encodes (disassembles the components) it into a series of words, each of which is marked by its location in the message to guide the receiver. In order to move the system to a new home (transmit it), the sender takes apart the ideas by putting it into words. The reassembly of the stereo system is similar to the receiver who takes the words (components) and mentally reconstructs them into ideas (complete stereo system).

The last step in the communication process is *feedback*, which enables the source to learn if the receiver has received and responded as desired to the message. The receiver's response or feedback to a source's message may be in the form of words, actions, or pictures. The receiver may ignore the message, perform an assigned task, or store the information. It is feedback that provides the basis for individuals to evaluate the effectiveness of their communication.

In adopting a behavioral perspective regarding organizational communication, we now turn to an examination of the functions served by communication in organizations.

Functions of Communication in Organizations

If we are to observe different organizations—a manufacturing company, school, hotel, or hospital—we would notice that communication serves four major functions: (1) informative, (2) regulative, (3) persuasive, and (4) integrative.[11]

The Informative Function

Employees in an organization require an enormous amount of information to operate effectively and efficiently. Managers need accurate, timely, and well-organized information to reach decisions or to resolve conflicts. Without a constant flow of information, managers must make decisions whose success may be more the result of chance than of anything else and conflicts may be exacerbated between personnel.

Organizations can be viewed as information-processing systems. All members of the organization are anxious to obtain more, better, and timely information; information enabling each employee to carry out his or her job. A college administrator, for example, must make decisions concerning which courses are to be offered in a particular semester based on information from the total academic environment, such as enrollment trends, student requests, course costs, and instructor qualifications. Workers also require information to do their jobs. As each worker is provided with information about his or her job performance, the employee sets new goals and develops the proper behaviors to achieve those goals.

Although the quality of job performance is dependent upon job-related information, many employees desire information that has very little to do with their work. Employees are concerned with the profits of their organization, the work standards of other employees, and security benefits such as retirement plans.

Employees also seek information that has no direct relationship to either their job or to organizational success. One frequently observes employees expressing a desire to know about the personal problems of fellow workers or about the conduct of an employee at a company picnic.

Most organizations also have regular meetings of managers to report the actions in each area of the total organization. Although the primary function of these meetings is informative, problems are shared and methods for developing and implementing solutions are adopted.

A survey of 219 banking personnel executives listed in order the kinds of information that are communicated most frequently in their organizations. Company news and future prospects are ranked first. This included company goals and achievements, business progress, new facilities, organizational changes, and future business and employee outlook. Next on the list was employee compensation, benefits, and services. This category includes changes in benefit programs, wage and salary changes, reports of profit-sharing results, holiday and vacation schedules, tax information, and information on community medical services. Other kinds of information mentioned by the survey respondents included company rules, policies, and programs, including working conditions and safety, absenteeism, equal employment opportunity programs, policy clarifications, promotions, and opportunities for training and advancement including changes, position openings, education programs, and social and other items.[12]

The Regulative Function

The operation of any organization is predicated upon its managers' ability to control and coordinate the activities of the organization. Manuals, policies, memos, and instructions comprise a set of guidelines for running the organization. In all organizations, two elements impact upon the regulative function. First, management controls the information transmitted. The manager sends orders downward to employees. The orders place the communicator in a position of authority with an expectation of compliance. However, the employees' acceptance of that order will depend upon (1) acceptance of the legitimacy of the source to send the communication, (2) power of the source to enforce sanctions, (3) perceived competence of the source relative to the issue communicated, (4) trust in the source as a leader and person, (5) perceived credibility of the message received, and (6) acceptance of the tasks and goals that the communication is trying to accomplish.[13] Second, regulative messages are basically work-oriented, concentrating on tasks that are necessary to accomplish a particular job. Employees need to know what is expected of them and what restrictions are placed on their behavior.

The Persuasive Function

In regulating the organization, managers quickly discover that power and authority will not always result in the desired control. Managers must often regulate through persuasion, which is used at all levels in the organization— such as the employee's requesting a raise from the boss or the manager's getting an employee to do tasks beyond his or her job description. Many superiors prefer to persuade a subordinate rather than issue orders. Successful managers realize that voluntary compliance by employees provides greater commitment than commands or appeals to authority.

The Integrative Function

Integrative communication functions are those that operate to give the organization unity and cohesion—defining objectives and tasks for the purpose of facilitating the entry and smooth absorption of appropriate participants; coordinating the activities and schedules of various individuals and departments; eliminating redundancy and wasted effort. Integrative processes serve to draw the organization's boundaries, taking in those individuals and activities that contribute to its objectives and excluding those that do not. The design of organizational structure—the provisions for channeling information and authority, power allotment, and the assignment of responsibility—represent an integrative function. The personnel function, at least in its recruitment and training aspects, accomplishes an integrative purpose. The principal thrust of integrative communication is in the direction of identity and uniformity.

Organizations attempt to provide the means by which employees will identify with the workings of the organization. Formal channels including newsletters, films, visits by top management, and yearly progress reports are developed to keep the employee informed. Integration comes from the type of information a person gets about the job. The best-integrated employees are those who are told what goals and objectives are, how their jobs fit into a total picture, and the progress they are making on the job. Developing upward channels of communication provides workers with a greater sense of participation in the organization. Suggestion systems, attitude surveys, and work conferences are often designed in terms of their integrative function. Integration also occurs through informal communication in the organization—conversations during coffee breaks, company picnics, athletic teams, and informal reports of personal achievements.

These four functions are not mutually exclusive, since any act of communication can fulfill several functions. For example, a foreman, John, wants to increase the output of an employee on the line. John might begin his conversation in the following manner:

"Bob, you must increase your productivity. It'll benefit us all."

Bob responds, "Why should I work any harder?"

John asks Bob to sit beside him at his desk, "Look, the company has got to increase the production to lower product costs. It's estimated that lowered costs will increase profits almost ten percent."

Bob reflects on John's comments and questions, "Does this mean increased salaries next year?"

"Yes."

In this situation, John has used his act of communication to fulfill three functions: informative (increased production leads to lower costs and higher company profits), regulative (Bob, you must increase your production), and persuasive (the foreman provides motivation for a behavior change by stating that the employee will be rewarded through an increase in pay).

Having examined the four major functions that communication serves in any organization, we now turn to the coordinating role of communication in organizations.

The Coordinating Role of Communication

Human activity is always directed toward the achievement of objectives. The object of a particular act may not be entirely clear at all times to all observers—or even to the actors—but it is difficult to conceive of any conscious action that is not aimed at producing some change.

Organizations exist because some objectives can be achieved only—or, at least, more efficiently—through the coordinated activity of two or more individuals. In fact, an *organization* may be defined as a *structured system of relationships that coordinates the efforts of a group of people toward the achievement of specific objectives*. Coordinating the actions of two or more individuals toward the achievement of a common goal is a problem for any organizational unit. It is only with the effective use of communication that coordination can be achieved.

As soon as an organized effort is proposed, it becomes necessary to communicate certain basic information in order to assemble the required participants. The organizational objectives must be defined and the role each individual will be expected to play, including the allotment of power and reward, must be described.

Once the enterprise is launched, the necessity for continuous multilevel and multidirectional communication becomes increasingly urgent. Information must be transferred regularly, accurately, and effectively from one individual and/or one department to another. Ideas have to be compared, conclusions reached, activities harmonized, and adjustments made to integrate all the individual activities into a working accord.

At the same time, the organization is in more or less continuous interaction with the society in which it exists. It interfaces with this external environment through an elaborate system of human and nonhuman intermediaries—products, documents, customers, vendors, directors, stockholders, representatives, competitors, the media, government agencies—which results in the exchange of information that enables the organization and its environment to respond to one another.

The internal and external processes by which all of the organization's informing, adjusting, and coordinating activities take place form a dense network of signals and responses, actions and reactions, effects and countereffects, which often operate to trigger, cancel, or reinforce each other in unpredictable chains and clusters.

The operation of this network varies from organization to organization. It is influenced by the structure and objectives of the organization, and by the philosophy and communication style of its management as well as its decision-making processes, motivating devices, and evaluation methods. It responds to the pressures and demands of the external environment. It is affected by the presence of each of its participants.

All of these influences come together to form the communication environment of the organization. Together with the physical setting in a particular office or area and the personalities and relationships of the participants, they strongly affect the climate in which communication takes place and the behavior of those taking part.

The relationship between communication and human behavior is a reciprocal one: each influences and is influenced by the other. An open communication environment encourages frank and open behavior; reticent and secretive behavior quickly taints the environment. The relationship between communication and behavior is, in fact, so close that it is impossible to study one without studying the other. Behavior is perhaps the most revealing mode of communication, and the individual who wishes to cut off communication entirely must first accomplish the impossible task of cutting off all behavior.

Communication is the mortar that holds our organizational structure together. It provides the basis for coordinating the relationship between individuals to reach the ultimate organizational objectives.

REVIEW QUESTIONS

1. What are the basic elements of the human communication process?
2. What are the functions served by communication in organizations?
3. What is the coordinating role of communication in organizations?
4. What is the behavioral perspective to organizational communication?

KEY TERMS AND CONCEPTS FOR REVIEW

- Organizational Communication
- Integrative Function
- Regulative Function
- Informative Function
- Persuasive Function
- Feedback
- Channel

- Source
- Receiver
- Message
- Encoding
- Decoding
- Ideation
- Behavioral Perspective

CASE STUDY

Pegasus Solar Corporation is a small solar conversion company in California. Its revenue is derived from converting heating systems for swimming pools from gas or electrical energy to solar heating. The company employs 200 persons. The ten managers hold bimonthly meetings.

At the managers' first meeting in November, the only item on the agenda involved the high turnover among its employees. George

Fredericks, the field manager and part owner of the company, called for reports on the number of employee turnovers during the past year. Each manager then provided his reasons for the turnover rate.

George Fredericks informed all the managers that the overall employee turnover rate must be reduced by 50 percent. In addition, each manager was responsible for some level of reduction. The managers shrugged their shoulders. Charles Bates, the supply manager, responded that the seasonal nature of the company's work made any significant reduction in employee turnover difficult. Furthermore, Bates noted that company profits were up 10 percent and that the time invested in reducing employee turnover would not be cost effective.

George Fredericks frowned and directed his response to the entire group. "Gentlemen, the turnover rate has tripled our unemployment obligations, which is actually reducing profits by 10 percent. Since each of you has been with us since the beginning, I know you all want to see the firm become even more healthy fiscally."

PROBES

1. Can you identify the elements of the communication process operating in the manager's meeting?
2. What functions of communication are illustrated in this meeting?

Recommended Readings

Dance, F. E. X. "The Concept of Communication." *Journal of Communication* 20 (1970):201–210.

DeVito, J. A. *Communicology: An Introduction to the Study of Communication.* New York: Harper & Row, 1978, Chapter 1.

Downs, C., W. Linkugel, and D. M. Berg. *The Organizational Communicator.* New York: Harper & Row, 1977, Chapter 2.

Fisher, B. A. *Perspectives on Human Communication.* New York: Macmillan Publishing Co., 1978, Chapter 1.

Swanson, D. L., and J. G. Delia. *The Nature of Human Communication.* Palo Alto, Calif.: SRA, 1976.

Thayer, L. *Communication and Communication Systems.* Homewood, Ill.: Richard D. Irwin, 1967, pp. 187–252.

Notes

1. J. R. Hinrichs, "Communication Activity of Industrial Research Personnel," *Personnel Psychology* 17 (1964): 199.
2. E. T. Klemmer and F. W. Snyder, "Measurement of Time Spent Communicating," *The Journal of Communication* 22 (1972): 142–158; D. Stine and D. Skarzensky,

"Priorities for the Business Communication Classroom: A Survey of Business and Academe," *The Journal of Business Communication* 16 (1979): 25.

3. H. L. Cox, "Opinions of Selected Business Managers About Some Aspects of Communication on the Job," *Journal of Business Communication* 5(1968): 7.

4. G. G. Alexander, "Planning Management Training Programs for Organizational Development," *Personnel Journal* 27(1964): 21.

5. P. F. Drucker, *The Effective Executive* (New York: Harper & Row, 1967), p. 65.

6. R. Killian, *Managing by Design . . . for Executive Effectiveness*, New York: American Management Association, 1968, p. 255.

7. B. A. Fisher, *Perspectives on Human Communication* (New York: Macmillan Publishing Co., 1978), p. 7.

8. C. Cherry, *On Human Communication* (New York: Macmillan Publishing Co., 1978), pp. 2–16, 217–255.

9. B. F. Skinner, *About Behaviorism* (New York: Alfred A. Knopf, 1974), Chapter 7.

10. F. E. X. Dance, "Toward a Theory of Human Communication," in F. E. X. Dance, ed., *Human Communication Theory* (New York: Holt, Rinehart and Winston, 1967), pp. 289–309.

11. L. Thayer, *Communication and Communication Systems* (Homewood, Ill.: Richard D. Irwin, 1967), pp. 187–252.

12. "How Do Your Communications Rate?" *Banking* 68 (1975): 8.

13. K. Davis, *Human Behavior at Work*, 5th ed. (New York: McGraw-Hill Book Company, 1977), p. 399.

Organizational Approaches to Understanding Communication in Organizations

LEARNING OBJECTIVES

After reading this chapter, you should be able to

1. Explain the theory of scientific management according to Taylor, Fayol, and Weber.
2. Explain the theory of humanistic management according to Mayo, McGregor, Likert, and Argyris.
3. Explain the systems approach to understanding communication in organizations.
4. Explain the decision-making approach to understanding communication in organizations.
5. Explain the communication approach to understanding communication in organizations.
6. Define the following terms: organization, "economic man," unity of command, authority, rabble hypothesis, Theory X-Theory Y, open and closed systems, adaptive-rational organization, programmed and nonprogrammed decisions.
7. Compare and contrast each of the five management approaches reported, and discuss their effects on the communication system in the organization.

Production organizations are commonly born in the perception of an unfilled need. For example, let us assume that there is a need for a more efficient, comfortable office chair. This need is perceived by an individual who has the initiative to act and the ability to design and build such a product. He or she assembles tools and materials, clears a space in the garage, and builds a demonstration model. One of the people to whom the model is exhibited is sufficiently impressed to buy it at a price that returns a satisfactory profit to the builder. Someone else notices the model in the first customer's office and places an order for one like it. In this manner the new chair gradually attracts wider attention until the builder has more orders than can be filled with the time and resources available. A partner is thus brought into the operation to provide both the additional capital and working skills required to raise production to the level needed to meet the existing demand. The partners work side by side, discussing and resolving business problems as they arise.

Their success is such that they decide to hire a helper. Eventually they take on another, then a third and a fourth. As the operation outgrows the garage, they lease a building with enough room for present production and future expansion. They consult an attorney on tax and legal problems arising from their growing business and are advised that it would be to their advantage to incorporate.

Incorporation requires a formal roster of officers, a definition of the company's purpose, and a description of its operation. Inexorably, the owners are drawn into the process of transforming a loosely structured operation into a formal setting for conducting business—an organization.

Organization was defined in Chapter 1 as a structured system of relationships that coordinates the efforts of a group of human beings for a specific objective. Many definitions of this term exist, testifying to the extraordinary difficulty encountered in pinning down the essence of the real functioning entity designated by the word "organization." For example, March and Simon[1] state "it is easier, and probably more useful, to give examples of formal organizations than to define the term."

Over the past two centuries social scientists and other observers of the social scene have produced many theories to account for the workings of organizations. Through the years these theories have grown in subtlety and sophistication along with their subject matter. But—as semanticists remind us—the map is not the territory, and none of the theoretical constructs has been sufficiently comprehensive to displace all others as *the* definitive universal model of the complex of interacting relationships that goes under the name of "organization."

The following sections examine the basic approaches that have been developed to explain the operation of human organizations.

The Scientific Approach

The founder of our chair firm assembled the tools and materials and personally designed, cut, shaped, assembled, finished, inspected, displayed, sold, and delivered the product. The partner did the same, although there might just as easily have been an agreement that one would handle "production" and the other would handle the "business" details.

When the partners begin to take on employees, however, they encounter an entirely new situation. Even if applicants with the required breadth of skills were available, it would probably not be practical from an economic standpoint to hire a work crew whose members are all competent to perform the full sequence of operations required to produce and market a finished product. Nor is it efficient to follow such a course in most manufacturing processes.

In the early stages of the organization, the partners might find it practical to assign one employee to assemble chair backs, another seats, another undercarriages, another the completed chair, and so on. As the work force continues to grow, the tendency to simplify will increase. Where one employee had been responsible for cutting, assembling, and finishing a subassembly, this assignment might be narrowed to the cutting of a single part, with half a dozen other employees assigned to the remaining operations required to produce the subassembly.

Our company will now exhibit the characteristics of the earliest stages in the industrial revolution, which was a revolution in productive relationships. The enormous significance of the *division of labor* in improving efficiency was first pointed out by economist Adam Smith in 1776.[2] The impact of that simple, logical development—not only on productivity but on ever-widening circles of human activity and thought—is yet to be measured. In this century, the phenomenon recorded by Adam Smith became the cornerstone of the first and most comprehensive effort to explain why organizations work the way they do and how they can be made to work more efficiently.

The basic theory that came to be known as *scientific management* was propounded by a remarkable trio of contemporaries—Henri Fayol, a Frenchman, Max Weber, a German, and Frederick Winslow Taylor, an American—whose lives spanned the period stretching from the middle of the nineteenth century to World War I.

Frederick Taylor

Frederick Taylor[3] founded and popularized the scientific management movement along with many of the techniques, such as time-and-motion study, with which scientific management has come to be identified.

Taylor's organization is built on the hypothetical "economic man," who is motivated and controlled by fear of hunger and desire for gain. Thus Taylor saw no reason to look beyond the pursuit of "maximum prosperity" for employer and employee alike in defining the ultimate objective of management. Success in this regard, he believed, could be achieved by applying scientific principles to the processes of production and management. Translated into practice, this consisted primarily of a systematic program of objective observations and adjustments designed to expose and correct inefficient operations. His famous study of "the science of shoveling" at a Bethlehem Steel Company machine shop around the turn of the century provides an impressive example of the method in action.

In the 1890s it was customary for each shoveler to provide his own tool, a practice that produced a bewildering range of performance on a job. In the Bethlehem yard the same shovel would be used to move both pea coal and iron ore, despite the fact that one averaged about three and a half pounds and the other thirty-eight pounds per lift.

Working with a select group of top shovel hands, Taylor determined that maximum efficiency in moving either material was achieved when the shovel-load weighed approximately twenty-one pounds. The total tonnage moved in a day's time dropped off significantly when a shovel was used that carried much more or less than that amount.

Accordingly, Taylor arranged for each shoveler to be issued a standard shovel with a capacity of twenty-one pounds. Each worker, in addition, was given instructions in the shoveling technique observed to be the most productive and least fatiguing. Pay incentives also were provided for superior performance.

The results were sensational. The average volume of material moved per day soared from sixteen to fifty-nine tons. Handling costs plummeted from 7.3 cents to 3.2 cents per ton (even after deducting the total cost of the experiment and incentive pay that boosted the average shovel pay from $1.15 to $1.88 per day). Bethlehem was able to reduce its yard crew from more than 400 to 140 employees.[4]

Thus, the results of "scientific shoveling" dramatically validated Taylor's time-and-motion theory, but they invalidated equally dramatically his contention that workers were misguided when they suspected increased production would lead to unemployment.

The general flavor of Taylor's work was to develop a true science of work; to use science in selecting and training and to gain cooperation between workers and management.

By "a true science of work," Taylor meant the establishment of an objective foundation for defining "a fair day's work." He proposed that for any job this standard should be set at the level of performance of a first-class operator working under ideal conditions, and that it should command a correspondingly high rate of pay.

Taylor assumed that every worker has the capacity for first-class performance at some task. He saw it as management's responsibility to select and train workers to do their "highest, most interesting, and most profitable" work—that is, to bring together the science of work and the selected workers. Through this process, he envisioned the elimination of strife through a close, mutually beneficial cooperation of management and labor.[5]

This faith in mutual labor-management interest in low labor costs and high productivity as the key to higher profits and higher wages is consistent with Taylor's belief that the hypothetical "economic man" is an accurate reflection of human reality. The theoretical acquisitor driven by fear of hunger and hope of material reward was a good deal less simplistic in Taylor's day than in our own. Accordingly, Taylor's incentive programs were designed to establish the closest possible correspondence between pay and performance. He regarded piecework as the ideal means of tying wages directly to productivity.

Henri Fayol

Henri Fayol[6] is generally credited with the earliest significant attempt to deduce the general laws of management, and the five components and fourteen principles of management he defined are still valuable to organizational analysis.

According to Fayol, management's five essential functions are planning, organizing, commanding, coordinating, and controlling. Besides the division of labor and its corollary, specialization, his fourteen principles included: unit of command and of direction, remuneration, order, equity, stability of tenure, initiative, hierarchy, and *esprit de corps*.

Although Fayol and Taylor tended to share the engineer's mechanistic view of humanity, their contributions to the scientific approach to formal organization were quite different. Fayol sought to define universal principles applicable to all management situations; Taylor created tools and methods for solving operating problems. Both men recognized the crucial significance of the division of labor, but Fayol's treatment of the subject remained essentially general and descriptive, while Taylor offered detailed prescriptions for maximizing task-division and specialization. Taylor was shop-oriented, and his concept of higher management lacked the insight that years of upper-echelon experience had provided Fayol.

Theoretically, both Fayol and Taylor recognized that division of labor demands a corresponding unification at the management level—that is, the greater the number of divisions of a particular task, the greater the necessity for a single controlling authority with a clear picture of the total operation. Nevertheless, Taylor proposed a "functional" system of control rather than a "military" chain-of-command hierarchy, without detailing how such a system could be made to work in upper management levels. Fayol criticized this proposal as a weakness in Taylor's approach and reemphasized the necessity for "unity of command" with clear lines of authority, preferably with each employee being responsible to only one superior.

According to the classical principles of scientific management, our hypothetical office-chair organization would be structured by one consideration— creating maximum material reward for company and worker by using rational methods to achieve the highest possible production at the lowest level.

Following Fayol, the task accepted by managmeent would consist of five elements: (1) *planning*—assessing market, economy, labor, materials, and other factors in order to devise a strategy for achieving company goals; (2) *organizing*—bringing together the equipment, workers, and materials required to achieve company objectives; (3) *commanding*—maintaining the goal-oriented activity of the company; (4) *coordinating*—unifying the organizational effort; and (5) *controlling*—maintaining compliance with established rules, plans, and commands.

The organization's structure would be contrived to preserve unity of command—classically, as a hierarchical pyramid, with a single executive or board at its peak, and the production workers at its base. Thus, in our model organization, the peak of authority would be occupied by the original partners (the founder, perhaps, formally designated president, and the partner vice-president) and the bottom tier by employees who performed tasks that physically convert raw materials into finished products—office chairs, in this case.

Between the two extremes, authority would be delegated to one or more levels of middle management. This sector would be required to carry out the basic organizational functions defined by Fayol as: *technical* (design, engineering, manufacture), *commercial* (buying and selling), *financial* (obtaining and using capital), *security* (protection of personnel and property), *accounting* (inventory, costs, income, records), and *managerial* (planning, organizing, commanding, coordinating, controlling). Like the workers, these employees would be selected, trained, and advanced according to procedures designed to (a) fill each position with the most competent person available and (b) reward and encourage the highest possible performance in the service of organizational goals.

Still following Fayol,[7] the principle of specialization would be applied rigorously at every level. The effect upon management would be the emergence of three specialized relationships known as "line," "functional," and "staff" positions. *Line* consists of the direct chain-of-command posts in authority from peak to base of the pyramid. *Functional* refers to the specialized positions (such as accounting) outside the direct chain of command. *Staff* refers to the agents of the line or functional authority to which they are attached.

No matter how complicated the organizational relations, however, a scientific management bureaucracy would reflect the principles of (1) *authority* (a clear, recognized line from the top of the pyramid to each individual in the hierarchy); (2) *unity* (each individual taking orders from and being responsible to one authority only); (3) *definition* (all duties, responsibilities, and relationships being defined and published); (4) *correspondence* (authority consistent with responsibility); and (5) optimum *span of control* (specialization and subdivision of a particular responsibility held to a specific number of subordinates, usually five or six, which one manager can supervise directly).

Max Weber

The third major contributor to the concept of scientific management is the German social philosopher Max Weber.[8] He created the first fully articulated theory of authority structure in formal organizations.

Why, Weber asked, do people voluntarily obey orders? From the outset he eliminated considerations of *power*, which he defined as the ability to compel obedience by force, and concentrated on *authority*, to which he felt the response was voluntary.

Under what circumstances, then, do people obey orders when they are not compelled to do so? People will respond to authority, Weber concluded, when they are convinced that the person exercising it has the "right" to do so.

How is the right to exercise authority validated or "legitimized?" Weber isolated three basic legitimizing methods, each associated with its own distinctive organizational structure. His analysis of the characteristics of these authority modes contributed to significant new insights into the nature of organizations—along with two durable concepts, "charisma" and "bureaucracy."

Charismatic authority, according to Weber, is legitimized by the personality of the individual exercising it. The charismatic individual is obeyed because of some extraordinary personal quality that carries a conviction of the right to give orders. This means that charismatic authority tends to be a one-generation phenomenon. When the charismatic leader dies or steps down, the organization crumbles unless a satisfactory method of legitimizing the authority of a replacement can be devised. If no new charismatic figure arises, which frequently happens, the organization will become traditional or bureaucratic in form, depending on the provisions it adopts for validating authority.

Traditional authority is derived through and sanctioned by custom. Succession to traditional authority can be legitimized in a variety of ways, depending on the custom that is in force. The right to govern may pass, for example, from parent to offspring, or to a successor designated by the leader, or by authorized representatives of the organization.

Bureaucratic authority is legitimized by "rational-legal" means—that is, by established rules and regulations. Weber viewed bureaucracy as a model of efficiency when compared to other forms of organization. Among its superior features he noted precision, speed, unambiguity, continuity, discretion, unity, and strict subordination. He considered reduction of friction, material, and personal costs by-products of these features.

Weber praised bureaucracy for exactly those qualities that distinguish it from charismatic and traditional organizations—its impersonality and its freedom from the dictates of outmoded tradition. Its authority is legitimized by compliance with regulations that ideally are designed to select the most effective leadership; its structure and procedures can be shaped to satisfy the requirements of their intended function rather than the whim of an individual or blind dictate of custom. Bureaucratic authority is respected because its legitimacy comes from the qualities that best equip it to accomplish the organization's purpose. This is what Weber meant when he called bureaucracy a "rational-legal" structure. It is rational because there is a functional relationship between its purpose and its form. It is legal because it is governed by rules that are consistent with its operation.

Scientific Management[9]

The image that emerges from the analyses of Weber, Taylor, and Fayol is admirably functional. It has a clearly defined purpose, and its form, procedures, and personnel are objectively selected to accomplish its purpose. The operations necessary to this accomplishment are broken down into simple tasks and equitably distributed among the personnel according to a system designed to take optimum advantage of their abilities and skills. Each employee is selected and trained, each task evaluated and adjusted for maximum efficiency. Those perennial wellsprings of conflict—productivity and pay rates—are arbitrated by ergonomic science and efficiency engineering.

The exercise of authority is neither a hereditary privilege nor a reward for popularity. Like any other responsibility, it is assigned in the manner that promises the greatest probable contribution to achieving organizational goals. Authority is, in fact, invested in organizational positions or offices, not in persons. No individual occupies an office by right, but by demonstrated ability to carry out the responsibilities of the office more effectively than anyone else available.

All positions and procedures in the model bureaucracy are governed by regulations designed to promote its objectives while preserving unity of control and directions over its efficiently divided operations. From top to bottom, positions are pyramided in an orderly hierarchy so that each position has authority that is superior to all positions below it and superior to those above it. Lines of authority and responsibility are clearly defined to provide each position with one—and only one—authority to which it is responsible. The ultimate governing authority is neither personal nor religious, but functional, and it is expressed in the requirements for achieving the organization's purpose.

In circumstances such as these, much obviously depends on the success of the organization in motivating its employees. For the "economic man" of the scientific management theory, this entails the development of devices for harnessing the employee's drive for material gain to the production process. Through the years, Taylor and the human engineers who followed his lead created an enormous variety of ingenious stratagems for this purpose, most of them based on his perception that piecework provides the most straightforward linkage between production and reward. Therefore, the "standard rate" of production for each operation—establishing, as it theoretically did, the human limit of performance for the average skilled worker under optimum conditions—is a key factor both in production and in pay rates.

Refinements of the basic incentive scheme are almost endless: individual and team competition plans, quota charts and boards, prizes, bonuses, and so on. The simple, direct system employed by Taylor at Bethlehem might well serve as an example for our model firm. Management's preparation for each "fair day's work" involved a detailed review of the previous day's individual performances. At the beginning of each shift, workers received a color-coded slip of paper reporting their production and earnings for the previous shift. "Yellow-slipped" employees would automatically be transferred or discharged if they failed to increase their production level.

Scientific management had two powerful factors in its favor: It provided the only comprehensive system of organization theory; and it offered solutions to management problems that had every appearance of being measurably and verifiably effective. However, one of these tenets—that the key to productivity is an economically motivated employee working under conditions scientifically designed for maximum efficiency—was empirically invalidated in a series of studies conducted between 1927 and 1932 at Western Electric Company's Hawthorne Works.[10]

The *Hawthorne Studies*, as they came to be called, were not designed to disprove Taylor's theory. On the contrary, they were initiated on the assumption that observation of the Hawthorne operations would scientifically establish the best working conditions for maximum productivity over a whole spectrum of tasks. One of the most celebrated of the studies was designed to pinpoint the level of illumination that resulted in maximum production. They compared the output of two groups of workers. One group was in a control room with customary lighting; the other was in a test room in which the light could be dimmed or brightened. The researchers discovered that productivity went up no matter what they did. When the two groups began work under the new conditions, output increased—in both rooms. Output continued to go up in the test room when the illumination level was increased and when it was decreased. Only when the room was made so dark that the workers could not see what they were doing was there a break in the increase of productivity.

Similar results marked experiments designed to establish an optimum schedule for rest breaks. Productivity went up with the introduction of a five-minute break. It continued upward with ten-minute breaks, with fifteen-minute breaks, with combinations of breaks of various lengths, and with the abolition of breaks altogether.

The researchers were forced to conclude that workers were not responding to illumination levels or rest periods but to nonmaterial incentives Taylor would have discounted—the amount of attention they were getting, the freedom to set their own pace conferred by their status as test subjects, and the excellent communications developed between the workers and the researchers, who had become "management" during the study.

Even more far-reaching were the findings of the study of "artificial restriction of output" in the "Bank Wiring Room" study. In this experiment the physical layout, tools, equipment, work methods, and incentive pay plan were scientifically designed to encourage maximum individual and group output by fourteen wiring room employees. The measures, which were already in effect when the study began, had improved productivity, but to a far smaller degree than had been expected. The study, which was undertaken to find out why, made a shambles of virtually every scientific management assumption about human motivation.

What the study revealed was that there was another force at work in the group—a force that paralleled and severely curtailed the formal authority of management in every area of work regulation. Where it did not actually countermand company authority, it limited and diminished the effect of formal orders and regulations in accordance with some mysterious system of its own.

This shadow force was the authority of the work crew itself. It arose somehow out of the interaction of the workers by a kind of unspoken consensus and was highly effective in establishing and policing its own regulations. Among other things, it rigidly enforced a production norm that had nothing to do with either the group's true ability or the company's quotas but was based on the group's concept of a fair day's work. This meant an output above the "chiseling" (too low) level but below a "rate-busting" (too high) level.

Confirmed and expanded by numerous subsequent investigations, the

Hawthorne studies served to call into question the basic tenets of scientific management and to encourage the development of alternate theories with broader application to observable facts.

Among the most significant of the new conclusions were the following:

1. Material incentives are far less effective than originally supposed, and nonmaterial values such as the acceptance and respect of peers may have equal or greater influence over the actions of individuals.
2. The group to which an individual belongs exercises an informal authority that affects individual actions, often to the apparent disadvantage of the individual.
3. Determining the amount of work an individual is physically capable of doing is usually less significant in predicting actual output than determining the amount of work the group believes is proper.
4. Learning to communicate and deal with the informal authority of the group may be of equal or greater importance to the formal authority of management than learning to communicate and deal with individuals.

Having been successfully challenged by the Hawthorne study conclusions,[11] the postulates of scientific management came under increasingly broad attack. Like many systems of thought rooted in the nineteenth century, the theory incorporated a great many philosophical and "common sense" assumptions. Not all of them were subject to verification, and many reflected organizational conditions as they should have been rather than as they were.

Critics questioned, for example, whether "a fair day's pay" could be scientifically established in the same way "a fair day's work" was determined— and whether management would accept the results if it could be so established. It was argued that for scientific management to be effective the organization would have to operate as though it existed in a vacuum, thoroughly insulated from such outside influences as the fluctuations of the market and of the general economy.

But it was the theory's assumptions about human nature that drew the sharpest and most sustained fire. The supposition that human motivation, except under conditions of extreme privation, is exclusively or even predominantly economic was assailed as a gross caricature. The narrowness of this key concept, it was suggested, led its proponents into a whole thicket of related errors, such as its neglect of the motivating power of social[12] and emotional factors, and its failure to deal with the critical role of communication in determining the organization's real ability to plan, direct, and monitor its own activities.

As an intellectual product of the industrial revolution, scientific management was dominated by the image of the machine. Its literature is filled with machine analogies, with the ideal formal organization typically and approvingly described as a well-oiled, unemotional, automatic mechanism chugging steadily toward its objectives.

As new data systematically reduced the status of the tenets of scientific management from that of governing principles to that of contributing factors in management, the importance of social and emotional factors in human motivation and behavior was reemphasized. It was therefore virtually inevitable that the influence of the "human factor" in organizations would become the next subject for intensified observation and analysis and new theoretical speculation.

The Humanistic Approach

The early organizational theorists were concerned primarily with the nonhuman elements of the organization. They seldom discussed communication, and they regarded organizations as closed and static systems, with work efficiency as their primary objective. Referring to these orientations, L. W. Porter and K. H. Roberts put it this way: "Downward (communication) would be emphasized, as would the use of communication systems for authority, coordination, and control."[13] The early theories never did adequately explain how and why individuals in the organization functioned as they did; it is, therefore, not surprising that the next wave of organizational theory was primarily concerned with the human elements. Among the later theorists were Elton Mayo,[14] Douglas McGregor,[15] Rensis Likert[16] and Chris Argyris.[17] Their work focused on human relations, interpersonal communication, and informal communication systems.

Elton Mayo

It is altogether fitting that the father of the "humanist" approach should turn out to be Harvard professor Elton Mayo, for it was he who had devised the Hawthorne studies that first challenged the basic tenets of Frederick Taylor and scientific management.[18] Mayo, who is also credited with pioneering the field of industrial psychology, used the term *human relations* to describe his organizational theory.

The humanist approach was in many ways the antithesis of scientific management, stressing forces and influences at work in the organization that the earlier theorists considered inconsequential. Scientific management viewed human behavior from the perspective of what Mayo termed the *rabble hypothesis*—the supposition that *each individual pursues self-interest to the exclusion of all other motivation.* Mayo countered this hypothesis by pointing to the existence of the "informal organization" demonstrated in the Bank Wiring Room study. Its existence, he argued, was made possible only by the "spontaneous cooperation" that takes place among human beings when they are brought together.

Mayo viewed with distress the progressive weakening of the individual's community and family ties and what he believed was a consequence—the withering of the traditional values of society. At the same time he saw the growing importance of the formal organization in its role as employer in the lives of individuals, and he concluded that the only hope of preserving the traditional values lay in finding ways for the organization to fill the void left in the individual's life by loss of community and family support. This, he believed, could occur only in a situation of mutual respect and trust between formal and informal organizations rather than the suspicion and antagonism exposed in the Hawthorne study.

To this end Mayo advocated more effective upward communication in organizations to provide management with greater insight into the attitudes, grievances, and aspirations of workers. He also urged the use of the tools provided by the social sciences to create an atmosphere in which there would be spontaneous cooperation from the employees to promote, rather than oppose, the objectives of the organization.

The Hawthorne studies opened the way for the exploration of uncharted "human" areas of the organization that had been ignored by scientific management—the influence of social, emotional, and other nonmaterial factors in human motivation and the role of communication, group interaction, leadership, and similar processes in organization effectiveness. In the years following the Hawthorne studies their conclusions were verified, amplified, and modified.

Douglas McGregor

In one of the most important humanist studies, the former president of Antioch College and MIT professor of management, Douglas McGregor, advanced what he called his *Theory X-Theory Y*. It was based upon the assumptions about human nature inherent in the theories of Henri Fayol and other scientific management advocates.

The basic assumptions of the early theorists, which McGregor designated Theory X, had been

1. That the typical person has a natural aversion to work;
2. Because of the first assumption, people will work effectively only when ordered, threatened, or forced to do so; and
3. That the typical person is indolent, irresponsible, unambitious, and inclined to value security above everything else.[19]

Conceding that Theory X may be valid for some human behavior under some circumstances, McGregor offered an alternate set of assumptions based on the perception that human beings can be more effectively "integrated" into an activity than ordered into it. These assumptions, labeled Theory Y, were

1. That work is as natural as play or rest, the given conditions making it onerous or rewarding;
2. That individuals committed to a particular objective will work to achieve it under self-direction and self-control;
3. That organizational objectives offering the individual an opportunity for the realization of personal potential can be highly rewarding and motivating;
4. That any human being welcomes responsibility under the right circumstances;

5. That most employees do not make the creative contribution to their organization that they are capable of making; and

6. That organizations waste the potential of most employees.[20]

We examine McGregor's theory more fully in Chapter 6.

Rensis Likert

A similar method of contrasting scientific management assumptions and practices with more human-oriented alternatives was employed by Rensis Likert in his studies of individual behavior in the organizational environment.[21] Seeking an explanation for the fact that some managers are far more effective than others in achieving organizational objectives, Likert concluded that supervisors who concentrate on "getting the job done" tend to achieve poorer results than those who devote most of their attention to developing productive human relationships. Thus he saw two basic forms of management: job-centered and employee-centered.

Job-centered management focuses on technical and operational details—precise job descriptions along with instructions, schedules, rates, and close supervision to keep up production and quality. *Employee-centered* management, in contrast, concentrates on building a healthy relationship with individual employees and among the work group, creating an effective team with maximum participation in decision making and high performance goals. Likert found evidence that employee-centered supervisors, who conceived their role as one of removing the obstacles to effective performance by subordinates, were actually more efficient than job-centered supervisors who emphasized "efficiency." He pointed out that whereas skillful, hard-driving scientific management techniques can result in operational efficiency and high productivity, these accomplishments are offset by job dissatisfaction, anticompany sentiment, turnover, labor troubles, and excessive scrap rates.

Likert described four different styles, or systems, of management, ranging from the extreme scientific management orientation labeled System 1 (*exploitive authoritative*) and System 2 (*benevolent authoritative*) to the ultimate humanist philosophy called System 4 (*participative*). System 3 (*consultative*) leans toward employee-centered management by seeking some employee involvement in lower-level decision making, but retains the authoritarian structure of Systems 1 and 2.[22]

The four systems are distinguished by characteristic styles in several areas—motivation, communication, and decision making. In System 1 motivation is based on fear, communication is downward, and decisions are made at the top. Systems 2 and 3 use both penalty and reward as motivating forces, with System 3 more likely to emphasize rewards. Upward communication tends to be confirmatory, moderate, and cautious in both System 2 and System 3, but System 3 employees often do influence decision, particularly at lower levels.

System 4 motivation combines external rewards with self-motivation based on the prospect of self-actualization through the achievement of organization objectives. Direct and frank communication is encouraged upward, downward, and horizontally in the organization. Employees participate in decision making at all levels.

Although many organizations do not conform to the characteristics of any single system, a great many others can be assigned definitely to one system or another on the basis of the dominant tendency of their management practices. Likert concluded that the closer an organization approaches System 4, the greater are its chances of achieving high efficiency and productivity, employee satisfaction, and good labor-management relations. (For a further discussion of Likert's theory, see Chapter 6.)

The increased emphasis placed on self-direction and self-motivation by humanists like McGregor and Likert involved a concept of individual fulfillment. This concept of personal development or *self-actualization* in organizational environments was studied by Chris Argyris.[23]

Chris Argyris

According to Argyris, every human being has a potential that can be developed. This process of self-actualization is highly rewarding to the individual, to the associates, and to the organization. But most organizations erect insurmountable barriers to such personal development. This is a critical problem, in Argyris' view, because he considers the organization for which the individual works to be one of the three decisive factors affecting self-actualization. The other two factors are *personal maturation* and *interpersonal competence*—a term Argyris used to describe interpersonal relationships marked by honesty and openness as against hostility and defensiveness.

The authority pyramid, division of labor, and intense specialization that are characteristic of the modern "rational-legal bureaucratic" organization promote shortsighted, self-centered, suspicious, and defensive attitudes that thwart self-actualizing impulses at every turn, Argyris concluded. Furthermore, he found that rather than encouraging personal and social maturation, or even interest in the challenge of a particular job or the fate of the organization, the organizational atmosphere promotes individual infantilism and traits such as passivity, dependence, irresponsibility, and indifference. This end result, in turn, would reinforce the assumptions that McGregor defined as Theory X, which had called for authoritarian control and task fragmentation, which would further alienate employees. Thus, it was a vicious spiral. Argyris argued that the organizational structure produced by adherence to the principles of scientific management does not conform with the principles of science.

Humanistic Management

How would humanist management work? Returning to our hypothetical chair manufacturer, let us assume that the promised results of scientific management practices—maximum productivity, strong motivation, and high morale—had not reached the expected levels. Employees had mysteriously failed to respond to process streamlining and incentive pay plans. The humanist team was then brought in to correct the situation. The humanists would arrive with tape recorders and sheaves of questionnaires instead of stopwatches and time-and-motion forms. Their initial move would be to make a scientific survey of the organization. They, however, would be concentrating on employee attitudes, communication, interactions, and participation.

Whereas the symbol of scientific management is the organizational chart, the symbol of the humanist approach is the suggestion box. What it symbolizes is the desire to impress upon the personnel that the company values the ideas of individual employees and encourages general participation in planning and decision making.

Other organizational humanist innovations might include the in-plant newsletter that becomes a vehicle for management's message while serving up chatty gossip and flattering features about the employees. Company-sponsored activities to encourage social interaction among employees and lower-level managers—parties, picnics, sports teams, and the like—might be instituted. There also would be frequent department meetings with general participation and occasional plantwide meetings at which the president might announce or explain company policies and plans.

Supervisory employees would be directed to seek out and establish cooperative relationships with the leaders of departmental groups, to learn and use employees' first names or nicknames, and to dispense praise. Under the humanist policy, rigid procedures, orders, and checkups would be replaced by dialogues about objectives, tolerance of individual work methods, and reliance on the employee's sense of responsibility for quality and quantity of production. Emphasis would be placed on the development of work teams with confidence in each other, pride in their performance, respect for their supervisors, and identification with company objectives.

In the humanist approach, managing personnel are encouraged to get to know their subordinates as human beings—to learn their interests, problems, and aspirations. In sum, this orientation believes in treating employees with the respect, consideration, and understanding they deserve as human beings in the expectation that they will learn to regard the organization as a supportive institution, identify their self-actualizing impulse with company objectives, and make it the beneficiary of their spontaneous cooperation.

Although the employee-centered policies of the humanist school have proved more effective than the job-centered policies of scientific management, neither has approached the level of efficiency and productivity promised by time-and-motion studies. The failure of scientific management has been attributed to its emphasis on material incentives and its equally mistaken disregard for human factors. In a not entirely unjustified caricature, Etzioni has suggested a possible explanation for the disappointing humanist results:

> In a typical Human Relations training movie we see a happy factory in which the wheels hum steadily and the workers rhythmically serve the machines with smiles on their faces. A truck arrives and unloads large

crates containing new machines. A person with long sideburns who sweeps the floors in the factory spreads a rumor that mass firing is imminent since the new machines will take over the work of many of the workers. The wheels turn slower, the workers are sad. In the evening they carry their gloom to their suburban homes. The next morning, the reassuring voice of their boss comes over the intercom. He tells them that the rumor is absolutely false; the machines are to be set up in a new wing and more workers will be hired since the factory is expanding its production. Everybody sighs in relief, smiles return, the machines hum speedily again. The floor sweeper is sad. Nobody will listen to his rumors anymore. The moral is clear: had management been careful to communicate its development plans to its workers, the crisis would have been averted. Once it occurred, increase in communication eliminated it like magic.[24]

Few would quarrel with the point that faulty communication creates problems whereas authentic communication creates understanding. But what if the rumor in Etzioni's scenario had been true? Automation *can* produce layoffs. Increased productivity *can* lead to reduction in force, as Taylor's shoveling experiment proved (unintentionally and somewhat embarrassingly).

Actually, the criticism is aimed at a conviction shared by both scientific and humanist management theories—the conviction that the interests of the individual employee are *always* served by the achievement of company objectives. Obviously, this is not always the case; individual and organizational objectives are sometimes unavoidably on a collision course. Ignoring this fact, most scientific management and humanist theorists have proceeded on the assumption that industrial peace would be an automatic product of honest communication between management and labor.

However, as Etzioni observed, conflict is not invariably negative. It can also lead to a healthy readjustment of power relationships and practices when it is a genuine conflict that is joined and resolved before it becomes a festering grievance. Papered over, it may produce long-term resentment and retaliation or seriously destructive anger.

A related criticism has been that the humanist approach, while promoting improved status for the individual employee, contented itself for far too long with serving as simply an elegant problem-solving tool for management. One of Elton Mayo's prime objectives, it will be recalled, was to enlist the tools of social science in the service of industry. In view of this initial direction of humanist management and its continual impulse to harmonize the interests of the individual and the organization, it is not surprising that the movement's techniques and vocabulary were often associated with cynical and manipulative programs designed primarily to substitute flattery for compensation.

Although the humanist approach was based on assumptions that were almost diametrically opposed to those of scientific management, it never produced a fully fleshed-out, comprehensive theory of organization to match the composite model that emerged from the writings of Fayol, Taylor, and Weber. Both approaches rely on objective observation and data gathering, and both are aimed at organizational problem solving. As a result, elements of the two approaches could sometimes be observed within the same organization—the old scientific structure, with its emphasis on incentive pay and mechanical efficiency, might remain in effect at the production level, coexisting with the suggestion box, the company bowling league, and participatory democracy in the white-collar departments. Although both theoretical approaches have provided valuable insights into certain aspects of organization functions, neither has proved adequate to the task of understanding and perfecting the organizational structure or removing the tension between it and the individual.

The Systems Approach

One profound shortcoming of both scientific and humanist management theories has received scant attention. This was the view of the organization as a "closed" system from which all outside influences could be eliminated. Even when the defect was noted, its consequences were seldom followed up. For example, H. A. Landsberger[25] complained in passing that the Hawthorne researchers had neglected to "draw attention to the fact that the rapidly worsening Depression in all probability had an important influence on the atmosphere in the Bank Wiring Observation Room." Observations such as these were not considered vital data in the Hawthorne method of study. One of the purposes of the Bank Wiring Room was the relative isolation of the workers under study, both from the outside world and from the rest of the organization. Thus, according to accepted laboratory procedure, the list of variables was narrowed by the exclusion of those that were prejudged to be irrelevant. This was precisely what Taylor had been so severely chastised for when he excluded all of the "human factor" variables that *he* considered irrelevant. In the case of the Bank Wiring Room, the observers assumed that everything significant in the subjects' working relationship would take place in that room. The Depression, like everything else that took place outside its walls, was irrelevant. It should be obvious, however, that the results might well have been affected by the anxieties carried into the room from the outside world by the test subjects.

If we operated from a closed system, we could gather all relevant data about an organization by studying each of its parts in isolation. The organization implied by these concepts is an aggregation of separate parts, each one of which—like the organization itself—functions in accordance with the design built into it, without being significantly affected by anything that goes on outside its boundaries. But an organization is more than a simple mechanical device closed to the influence of the environment in which it exists. This is the essential point made by the advocates of the "systems" approach to organizations.

System theory, according to Katz and Kahn,[26] "is basically concerned with problems of relationships, of structure, and of interdependence rather than the constant attributes of objects." Its focus is on the whole system rather than on parts of the system. It is only concerned with parts of the system as they are related to the whole.

Huse and Bowditch,[27] using a systems approach as a foundation for understanding and managing behavior in organizations, suggest that an organization has numerous subsystems which are interdependent and interrelated. They view an organization as effective and efficient when it has ". . . the ability to adapt, a sense of identity, the capacity to test reality, and the ability to be well integrated and to simultaneously consider" three different perspectives: (1) structural design, (2) flow, and (3) human factors.

Open and *closed* are relative terms as applied to organizational systems. A system is relatively more or less open or closed, depending on the degree of interaction permitted across its boundaries within its environment. A windmill-driven water pump is a good example of a relatively closed mechanical system. As inputs from the environment it receives water and wind energy; its output is water transportation. It is engaged in a slow exchange of energy with the environment through oxidation and wear. Otherwise, it carries on its activities from season to season virtually unchanged by influences from the world outside its boundaries.

By contrast, the Hawthorne organization was an "open" system, characterized by many varied interactions with its environment. Not only did its inputs of raw materials and energy and its output of products involve dynamic interaction, but they also affected its relations with diverse entities—the market, both economic and labor; the competitors; and the parent organization.

The typical organization is in a process of constant dynamic response to general and specific inputs from its environment. It is continually reacting to feedback. Greater interaction takes place at the level of internal management because continuous adjustments are required by the often conflicting influences of individuals and organizational subsystems. According to the evaluation of Cyert and March,[28] governing the organization "coalition" may require greater time, energy, and skill than dealing with the outside world.

Although it is by no means a new concept, the systems approach to organization theory has begun to receive the attention it deserves only in recent years. It was prompted, in part, by the explosive development of computer science and technology, with the attendant emphasis on systems analysis. This approach to organization has both philosophical and practical dimensions to the communication specialist. It broadens the communication perception of individuals in organization, and it helps individuals understand the function of communication in linking subsystems within the larger system.

The Decision-Making Approach[29]

Decision-making theory begins with a critical examination of the nineteenth-century concept of "economic man" within the economic organization, both of which are motivated by rational self-interest to seek the highest possible material gain. Besides the assumption that acquisitiveness is the prime motivating force, this theoretical approach further assumes that the individual or organization is "omnisciently rational"—that is, in possession of all the information required to determine which is the most profitable course to follow.

Unfortunately, of all the possible data affecting even the simplest decision generally few are known, and only a fraction of these are available to the individual making the decision. Much of the relevance of what is known will doubtless go unrecognized, and some will be diverted by social and emotional filters—custom, habit, convention, bias, fear, and the like. Whatever information survives after that will figure in the final decision. In view of this reality, the decision-making analysis substitutes an "adaptive rational" organization and an "administrative man" for the entrepreneur organization and the "economic man."

The adaptive-rational organization seeks to maintain balance among the internal and external forces affecting decisions; the administrative man seeks satisfactory rather than ultimate solutions—that is, acceptable rather than maximum results. For example, relevant information might show that a given product or unit of work could command a maximum price of $50. In the absence of an ideal level of information and rationality, the acceptable satisfactory figure might be set at "anything over $45." To employ Simon's analogy, you do not necessarily sift the haystack until you find the sharpest needle, but merely until you find one sharp enough with which to sew.[30]

In this environment the role of the senior executive is likely to be less like that of the captain of a ship steering a steady course toward a chosen port and more like that of a prime minister mediating among a coalition of warring factions. No decision can be taken without a careful weighing of the interest and clout of the various contenders.

What usually results, according to Cyert and March, is a "quasi-resolution of conflict"—a temporary state of balance or standoff among the combatants that permits the organization to function at an acceptable level.[31] Some of the quasi-resolution tools are "local rationality" (each department makes policy for its own sphere of competence, even if the "local" policy is not completely compatible with organizational policies); "acceptable level" decision making (decisions and goals reflect existing inconsistencies rather than theoretical possibilities); and "sequential attention to goals" (commitment to a single goal is avoided by emphasizing first one goal and then another so that each of several goals gets some attention).

The majority of day-to-day organizational decisions are not organization-wide, of course. Most decisions involve routines that are repeated over and over with little or no change of procedure. In most firms, for example, the series of decisions and actions required to process a shipping order is reduced to a set procedure that trained employees can follow by rote. H. A. Simon[32] calls such procedures *programmed decisions*—that is, they are standardized and can be carried out without separate evaluation and decision each time.

Some complicated sequences of actions can be completely programmed from beginning to end; others require a certain amount of judgment. Some decisions are so new, important, or difficult that they must be thought through step by step. These Simon calls *nonprogrammed* decisions.

Traditionally, managers have been selected at least partly for their ability to make nonprogrammed decisions and to devise and supervise programmed procedures. Today, however, the rapid development of cybernetic management devices promises changes in decision-making processes that may be as profound as any that have taken place since the industrial revolution.

The computer has already converted many previously nonprogrammed decisions into programmed ones. Simon, who has done extensive work with complex decision making by computers that simulate human thought processes, predicts that the nonprogrammed decisions will eventually become passé, along with many features of today's organization and management.[33]

Our hypothetical chair-manufacturing organization began as a single craftsman's venture and eventually became a major corporate bureaucracy, reflecting in the process the increasing complexity of twentieth-century society and its institutions. Tracking these developments with growing sophistication have been the analytical tools with which the social sciences have attempted to understand organizations and the principles governing their operation. These have made it possible to focus attention on the structure from the perspective of each principal point of view, examining it successively as a job-centered, person-centered, process-centered, and decision-centered activity. Each has added a new dimension of understanding, but none has provided all the missing pieces required to construct a comprehensive theory of organizations. If, as Simon suggests, the contemporary organization is on the threshold of a technological revolution brought about by new methods of processing information, it is appropriate now to take a more detailed look at the organization in one of its most significant and most neglected roles—as a communicating organism.

The Communication Approach to Organizations

The organizational theories discussed to this point treat communication as a passive tool through which managerial will is expressed. Attention given to communication was essentially prescriptive—suggestions for improving the clarity, force, and distribution of the necessary information.

Classical scientific management theory, for example, seldom accorded communication individual significance in the organizational scheme. Preoccupied as they were with the effective exercise of authority in achieving organizational goals, these theorists conceived of the corporate communication system as a conduit for transmitting instructions downward to those who would carry them out and confirmation upward that they had been carried out.

Partly because of the Hawthorne experience, the humanists paid greater attention to communication than did the advocates of scientific management. Having discovered that rapport between management and worker improved morale and productivity and that informal communication channels can be as effective as formal ones, those who sought to apply the lessons of Hawthorne made improved communication an important element of their program. Supervisors were encouraged to establish contact with the informal organization, to break down the barriers to human interchange, and to communicate approval and friendly encouragement in every possible way.

Even so, the humanists continued to regard communication much as their scientific management counterparts did. Essentially the humanists thought of communication as an instrument that interferes with the efficient exercise of authority when it is faulty, and promotes harmonious operation when it is properly adjusted.

It was only with the view of the organization as process rather than structure—as a product of the interaction of its components, objective and subjective alike—that the communication function began to be perceived as a crucial force in the life of the organization. Particularly for those who viewed the organization as an *adaptive social structure* no less than an *economy*, and those who were concerned with the decision-making processes, it became increasingly difficult to regard communication in the old static way as a neutral courier service for transmitting packages of meaning from point to point.

The conventional view of communication assumed that the message transmitted would be rational (that is, logically related to meaningful data), the meaning received would be the same as the meaning transmitted, and the meaning transmitted would evoke an appropriate response. If we apply these assumptions to our hypothetical chair-manufacturing firm, however, we will discern some of the reasons why the conventional view was inadequate in accounting for real communication processes in modern organizations.

As the individual venture of one person, our model firm encountered no internal communication problems. All the communication processes were carried out intrapersonally, within the consciousness of its single participant. (And although psychologists and general semanticists warn that both the structure of our language and the habits of our thought make such inside communication less objectively meaningful than we like to believe, it is still the most direct form of communication available.)

The first internal interpersonal communication problems arise with the arrival of the partner. But these problems are likewise minimal because the two individuals share a common objective and deal with each other on a face-to-face basis as equals.

With the development of an organization, however, the communication difficulties begin to multiply. At first the partners are able to interview new employees personally, describing the kind of performance they expect and the inducement they will offer in return. They also share the work process, monitoring performance and behavior directly. In these simple organizational stages the lines of communication do have the uncomplicated linear appearance described in earlier theory.

Even after they abandon the workbench, the partners will be able to maintain rapport with the shop for a period, boosting morale by direct encouragement and camaraderie, or discipline by the visible exercise of authority. Eventually, however, direct communication will be replaced by formalized company rules and regulations—*programmed* instructions and decisions—and direct contact by an intermediate tier of supervisors between the partners and their employees.

As the organization grows, the owners will discover the limits of their "span of control," and develop a second tier of managers to supervise the supervisors. At a certain stage the company begins to develop vertical divisions in addition to the tiers of management. This would happen about the time departments begin to appear, each with its own vertical hierarchy. With the addition of each new tier and division the chief executives find themselves further removed from the basic operations of their organization.

At first the consequences will be slight. At the stage in which the partners continue to act as direct supervisors of operations inadequacies of instruction or understanding can be detected by a simple form of feedback. The owner-supervisor personally instructs a worker in the desired procedures and directly observes the results. This makes it possible to correct any deficiency immediately.

Everything changes with the interposition of middle tiers of management. Direct instruction and observation are replaced by ever-longer systems for transmitting messages. Messages that were suitable for face-to-face exchanges with specific individuals must be standardized for general distribution. Some messages mysteriously lose their meaning or acquire new shades of meaning with every way station they pass through, and ambiguities and misunderstandings multiply. Constantly increasing effort is devoted to improving procedures for transmitting instructions to the periphery of the organization and getting back some sort of accurate signal that the instructions have been followed and what the results have been. But no matter what the owners do, it is all but certain that as the organization grows they will sense increasing isolation from its reality.

The causes for change in the organizational complexity are readily apparent. The first is simple communication entropy—some loss of meaning, however slight, inevitably takes place whenever a message is transmitted from any sender to any receiver through any medium. A second cause is the inevitable disparity between organizational and personal goals, and among goals and directions of different groups and individuals within the organization's coalition.

It is the role of communication as an independent and dynamic force that is missing in the humanist and scientific management models. Both regard communication as an essentially controlled, passive instrument of authority; neither treats it as a force that shapes and is shaped by the environment in which it operates. Plausible and self-evident as the classical assumptions about communication appear to be at first glance, all management experience, decision-making theory, and communication analysis indicate that they are invalid for any serious examination of the function and effect of real communication systems in real organizations in the modern world. The alterations in meaning that take place in messages transmitted in organization communication systems are not simply the result of the distance they must travel. Meaning does suffer general attrition in transit. But more importantly, meaning undergoes certain *characteristic deformations* in passage through the organizational communication channels. How these systematic changes take place and the role they play in the life of the organization are crucial questions in the study of both communication and organization theory.

March and Simon[34] analyzed the built-in provisions that organizations have for making new information compatible with existing policies. Incoming data, they found, are either excluded altogether or subjected to successive "editings" until they are in conformity with information already in the system. By the time data—particularly upward-moving data—reach the decision-making level, they usually have been strongly tilted toward optimism, support for existing policy, and conformity to the known preconceptions of the intended receiver.

In a closely reasoned analysis of the decision-making process, M. F. Hall demonstrated that decisions are commonly founded on premises that are considered "probably true" in the light of information in the organizational communication system at the time of decision.[35] He concluded: "It is the information-structuring clique in an organization which is the one in which decisional (as opposed to merely formal) power resides." Hall saw the chief executive as a link between this informal "clique" and the formal decision-making structure.

Many observers now believe that just as neglect of the positive role of communication led to serious weaknesses in the scientific management and humanist theories, understanding of the communication role makes it possible to structure the organization and control its activities. This approach, then, assumes that the organizational structure can be made to emerge from an effective communication system rather than the other way around.

This is not a new idea. In 1938, Chester Barnard maintained that "the first function of the executive is to develop and maintain a system of communication."[36] The purpose of this system, according to Allen and Koehler, should be to "stimulate desired behaviors."[37] This means not only a strong system for transmitting messages but an equally strong program for obtaining the feedback. The latter has an important place in communication. It provides the return signals that supply continuous data on the effectiveness of the communication system in transmitting the intended message, as well as on the effectiveness of the policies communicated and the organizational structure designed to carry them out. Also it means that managers must have an effective communication system that stimulates people (persuasive influence) to want to achieve desired outcomes (organizational goals).

The communication system therefore creates powerful tools for continuous adjustment of the structure and processes to meet changing circumstances. In the absence of an arbitrary display and use of authority, it can create a nonpunitive organizational climate in which most of the ill effects of artificially stimulated motivation and other pressures are minimized.

REVIEW QUESTIONS

1. What is an organization?
2. Describe the objectives and rationale of scientific management and its effect on communication in organizations.

3. Describe Fayol's "five functions of management" and give an example of each where communication was necessary to complete the function successfully.
4. Explain line, staff, and functional positions, and their relationship in the organization structure.
5. What is the "principle of specialization," and what are some of the advantages and disadvantages of using this principle in organizations?
6. Analyze Weber's discussion of power and authority, and give an example of each as they might occur in organizations.
7. What is the "rabble hypothesis?" Discuss its contribution to understanding organizational theory.
8. Compare and contrast Likert's discussion of "job-centered" management and "employee-centered" management.
9. Using Likert's four systems of management, which system most closely represents the system used by your instructor in class? Support your answer with numerous examples.
10. What are "human factors," and how do they affect communication in organizations?
11. What is the difference between an "open" and "closed" system?
12. What are social and emotional filters, and what are their effects on the information and decision-making process?
13. What do the authors mean by "administrative man," and how does such a manager operate in the organization?
14. Give three examples each of programmed and nonprogrammed decisions in the organizational context?
15. Scientific management and humanistic management seem to be dichotomous in their perspectives of managerial behavior. What, if anything, do they have in common?
16. Why is the organizational chart associated with scientific management and the suggestion box associated with humanistic management?
17. Why did both scientific and humanistic management theorists fail to recognize the significance of communication in organizations?

KEY TERMS AND CONCEPTS FOR REVIEW

- Organization
- Economic Man
- Maximum Prosperity
- Fayol's Five Functions of Management
- Line Positions
- Staff Positions
- Functional Positions
- Power

- Authority
- Charismatic Authority
- Traditional Authority
- Bureaucratic Authority
- Hawthorne Studies
- Bank Wiring Room
- Chiseling
- Ratebusting
- Rabble Hypothesis

- Theory X-Theory Y
- Job-Centered Management
- Employee-Centered Management
- Open System
- Closed System

- Adapted Rational Organization
- Administrative Man
- Characteristic Deformations
- Programmed Decisions
- Nonprogrammed Decisions

CASE STUDY

David Larson is the assistant editor of the college newspaper. Two of his many responsibilities include performing the duties of editor when that individual is absent and being responsible for the advertising department budget and sales. David also writes a daily news column that reports on upcoming campus activities and programs. Everyone on the newspaper staff seems to get along well together. In fact, many of the staff people usually get together a few times a week at the local pub after work and socialize.

PROBES

1. Assume that you are the editor in chief of the college newspaper, and you prefer to use the scientific management approach to managing your organization. You must leave town for one week and your assistant editor will be in charge. Your style of management is unpopular among staff members. How would you communicate to David about the responsibilities of being editor in chief?
2. Using the systems approach to management, what effect would keeping some staff members after work, which would cause them to miss the occasional "after hours" party, have on the other members of the staff who are allowed to leave?

Recommended Readings

Aldrich, H. E. *Organizations and Environments.* Englewood Cliffs, N.J.: Prentice-Hall, 1979.

Altman, S. and Hodgetts, R. M. *Readings in Organizational Behavior.* Philadelphia: W. B. Saunders, 1979.

Brooks, K., Callicoat, J. and Siegerdt, G.,"The ICA Communication Audit and Perceived Communication Effectiveness Changes in 16 Audited Organizations," *Human Communication Research,* 5 (1979): 130–137.

Goldhaber, G. M. *Organizational Communication.* 2nd ed. Dubuque, Iowa: William C. Brown, 1979.

Hodgetts, R. M. and Altman, S. *Organization Behavior.* Philadelphia: W. B. Saunders, 1979.

Huseman, R. C., Logue, C. M. and Freshley, D. L. *Readings in Interpersonal & Organizational Communication.* 3rd ed. Boston: Holbrook Press, Inc., 1977.

Porter, L. W., Lawler, E. E. and Hackman, J. R. *Behavior in Organizations.* New York: McGraw-Hill Book Company, 1975.

Notes

1. J. G. March and H. A. Simon, *Organizations* (New York: John Wiley & Sons, Inc., 1958), p. 1.
2. A. Smith, *The Wealth of Nations*, Cannan edition (New York: The Modern Library, 1937). Originally published in 1776.
3. F. W. Taylor, *The Principles of Scientific Management* (New York: Harper & Row, 1911).
4. H. Albers, *Organized Executive Action* (New York: John Wiley & Sons, Inc.), p. 28.
5. Ironically, Taylor's theories gained their widest publicity as a result of a congressional investigation into labor unrest in the federal arsenal at Watertown, N.Y., following the introduction of "scientific management."
6. H. Fayol, *General and Industrial Management* (New York: Pitman, 1949).
7. Ibid.
8. M. Weber, *The Theory of Social and Economic Organization*, trans., A. M. Henderson and Talcott Parsons (New York: The Free Press, 1947).
9. The basic ideas now generally associated with the theory of scientific management did not arrive neatly packaged. In fact, their developement was an extraordinarily protracted process. Adam Smith first pointed to the significance of the division of labor in *The Wealth of Nations*, published in 1776 (Modern Library, 1937). Frederick W. Taylor launched his time-and-motion studies at the Midvale Steel Company more than a century later, in 1881, and the famous Bethlehem experiments in 1898. The seed of "Taylorism" appeared in papers presented to the American Society of Mechanical Engineers in 1895 and 1903—expanded into a book, *The Principles of Scientific Management,* in 1911 (Harper). Henri Fayol's main ideas on management were contained in an article published in a French journal in 1916, but did not appear in English translation until 1929. An English translation of Max Weber's *The Protestant Ethic and the Spirit of Capitalism* was published in 1930 (London: Allen & Unwin) and *The Theory of Social and Economic Organizations* in 1947 (The Free Press). In the United States "scientific management" became a household term largely through the evangelical efforts of disciples of Taylor and Fayol. Testimony before a hearing of the Interstate Commerce Commission that the application of Taylor's principles could save the floundering railroads was headlined in the press. A number of popular and scholarly books published in the 1930s— *Onward Industry!* by James D. Mooney and Alan C. Reiley (New York: Harper, 1931) was one of the earliest—interpreted and expanded on the principles of effective organization laid down by Fayol and Taylor. In 1937, *Papers on the Science of Administration*, edited by Luther Gulick and Lyndall Urwick, brought a comprehensive collection of views on the administrative principles of scientific management to a wide audience (New York: Institute of Public Administration, 1937).
10. See F. J. Roethlisberger and W. J. Dick, *Management and the Worker* (Cambridge, Mass.: Harvard University Press, 1939).
11. The conclusion of the Hawthorne experiments have been widely accepted, but the

actual research has come under considerable attack. For example, see A. Carey, "The Hawthorne Studies: A Radical Criticism," *American Sociological Review*, 32 (1967): 403–416.

12. The founders of scientific management were by no means unaware of social factors in motivation. Taylor, for example, described with some outrage the intense pressure the other workers could bring to bear on those workers who cooperated with his programs for increasing production. At Bethlehem, Taylor took considerable pains to disrupt social interaction on the job by isolating workers whenever the nature of the work permitted, by forbidding crews of more than four workers, by seating small-parts inspectors too far apart for conversation, and so on, in order to prevent distractions from what he considered their principal motivation, the desire to earn more money.

13. L. W. Porter and K. H. Roberts, "Communication in Organizations." In D. Dunnette, ed., *Handbook of Industrial and Organizational Psychology* (New York: Rand McNally & Company, 1976).

14. *The Human Problems of Industrial Civilization* (New York: The Macmillan Company, 1933).

15. *The Human Side of Enterprise* (New York: McGraw-Hill Book Company, 1961).

16. *New Patterns of Management* (New York: McGraw-Hill Book Company, 1961).

17. *Personality and Organization—The Conflict Between System and the Individual* (New York: Harper & Row, 1957).

18. Mayo, op. cit., pp. 33–35.

19. McGregor, op. cit., pp. 33–34.

20. Ibid., pp. 47–48.

21. Likert, loc. cit.

22. Ibid., pp. 5–25, 222–236, 237–248.

23. Argyris, op. cit.

24. A. Etzioni, *Modern Organizations* (Englewood Cliffs, N. J.: Prentice-Hall, 1964), p. 43.

25. H. A. Landsberger, *Hawthorne Revisited* (Ithaca, N.Y.: Cornell University Press, 1958).

26. D. Katz and R. Kahn, *The Social Psychology of Organizations* (New York: John Wiley & Sons, 1966), p. 18.

27. E. Huse and J. Bowditch, *Behavior in Organizations* (Reading, Mass.: Addison-Wesley, 1973), pp. 37–38.

28. R. M. Cyert and J. G. March, *A Behavioral Theory of the Firm* (Englewood Cliffs, N.J.: Prentice-Hall, 1963).

29. J. G. March and H. A. Simon, *Organizations* (New York: John Wiley & Sons, 1958) advanced a view of the organization as a system of decision-making individuals. Each man has expanded and developed the concept in subsequent works, Simon in his *The New Science of Management Decision* (New York: Harper & Row, 1960), and March, in collaboration with Richard M. Cyert, in *A Behavioral Theory of the Firm* (Englewood Cliffs, N.J.: Prentice-Hall, 1963). Simon, who has done extensive research in the decision-making process using computerized models, treats management as essentially a decision-making function.

30. J. G. March and H. A. Simon, *Organizations* (New York: John Wiley & Sons, 1958); H. A. Simon, *The New Science of Management Decision* (New York: Harper & Row, 1960); R. M. Cyert and J. G. March, *A Behavioral Theory of the Firm* (Englewood Cliffs, N.J.: Prentice-Hall, 1963).

31. Cyert and March, loc. cit.

32. *The New Science of Management Decision* (New York: Harper & Row, 1960).
33. *The Shape of Automation* (New York: Harper & Row, 1965).
34. March and Simon, loc. cit.
35. "Communicating within Organizations," *Journal of Management Studies* 2 (1965); 54–69.
36. C. I. Barnard, *The Functions of the Executive* (Cambridge, Mass.: Harvard University Press, 1938), p. 225.
37. R. W. Allen and J. W. Koehler, "A Conceptual Approach for Analyzing the Impact of the Power Variable on Communication in Organizations." Paper presented at the Academy of Management annual meeting, New Orleans, 1975.

PART TWO

The Organizational Message

3 | Message: Content and Form

LEARNING OBJECTIVES

After reading this chapter, you should be able to

1. Explain the characteristics of symbols and forms in message sharing.
2. Describe the nature and effect of the six basic communication styles.
3. Explain the differences in content and form of verbal messages and nonverbal messages.
4. Describe the relationship between verbal and nonverbal messages.
5. Discuss the six broad categories of nonverbal messages.
6. Understand the functions that nonverbal messages perform.
7. Identify and describe the six common message barriers.
8. Identify and discuss the three common types of semantic problems.
9. Identify and discuss the characteristics of two types of organizational climate.

Success or failure in achieving organizational goals depends, to a large extent, upon the effectiveness with which messages are shared among members of the organization. Most of the time spent in organizations involves the sharing of messages as the members discuss problems; study and prepare reports; give and receive instructions; talk or listen on the telephone; read, write, or dictate correspondence; give speeches; measure performance; and so on. Message sharing, the process used by one person or agency in order to achieve common understanding, is a two-way process by which people communicate *with* one another rather than *to* one another. Message sharing is initiated by the sender, who produces a message designed to elicit a specific response from the receiver. The receiver, interpreting the message according to his or her own understanding, conveys a reaction to the message back to the sender. When the intent of the sender and the response of the receiver are incompatible, a breakdown of communication results. Thus, message sharing may be viewed as a continuous, interpersonal, and organizational process.

The importance of messages, the skills that must be cultivated to become effective message sharers, and the losses that may be engendered when communication fails, make it worthwhile to study the various features that constitute the content and form of messages. In this chapter, we discuss the characteristics that make up the content and form of verbal and nonverbal messages. We consider communication styles, the basic areas of nonverbal communication, the various cues and signals that constitute nonverbal messages, the function of some of the cues, the inherent qualities or factors that lead to message sharing barriers, and a few of the faulty assumptions that can create problems in message sending.

We begin by discussing the symbols and forms of the message.

Message: Symbols and Forms

A *message* is the product of a source's ideas and feelings translated (encoded) into a set of symbols. Symbols are grouped or listed under two separate forms—verbal and nonverbal—and generally consist of words, actions, pictures, or numbers that take the place of, stand for, or refer to something else. For example, the word *manager* represents a position in the hierarchy of organizations. The source—person, group, or organization—transmits the message to the receiver or receivers by speaking, writing, drawing, or acting. The structured symbols are received by listening, reading, or observing. *Feedback* enables the source to learn if the receiver has received the intended message. The receiver's response, or feedback, to a source's message may be in the form of words, actions, or pictures.

When employers wish to communicate an idea to their employees, they formulate a message—that is, they organize their ideas into a series of symbols designed to communicate with their employees and select the appropriate format for transmission. Many messages transmitted in an organization are composed of verbal symbols. Verbal symbols are words like *product* or *manager*, which refer to specific objects and people, or *dislike* and *hate*, which refer to inner feelings. The verbal symbols are transmitted within the oral or written structure of our language. As Korzybski pointed out, language is a map of the ideas conceived, not the ideas themselves.[1]

Total understanding or sharing by communicators depends on whether both the message sender and message receiver have similar experiences with the ideas, objects, or *referents* that are alluded to in the message. Verbal messages use word-labels, which have no meaning in and of themselves. Rather, they act as triggers to stimulate or evoke meaning in us. The key is to understand the *arbitrary* nature of the words that we use daily in constructing messages. We may, for example, *arbitrarily* decide to label a certain gadget an accelerator, a facilitator, a gizmo, a hyperactivator, and so on. None of these labels is able to describe the object adequately; labels never do, and our intended receivers seldom understand us fully.

The sharing of meaning also depends on the *style* with which messages are exchanged. A *communication style* is a specialized set of interpersonal behaviors that are used in a given situation. Each communication style consists of a constellation of communication behaviors or "traits" that are used to elicit certain responses in certain situations. Moreover, a particular style will be consistently used by a person for similar situations. As a general rule, we can distinguish one communication style from another. For example, we have a remarkable ability to differentiate "apple polishers" from "flatterers," from "condescenders," and so on. The appropriateness of a particular communication style depends on the intent of the sender, the expectations of the receiver, and the "behavior protocols" or requirements of the setting in which the message exchange occurs.

Six basic communication styles prevail in organizations: a controlling style, an equalitarian style, a structuring style, a dynamic style, a relinquishing style, and a withdrawal style.[2] We now examine these communication styles and their impact on task performance and organizational behavior. Some communication styles are more effective than others in certain situations. Table 3-1 provides an overview of these styles.

The Controlling Style   A controlling style of communication or message sending is characterized by an intent to limit, coerce, and direct the behaviors, thoughts, or responses of others. People who resort to the controlling style of communication, called *one-way* communicators, are interested mainly in sending messages rather than in sharing messages. (See Figure 3-1.) They are not interested in receiving feedback unless it can be used to their own personal advantage. They do not care about the points of view of others and generally try to use their authority and power to force the compliance or obedience of others to their own points of view. The messages of these one-way communicators do not attempt to "sell" an idea; they tell others what they are to do. A source who is viewed as an expert at a particular task may be able to get by with

TABLE 3-1   Six Communication Styles

Style	Communicator	Purpose	Technique
Controlling	Directive, demanding	To persuade others and gain compliance	Use power and authority and sometimes manipulation
Equalitarian	Friendly, warm	To stimulate and draw out others	Stress mutual understanding
Structuring	Objctive, detached	To systematize environment; to clarify or establish structure	Cite applicable standards, procedures, or rules
Dynamic	Direct, aggressive	To arouse to action	Be brief and to the point
Relinquishing	Receptive to others' ideas	To shift responsibility to others	Support others' points of view
Withdrawal	Independent	To avoid communication and influence	Talk about something else; use a verbal attack

an occasional use of the controlling style. However, a source who is viewed as being incompetent cannot get results through the use of this style. The controlling style is often used to persuade people to perform effectively and generally takes the form of criticism, which can in some cases be benevolent and gentle. Unfortunately, a controlling style of communication often has negative overtones, and generally evokes negative responses. In a series of studies at General Electric,[3] researchers analyzed the effects of criticisms used by supervisors to improve the job performance of their employees. Results showed that constant criticism and controlling had a disastrous effect on goal achievement, especially among those employees with low self-esteem.

The Equalitarian Style   The equalitarian style of communication is marked by a two-way flow of verbal messages—oral or written—with influence and initiative being shared by sender and receiver. In equalitarian message exchanges, communicators stimulate one another to plan, set goals, take action, or think. Communication is open, with members of the organization expressing ideas and opinions in a relaxed and informal atmosphere that promotes acceptance and mutual understanding. Those who use the equalitarian style are characterized as having high concerns for both good relationships and task performance. The message sender assumes no personal superiority or expertise and is willing to receive and give information.

The equalitarian style facilitates organizational communication by drawing

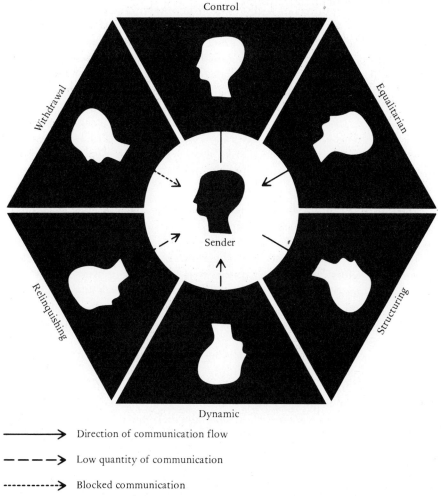

Control

Withdrawal

Equalitarian

Sender

Relinquishing

Structuring

Dynamic

⟶ Direction of communication flow

- - -➤ Low quantity of communication

∙∙∙∙∙∙∙∙➤ Blocked communication

Figure 3-1 Direction and Flow of the Six Communication Styles. The equalitarian style and, to a certain extent, the dynamic style involve two-way communication, whereas the other styles are one-way. When a controlling or structuring style is used, the sender takes the initiative and assumes a more active role. In using the withdrawal or relinquishing styles, the sender tends to be passive.

out the ideas of all who must share the communication network. It is effective to foster empathy and cooperation especially in situations involving complex decisions largely because it ensures the sharing of vital information.

The Structuring Style   A structuring style of communication uses verbal messages to establish order, organization, scheduling, and structure. The message sender is basically interested in influencing others by sharing with them the goals, standards, schedules, rules, or procedures that apply to the situation at hand. Messages incorporating a structuring style are necessary in environments involving complex tasks. Following the establishment of goals, procedures, objectives, and policies, structuring messages must be continually produced in order to clarify and interpret issues. Job descriptions, operating manuals, and policy statements also require structured verbal messages.

Stogdill and Coons[4] of the Bureau of Business Research at Ohio State University discovered a dimension of effective leadership that they labeled "initiating structure." Efficient initiators of structure are sources who draft verbal messages that establish goals, outline the necessary assignments, and provide answers when questions are raised. Although the structuring style is necessary for the proper conduct on tasks, it is a good idea to use the equalitarian style occasionally in order to allow for some relaxation.

The Dynamic Style   Messages incorporating the dynamic style of communication tend to be highly "charged up" and aggressive in tone, largely because the sender perceives that the task environment calls for action-oriented, "gung-ho" involvement. It is the style of cheerleaders, coaches, sales leaders, and campaign directors; its primary purpose is to stimulate workers. At the beginning of a project, a supervisor may say or write: "We all know that this is a difficult project and that the next few days will really wear us down. But tackling difficult projects is what we're really all about. Everybody knows what we can do, that's why they asked us to do this job. So go home, get a good night's sleep, come back tomorrow, and let's start showin' 'em what this team is made of." This is a succinct and straightforward statement made by a pragmatic person. No attempt is made to spell out procedures about what is to be done. Rather, the communicator is intent on boosting group morale.

The dynamic style is effective in dealing with frequent crises if the workers are mature and competent enough to handle the problems. Practically all coaches can deliver pep talks, but not every team can win; if workers feel inadequate to perform in the manner called for by the communicator, they may feel frustrated.

The Relinquishing Style   The effective use of the relinquishing style of communication involves a declaration of willingness on the part of the sender to take a back-seat role. Although given the right to command, control, and direct, the sender using the relinquishing style is willing to defer to the judgment of others. The posture is receptive rather than directive. The relinquishing style is often used by a source who is interested in team building, as can be seen in the team-building intent in this verbal message: "We are aware that most of you feel a bit hesitant to be outspoken with your ideas simply because you're newcomers. However, I want you to know that we old-timers don't have all of the answers. We could all use some fresh ideas around here. So we are going to back off for a while and let all of you bright, new people take a fresh look at the problem. Make some decisions, and let's see if we can implement them."

Messages of this type are particularly effective when the sender is working with people who are clearly knowledgeable, experienced, conscientious, and understanding, and are willing to assume responsibility.

The Withdrawal Style   A withdrawal style of communication is manifested in rather impoverished communication. People adopt this pattern when they do not want to communicate because of some type of interpersonal problem or difficulty they may have. Orally or verbally, the message is clear: "I don't want to be involved." In this case, the individual is not merely relinquishing responsibility but is indicating a desire to avoid all communication. Obviously, this style of communication does not facilitate organizational communication.

From the brief descriptions of each of the six communication styles, it appears that the *equalitarian* style constitutes the ideal. Three other styles—*structuring, dynamic,* and *relinquishing*—may be used tactfully and strategically with good effect. Both the *controlling* and *withdrawal* styles tend to hinder productive interaction.

The importance of verbal messages and communication styles notwithstanding, they do not constitute the totality of components of organizational communication. *A considerable amount of organizational communication is never verbalized.* A major part of a message is communicated by the source's actions. If an employee came to work and found that the manager had moved his or her desk from a location in a private office to one in an open area, communication has taken place. If no verbal explanation accompanies the action, the employee will interpret the action in his or her own way. The movement of the desk could be interpreted as a symbol of demotion. Messages can be transmitted by smiles, headshaking, frowning, and a wide variety of gestures; they can take the form of some direct action—slapping, touching, patting, and so on. These messages are called *nonverbal* messages.

Verbal and nonverbal messages are dependent on each other. Even the simplest verbal expression can be modified by nonverbal behavior. Edward Hall in *Silent Language* illustrates the fact that gestures, tone of voice, and environment, as well as cultural and social referents, cannot be dissociated from the spoken language. In fact, without nonverbal symbols the spoken word has little meaning. Vocal and facial nonverbal symbols have a critical effect on the way a verbal message is received. Mehrabian claimed that as much as 93 percent of a message's impact depends on nonverbal cues. In addition, he estimated that 65 percent of the social meaning of a message in face-to-face interaction is transmitted through nonverbal symbols.[5] The same words—for example, "I feel the manager is doing an adequate job"—can be heard with a variety of meanings. Whether they are interpreted as positive or negative, acceptance or rejection, depends on the occasion and/or tone of voice. More importantly, we cannot give adequate meaning to the verbal message outside its nonverbal context. Take the following situation, for example. A personnel director is convinced she can persuade a union representative that the company cannot afford to institute new hiring policies. She suggests a compromise. The union negotiator is sharply opposed to this action.

Personnel Director   Will the union consider a plan less costly to the firm?
Negotiator   Yes!

The verbal symbol "yes," would indicate an affirmative response to the personnel director's question. However, let us suppose that the union negotiator paused ten seconds before responding, bowed his head, slouched deeply in his chair, and frowned. This would have to be interpreted by the personnel director as a negative response. Even the simplest words can have a variety of meanings when modified by nonverbal symbols. A manager who reports that he "asked" his subordinate to do something may have resquested it, suggested it, or ordered it. Problems are constantly arising when there is a conflict between verbal and nonverbal symbols.[6] The boss who boasts of an open-door policy but requires employees to schedule appointments presents inconsistent verbal and nonverbal messages. If nonverbal messages do conflict with verbal messages, a receiver is more likely to find the nonverbal message believable. The ability to understand the relationship between verbal and nonverbal messages is vital to effective management. Therefore, it is important that we look very carefully at a few of the crucial kinds of *nonverbal messages* that influence the quality of organizational communication.

Nonverbal Messages

The floor manager of a department store constantly pointed out to his salespersons that he depended upon them "100 percent" to help him do a good job. The manager was often heard to remark: "You guys are the only people who know what selling is all about. You are the ones who deal with the customer ... and that is why you have more information for coming up with good suggestions. I need you guys." In staff-management meetings, however, the agenda was usually so crammed with the floor manager's items that there was never any time for anyone else to present their problems, ask questions, or make suggestions. When someone tried to interrupt him, he would frown or scowl while saying something like: "You'll get your turn; just let me get through a couple of these more important issues, and I'll get back to you. I really want to key in on your idea." Several minutes later, the floor manager would apologize for "taking up so much time" at the meeting, and announce that he was late for an appointment and had to rush.

We often forget that what we *do* communicates a message. Scowling, frowning, cramming an agenda with certain issues, ignoring questions, and the like invariably communicate certain attitudes to our colleagues, superiors, and subordinates. Our actions speak louder than our words in the long run. People believe actions more than they do words. Many research studies have been conducted to assess the influence of nonverbal behaviors or cues on verbal messages. In one study,[7] the subjects were asked to evaluate messages that were sent by a speaker who deliberately controlled nonverbal cues in order to determine if they were more convincing than the verbal messages. The subjects rated the speaker as less sincere than the verbal message would indicate when "insincere" nonverbal cues were used (e.g., nervous deferential smile, lowered head, and nervous eager-to-please speech indicating submissiveness) as opposed to another presentation. In this presentation the same speaker used "sincere" nonverbal cues (e.g., stern, unsmiling facial features, raised head, and a loud dominating tone). The results support the contention that listeners discriminate between the statements made by a speaker and the speaker's intention. When verbal and nonverbal cues are "out of sync," we tend to attribute meaning or intention to the source on the basis of the nonverbal cues.

Thus, even though the manager in the example given spoke the "proper" words to indicate a responsiveness to the opinions of his staff, his real attitude of intolerance and unwillingness showed through his nonverbal message. When we consider Mehrabian's suggestion that 93 percent of a message's impact depends on nonverbal cues, the results in the experiment and in the example are not surprising. The impact of nonverbal messages is manifested in a wide variety of situations and contexts. There is evidence that management is beginning to take nonverbal messages into greater consideration when they are making personnel decisions. One management consultant firm has developed a new personnel evaluation scheme called *movement analysis*.[8] During interview sessions, the consultant in this process studies the candidates' movements and attaches meanings to them. This process is described in some detail later in the chapter, but a wide range of nonverbal messages can now be considered. The following definition gives some idea about the many cues, signs, messages, or signals that are involved:

> Nonverbal communication involves the exchange of meanings largely through such signals as (1) proxemics—i.e., the utilization of personal space and physical environment, (2) body movement or kinesics, (3) facial expressions, (4) eye contact or visual interaction, (5) vocalizations or paralanguage, and (6) chronemics or attitudes toward time, schedules, and appointments.

We now consider each of these six areas from which nonverbal messages are emitted.

Proxemics

In interaction with visitors to her office, the manager usually sat rigidly behind her desk, leaving the other person somewhat distant on the other side of the desk. This arrangement created a psychological distance and clearly established her as the leader and superior in the interaction. The manager then rearranged her office so that a visitor sat beside her on the same side of her desk. This suggested more receptiveness and equality of interaction with visitors, and had the additional advantage of providing a work area on her desk for mutual examination of appropriate documents. When she wished to establish a more informal relationship, particularly with her subordinates, the manager came around the desk and sat at the front of the desk in a chair near the employee.

This story provides an excellent example of what is meant by *proxemics*. Proxemics is the study of the relationship between space and communication; it involves the study of our attitudes toward personal territory, arrangement of furniture and fixtures, and the like. We communicate with others around us through our use of space. As Tortoriello, Blatt, and DeWine put it:

Each person's identification of his own personal space, as well as his use of the environment in which he is located, influences his ability to send and receive messages effectively. How close we stand to one another, where we sit in a room and how we generally position ourselves in relation to others will certainly affect our own as well as our listener's level of comfort in the conversation.[9]

Our habits, attitudes, and responses concerning our perceptions of space, environment, and territory within the organization may be based on our psychological needs, physiological needs, or a combination of both. Researchers such as Hall[10] and Hayes[11] have pointed out the importance of maintaining "proper" personal and social distance in order to provide an ideal climate for productive interaction in human communication. Hall, in particular, deals with the dimensions or zones of comfortable personal and social distances.

Gerald Goldhaber[12] provides three principles that describe the use of personal space in organizations. These principles help to demonstrate the link or relationship that exists between proxemics and status.

Principle 1: The higher the status that one occupies in an organization, the more and better is the space that he or she will have. The size of an office—its furnishings, number of windows, number of occupants—all provide information not only about the occupants but about the organization as well. Preston and Quesada relate the story of an executive who upon being promoted to a new job was transferred to an office at company headquarters. The office to which he was moving was formerly that of a vice-president—although the executive's promotion was to a position lower than that of vice-president. Preston and Quesada describe what happened.

> The new office was well furnished, including wall-to-wall carpeting, paintings, and the other amenities of a high-status business office. Before top management would let the executive occupy his new office, however, they told maintenance to cut a 12-inch strip from the entire perimeter of the carpet. Why? Because wall-to-wall carpets convey a message of position and power in the company and belong exclusively to executives of vice-presidential rank or above. With a single action, the company had put the executive "in his place" and had conveyed the message to all his future visitors.[13]

In the absence of such clear-cut signals or nonverbal messages, people may feel uncomfortable in their surroundings. Many organizations take advantage of this unwritten code to arrange desks, space, and furniture in offices.

Next to size and furnishings, the *location* of an office is the chief indicator of organizational status. Corner offices—and prime window views—belong to only the "top" people. Status increases with the number of windows an executive can manage to acquire.

Principle 2: The higher one's status in an organization, the better protected one's territory is. Have you noticed how difficult it is to gain direct access to certain executives and officials? Important individuals in an organization appear to be protected from intruders and invaders by doors, secretaries, and protocols. Visibility and accessibility decrease as one's importance and status in the organization increase.

Principle 3: The higher up one is within an organization, the easier it is to invade the territory of lower-status personnel. Your manager or supervisor may enter your territory at will; you, on the other hand, may not exercise the same prerogative concerning his or her space or territory. A supervisor or boss may call you to a meeting at any time; the supervisor, on the other hand, may be called upon usually through appointment. This right to invade or encroach upon a subordinate's territory may lead to great dissatisfaction if it is abused. Typically, we do not like people who continually barge in on us—regardless of how high their status might be.

Kinesics

Kinesics refers to body motion and includes gestures, movements of the body, and posture. Reference was previously made to the use of *movement analysis* by certain organizational consultants as they screen personnel. Generally, these consultants watch for certain movements in order to characterize a particular candidate or applicant. Here are a few examples:

> *Side-to-side movements*—a person who takes up a lot of space while he talks by moving his arms in large circular motions will do much informing and listening and will be best suited to companies that are seeking a sense of direction. *Forward and backward movements*—a person who extends her hand straight forward and tends to lean forward during the interview is identified as an "operator." This is the kind of manager whose need for action best suits her to companies that need an infusion of energy or a dramatic change of course. *Vertical movements*—this individual "draws himself up to his tallest" during the handshake. He is characterized as the "presenter"—a master at selling himself and the company.[14]

Researchers say that body movements hint at *responses to feelings* rather than to the feelings themselves. Body movements tell us *how* people are dealing with their feelings at a given moment, whereas their facial expressions may show their feelings themselves.[15] For example, when a supervisor is refraining from berating a delinquent employee, his or her reddened face and furrowed brow will inevitably show the rage or the emotion while the clenched fist and tightened shoulders will give some clue about the control being exercised. Although body movements offer cues that can be interpreted fairly accurately, our ability to interpret these movements depends on our sensitivity to how we ourselves normally behave when we feel angry, elated, fearful, insecure, and so on.

Facial Expressions

The face is the most reliable indicator of emotion, intention, attitude, and orientation. Notice the raised eyebrows for disbelief, the rubbing of the nose in disbelief, the gaping jaw for astonishment, the pursed lips in frustration, and the quick wink in friendliness. We should be more mindful of these nonverbal cues since they play such an important role and exert such strong impacts on organizational communication. These facial expressions also serve to encourage or discourage feedback or productive interaction.

"Slugs" Magruder, the campaign manager of a fund-raising organization, has been known to squelch complaints, gripes, and feedback concerning his strategies quite effectively. For example, when he is approached by his assistant manager, Sally Jones, who is really not too happy with the way things are going, "Slugs" realizes her intent, and immediately indicates his unwillingness to listen to her by frowning, lowering his head, glancing at the floor, and tightening his jaw. If Sally is wise, she will realize the futility of attempting honest, two-way communication with "Slugs" at that point. She may decide to bring up the issue in a different context, at a different time, or maybe with someone else if that is feasible.

Visual Interaction

The eye contact between communicators affects how each one perceives and reacts to the other. During a conversation, there is more visual interaction when a person is listening than when the person is speaking. When two people are interested in establishing or continuing communication, they tend to engage in direct interaction, keeping eye contact with each other. If, on the other hand, individuals are not interested in establishing or continuing communication they tend to let their visual attention drift.[16]

Generally, one increases eye contact with another person when one is being praised and avoids visual interaction when one is being criticized. An employee's lack of visual interaction may indicate, for instance, a fear of criticism.

Visual interaction also plays a role in feedback. Increased eye contact tells one that the receiver may be interested or involved. If, however, the listener does not look up during a message presentation, it may be out of boredom or indifference. The source that perceives the receiver's visual interaction positively may be stimulated to continue speaking. The conversation may halt if the receiver shows signs of impatience or eagerness to break in.

Vocalization or Paralanguage

Vocalization or paralanguage refers to cues transmitted by the voice but not through language—vocal tone, stress, length of hesitations, and pauses. For example, in an office we may need to be firm in handling an employee. We may verbally command the employee to carry out some action, but because the employee is a friend, we might use vocal tones that are not too harsh. The employee may fail to view our message as a command. Vocal cues communicate our emotions and feelings. Davitz found that people could communicate their emotional feelings entirely through their voices.[17] Our rate of speech also is an indicator of our inner feelings. For example, faster rates, short comments, and frequent pauses reflect anger, stress, or fear, whereas slower rates of speech, extended comments, and less frequent pauses may reflect grief or depression. Mehrabian suggests that nonfluencies or speech errors become more frequent as our discomfort or anxiety increases.[18]

Research indicates that we can tell much about a person's physical characteristics, interests, aptitudes, personality traits, and education just by being aware of their vocalizations or paralanguage. Tortoriello, Blatt, and DeWine wrote of the following circumstance:

In one organization a woman was next in line for a promotion. However, her boss told her that certain personal characteristics kept her from getting the job. Only after asking a colleague for advice did she learn that one of her most annoying personal characteristics was her high-pitched, strident voice. Since the new position would require her to be involved in public relations work and to represent the company to the public, it was felt that the image she would present would be a negative one.[19] In our culture, the high-strung, extremely tense individual is generally (and perhaps stereotypically) associated with having a high-pitched voice.

Chronemics

People's use of time is no less important than facial expressions or gestures as an indicator of their feelings of confidence, aggression, inferiority, superiority, or anxiety. For instance, whereas the subordinate will tend to be on time for a meeting, the superior may arrive late.

Similarly, if we measure the time that elapses between knocking on the office door and entering a room, when the superior comes to visit the subordinate, the delay will probably be minimal. On the other hand, if the subordinate visits the superior, there may be a considerable interval between knocking on the door and entering.

Another example is the time span that a person uses before answering a question. In general, subordinates tend to reply immediately to a question, whereas superiors may take their time in answering.

It is easy to see why such gestures of time are indicative of the subjective importance of people. Time is precious, and the more important we feel we are, the more jealous we are of our time. Hence, we may feel that we cannot keep our superior waiting at our doorway or take up his or her time as we deliberate to come up with an intelligent answer. On the other hand, it seems perfectly all right for the superior to use the subordinate's time as he or she thinks about the correct answer.

The more important one is, the more time one can claim, and extra time is obtained by taking it from others. Americans are socialized, usually by their families and school systems, to be very sensitive to time. These norms about time are not shared by other cultures. Hall reported that members of many cultures do not plan or schedule events very far in advance and are much less precise in meeting time deadlines. For example, many people of the Middle East tend to lump all time beyond a week into one undifferentiated category, the future. As a result, Middle Easterners are likely not to keep appointments set too far in the future, much to the dismay of Americans who attempt to plan with them. Americans tend to arrive very promptly (that is, within a few minutes of the hour agreed upon) for an appointment, whereas in other cultures it may not be considered impolite to keep someone waiting for hours.

Regardless of our roles in the organization, we stand to profit from a growing awareness of nonverbal messages and their impact. Nonverbal messages serve to *repeat, contradict, substitute, complement,* and *regulate* communication. We earn better cooperation from others if we recognize and respond appropriately to nonverbal cues. By becoming more observant of posture, facial expression, the use of personal space, spatial arrangements, the use of time, and similar nonverbal cues we can become more effective in exchanging messages in the organization.

Thus far, we have seen how both verbal cues and nonverbal cues combine to form message elements. However, the knowledge of the mutual importance of these two components of communication is of limited value in ensuring that we shall perform with total efficiency as communicators. Our efficiency and effectiveness as communicators will be even further increased when we fully understand the nature of the *communication* barriers that are inherent in any given message sharing environment. The following section discusses some of the crucial barriers that can contribute to communication breakdowns when efforts are not made to circumvent them.

Message Barriers

A manager discovers a long-standing and unattended employee problem and reprimands his staff for failing to bring the problem to his attention. Employees complain that management forgot to inform them of new policies. Executives, top and middle management, supervisors, and workers complain about the inadequate communication that each receives. Few, if any, organizations have an uninterrupted flow of messages, horizontally or vertically, within their hierarchical structure. Messages conveyed to individuals are often inaccurate, biased, incomplete, and distorted.

This section attempts to explain a number of major message problems that are commonly found in organizations. An understanding of the potential for message problems that are inherent in an organization should make one more aware of personal message needs in the organizational context. Although it is not possible to cover every type of message or communication barrier that prevails in the organizational setting, we provide extensive coverage of those barriers that we have discovered most commonly in the several organizations that we have studied. According to our observations, the following represent six common *message barriers*:

1. Message meaning
2. Faulty feedback loops
3. Message overload

4. Message transmission effects
5. Semantic problems such as "allness," semantic information distance, and inference-observation confusion
6. Organizational climates

Let us discuss the kinds of problems that are engendered by each of these barriers.

Message Meaning

It is impossible to predict exactly how one will encode, transmit, or decode a message. One may take independent, inner-directed action or be affected by factors that are not under one's control.[20] Communicators are influenced by their own cultural heritages, social environments, and previous experiences. For example, when a foreman receives a written directive that is to be disseminated orally to his fellow workers, what he does to that message and how he translates that message into spoken form depends in part on his previous experiences. When the spoken message is received by the fellow worker, how that individual translates the message and responds to it is dependent upon his or her own perception of what has been transmitted by the foreman. The prior experiences of the employees provide them with their own unique perception of things, or their own frame of reference. If the foreman is viewed as a "father figure," the employees may accept or reject what he says, depending upon the type of relationship they had with their own father.

In Plato's *Phaedrus*, Socrates points out that to talk to others one must do so in terms of their own experiences—that is, one has to use a manager's language when talking to managers, and so on. The language of the message is based within the experiences of the source. If a manager, in attempting to communicate a specific message to either a superior or subordinate, is met with a failure of others to comprehend the language of the communication, repetition of the message would be worthless. Clarification of the message can only be successful if it is received in relationship to the employee's experiences. As Peter Drucker points out, "we cannot perceive unless we also conceive. But we also cannot form concepts unless we can perceive. To communicate a concept is impossible unless the recipient can perceive it; that is, unless it is within his perception."[21] Disagreement or conflict is likely to occur not about answers or anything ostensible but rather as the result of incongruity in perceptions. What A sees so vividly, B does not see at all; and, therefore, what A argues has no pertinence to B's concerns, and vice versa.

In the story of the three blind men and the elephant, each man felt a different part of the animal—its trunk, its tail, and its ears—and proceeded to describe the entire beast. Each man's description of the animal was different. Each man's experiences were incomplete and, thus, their attempt to communicate an accurate description of the elephant was doomed to failure. Accurate communication can take place only when one knows what the receiver can see and why. Experiences with people, places, objects, and ideas give meaning to what is taken in.

The meaning of a message is not the same for everyone. Instead, the meaning for the words transmitted is unique for each individual, and it is always changing. Changes in meaning occur whenever a message is received. Furthermore, meanings for words or nonverbal symbols change during a lifetime. Experiences alter the context within which one interprets incoming or outgoing messages. Hayakawa has pointed out that "the meanings of words are not in the words. They are in us... no word ever has exactly the same meaing twice."[22] Figure 3-2 illustrates the message-meaning process. The following example illustrates this process: One Monday morning in the spring a manager arrived at the building in which his office was located. Before starting to work he crossed the room to a subordinate's desk. While surveying the top of the desk, he noticed a clutter of crumpled papers piled in the form of a pyramid. The manager, who had spent his entire weekend doing paperwork, thought (A_1) "Fantastic, this man is really working hard." As the employee approached his desk, he was somewhat apprehensive about the manager's presence. It occurred to the manager that by saying something friendly, he could provide the employee with some encouragement (A_2). But how could the manager word the message (A_3)? The pile of papers appeared to provide him with the natural lead.

Manager   (Pointing to papers)   Isn't that a sight!
Employee   (Bows, speaks softly)   I'm sorry, it'll never happen again.

The manager immediately recognized that the employee had misinterpreted his remarks. Perhaps the employee felt the manager meant that the desk was disorganized or messy (A_5).

Manager   I only meant that you had been working hard. I wasn't criticizing.
Employee   (No response)

The employee was preoccupied with the initial message. He was no longer receptive to words from outside. The explanation was mere "noise." The receiver's inner circuit $(B_1$ through $B_6)$ was operating differently from the inner circuit of the source $(A_1$ through $A_6)$. Meaning is assigned by individuals to the messages they create, transmit, and receive.

Faulty Feedback Loops

Another important part of the sender-receiver model involves the feedback loop. As long as A is getting feedback from B, he can monitor what he is sending and thus try to keep the communication as effective as possible. This is called *two-way* communication. When communication is only one-way—that is, when there is little or no feedback—A has little or no idea as to the effectiveness of his communicative attempts. Therefore, it is more important for A to obtain as much feedback from B as possible. Message evaluation is impossible without accurate and timely feedback. (In fact, it is a misnomer to describe one-way communication as being communication at all. Rather, it is more like an insensitive transmission of information.)

Unfortunately, much of the communication that takes place in an organi-

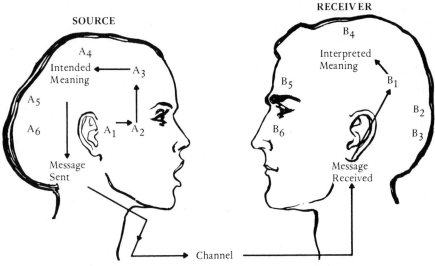

Figure 3-2 Perceptual Differences among Employees of the Organization
A_1 to A_6 = experiences, feelings, ideas, language system of source
B_1 to B_6 = experiences, feelings, ideas, language system of receiver

zational setting is exclusively one-way or "sending only" communication, and the lack of feedback one sees in such organizational communication channels as memos and written directives all too often carries over with interpersonal communications. Consequently, each individual acts more or less as an autonomous sender and mistakenly assumes that all the other senders are very attentive listeners. We expect others to act on our ideas and thoughts and to give us feedback, but we often fail to reciprocate. Thus, it would seem that feedback is one of the few things that is easier to give than receive.

The more one investigates the problems associated with communication, the more it becomes apparent that *complete* communication is impossible. This does not mean that communication attempts should be abandoned, because communication can be made more effective by individual managers who are willing to work diligently at improving their communication skills.

Message Overload

A woman in the office was known as Ms. Memo because she was always sending subordinates, superiors, and peers a barrage of memos; it seemed as if she would rather write memos than talk. Unfortunately, her memos only added to the stockpile that already existed in the employees' in-box. Since the employees could not handle all these bits of information, the memos would languish in the box without being read. This case illustrates a problem that is common in most organizations—*message overload*, which refers to the input of messages to employees that exceeds the latter's ability to process the incoming material. For example, a survey of 3,000 executives by Dartnell Institute for Business Research reported in 1967 that the "average businessman spends two to three hours a day reading and answering mail." If some of these tasks were not delegated to others, "keeping up with the mail would take . . . more than one-third of a regular business day."[23] We can deal only with a limited amount of information at one time. If we are asked to handle a quantity exceeding our channel capacity, our performance will result in confusion. People do have limits to the amount of information they can handle. Restrictions must be placed upon communication in an organization because of the complexity of the communication. According to W. C. Redding: "Without restrictions on communication, any organizational member—especially if he occupies a position requiring coordination or decision making—could be buried under an avalanche of incoming messages from all the other members."[24] Managers at the upper levels of an organization are the potential, if not the actual, recipients of innumerable messages from subordinates. Message overload is part of the organizational structure, especially as the individual moves up the hierarchical ladder in management.

The organization, as well as its employees, may face message overload problems. Meier investigated a research library that was confronted by rapidly increasing overloads of messages in requests for new acquisitions and in circulation. He found that information overload led to the use of priority rules for storing incoming messages, the downgrading or ignoring of lowest priority messages, the creation of branch facilities, the delegation of activities to outside agencies such as bookstores, the modification of performance standards to allow higher rates of errors, the development of rigid rules to reduce services and eliminate tasks, and, ultimately, the resignation or transfer of personnel. Many of these actions led to a drop in employee morale, especially when the performance standards were lowered. The organization exhibited confusion, evasion, and inefficiency. Meier suggested that the capacity of the institution to complete the flow of transactions is equivalent to the channel capacity of a communication system for decoding and coding messages.[25]

Should communication channels be open or restricted in an organization? Rosengren contrasted basic communication climates in two hospitals, a large, state-operated organization with rigid routines and highly restricted channels, and a small nonbureaucratic hospital possessing looseness of structure with permissive and spontaneous communication. The spontaneity in the small hospital led to a state of maximum communication but was characterized by interpersonal tension and message overload.[26] In any large organization a far greater number of potential messages can be sent than any single message receiver could even cope with. The organization must thus restrict the communication that does take place.

The alleviation of the message-overload problem is crucial to the efficiency and effectiveness of the organization. One technique for handling message overload is the "exception principle." In Scott's words, ". . . only significant deviations from standards, procedures, and policies should be brought to the attention of the superior. The subordinate should transmit messages to his supervisor only on matters of exception and not of standard practice."[27] The exception principle implies downward delegation of authority and is consistent with McGregor's Theory Y. It suggests that "all decisions should be made at the lowest organizational level commensurate with personal ability and availability of information."[28]

The concept of uncertainty absorption can be applied to the handling of message overloads. It refers to the increasing omission of detail as messages move through the echelons in an organization, especially upward-directed messages. The individual closest to the facts possesses the details, qualifications, limitations, and uncertainties involved. As messages are transmitted in serial fashion upward, certain information is omitted—for example, factual uncertainties or limitations—and, thus, the message overload is decreased. Uncertainty absorption may create a problem in that "each layer of management becomes a filter" and, in many instances, only a "trickle of information comes through to the chief executive." As the executive becomes isolated, he or she is removed from "specific knowledge of action in the enterprise."[29]

Managers also can become isolated from the "facts," because the organizational barriers protect them from overload. In that event, the managers may not possess the information needed to make a correct decision. As Redding suggests, there is an "inverse relationship between hierarchical position and ability to know all the 'facts' required for decision making (i.e., the higher one ascends in management levels, the farther the decision maker gets from . . . lower order events)."[30]

A major problem of overreacting to message overload is that we may remove a great deal of needed information. In large organizations it is difficult to get relevant information to decision makers from all parts of the organization; that is, in a form that contains crucial facts and screens out those of secondary importance.[31]

J. G. Miller proposes that when individuals and organizations are confronted with message overload, they may adopt a number of detrimental strategies to handle the problem:

1. Omission—failing to handle some of the input
2. Error—ignoring or failing to correct errors
3. Queuing—letting things pile up until a later date
4. Filtering—dealing with input categories ranked according to some priority system
5. Approximation—lowering of standards of precision
6. Multiple channels—decentralization or delegation of information processing to others
7. Escape—refusal to handle the input at all[32]

Organizations must resolve the problem created by conflicting needs. They must open up communication channels and restrict certain messages to avoid breakdowns. Selectivity of information channeling may be the answer. Management may need to decentralize the delegate decision-making powers so that decisions are made where the facts are available to the decision maker. Message overload is an inherent problem of the large organizational structure, which one can reduce but never eliminate.

Message Transmission Effects

As a message is passed from employee to employee, either vertically or horizontally, the content of the message is usually modified. We have all played the game of rumor as children, when we would pass a message from friend to friend to see how funny it would be by the time it reached the last person. Perhaps you will remember how the message, content, meaning, and structure changed after passing through only a few receivers. In organizations we have a similar phenomenon; parts of instructions never reach a subordinate, reports from subordinates to superiors are garbled, and so on.

Researchers have studied the manner in which message content is transformed between source and receiver as it is relayed through several individuals under the concept of *serial transmission effect*. As Redding remarks, ". . . serial transmission effects can only be regarded as one of the most pervasive and most troublesome phenomenon in organizational communication."[33]

An organization is made up of individual positions and communication channels connecting them. All messages are required to move along these positions, or relay points, as they are transmitted vertically or horizontally. Our concern is the role of the individual who passes information along the communication channels. The employees play two roles: (1) duplicatory and (2) reductive. An individual playing a duplicatory role transmits the message without significant change. However, according to D. T. Campbell, an individual playing a reductive role reduces "complex input signals into a simpler output language such as off-on, start-stop, good-bad, safe-danger, and the like."[34] Errors that occur when individuals play a reductive role are:

1. Simplification
2. Filling of gaps
3. Accentuating of contrasts

Perhaps the greatest problem is that employees tend to interpret new messages in terms of similar prior messages. As Campbell puts it:

> This bias toward prior input, this influence of memory, meaning, and the like, is protean in its manifestations . . . Note that in the communication of words, this principle implies a pervasive bias toward ordinary, typical, popular outputs.[35]

Although this bias may be reduced by message redundancy and the elimination of managerial levels, it can never be totally eliminated. We are dependent upon past experience to structure the world around us.

Semantic Problems

Allness   When we use language, we abstract; that is, we focus on some details while neglecting the rest. When we speak, write, listen, or read, we are constantly abstracting. For instance, when one receives a memo from a superior, one attends to certain details in the message while overlooking some of the other information. One problem that arises from abstracting is a phenomenon known as *allness*. It is easy to believe that we possess all the answers to a subordinate's question or understand all the ideas contained in a memo. However, by the very nature of abstraction, we are fooling ourselves. Let us examine the phenomenon of allness in detail.

The organizational employees who are close-minded and categorical in their message production and reception are assuming that they know all the information that applies to the message topic and can state this information succinctly. The validity of such an assumption is absurd. As Bois states, we need to go beyond the obvious.[36]

You can try an experiment on your own. Talk to a friend or co-worker for five minutes about a superior's behavior—perhaps the superior's inefficiency. After the discussion, attempt to describe everything that occurred and every impression you gained from the conversation. For instance, you might discuss the superior as a person or as a boss, the reasons for his or her inefficiency, the inconsistencies between your perceptions of the superior and those of the source, and so on. When you have completed your description of the source's message, then ask yourself the question: Have I said everything about it? The answer inevitably will be no, because it is impossible to consider all information, its innumerable interpretations, or the disparities between two individuals' perceptions of the same person, object, or event.

As noted previously, the process of abstraction can lead to a belief that we can know all or say all about someone or something. What actually happens when we describe a superior in an organization? Let us assume that we say, "the boss is inefficient." This could mean anything from "the boss never gets work done on time," to "the boss's orders are ambiguous." But, we are also neglecting facts such as the boss is "an excellent problem-solver," "friendly with co-workers," and the like. One piece of neglected information particularly relevant to the perception of the individual might be, "the boss allows (or encourages) co-workers to assist in the decision-making process." This could explain the inefficiency, because the time consumed to permit more active participation by co-workers might prevent the completion of tasks within a specified time. Recognizing that allness can be created by our own abstracting when we categorize people, events, or objects may be difficult. It is much easier for us, psychologically, to believe that we have all the facts to make a decision. Permitting ourselves to perceive inordinate amounts of missing information could cause perceptual inconsistencies and doubts about our own conclusions or decisions.

A close-minded individual will find it difficult to accept other points of view about a particular topic, decision, or person within an organization. Employees who contradict or transmit inconsistent messages may be perceived as ignorant, or even as a threat. Consider the problem that might arise if a close-minded production expert is told by a sales expert how important public relations is to the activities of an organization. Figure 3-3 illustrates how a

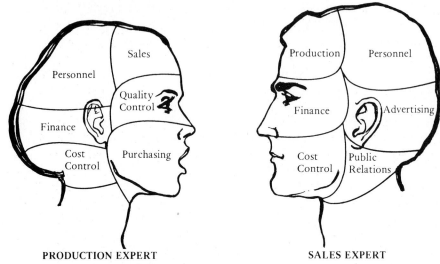

PRODUCTION EXPERT   SALES EXPERT

Figure 3-3 The Allness Problem

production expert's perception of relevant areas in an organization differs from that of the sales expert. The production expert has deleted public relations from her recognition of relevant areas of concern in the organization, and may subsequently filter out information relating to the role of public relations in the organization. Thus, breakdowns will occur between the production expert and the sales expert. It is as if the sales expert were talking to a brick wall rather than a thinking, reasoning human being. If individuals establish barriers to filter out new information, they can shield themselves from learning anything new or different. Haney has developed a diagram to illustrate the effect of the *allness* phenomenon upon learning (see Figure 3-4).[37] Haney also has suggested the following activities to reduce allness:

1. Recognize that you will *never* know or say everything about anything.
2. Do not build barriers or an "all wall." Keep your mind open to new ideas and alternative courses of action.
3. Remember that what you know or say is not all there is to know or say.
4. Recognize that to communicate a message you must abstract and thus potentially lose significant elements of your message topic.[38]

Semantic Information/Distance

The term *semantic information/distance* refers to the difference in understanding and/or information between groups in an organization—for example, between management and union, management and employees, various departments, and so on. Tompkins found a statistically significant "semantic distance" between rank-and-file members and the staff of a union.[39] Triandis, who explored the degree to which various occupational and hierarchical groups understood certain jobs and individuals, discovered consistent differences. Upper management would stress socioeconomic class as primary criteria for judging individuals; lower management would tend to differentiate individuals on the basis of power and authority; and workers would make their distinctions upon pay, authority, and reliability.[40]

Schiffman, comparing two levels of union officers and two levels of management, found significant semantic differences with such concepts as sensitivity, solidarity, management, and strike. Differences occurred within and between the two levels of each group.[41] It would appear that managers and subordinates differ in their perception of a subordinate's job duties, job requirements, future changes in the job, and obstacles to performance.[42] There seems to be no real gain in understanding if a manager has held the subordinate's job at a previous time.[43]

Minter, who examined sixty-five managers in two divisions of a manufacturing company, made comparisons among responses of three levels of supervisory/managerial personnel. He utilized what he called *congruence analysis* to "ascertain the degree to which managers occupying contiguous levels in the same department or division agreed with one another on a given topic." The managers in Minter's study manifested serious degrees of semantic distance (on specified topics) almost two-thirds of the time.[44]

Tompkins discovered differences between "actual" semantic distances and "perceived" semantic distances between individuals.

> ... semantic/information distance ... is a barrier to communication primarily when it is not perceived by the people involved ... It may be that perceived distance is ... more important than actual distance ... The speaker who correctly perceives the actual "semantic/information distance" at least has the opportunity to reduce the gap.[45]

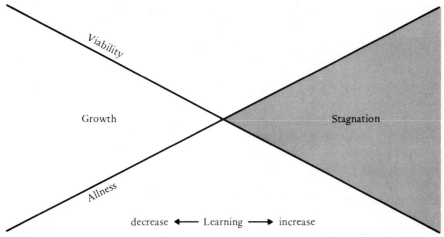

Figure 3-4 Allness and Learning. As one's allness increases, one's viability decreases and vice versa. Growth and development tend to cease as one's allness exceeds one's viability. The diagram, however, does not take time into account. It is evident that one's allness-viability ratio fluctuates from time to time and from employee to employee.

Tompkins suggests that feedback by an individual enables one to change actual semantic distance into perceived semantic distance. The managers' or employees' ability to receive and respond to feedback increases their sensitivity and could decrease semantic distance.

Semantic misunderstandings also may arise because the two communicators hold different values or sets of values. McMurray noted the relevance of the communicator's value system:

> Communication must express only those values of management . . . which are reasonably consonant with the recipient's ideologies . . . Thus, direct pleas for greater productivity reinforce the belief that the company is greedy and seeks to exploit its employees . . . All communication should be designed to emphasize common values.[46]

Guth and Tagiuri found a number of value differences between scientists, research managers, and executives. In addition, they found differences between actual and perceived values, which, in some cases, exaggerated the value differences.[47] In a related research project, Sykes observed that union employees perceived foremen as "brutal" and, thus, tended to denounce them as a group in union meetings and interviews. However, the employees were generally satisfied with the foremen with whom they associated on the job. It would appear that the workers' perception of the foreman was rooted in a value which looked upon managers as selfish and harsh.[48] We can conclude, therefore, that semantic differences, actual or perceived, can cause problems in message understanding. These problems may be reduced by accurate and open feedback between employees in an organization.

Inference-Observation Confusion

You are walking down the street with a group of friends when two cars collide in front of you. The police arrive, ascertain that you and your friends have witnessed the accident, and ask you to write down what you have observed, saying, "you may be called to give testimony in the future." Thereupon each witness describes the collision. An officer collects the statements, reads them, and grimaces; the witnesses' descriptions are all different. Was the policeman surprised? Of course not. He knows that two people observing the same event will never see, remember, or report it identically. As noted in the discussion of semantic/information distance, individuals do not understand or perceive the same event, topic, or individual in the same manner. One reason for the inconsistency in reporting—as in a car accident—is the form of language we use to describe the event.

When we witness an event, we can make two kinds of statements about our observation. For instance, we see an employee sitting in the corner of the packing room and say: "That employee is sitting in the corner of the packing room." This description is called a *statement of observation*. Statements of observation directly match what we observe. However, we can also say: "The employee is sick." Unless we ask the person directly whether he or she is sick, we have made a *statement of inference*. We have inferred that the employee was sick because: (1) the person looked sad; (2) the person was slumped in a chair; (3) employees in the packing room do not sit in the corner during breaks. Our inference may be probable or highly improbable. We do not know positively that the person was sick; he or she may have been tired or lazy. As Haney notes:

> Observational and inferential judgments are often extremely difficult to distinguish. Certainly the structure of their language offers no indication of their differences. There may be no grammatical, syntactical, ortho-graphical, or pronunciational distinctions between them whatsoever. Moreover, the tones or inflections in which they are uttered may sound equally "certain."[49]

The failure to differentiate between these two types of message statements can lead to communicator misunderstandings. We may confuse inferences for observations, subjective judgments from "facts." Thus, we may act as if inferential judgments are facts. For example, if a manager tells a subordinate that the company retention policy will demand new behaviors in the future, the employee may become anxious or threatened. If the superior's statement is based on an inference rather than an observation, the anxiety and possible defensiveness is unwarranted. Should the employee acting upon the inferential statement modify this behavior, he or she may manifest behaviors that are appropriate to the new circumstances but not the old, and the employee may thereby be jeopardizing the present position.

The inference-observation problem can lead to the taking of "uncalculated risks." For instance, an employee must meet with her immediate superior regarding the rumor of employee layoffs. The employee assumes that she is to be laid off. The manager, on the other hand, intends only to inform all employees of the company's future actions. Upon meeting with the superior, the employee is truculent; she is unresponsive and defensive. The employee behaved according to her inferential judgment and, thus, took an uncalculated risk that could harm her present position with the organization. She has forgotten that her new behavior is based upon an unsupported inference. Haney states: Confusion occurs "when (1) someone makes an inference, (2) fails to recognize or remember that he has done so, (3) thus does not calculate the risk involved, (4) proceeds to act upon his assumption as if it were 'certain,' and (5) ends by taking an unrecognized and uncalculated risk which may sometimes prove costly, dangerous, or even fatal."[50]

In order to decrease the negative effects of the observation-inference confusion, we should (1) be aware that we are making inferences rather than observations, and (2) calculate the degree to which our inferences are correct. Table 3-2 lists the characteristics of observation and inferential statements.

Once we recognize that we are dealing with statements of inference, we must ascertain the probability of their being true. Taking risks is usually warranted only when the probability of the statement is high. Finally, and perhaps most importantly, as communicators we can prevent confusion by

TABLE 3-2   Statements of Observation and Inference

Statements of Observation

1. Can be made only after or during observation.
2. Must stay with what one has observed—must not go beyond.
3. Can be made only by the observer.
4. Statements of observation approach "certainty."

Statements of Inference

1. Can be made at any time.
2. Can go beyond the observation—well beyond.
3. Can be made by anyone.
4. Statements of inference involve only degrees of probability.

---

labeling our inferences for others—for instance, "It would appear that our company policy will change based upon previous management actions" as opposed to the statement, "Company policy will change."

Organizational Climates

When we feel threatened psychologically, we normally react by throwing up barriers against the threat. This type of response is what is referred to as a *defensive reaction*. Once that defense reaction occurs, effective communication is drastically curtailed. Frequently, our messages are constructed in such a manner as to pose some degree of psychological threat to the receiver. Thus, it is worthwhile to learn of those message characteristics that may contribute to the arousing of defensive postures. Jack Gibb[51] describes differences that characterize messages and influence the *defensive* and *supportive* climates that prevail in organizations. Gibb distinguishes between a defensive and a supportive climate in the following manner.

A *defensive climate* is one in which you feel threatened. You perceive that your communication is used against you, carefully edit your comments to protect yourself from real or anticipated threat, and mistrust others and, therefore, are closed to them.

A *supportive climate*, on the other hand, is one in which you feel free from threat. You perceive that, although the content of your communication may be evaluated and even rejected, no one is passing judgment upon your personal worth. In the absence of threat, and perceiving that others are open and honest, you freely express opinions and feelings, trust others, and are open with them.

Gibb developed a system of categories of behavior that lead to supportive and defensive climates as shown in Table 3-3.

When we feel as if we are being evaluated or criticized unduly, we are likely to become defensive—the message climate makes us defensive. But when the person objectively and unjudgingly describes us without becoming evaluative, circumstances appear somewhat more supportive and we are not likely to become so defensive as to withdraw from communication. We do not like people to control or coerce us; it is much better when they seek to solve the

TABLE 3-3 Climates of Organizational Communication

Defensive	Supportive
1. *Evaluation:* To pass judgment on another; to blame or praise; make moral assessments of another or question his motives; to question the other's standards.	1. *Description:* Nonjudgmental; to ask questions which are perceived as requests for information; to present feelings, emotions, events which do not ask the other to change his behavior.
2. *Control:* To try to do something to another; to attempt to change behavior or attitudes of others; implicit in attempts to change others is the assumption that they are inadequate.	2. *Problem Orientation:* To convey a desire to collaborate in solving a mutual problem or defining it; to allow the other to set his goals and solve his own problem; to imply that you do not desire to impose your solution.
3. *Strategy:* To manipulate another or make him think he was making his own decisions; to engage in multiple and/or ambiguous motivations; to treat the other as a guinea pig.	3. *Spontaneity:* To express naturalness; free of deception; a "clean id;" straightforwardness; uncomplicated motives.
4. *Neutrality:* To express a lack of concern for the other; the clinical, person-as-an-object-of-study attitude.	4. *Empathy:* To respect the other person and show it; to take his role; to identify with his problems; to share his feelings.
5. *Superiority:* To communicate that you are superior in position, wealth, intelligence etc.; to arouse feelings of inadequacy in others; to express that you are not willing to enter into joint problem solving.	5. *Equality:* To be willing to enter into participative planning with mutual trust and respect; to attach little importance to differences in ability, worth, status, etc.
6. *Certainty:* Dogmatic; to seem to know the answers; wanting to win an argument rather than solve a problem; seeing one's ideas as truths to be defended.	6. *Provisionalism:* To be willing to experiment with your own behavior; to investigate issues rather than taking sides; to solve problems, not debate.

Adapted from "Defensive Communication" by Jack Gibb, *Journal of Communicaton*, 1961, 11: 141-148.

problem without forcing us to go along with a particular solution. Then too, we usually act coldly toward a person who has a preset plan as opposed to one who spontaneously reacts to situations. Strategy often implies the use of a gimmick or some deception. Similarly, when a person is neutral toward us, as opposed to empathic or sympathetic, it usually makes us more defensive. When a person acts in a superior manner to us instead of as an equal, we say that he or she is on an ego trip. Such superior behavior is deflating to our self-esteem and arouses our defenses. Finally, when someone acts as a "know it all" this attitude of certainty or dogmatism is less pleasant than when the person is willing to have an open mind and act with a degree of provisionalism. Gibb found that groups with more defensive climates got more bogged down in worthless ego-protecting discussion and accomplished less than did groups which had a more supportive climate.

In this chapter we dealt with the nature of verbal and nonverbal messages, their functions and impact, the various communication styles that affect human interaction in the organization, and the barriers that frustrated efficient organizational communication. Words do not have inherent meanings; they are simply labels that we attach in unique and individual ways to our world of experiences. And since labels trigger meanings in others, the degree to which we achieve true communication is determined in part by how accurate we are in relating these labels to reality. If we are inaccurate, we describe a world that is not there. Carried to the extreme, inappropriate uses of language can affect our personal performance as well as that of the organization. Our well-being can depend upon our being aware of the important ways in which language reflects and influences the way we think and communicate.

Many communication problems arise from a lack of awareness about "the way we word." When the many pitfalls of language processing are pointed out, it seems amazing that people can communicate at all. Our sense of what accounts for effective message sharing will improve considerably if we rid ourselves of six faulty assumptions.

1. Don't assume that the message sent is going to be identical with the message received.
2. Don't assume that you can communicate only when you consciously choose to do so.
3. Don't assume that meanings are inherent in words.
4. Don't assume that the communication process ceases after the message has been received.
5. Don't assume that if a communication breakdown occurs, it is invariably the receiver's fault.
6. Don't assume that the addition of electronic gadgets and assorted communication devices will alone be responsible for creating better communication climates.

REVIEW QUESTIONS

1. What is the nature of the relationship between symbols, words, and meanings in organizational messages?
2. How does each of the six communication styles effect interaction and communication?
3. What is the nature of the role and function of nonverbal messages in the overall message environment?
4. What are the various situations inherent in the organizational setting that create message barriers?
5. What is the nature of the semantic problems that arise to create communication breakdowns?
6. How does one counteract the prevalence of defensive climates and build supportive communication climates in the organization?

KEY TERMS AND CONCEPTS FOR REVIEW

- Message
- Symbols
- Communication Style
- Verbal Message
- Nonverbal Message
- Proxemics
- Kinesics
- Facial Expressions
- Visual Interaction
- Paralanguage
- Chronemics

- Message Barriers
- Meaning
- Feedback Loop
- Message Overload
- Message Transmission Effect
- Semantic Problems
- The Allness Problem
- Semantic Information Distance
- Inference-Observation Confusion
- Organizational Climates

CASE STUDY

Alice has been recently appointed as project manager of a campaign to raise funds for the Associated Student Body. She and Bill, one of her "project captains," have met to discuss the progress and problems of the fund-raising drive. The following represents a small segment of their discussion:

Alice   Bill, I know how most of you guys around here feel about a woman being put in charge of the drive, but I've got a job to do ... and I don't care what anybody thinks.

Bill   Cool the malice, Alice! Nobody's got anything against a woman being put in charge. Hey, how do you like my rhyme—malice ... Alice! Pretty neat, huh?

Alice   Okay, let's quit with the silly rhyme and get down to business. I know that the crew feels that I am trying to control things but I can't help but tell you that you are getting the campaign off to a bad start.

Bill   What do you mean by a "bad start"?

Alice   You know darn well what I mean by a "bad start." This drive costs a lot of money, you know. Mess up at the beginning and you could just about forget it.

Bill   Alice, wait a second. Don't get emotional.

Alice   Emotional? Is that one of your stereotypes? Are you insinuating that ...

Bill   Look, I didn't mean anything personal.... I'm sorry if I upset you.

Alice   That's okay. I'll be all right.

Bill   Alice, you may not believe this, but I am perfectly willing to listen to your ideas about the campaign. If you think that we are heading in the wrong direction . . . or getting off to a bad start as you say, I'll be very . . .

Alice   Do you know what your problem is, Billy-boy? Do you know? I'll tell you. You've got this real condescending attitude about everything.

Bill   I give up! I'll never understand women! And don't you go calling me Billy-boy.

Alice   Bill, I'm sorry. Fighting isn't going to get us anywhere. This campaign's got me real edgy.

Bill   It's got everybody edgy. I'm already two weeks behind on my class assignments.

Alice   Maybe we could put our heads together and come up with a plan really fast. When this thing gains some momentum, we'll be able to relax and get back to our schoolwork. We've got to remember that that's what we're here for.

Bill   Boy, I couldn't agree with you more. Okay, what's your plan?

Alice   Bill, the first duty for your group is to "zone" the various territories and to find out how the telephone campaign is going.

Bill   Yes, I think I should definitely get around to that today. Our number of pledges seems to be decreasing, and I need to get to the bottom of it. What do you think?

Alice   I'll leave that entirely up to you, Bill. You know that I don't want to tell you how to do your job.

Bill   Alice, I've gotten some very good feedback from businessmen in town, and the follow-up on them looks pretty good. I think we should put them on top of our list.

Alice   Businessmen, businessmen. . . . Everytime it's the businessmen. They don't care about anybody but themselves. You overrate those guys. I know you've been sold on the idea of canvassing businessmen from the very beginning, Bill, but you are off on a wild-goose chase. You've put a lot of effort into that idea and yet your donations from them is only a trickle. I want to make it clear that not only am I encouraging your people to stop canvassing the business sector, but I'm telling you to stop wasting your time with them. Stick with the students, the faculty, and the alumni. And, that's an order!

Bill   If that's what you want, all right, boss. I'll go along with you on it. I'm tired of this. . . .

Alice   Bill, you have a tendency to come up with some really wild schemes. What's the matter with you, anyway?

Bill   Look, I thought that a campaign in the business sector would go, but since you feel so strongly about it, let's drop it. Maybe I should come back when you're not so emotional . . . so high-strung.

Alice   Hold it! I'm not being emotional. I just happen to believe that businessmen don't give money to anything unless you promise to give them publicity. Let's not waste time and energy on losers.

Bill   I like to ride a winner, too!

Alice   What do you think of the campaign-button drive in our project?

Bill   That drive was launched the wrong way. We should make it standard procedure to find out from suppliers whether they can really get the printing done on time. We should tell them what we want, rather than let them dictate to us. As it is, we don't have enough buttons; and at a 50 percent profit on each button, we're losing money.

Alice   You're right, Bill. I told Debbie to make sure that the "buttons" guy could make good on the order, but she never listens.

Bill   It surely would make things easier for us. Keep after Debbie. We have to have a serious talk with that "button man."

PROBES

1. Identify the various elements of the language that contribute to communication breakdown in this dialogue.
2. What are the terminologies and statements that one may be inclined to label "sexist?" Why do they bear such negative connotations to the participants in situations such as the one described in the case study?
3. Identify and discuss the various communication styles that prevailed in the dialogue.
4. Were there times when the communication climate was supportive? Defensive? If so, identify the statements that contribute to the two types of communication climates.

Recommended Readings

Davis, K. *Human Behavior at Work: Organizational Behavior*, 5th ed. New York: McGraw-Hill Book Company, 1977, Chapter 21.

Goldhaber, G. *Organizational Communication*, 2nd ed. Dubuque, Iowa: William C. Brown Company, 1979, Chapters 4 and 5.

Haney, W. *Communication and Organizational Behavior: Test and Cases.* Homewood, Ill.: Richard D. Irwin, 1973, Chapters 6, 7, 8.

Sigband, N. *Communication for Management and Business.* Glenview, Ill.: Scott, Foresman and Company, 1976, Chapter 1.

Tortoriello, T., S. Blatt, and S. DeWine. *Communication in the Organization: An Applied Approach.* New York: McGraw-Hill Book Company, 1978, Chapter 6.

Wofford, J., E. Gerloff, and R. Cummins. *Organizational Communication: The Keystone to Managerial Effectiveness.* New York: McGraw-Hill Book Company, 1977, Chapter 9.

Notes

1. A. Korzybski, *Science and Sanity*, 3d ed. (Lakeville, Conn.: The International Non-Aristotelian Library Publishing Co., 1948), p. 58.
2. J. C. Wofford, E. Gerloff, and Robert Cummins, *Organizational Communication: The Keystone to Managerial Effectiveness.* (New York: McGraw-Hill Book Company, 1977), pp. 147–168.
3. E. Kay, J. French, and H. Meyer, *A Study of the Performance Appraisal Interview* (New York: Behavioral Research Service, General Electric Co., 1962).
4. R. Stogdill and A. Coons, eds. *Leader Behavior: Its Description and Measurement* Research Monograph No. 88. (Columbus, Ohio: Bureau of Business Research, Ohio State University, 1957).
5. A. Mehrabian, "Communication Without Words," *Psychology Today* 2 (1968): 53.
6. N. B. Sigband, *Communication for Management* (Glenview, Ill.: Scott, Foresman and Co., 1969), p. 20.
7. Eva M. McMahan, "Nonverbal Communication as a Function of Attribution in Impression Formation," paper presented at the Speech Communication Association Convention, San Francisco, December 1976.
8. J. Ross-Skinner, "Those Telltale Executive Gestures," *Dun's Review* 95 (March 1970):61–67.
9. T. Tortoriello, S. Blatt, and S. DeWine, *Communication in the Organization: An Applied Approach* (New York: McGraw-Hill Book Company, 1978), p. 127.
10. E. T. Hall, *The Hidden Dimension* (Garden City, N.Y.: Doubleday & Co., 1966).
11. M. Hayes, "Nonverbal Communication: Expression Without Words," in Richard Huseman, C. Logue, and D. Freshley, eds., *Readings in Interpersonal and Organizational Communication* (Boston: Holbrook Press, 1973), pp. 25–39.
12. G. Goldhaber, *Organizational Communication* (Dubuque, Iowa: William C. Brown Company, 1974), p. 150.
13. P. Preston and A. Quesada, "What Does Your Office 'Say' About You?" in P. Frost, ed., *Organizational Reality* (Santa Monica, Calif.: Goodyear Publishing Company, 1978).
14. Tortoriello, Blatt, and DeWine, op. cit., 128.
15. P. Ekman and W. Friesen, "The Repertoire of Nonverbal Behavior: Categories, Origins, Usage and Coding," *Semiotics* 1 (1969): 63–92.
16. R. V. Exline and L. C. Winters, "Affective Relations and Mutual Glances in Dyads." In S. S. Tompkins and C. E. Izard, eds., *Affect, Cognition, and Personality* (New York: Springer, 1965), p. 319.
17. J. R. Davitz, *The Communication of Emotional Meaning* (New York: McGraw-Hill Book Company, 1964), p. 14.
18. A. Mehrabian, "Influence of Attitudes from Nonverbal Communication in Two Channels," *Journal of Consulting Psychology* 31 (1967): 248–257.
19. Tortoriello, Blatt, and De Wine, op. cit., 136.
20. P. Pigors and C. A. Myers, *Personnel Administration*, 6th ed. (New York: McGraw-Hill Book Company, 1969), p. 123.
21. P. F. Drucker, *Technology, Management and Society* (New York: Harper & Row, 1970), p. 7.
22. S. I. Hayakawa, *Language in Thought and Action* (New York: Harcourt Brace Jovanovich, 1949), p. 60.
23. *Commerce* (December, 1967):12.

24. *Communication within the Organization* (New York: Industrial Council, 1972), p. 92.
25. R. L. Meier, "Communication Overload: Proposals for the Study of a University Library," *Administrative Science Quarterly* 7 (1962): 541.
26. W. R. Rosengren, "Communication, Organization, and Conduct in the Therapeutic Milieu," *Administrative Science Quarterly* 9 (1964): 70–90.
27. W. G. Scott, *Human Relations in Management* (Homewood, Ill.: Richard D. Irwin, 1962), p. 201.
28. J. L. Massie, "Management Theory." In J. G. March, ed., *Handbook of Organizations* (Chicago: Rand McNally & Company, 1965), p. 398.
29. S. Edmunds, "The Reach of an Executive," *Harvard Business Review* 37 (1959): 95.
30. W. C. Redding, "The Empirical Study of Human Communication in Business and Industry." In P. E. Reid, ed., *The Frontiers of Experimental Speech Communication Research* (Syracuse, N.Y.: Syracuse University Press, 1966), p. 75.
31. D. R. Daniel, "Management Information Crisis," *Harvard Business Review* 39 (1961): 111–121.
32. Redding, op. cit., p. 103.
33. Redding, Ibid., p. 106.
34. D. T. Campbell, "Systematic Error on the Part of Human Links in Communication Systems," *Information and Control* 1 (1958): 334–369.
35. Ibid., p. 348.
36. S. Bois, *Explorations in Awareness* (Dubuque, Iowa: W. C. Brown Company, 1966).
37. W. V. Haney, *Communication and Organizational Behavior: Test and Cases* (Homewood, Ill.: Richard D. Irwin, 1967), p. 260.
38. Ibid., p. 262–263.
39. P. K. Tompkins, "An Analysis of Communication between Headquarters and Selected Units of a National Labor Union." Phd. diss. (Lafayette, Ind.: Purdue University, 1962).
40. H. C. Triandis, "Categories of Thought of Managers, Clerks, and Workers about Jobs and People in an Industry," *Journal of Applied Psychology* 43 (1959): 338–344.
41. M. Schwartz, H. Stark, and H. Schiffman, "Responses of Union and Management Leaders to Emotionally-Toned Industrial Relations Terms," *Personnel Psychology* 23 (1970): 361-367.
42. N. R. F. Maier, "Super-Subordinate Communication: A Statistical Research Project." In *AMA Research Report No. 52* (New York, 1961), pp. 9–30.
43. N. R. F. Maier, R. Hoffman, and W. Read, "Super-Subordinate Communication: The Relative Effectiveness of Managers Who Held Their Subordinate's Positions," *Personnel Psychology* 16 (1963): 1–11.
44. Redding, op. cit., pp. 455–457.
45. Tompkins, op. cit., pp. 223–224.
46. R. N. McMurray, "Conflicts in Human Values," *Harvard Business Review* 42 (1963): 139.
47. W. D. Guth and R. Tagiuri, "Personal Values and Corporate Strategies," *Harvard Business Review* 43 (1965): 123–132.
48. A. J. M. Sykes, "A Study in Changing the Attitudes and Stereotypes of Industrial Workers," *Human Relations* 17 (1964): 143–154.
49. Haney, op. cit., 96.
50. Ibid., p. 97.
51. Jack Gibb, "Defensive Communication," *Journal of Communication* 11 (1961): 141–148.

4 | Message: Direction of Communication

After reading this chapter, you should be able to

1. Identify and differentiate between the three directions that messages flow in organizations.
2. Explain the five elements in downward communication.
3. Identify the channels of downward communication.
4. Explain the communication problems associated with downward communication.
5. Identify five factors that influence upward communication effectiveness.
6. Explain the functions served by upward communication.
7. Identify the channels of upward communication.
8. Explain the communication problems associated with upward communication.
9. Explain the functions of horizontal communication.
10. Identify the channels of horizontal communication.
11. Explain the communication problems associated with horizontal communication.

"Relax—the foreman can be trusted with the information."

"There are too many memos around here . . . combining them into one or two weekly reports would be more meaningful."

"If we don't guarantee our staff anonymity when completing the questionnaire, the answers may not be completely honest or accurate."

"I think it's pointless to give all the employees our financial picture."

"We need to set up a meeting between the engineering and quality control departments to resolve the conflict."

Such comments can be heard in any organization. In each instance, the topic of conversation relates to the direction the message flows within the hierarchical structure of the organization. Over a decade ago, the communication policy of American Airlines recognized the importance of communicating messages in three directions.

> The success of American Airlines, and in turn the success of its employees, is greatly dependent upon the teamwork of personnel at all levels— between staff and line, and between all functions. This teamwork will be in direct ratio to the quality of our communications.
> It is therefore the policy of the company that communications will be imaginative, timely, appropriate, and free flowing—that there will be communication downward, upward, and laterally throughout the company.[1]

Organizational theorists and researchers have examined and explained the flow of messages in those three basic directions—downward, upward, and lateral or horizontal. In this chapter we examine upward, downward, and horizontal communication. Although the direction of transmitting the message is the major difference, each message system uses some unique channels, serves different functions, and presents different problems that must be resolved in attempting to communicate effectively in organizations.

Downward Communication

Early organizational theorists viewed the organization structurally as an authority pyramid, and communication was viewed principally as a tool for transmitting orders downward from superiors to subordinates. Today, the crucial role of downward communication remains unquestioned. William M. Allen, former chief executive officer of Boeing stated, "The task of communication in business takes on larger dimensions . . . where once it may have been concerned primarily with publications, news service, and appropriate management messages, now it must be regarded as an integral part of managing."[2] Executives are aware that "informed employees are better, more productive employees. They get more out of their work, and they do a better job for the company."[3] Organizations are aware of the need to do more than merely transmit orders downward. Large companies have used a number of special downward-directed methods to effect successful communication with their employees.

- *Connecticut Mutual Life Insurance Company* offered employees free breakfasts if they signed up to sit at an executive's table in the cafeteria and participated in a rap session at which no questions would be considered out of bounds.
- *Xerox* produced a filmed interview with its president to inform employees on problems facing the company.
- *Du Pont* videotaped monthly programs of company news and information for noontime viewing by employees. The company also established a telephone newsline system with a recorded message on company news, emergency weather, and traffic information.
- *Citibank* posted a daily news sheet, "What's Up?" in the elevators of its New York City headquarters building. The sheet contained information on changes in personnel policies, employee programs, and important information on the banking business.
- *NCR (National Cash Register)* used a periodic news sheet, "NCR Noon Headlines," to tell employees about major company announcements.

Katz and Kahn have identified five different elements in downward communication: (1) job instruction, (2) rationale, (3) ideology, (4) information, and (5) feedback.[4]

(1) *Job instruction* is conveying to organization subordinates what they are expected to do and how they are to do it. It may be carried out through a wide variety of means—direct orders, job descriptions, procedure manuals, special training programs, audiovisual aids, and so on. The principal factors affecting the content of job instructions appear to be job complexity and the skill or experience required to do the work. Job instructions that are precise and direct tend to be associated with simple jobs to which the employee brings minimal skill and experience. More generalized instructions usually apply to complex jobs, in which the employee is expected to demonstrate judgment, skill, or experience.

(2) *Rationale* is the explanation of an activity's purpose and how it fits into the overall activity or objectives of the organization. The quantity and quality of rationale communication is determined to a large extent by management philosophy and its assumptions about subordinates. Managers who regard employees as lazy adults who will work only when forced or bribed to do so tend to engage in little or no valid rationale communication. All organizations deliberately conceal the rationale for some actions at some times. But organizations whose management habitually regards subordinates with suspicion and contempt seldom see any virtue in providing employees with information about organizational objectives and operations. Managers who perceive employees as self-motivated and productive, on the other hand, usually give high priority to rationale communication.

(3) *Ideology* is, in a sense, an extension of rationale. The emphasis in rationale communication is on explaining the task and placing it in organizational

perspective. Ideological communication, on the other hand, seeks to justify the organization's objectives and to enlist the subordinate's support and enthusiasm for them in order to strengthen loyalty, morale, and motivation.

(4) *Information* is intended as a means of acquainting subordinates with the organization's practices, regulations, benefits, customs, and other appropriate data not directly involved with job instruction and rationale. The typical employee handbook is an example of information communication.

(5) *Feedback* is a provision for giving employee information about the adequacy of his or her job performance. The simplest form of downward feedback is the paycheck which, in the absence of information to the contrary, tells the employee that performance is satisfactory. Where jobs are relatively simple and instructions detailed, poor performance is often attributed to gross ineptitude or unwillingness, and feedback may consist of a routine warning, transfer, or dismissal. Where jobs are complex and instructions general, or in organizations with a "human-centered" philosophy, downward feedback becomes a difficult and delicate undertaking for the manager who must evaluate the performance of subordinates, often without any clear guidelines. Attempts to institutionalize this problem with periodic formal job evaluations, or to shift a part of the burden to the subordinate by basing the performance criteria on self-imposed job objectives, do not appear to have met with spectacular success.

The single most powerful influence on all downward communication undoubtedly is the hierarchical structure of the organization. Downward-moving messages tend to grow as they move through successive levels of the hierarchy. The message from the peak of the pyramid may be a bare statement of a desired result. The means for achieving the desired result may be added at the next lower level. Procedural details follow at the next level. In that way the order to achieve a particular result may well reach the operational level as a fully detailed plan.

Employees want information from their superiors and seek instructions about their work, information regarding things affecting them, and the latest news.[5] As the amount of information they obtain increases, employees will seek additional information.[6]

Managers generally believe that their messages reach the subordinates for whom they are intended. However, in a survey of workers and foremen, Likert found that superiors overestimate both the amount of information known by subordinates and the degree to which the superiors understand their subordinates' problems.[7] Although employees want information from their superiors, they often do not receive it. Many employees complain that they are not properly informed regarding their job performance.[8] Before exploring in depth the communication problems associated with downward-directed messages, we look at the channels used to transmit downward communication.

Downward Communication Channels

In selecting the proper vehicle for transmitting the message, the superior must consider who the receiver will be—skilled mechanic, union steward, or foreman. The superior will be concerned with the desired response, whether it be attitude

TABLE 4-1   Downward Communication Channels

Oral	Written
Personal Instructions	Instructions and Orders
Lectures, Conferences	Letters and Memos
Committee Meetings	House Organs
Interviews	Bulletin Boards
Counseling	Handbooks, Manuals
Telephone, Public Address System	Pamphlets
Movies, Slides, Television	Posters
Social Affairs, Union Meetings	Information Racks
Grapevine	Handouts
Gossip, Rumor	Union Publications
Speeches	Pay Inserts
Training Programs	Annual Reports

and/or behavior change. Timing must be considered, because a particular message channel may be acceptable at one moment and not at another. Communication channels may depend on the size of the business establishment, and the selection of the channel will depend on what is to be communicated, for example, payroll information is provided in pay inserts. In any organization, the communication channels used should be "on a consistent basis for definite types of communication."[9] Table 4-1 lists the most often utilized channels for downward communication in organizations.

We now examine a number of these communication channels in greater depth.

Instructions and Orders   Orders and information can be given in oral or written forms and transmitted from one level to another. The superior is required to have—or know where to get—complete and accurate information in case the message should be wrong, incomplete, or unclear.

Posters and Bulletin Boards   In most organizations, bulletin boards are used to recognize outstanding achievement, make motivational announcements (e.g., safety and quality control), and for general interest announcements such as scheduled meetings or approaching holidays. If properly located and handled, bulletin boards can be a valuable tool for employee communication. If members of the employee group share responsibility with management for the bulletin boards, the channel can facilitate the participatory process of management. One potential problem with this channel is that many employees do not carefully read bulletin boards or posters, which should, therefore, only be utilized as supplementary message devices when communicating important information.

Company Magazines   The company magazine generally falls into one of three categories:

1. The most popular is the magazine that runs several features on the industry of which the company is part, the latest speech of the company president, and a story on government affairs. A fair percentage of the

issue is devoted to employee activities, including weddings, births, retirements, vacations, sports, deaths, awards, and educactional activities.

2. A second type is the tabloid, which may concentrate on company news, is written in a rather breezy style, and may very well have an employees' classified ad section.

3. The journal type of company magazine usually carries several articles of a broad, general nature. There is no news of employees or discussion of the day-to-day activities of the company. An attempt is made to publish only material of a fairly high level. Examples are *The Western Electric Engineer*, and Standard Oil's *The Lamp*.[10]

Controversial topics are generally avoided. Tingley suggests that successful company publications report on internal technological matters, the internal social environment, the external environment, and the organization's social responsibilities and dynamics.[11]

Letters, Pay Inserts, and Memos   Letters and pay inserts are usually directed to the employees' home address. The letter, which provides the most personalized channel, is addressed to the employee and can be read carefully in the home atmosphere. Letters can be used to discuss organizational issues such as safety programs and company developments (mergers, expansions, or acquisitions) or to express appreciation for the employee's contribution to the organization. Letters have the advantage of low cost, speed of delivery, and the ability to reach all subordinates.

Pay inserts also ensure message exposure to every employee. The message is printed on a small card or slip of paper, which is often attached to the check. The pay inserts are used to transmit short announcements or news bulletins. If this channel is to have a continued impact on employees, it should not be used routinely but only for special occasions.

Handbooks, Manuals, and Pamphlets   Handbooks provide information of immediate concern to the employee. They may offer information regarding employment services, benefits, and policies. Management can also reach the employee's family through this channel, and thereby increases the family's understanding and appreciation of the company.

Because they are so complex, most large organizations provide employees with a company orientation manual. The value of the manual is threefold: (1) employees receive the same information on topics ranging from fringe benefits to rules and regulations; (2) it saves time for superiors, thereby eliminating the need for individual conferences; and (3) the manual eliminates informational errors.[12]

Information Racks and Handouts   Some organizations provide racks containing free literature of all types. Handouts may include information on company services, management techniques, benefits, social activities, and the like.

Annual Reports   Annual reports are generally written for the owners or stockholders of the company. However, increasing numbers of employees and union personnel have, in recent years, become part of the annual report readership. Annual reports provide employees with a list of corporate goals and objectives, a listing of income and expenditures, changes in personnel, and, usually, some discussion of new processes and developments. One judge of annual reports suggested that the annual report should make employees aware of the fact that they are in partnership with the shareholders and thus, provide employees with a sense of personal involvement in the success of the partnership. This action should contribute to the employees' job satisfaction.[13]

Union Publications   Union publications transmit to employees information regarding policy, services, and activities in their behalf.

Public Address System   The public address system serves not only for paging purposes but also for making important announcements. Such systems can be misused and overused by superiors. Its major drawback is that one never knows if subordinates are listening to the message.

Many other downward channels have not been detailed here. External means, such as radio, television, and the press, can be utilized to communicate with employees as well as the general public. Top management may reach middle and lower management through personal contact or through such written forms as policy manuals or authorized schedules. However, management will never know if effective communication has been achieved until it determines the employee's response through upward communication channels.

The Bureau of National Affairs recently surveyed banks to discover which downward communication channels were the most effective. The bank personnel indicated that the best way to relay management messages to employees is by meetings in small groups. The small group is most effective because it permits two-way communication, allows full explanation "implemented by questions and answers," and permits free discussion. The result is "full understanding and personal commitment." Other channels in order of effectiveness were company publications on a regular basis, supervisors' meetings, employee mass meetings, letters to employees' homes, pay inserts, and bulletin boards. The downward channels that were considered least effective included posters, plant tours, public address system, and memos to employees.[14]

Since both employees and management are concerned with downward communication, why does it fail so frequently? We examine the problems of downward communication in the next section.

Downward Communication Problems

When the supervisor called a meeting to explain a new company policy, he sent out a poorly written memo. Then he began the meeting with a poorly worded statement about the new policy, which he had not taken time to understand himself. The discussion that followed was imprecise, loosely structured, and disoriented. When the meeting was finally over, his subordinates—obviously worried and concerned about the new policy—reluctantly went back to their desks. Conclusion: managers who do not choose their words carefully and plan what they are going to say should not be surprised to find that whereas they know what they mean, their subordinates do not.

The amount of information accurately understood by a group of employees varies with the communication situation. However, tests have shown that employees and supervisors have serious inadequacies of information.[15] D. A. Level, in a survey of nonsupervisory employees of a small urban bank, found that employees identified between 46 and 96 percent of information deemed essential by management.[16] A. B. Chase in a survey of over 150 firms of various kinds and sizes suggests a general presence of ineffective downward-directed communication.[17]

It is difficult to determine whether managers or employees are to blame for the lack of correct information. In E. Walton's opinion,

> If each employee really mastered *all* the communications humming about him, he would have precious little time for anything else but that. Management's . . . expectations that employees will absorb a large percentage of all the messages directed at them is very optimistic and quite unrealistic.[18]

Walton proposes what might be called the general principle of *relevancy*—that is, supervisors and employees develop their own methods of selecting information from messages. They take from the message only what is perceived as "needed to do the job."[19]

There appears to be no absolute relationship between information adequacy and employee satisfaction within the organization. However, the type of information contained in messages may make a difference. It is possible that employee satisfaction is not related to information that has little relevancy to the employees or that is complex and difficult to remember. On the other hand, if the employees are missing information that they perceive as relevant, there may be a decrease in employee satisfaction and morale.[20]

As messages pass from superior to subordinate, a filtering process is operating. Filtering can occur in either direction, up or down. K. Davis writes: "The idea of upward filtering to tell one's manager mostly what he wants to know has been extensively discussed in the literature, but the idea of downward filtering by which a manager tells his subordinates only what he thinks is important has been less developed."[21]

Nichols found that the information content of messages is substantially reduced as one moves down through the hierarchy. Table 4–2 demonstrates that a dramatic reduction in information content occurs as the message moves from high to low levels in the organization.[22]

Brenner and Sigband found, in a survey of over 500 executives and managers, that managers who are higher in a structured hierarchy tend to be better informed than those at lower levels. Individuals at higher levels in the

TABLE 4-2   Information Reduction in Downward Communication

Level of Hierarchy	Percentage of Information Received
Board	100
Vice-President	63
General Supervisors	56
Plant Managers	40
General Foremen	30
Workers	20

hierarchy appear to possess more of the information needed to do their jobs than do individuals who are lower-level managers.[23]

A prime example of downward filtering is the study by R. A. H. Rosen. Management was to transmit information regarding the handling of a new plant hiring program for minority employees to first-line supervisors (foremen). The foremen who were to deal with the new program "lacked clarity with respect to management's expectations of them." The policy itself was poorly communicated, sometimes "hastily and tardily formulated." After the program was in force one year, questions still "remained unanswered." The filtering of information from management to subordinates (foremen) led to role ambiguity regarding the program; conflicts among management filtered down to the foremen in the form of contradictory expectations or as a lack of knowledge about what the company wanted.[24] Filtering of the message between superior and subordinate led to message distortion and information inadequacy. This led to a decrease in organizational effectiveness.

The *lack of openness* between management and employees also can produce blockages and distortions of downward-directed messages. P. K. Tompkins concludes that "many members of management seem to care little for facilitating upward communication and that there is a preoccupation with downward communication to the detriment of upward communication."[25] Culbert and Elden declared:

> In general, management has not concerned itself with *downward* flow. Executives justify the wisdom of their decisions by saying, "You don't understand. If you had my information, you would have decided as I did." In other words, executives base their power on withholding, rather than sharing, information.[26]

Managers may supply downward information when they feel it is necessary for accomplishment of the task, but they may withhold information if they perceive it as irrelevant or potentially harmful if possessed by subordinates.[27] For instance, a manager will transmit information to motivate an employee to improve productivity, but hesitate to discuss a new policy for handling management-union problems.[28] Basically, communicators, whether superiors or subordinates, will only send messages that appear to be in their best interests. Superiors will suppress messages to subordinates if they perceive such messages as having a damaging effect upon themselves or the organization. Managers will filter out, distort, or even forget information that is not perceived as relevant to their needs and interests.

The openness of downward communication by the superior is affected not only by the superior's "openness" in sending messages down the line but also by the subordinate's "openness" in receiving and assimilating the messages. Thus, it may be either the sender or the receiver who is affecting the total information communicated in a message. Surveys conducted in organizations generally show a large number of employees not getting the information on matters that concern them. In other words, information inadequacy is a common problem in organizations. Although in some cases management suppression is the cause of information deficiencies, it is more often managerial selectivity in message sending that creates problems.

One index of information filtering by management is whether the subordinate receives important news from the grapevine prior to receiving the "official" news sources. Level and Walton found that between 20 to 38 percent of employees frequently receive important information first from the grapevine. We may conclude that in a typical organization subordinates experience significant degrees of "information deprivation."[29] Katz and Kahn summarize the problem in terms of both upward and downward communication.

> The information requirements of superior and subordinates are not *symmetrical*. What the superior wants to know is often not what the subordinate wants to tell him; what the subordinate wants to know is not necessarily the message the superior wants to send.[30]

The Pillsbury Company in 1967 initiated a program to open up downward message transmission. By late 1970 the program was in all seventeen plant locations. Superiors acted as chairmen for in-plant meetings with supervisors. The meetings were held once a week and lasted about fifteen minutes. Each session included brief reports from the supervisor on "matters that interest them" and discussions to learn what "is on the minds of the employees." The primary objective of the program was to provide employees with more information about what was going on and why it was being done. Topics such as rumors, production statistics, and new products were discussed. The effect was increased downward message transmission.[31]

As Gemmill suggests, any company attempting to improve the transmission of messages must examine its system of rewards and punishments. Rewards must be clearly visible for facilitating the behaviors that provide true openness from superior to subordinate. "Mere lip service will not only be inadequate, it can easily undermine (source) credibility and thus produce a boomerang effect."[32]

Goldhaber suggests that many organizations rely heavily upon mechanical and written communication media and neglect oral, face-to-face transmissions.[33]

How should management transmit information to employees? We suggest that a combination of oral and written (printed) media are more effective in achieving employee understanding than either oral or written messages alone. Altogether, oral messages may be more effective than written ones. Dahle found that the most effective media in rank order were (1) oral and written combined; (2) oral; (3) written (print or mimeograph); (4) bulletin board; and (5) grapevine.[34]

Two conclusions emerge relative to the effectiveness of various media in organizations. First, oral, face-to-face communication is generally preferred by employees to impersonal printed media, such as management letters or house organs. Second, group meetings are regarded as effective media of downward communication.

When deciding which media to use, Davis's recommendations are valuable:

> Written communication provides an official record and is less likely to be filtered because it can be sent in exactly the same form to all persons involved. However, written communication lacks face-to-face contact, tends to formalize relationships . . . often requires excessive detail for completeness, and cannot be easily adjusted to fit different information needs of receivers.[35]

Melcher and Beller recommend the use of more than one message channel or medium. For instance, oral media, employed first, should be followed by written ones. They argue that the use of formal written communication in controversial settings may have a polarizing effect. It is inappropriate to attempt "to achieve consensus on the formal level" prior to reaching agreement through the give-and-take of informal, oral communication.[36]

> Where persuasion or arriving at consensus is involved, it is essential to operate on the informal verbal (i.e., oral) level as positions can be changed without loss of official status. When agreement is achieved, the decisions should be formally processed and written.[37]

Goldhaber has identified two additional problems associated with downward communication. First, employees may become saturated with messages directed downward. An overload of memos, letters, house publications, and the like may cause employees to ignore some vitally important messages. Second, the timing of some messages is inappropriate. Criticizing a subordinate in the weekly information-sharing meeting, for example, would be inappropriate and, possibly, counterproductive.[38]

Davis has suggested that to improve downward communication managers must lay a foundation for effective communication.[39] The basic requirements of that foundation are

1. Managers must have the ability to provide information for employees when needed. If the manager does not possess the needed information, he or she should say so and find the information.
2. Managers should share information that is needed by the employees. The manager not only keeps the employee informed but also helps the employee feel informed.
3. Managers should develop a plan of communication (policies and procedures) so that employees can expect to obtain information regarding managerial actions that affect them.

4. Managers should seek to establish trust between sender and receiver. Trust leads to open communication which facilitates agreement between subordinates and superiors as needed.

Downs, Linkugel, and Berg have recommended a set of guidelines to assist an organization's downward communication:

1. The channels and the types of information they carry should be definitely known by management and employees alike. This may occasionally require some publication about channels, since people tend to forget what is available to them.

2. Management should know exactly what it wants its communication to achieve . . . A consultant once pointed this out dramatically to a railway company by asking what it hoped to achieve through its house organ. Apparently no one had ever asked that question, and no one could give an answer. Even the editor showed great discomfort because he did not have identifiable goals in mind.

3. Lines of communication should be as direct and as short as possible. Generally, personal channels are preferred by employees because of their speed, the kind of information that goes through them, and the opportunity to get clarification of the message.

4. Human communication is never exact, and management may need to spend extra effort in an attempt to be clear and consistent. Clarity and consistency are judged by the receiver, so management needs to be oriented toward employee reactions.

5. Timeliness is important. There may be an optimum time to disseminate information. It is possible to communicate too early as well as too late. During labor negotiations, for example, it may be extremely unwise to announce the company's position before the negotiations are completed. Or a company may censor information about a new product in order to maintain its competitive edge. . . . A more common complaint is that it takes too long to process information or information does not get to the worker until it's too late. . . .

6. Distribute the information when and where it is most likely to be comprehended. . . . A company may have to study the unique behavior of its workers in order to make such a decision.

7. Use finances as a means of evaluating the communication program. . . . One may wonder, for example, whether it is more economical to pull employees off their jobs to listen to a speech on new staff benefits or to prepare an elaborate written explanation and mail to their homes.

8. Generally, sending messages through two channels rather than one is more effective.

9. Even though it may be necessary to pay special attention to periods of stress and change, communication must be continuous. Employees will not tolerate a communication vacuum.[40]

In summary, the selection of the appropriate channel is important to provide effective downward communication. However, there are no universal channels that guarantee the correct medium or accurate information through a particular channel selection. Downward-directed organizational messages have been stressed but messages also flow from subordinates to superiors. We now examine upward-directed organizational messages.

Upward Communication

Upward communication often undergoes both condensation and editing as it moves from lower to higher levels of authority. The remarkable variety and force of the influences that tend to lead to the transmission or distortion of information moving upward in organizations has provided one of the most fruitful areas for modern organizational research.

Several different theories have been developed to explain the functions of upward communication. One of the first was the *substitute locomotion theory*, which held that upward communication serves as a substitute for actual movement or promotion in the organizational hierarchy. Kelly, in comparing the communication behaviors of upwardly mobile and nonmobile workers, found that upward communication was most frequently initiated by individuals desiring but unable to achieve improvement in their rank.[41] An alternative explanation is that people who can move upward avoid communication for fear that they will damage their chances for advancement.

A second theory, *need satisfaction*, suggests that employees seek to achieve certain internal needs through upward communication. Cohen found upward communication useful in achieving increases in status by promoting actual movement upward in the organizational hierarchy.[42] Employees prefer to speak with others who have the capacity to gratify or deprive them through tangible decisions and rewards or through expressions of approval and confidence. Employees distort upward messages to obtain better evaluations from their superiors. Mulder suggests that upward communication serves the function of reducing the psychological distance between status levels. Subordinates wish to be closer to, or identify with, their superiors, and upward communication helps them to achieve that aim.[43]

According to Katz and Kahn,[44] subordinates may elect or be required to transmit information upward about (1) the assigned job, performance, and problems; (2) fellow employees and their problems; (3) organizational practices and policies; and (4) tasks to be done and how to do them.

Koehler and Huber[45] described five factors that appear to have significant influence on upward communication effectiveness:

1. *Positive upward communication is more likely to be utilized by managerial decision makers than negative upward communication.* That is, there is a consistent tendency for middle managers to believe good news and pass it along to their superiors, while discounting and suppressing bad news.
2. *Upward communication is more likely to be utilized by managerial decision makers if it is timely.* Decision making is not a continuous activity. Conse-

quently, pertinent data that arrive on the eve of a decision are more likely to be used at that time than old information because the employees will tend to interpret or accommodate the new data to fit those already in hand.

3. *Upward communication is more likely to be accepted if it supports current policy.* Once policy is set, it is typically sustained by resistance to change throughout the system. Evidence of policy effectiveness is welcomed and publicized; criticism, particularly from subordinates, is likely to be ignored.

4. *Upward communication is more likely to be effective if it goes directly to a receiver who can act on it.* Messages are generally treated with a great lack of urgency. In addition, communications that must pass through several intermediaries suffer the risk of being discarded or distorted at every station on their way up.

5. *Upward communication is more effective when it has "intuitive appeal" to the receiver.* Messages from subordinates are more readily acceptable if they conform to the "common sense" awareness of the preconceptions of those they are intended to influence.

C. I. Barnard also stressed the crucial role played by the *receiver's* perceptions in the interpretation of the message, regardless of the sender's intention.[46] For downward communication, this suggests that the receiver of a message might extract an entirely unintended meaning from it because of a difference in perception and understanding from that of the sender. For upward communication, as Campbell[47] and others have shown, it often means that the sender distorts the message to conform to a conception of what the receiver wants to hear.

Gouldner[48] found that when labor and management represent polar forces, upward communication may become an effective vehicle of subordinate pressure against "programmed" authority such as rules and regulations. This can serve an important function in organizational dynamics, forcing changes that reflect the true relationship of power groupings before really explosive pressures build up.

Roberts and O'Reilly[49] found considerable evidence of a correlation between effective upward communication and the subordinates' *trust* in the superior. Evidence was less clear for a similar correlation with the subordinates' perception of the superior's *influence* over their future, and with the subordinates' ambition to move up in the organization, or *mobility* aspirations. A number of interesting relationships affect the three interpersonal factors and effective upward transmission of information.

Trust, for example, appears to be significantly related to a large number of communication factors. As might be predicted, a subordinate who trusts a superior also trusts the accuracy of the information received from the superior. A trusted superior is more likely to be perceived as having high influence. A subordinate is more likely to seek interaction with a trusted superior and to express satisfaction with communication in general. Subordinates who do not trust their supervisor, on the other hand, are likely to engage in *gatekeeping*— that is, to block or withhold information—and to acknowledge the existence of distortions in upward communication.

The subordinate's perception of the superior as having high influence shows some degree of association with the desire for interaction and with satisfaction with communication, though the linkage between these factors and trust is less pronounced. Perceived influence is also less consistently related to gatekeeping than is trust.

The subordinate's mobility aspirations exhibit some positive correlation with perceived influence of the superior, perceived accuracy of the information transmitted by the superior, and general satisfaction with communication. Throughout, mobility displays fewer and weaker associations with communication factors than either trust or influence.

As an element of downward communication, feedback serves to provide employees with information on the effectiveness of their performance, as perceived by superiors. As an element of upward communication, feedback supplies management with information on the effectiveness of directives and policies. Broadly defined, it represents the principal function of upward communication.

A familiar example of a mechanical feedback system is a thermostatically controlled furnace, in which a temperature-actuated switch turns the furnace on automatically when the temperature falls below a set lower limit and turns it off again when the temperature rises to a selected higher limit. Some analogous form of self-monitoring or self-regulation is the objective of feedback systems in general.

Obviously, the key to effective feedback is the system's ability to supply the control point with timely, accurate information on the status of the monitored activity. In a hierarchical structure such information travels through upward communication channels in which it may be subjected to an enormous number of impeding and distorting forces. Not only do the individuals at the operations level tend to report favorable results and conceal unfavorable results, for example, but those in higher echelons exhibit a corresponding tendency to resist acknowledging unfavorable information as long as possible.

The existence of effective upward communication provides several immediate and important rewards. According to Planty and Machever, these rewards include the following:

1. Management gets an improved picture of the work, accomplishments, problems, plans, attitudes, and feelings of subordinates at all levels.
2. Before becoming deeply involved, management spots individuals, policies, actions, or assignments that are likely to cause trouble.
3. By helping lower echelons of supervision to improve their selection of those things that are to be communicated upward, management gets the lower echelons to do a more systematic and useful job of reporting.
4. By welcoming upward communication, management strengthens the only device for tapping the ideas and help of its subordinates. This gives management a better answer to its problems and eases its own responsibility.
5. By opening the channels upward, management helps the easy flow and acceptance of communications downward. Good listening makes good listeners.[50]

We now turn our attention to the channels used to direct messages upward in the organization.

Upward Communication Channels

All employees, except those at the highest level of management, must communicate upward. Most of the channels that are useful for downward communication are also used in upward communication. Table 4-3 lists some of the most common upward communication channels used in organizations.

We now examine a number of the upward message channels.

TABLE 4-3   Upward Communication Channels

Oral	Written
Face-to-Face Interviews	Reports
Interviews	Personal Letters
Telephone	Memos
Meetings, Conferences	Grievances
Social Affairs	Suggestion Systems
Grapevine	Attitude/Information Surveys
Union Representatives	Union Publications
Counseling	

Suggestion and Complaint Systems   IBM established a "Speak Up Program" to provide answers to complaints, comments, and questions. If employees signed a certain form, an answer was mailed to their home. These employees were also given an opportunity to indicate a preference for discussing the problem with a qualified person. IBM found over 90 percent of the letters received were signed and about 80 percent asked for interviews.[51]

The suggestion system is meant to stimulate participation of employees in all aspects of the organization, usually by rewarding them for ideas that may benefit the company. It also provides an opportunity for employees to express criticism and relive their frustrations.

The suggestions are usually evaluated by a committee of superiors. The average suggestion input per year is about 200 to 300 per 1,000 employees. One-tenth to more than one-half of all employees who make suggestions receive some reward.[52] Supervisors are sometimes excluded from suggestion plans because managers and employees often charge that supervisors steal ideas from subordinates.[53] Rewarding the supervisor as well as the employees for their suggestions might decrease the implied threat of having their ideas stolen by superiors.

Although the suggestion programs can improve organizational operation, certain problems can arise.

Sometimes the suggestion made by a worker makes a supervisor appear inefficient or incompetent because the change was not already instituted by the supervisor. Then there is the delicate task of telling someone that his suggestion has no merit and is not eligible for an award. Still another problem is the amount of money to be awarded.

In some instances the suggestion made may cause the routine of an entire work group to change, or may result in eliminating one member of the group because of a more efficient production procedure. This obviously results in lowered group morale, ill will, and antagonism. The gain made through the suggestion may be lost twice over as a result of worker resentment.[54]

Face-to-Face Conversations and Reports   Ideally, a two-way system of communication should exist in every organization. Subordinates should feel as free to communicate with their superiors as superiors with subordinates. However, subordinates may not communicate unless the superior has an open-door attitude or encourages the expression of feelings and attitudes.

Reports may be of two kinds: oral and written. Oral reports can be presented in formal fashion before a group, with the presentation being accompanied by charts, graphs, and other visual aids. The oral report can also occur as a statement between subordinate and superior. Written reports come in a variety of forms and serve a number of functions. One author classifies the forms of reports according to their function (analytical, informative, persuasive). Another writer classifies them by type (credit, periodic, memo, examination, progress), whereas others prefer to classify reports by fields (medicine, management, marketing, sales, engineering) or area of activity (research, public, annual).[55]

Grievance Procedures   Subordinates are provided with the means—for example, a grievance panel—whereby they may appeal decisions of their superior or the actions of their fellow employees. Grievances may be concerned with promotions, workload, interpersonal relationships between employees or employee-subordinates, and so on. If the subordinates' grievances are supported by the labor union, for instance, the message will have a greater impact upon their superiors.

Attitude and Information Surveys   This channel usually helps to obtain employee responses to specific questions about the firm and its management. Surveys can provide superiors with information regarding morale problems, attitudes toward specific jobs, management, the organization, and misunderstandings with fellow employees, management, and the organization.

Grapevine   The grapevine serves as a means of emotional release and provides management with significant cues concerning the attitudes and feelings of organizational members. Although management may not wish to encourage the grapevine, its existence is inevitable. Consequently, management should utilize the information that evolves from it.

Many other channels of communication can be set up for increased upward communication. Whatever the channel, upward communication is beset with inherent problems. Generally, messages communicated upward serve two basic purposes: (1) to aid management in controlling and directing the firm and (2) to evaluate job performance. Consequently, employees may filter or change information to have the most favorable effect upon themselves. For instance, it was discovered that superiors were less aware of their subordinates' work problems when these subordinates were anxious to be promoted.[56] When employees do not care for their firm, they also may restrict or alter negative information about errors and problems. It is ironic that many times the individual who has the most to gain by upward communication refuses to communicate vertically.

A number of large organizations have used special techniques for channeling messages upward from employees. For example:

Southern California Edison Company has used a special "action reporter" in its biweekly newspaper who answers questions from employees about the company and related subjects.

Burlington Northern has used a "Dial-the-Boss" internal telephone system that records and passes employeee queries on to the chairman of the board or vice-chairman. Telephoners receive an answer by mail from one of these officials.

Connecticut General Life has used the "lunch on the house" day, during which the lunch period is extended from forty-five minutes to ninety to permit officers and supervisors to trade ideas with employees.

The BNA survey of banks reported earlier also rated upward communication channels, the most effective of which was "employee meetings." The sample gave several reasons—"employees seem to relate their feelings more freely," "they tell it like it is, not what (management) wants to hear," and "atmosphere of mutual trust and respect fosters honest discussion.." Formal attitude surveys, grievance or complaint procedures, counseling, exit interviews, talks with union representatives, formal meetings, and suggestion systems were all rated as effective upward channels.

A number of channels were not rated as particularly effective in the bank organization—grapevine, gripe boxes, a Q & A section in the employee magazine, open-door policy, employee committees, and special feedback procedures.[57]

The organizational hierarchical structure should permit communication to flow upward as well as downward. Unfortunately, communication from the bottom does not flow as freely as communication from the top. Problems in upward communication are now examined.

Upward Communication Problems

Likert stated that upward communication is at least as inadequate as downward communication and probably is less accurate because of selective filtering of the information that subordinates feed their superiors.[58]

It is difficult to determine whether upward- or downward-transmitted messages create the most serious problems in organizations. Cuttip and Center state: "The most pressing need is for more adequate upward communications, a management that operates from the bottom up."[59] Guetzkow suggests that "when there is contact between individuals of different status, communication from superior to the subordinate generally takes place more easily than communication from the subordinate to the superior."[60] As previously noted, employees are more likely to communicate pleasant messages upward than unpleasant ones; achievements are more often transmitted upward than information about errors or difficulties at lower levels.[61] Katz asserts that the "voice of the rank-and-file member of the organization is greatly attenuated as he attempts to get his message up the line."[62]

Subordinates are likely to screen out information passed up the line when they believe that this information "might reflect negatively" on their competence and, hence, their chances for "security or progress" in the organization. Citing Tompkins,

> There is . . . some research evidence to support the common-sense observation that subordinates are often reluctant to ask supervisors for help when they need it—because this might be perceived as a threatening admission of inadequacy.[63]

There is also a tendency in large organizations to block or distort upward-directed messages that are perceived as disadvantageous to either sender or receiver. Subordinates will only facilitate upward-directed messages when they believe that the message will either please the boss or enhance their own welfare. Subordinates who most desire promotion, for example, are least likely to communicate with their superiors.[64]

Athanassiades investigated the distortion of upward communication in two different types of organizations, a university faculty and a police department. The results of this study suggest that three factors distort upward-directed communication by subordinates: (1) degree of subordinate autonomy, (2) subordinate's security level, and (3) aspiration for upward mobility. The degree of upward message distortion is positively related to the subordinates' level of insecurity and mobility. And, the degree of autonomy contributes to the clarity of a subordinates' perception of his or her own security or mobility. Athanassiades suggests that distortion of upward communication provides a mechanism with which the subordinate can cope with the organization. If the upward distortion provides the organization with the means of using subordinates who possess mobility drives and/or feelings of insecurity, the upward communication can still be considered functional by the organization.[65]

Upward communication is a broad label, which describes subordinate-to-superior communication. A number of terms have been used to denote the level at which superiors are willing to hear the ideas and complaints of subordinates. They are upward communication freedom, upward receptiveness, and upward permissiveness. G. A. Sanborn discovered in a study that one-third of the employees examined did not perceive superiors as welcoming their comments. Furthermore, a third of the subordinates did not feel free to approach *appropriate* superiors regarding suggestions, personnel policies, benefits, company rules, regulations, and complaints.[66] R. L. Minter also found that many topics are taboo and not talked about between subordinates and superiors.[67]

Willits' investigation of "open communication" is of particular relevance. Open communication is defined as the probability that an individual will attempt to share accurately his or her views, feelings, and intentions with another, on matters that are pertinent to organizational objectives.[68] Willits was concerned with the message-sending side of openness, that is, the degree to which a subordinate could be open, authentic, or self-disclosing to a superior. He differentiates between two dimensions of open communication: (1) open communication of ideas, and (2) open communication of feelings. Willits found that open communication of ideas correlates positively with performance, whereas open expression of feeling and performance are negatively related.[69]

> . . . the negative correlations suggest that need to distinguish between open communications of feelings, and open communication about feelings. It may be one thing to tell the president matter-of-factly that you find his actions insulting, but another to act insulted. It may be functional for managers to be able to discuss feelings openly; however, it may be dysfunctional for them to vent those same feelings emotionally. As a result . . . three kinds of open communication are distinguishable:
> 1. Open communication of ideas
> 2. Open communication *about* feelings
> 3. Open communication *of* feelings[70]

Willits predicts that open communication about feelings will be associated with effective company performance, but open communication of feelings will probably be associated with ineffective communication. Lack of communication openness can lead to restricted commitment to the organization, subordinate gamesmanship, and the failure by executives to understand subordinates' perceptions of themselves.

Employees complain of the inability to make contact with superiors. As Vogel points out, "typically only about a third of the employees rate their boss as 'good' on being easy to see with a problem and only about a quarter rate him good on such matters as ability to handle complaints and encourage suggestions."[71] Most supervisors do not realize they are not accessible to their employees. Many managers believe that they deserve a greater voice with their own superiors than their own subordinates deserve with them. "To put it another way, many managers tend to be overly optimistic when assessing the blockages to upward communication experienced by their subordinates."[72]

"Someday I'm going to tell my boss what I really think about his work," is one of the most recurrent, and least honored, pledges of the frustrated subordinate. Superiors do want to know where they stand with their fellow employees and do welcome constructive criticism. Moreover, in many cases they are willing to take corrective action when they learn that their subordinates think their performance needs improvement. It is difficult, however, for superiors with years of experience to change quickly.

Superior evaluation builds a safety valve into the managerial system. It enables bosses to get a direct and accurate feedback on how their performance helps or hinders their employees. The superiors have an opportunity to explain or alter their behavior by listening to employee gripes, and sometimes, by altering their own behavior, they build confidence and trust, increase openness, and show willingness to help subordinates improve.

It is probable that superior preferences are communicated either consciously or unconsciously to subordinates when they communicate with their superiors. The subordinates may learn to avoid communication with superiors. It would seem that effective upward communication is dependent in part on the superior's willingness to permit open communication from subordinate to superior. As Redding suggests, "upward permissiveness" on the part of superiors is (a) a crucial dimension of organizational communication and (b) an essential ingredient in any overall managerial climate associated with organization effectiveness.[73]

Interpersonal trust seems an important antecedent to the openness and accuracy between employees, including superiors and subordinates when interacting. Gibb noted that the lack of trust leads to "inadequate data-flow,"[74] and that the lack of trust leads to distortion of data through channels, grapevine behavior, ambiguity, and protective phraseology. Expressions of low trust in superiors are related to: "(a) those variables which may signify potential gatekeeping and distortion of information (acknowledgment of the presence of influences leading to distortion of upward information flow, propensity to withhold information, and lack of desire for interaction); and (b) attitudinal variables (doubts about the accuracy of information received and dissatisfaction with communication in general). In these circumstances, the untrusting subordinate has little desire for interaction with supervisors."[75]

The relationship of the superior's influence over subordinates on upward communication is not as clearly defined as trust in superiors. Kelly, for example, concluded that the hierarchy produced a restraining force "against communicating criticisms of persons at the other levels."[76] Festinger pointed out that hierarchies restrain free communication, particularly criticism and aggressively toned comments, by low-status members to high-status members.[77] Roberts and O'Reilly, however, found that subordinates with high-influence superiors desire interaction and believe that accurate information is received from them. Furthermore, influence may not be dependent on trust and trust may predominate over influence.[78]

Read has suggested that there is a negative relationship between upwardly mobile members of an industrial organization and the accuracy of the upward communication. In addition, high-mobility aspirations by subordinates mitigate against accurate communication of potentially threatening information even when high trust of superiors exists.[79] Intuitively, the view that ambitious, upwardly mobile subordinates restrict their messages to exclude unfavorable or critical information is logical. Roberts and O'Reilly suggest this behavior may operate only in some groups. There was some evidence that upward mobility may influence upward communication in highly structured organizations such as military units.[80]

Davis has suggested that upward communication could be improved by better listening, building trust, and responding to messages that are received (feedback). He suggests a general policy to define which kinds of upward messages are desirable:

1. Any matters in which the supervisor may be held accountable by those at higher levels. (This includes all basic accountability for performance on one's assigned job.)
2. Any matters in disagreement or that are likely to cause controversy within or between any units of the organization.
3. Matters requiring advice by the supervisor or coordination with other persons or units.
4. Any matters involving recommendations for changes in, or variance from, established policies.
5. Any other matter that will enable higher management to improve economic and social performance.[81]

Downs, Linkugel, and Berg have also established some guidelines for use with upward communication:

1. Management should know what kinds of information it wants to have communicated upward and provide appropriate channels to get it.
2. Upward communication must be solicited. Many employees feel that communication is not wanted unless it is specifically requested.
3. Upward communication cannot be forced; it can only be invited. Open upward communication requires a basic trust of management.
4. In general, personal channels are preferable to impersonal ones, except in cases where the employee feels a need to remain anonymous. Consequently, both types should be available to the employee.
5. Listening must be active. There should be a concerted attempt to understand the messages employees send.
6. Upward communication requires a downward response. Employees who ask questions expect that they will be answered.[82]

Thus far we have been discussing messages flowing between superiors and subordinates in a vertical direction—upward or downward. In the next section we examine messages that flow horizontally or laterally within the organization.

Horizontal Communication

Horizontal communication is looked upon by many modern managers as being more crucial for organizational success than vertical communication. A study by Hage, Aiken, and Marrett found that as organization diversification and personal specialization increased, the volume of communication also increased in order to maintain coordination. They concluded, that: "The major direction of this increased flow of information is horizontal, especially cross-departmental communications at the same status levels."[83] Internal relationships are almost entirely lateral; they are with other functional departments of the same rank in the organizational hierarchy—departments such as production, scheduling, and quality control.

Horizontal communication consists of messages between employees on the same hierarchical level. Students of organizational communication have noted for some time that organizations emphasize and reward vertical communication, but virtually ignore horizontal communication.[84]

Early studies of organizations had largely ignored horizontal communication because there was no place for it in the model. Classical theorists focused on the hierarchical structure, and communication—when it was examined at all—was considered significant only to the extent that it was formalized in channels paralleling the chain of command.

It, therefore, came as something of a shock when the Hawthorne studies revealed that organizational personnel, even at the lowest level, talk to each other and sometimes achieve levels of understanding and coordination that challenge the organization's formal authority. Once recognized, however, this informal intraunit communication system became the object of study and efforts designed to integrate it within the formal structure. Managers were encouraged to identify and cultivate contact with the leaders of informal groups, and certain task functions, such as filling in job instruction details for new employees, were often turned over to the peer group. Although this was no doubt a sound move from an economic standpoint, it was sometimes calculated to achieve an additional purpose, as Katz and Kahn indicate:

> . . . if there are no problems of task coordination left to a group of peers, the content of their communication can take forms which are irrelevant to or destructive of organizational functioning.[85]

Obviously, this does not refer to the kind of horizontal task coordination across departmental lines that Hage, Aiken, and Marrett described as increasing in volume with growing organizational diversity. Like informal communication within a unit, cross-department communication undoubtedly involved a great deal of nontask conversation, but its principal function was to get the job done.

It is probably a safe assumption that some degree of such informal coordination and problem solving takes place through horizontal communication between members of different departments in every organization. Most communication systems would be swamped immediately if each interdepartmental message was sent "through channels." Such unacknowledged short-circuiting of the communication system probably accounts for missing pieces in the incomplete picture a manager often has of departmental activities. Like horizontal communication, informal cross-departmental communication appears to have been neglected by researchers principally because, as Hall puts it, "such communications are not supposed to occur."[86]

Horizontal communication performs several important functions in organizations. First, it allows coordination between departments to maximize productivity. Second, it allows problem solving at the level of origin and thus increases the morale and confidence of the individuals involved in the problem-solving process. Third, it allows sharing of information among departments—

which often contributes to task effectiveness. Fourth, it is useful in solving intradepartment and interdepartment conflict without intervention. Fifth, by allowing interaction among organizational peers, horizontal communication furnishes social and emotional support to the worker. Sixth, it serves as a substitute for upward and downward communication in some situations. Some employees find it more comfortable to interact with peers and their interaction thus serves as an outlet for their problems, frustrations, and fears.

Horizontal Communication Channels

Horizontal communication is important among employees in the development of group coordination and teamwork; it facilitates their interaction and the performance of their job responsibilities. In some organizations the amount of horizontal communication is as great as the amount of vertical communication. Take, for example, an advertising agency where the layout department depends on the art department for incoming work that supplies the production department, and which, in turn, receives special services from a number of special organizations; each department and organization is on the same hierarchical level. Most of the channels discussed earlier also are employed in horizontal communication. Table 4-4 illustrates some commonly used horizontal channels. We now examine two additional channels.

TABLE 4-4   Horizontal Communication Channels

Oral	Written
Lectures, Conferences, Committee Meetings	Letters, Memos, Reports
Telephone, Intercom Systems	House Organs
Movies, Slides, Television	Bulletin Boards, Posters
Social Affairs, Union Activities	Handbooks and Manuals
Grapevine, Rumor, Gossip	Annual Reports

Committees   Committees serve for both vertical and horizontal communication, and assist or hinder both the informal and formal communication structures in an organization. Usually appointed from within the organization, committees assist in the exchange of oral and written messages and can overcome weak links or barriers in the formal communication structure. However, the mere formation of a committee will never guarantee that a task or goal will be accomplished either efficiently or effectively. The success of committees is largely dependent upon the abilities of group members and their leader or chair. Price has given the following suggestions for an effective chair in organizations:

1. Never compete with group members.
2. Listen to the group members.
3. Don't permit anyone to be put on the defensive.
4. Use every member of the group.

5. Keep the energy level high.
6. Keep the members informed about where they are and what is expected of them.
7. Keep your eye on the expert.
8. Remember that you are not permanent.
9. Do not manipulate the group.
10. Work hard at the technique of chairmanship.[87]

In addition, the chair must utilize a leadership style that is appropriate to the situation (see Chapter 9 for a discussion of leadership styles in the organization).

Conferences   Managers and employees may arrange conferences or retreats in which associates meet for one day or several days to confer without the usual interruptions of offices and assembly lines. Dinners, picnics, and other social affairs may be held to permit extra contacts and freer exchanges.

Horizontal communication may be perceived as threatening by an authoritarian manager, foreman, or union steward. When subordinates develop an effective horizontal communication network and increase their knowledge of the overall organizational structures, the likelihood of authoritarian leadership declines.

In any organization it is important for management and employees to create conditions that are conducive for the transmission of messages both vertically and horizontally. A free flow of messages, vertically and horizontally, is dependent not only on the organization structure and communication climate but also upon the media that are appropriate for different levels in the organization.

We now turn our attention to several organizational communication problems associated with horizontal communication.

Horizontal Communication Problems

Horizontal communication is vital in providing coordination between organizational subdivisions. However, the subdivisions themselves may impair horizontal communication. Katz and Kahn noted that organizations with a more authoritarian structure control more closely the flow of horizontal information. The highest level manager possesses information about each subdivision under his or her control, but the lower level managers are only familiar with the operations of their own subdivisions. Restricting the information increases the power of the superior manager. By imposing restrictions on horizontal communication, the subordinate becomes dependent on information that is communicated by vertical channels. A totalitarian government is the extreme example of control over horizontal communication.[88]

Horizontal communication also can show uncontrolled proliferation. As an organization's structure becomes more diversified and as individuals become increasingly specialized, the need for coordination increases horizontal communication.[89] Horizontal communication increases as power or authority be-

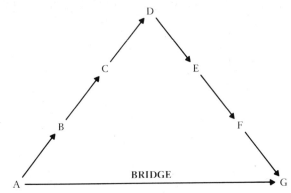

Figure 4.1 Fayol's Bridge

comes less centralized and shared throughout the organization. Horan found in organizations characterized by unrestricted horizontal communication that there were frequent instances of conflict and misunderstanding.[90]

When employees have no questions of task coordination, problem solving, or information sharing about whch to communicate, they may turn to gossip and rumor that is irrelevant and potentially destructive to organizational operations. As Katz and Kahn state, "If there are no problems of task coordination left to a group of peers, the content of their communication can take forms which are irrelevant to or obstructive to operational functioning."[91]

Finally, there exists at times a tendency among peers not to formally communicate task-related information horizontally. Rivalry for recognition and promotion may cause competing subordinates to be reluctant to share information. Subordinates may find it difficult to communicate with highly specialized people at the same level but in other technical departments.

Organizational structures may discourage horizontal communication between individuals in different divisions. Messages are supposed to follow a "chain of command," that is, messages pass up to the superior and then back down. The passage vertically within the organizational structure as part of the horizontal flow increases the time it takes individuals to communicate. Fayol proposed a formal channel called "Fayol's Bridge" (shown in Figure 4.1) to eliminate this problem.[92] Normally, messages in formal channels will pass from individual A upward through individuals B and C to individual D and then downward through individuals E and F to individual G. Using Fayol's Bridge, when organizational success depends on quick action, the message can be sent directly from individual A to individual G.

Galbraith has suggested in order of increasing cost a variety of horizontal communication forms that will increase the effectiveness of horizontal interactions in the organization.

1. Utilize direct contact between managers who share a problem.
2. Establish liaison roles to link two departments that have substantial contact.

3. Create temporary groups called task forces to solve problems affecting several departments.
4. Employ groups or teams on a permanent basis for constantly recurring interdepartmental problems.
5. Create a new role, an integrating role, when the leadership of lateral processes becomes a problem.
6. Shift from an integrating role to a linking-managerial role when faced with substantial differentiation.[93]

REVIEW QUESTIONS

1. What are the five elements in downward communication?
2. What problems of communication are associated with messages transmitted downward in the organization?
3. How should one transmit information downward?
4. How can one improve downward communication?
5. What organizational functions are served by upward communication?
6. What problems of communication are associated with messages transmitted upward in the organization?
7. How can one improve upward communication?
8. What organizational functions are served by horizontal communication?
9. What problems of communication are associated with messages transmitted horizontally in the organization?

KEY TERMS AND CONCEPTS FOR REVIEW

- Downward Communication
- Job Instruction
- Rationale
- Ideology
- Information
- Feedback
- Substitute Locomotion Theory
- Need Satisfaction Theory

- Relevancy
- Openness
- Information Deprivation
- Trust
- Mobility
- Gatekeeping
- Upward Communication
- Horizontal Communication

CASE STUDY 1

Seymour Hymen is director of personnel for Diet, Inc. He has 330 employees under his supervision. Ten employees are managers, each supervising units of thirty workers. The work units are deployed in the field to conduct seminars in weight control.

Recently, Seymour has noticed that the company's new policies and procedures were not being implemented immediately by the managers. Furthermore, the field-workers were not receiving some of his directives.

PROBES

1. If you were the company director, how would you transmit the directives to the workers?
2. If you were the company director, how would you oversee the implementation of new policies and procedures?

CASE STUDY 2

The chairperson of the Accounting Department in a large university complains to the school dean that his faculty are frustrated with new university scheduling policies. Faculty are not getting to teach their preferred courses, classes have been dropped from the schedule without notice, and the scheduled class times do not consider the other obligations of the instructional faculty.

The president and vice-president for Academic Affairs are sympathetic to the faculty complaints. To help solve the problem, the dean is requested to develop a new set of scheduling policies and procedures.

PROBES

1. What channels of communication should be used to develop the new policies and procedures? Why were these channels selected?

Recommended Readings

Athanassiades, J. C. "Distortion of Upward Communication in Hierarchical Organizations." *Academy of Management Journal* 16(1973): 207–225.

Baird, J. E. Jr. *The Dynamics of Organizational Communication.* New York: Harper & Row, 1977, Chapter 7.

Katz, D., and R. L. Kahn. *The Social Psychology of Organizations* New York: John Wiley & Sons, 1966.

Planty, E. and W. Machever. "Upward Communication: Project in Executive Development." *Personnel* 28(1952):304–319.

Reitz, H. J. *Behavior in Organizations.* Homewood, Ill.: Richard D. Irwin, 1977, pp. 355–363.

Sigband, N. B. *Communication for Management and Business,* 2d ed. Glenview, Ill.: Scott, Foresman and Co., 1976, pp. 26–44.

Notes

1. G. Seybold, *Employee Communication: Policy and Tools* (New York: National Industrial Conference Board, 1966), pp. 31–34.
2. *Boeing Management Perspective*, July/August 1968.
3. C. B. McCoy, *Better Living* (Fall 1971): 3.
4. D. Katz and R. Kahn, *The Social Psychology of Organizations* (New York: John Wiley & Sons, 1966), pp. 239–243.
5. W. Kirchner and J. Belenker, "What Employees Want to Know," *Personnel* 32 (1955): 379; J. Miner and E. Heatin, "Company Orientation as a Factor in the Readership of Employee Publications," *Personnel Psychology* 12 (1959): 607–618.
6. S. Habbe, Communicating with Employees, Student Personnel Policy, no. 129, New York: National Industrial Conference Board, 1952.
7. R. Likert, "Motivational Approach to Management Development," *Harvard Business Review* 37 (1959): 75–82.
8. Katz and Kahn, op. cit., p. 239.
9. "How Do Your Communications Rate?" *Banking* 68 (1975): 8.
10. N. B. Sigband, *Communication for Management and Business*, 2d ed. (Glenview, Ill.: Scott, Foresman and Co., 1976), pp. 37–38.
11. S. Tingley, "Six Requirements for a Successful Company Publication," *Personnel Journal* 46 (1967): 638–642.
12. Sigband, op. cit., pp. 38–39.
13. "How to Keep Employees Well Informed," *Personnel Management* 9 (1977): 13, 15.
14. "How Do Your Communications Rate?", loc. cit.
15. W. C. Redding, *Communication Within the Organization* (New York: Industrial Communication Council, 1972), p. 425.
16. D. A. Level, "A Case Study of Human Communications in an Urban Bank," Ph.d. diss. (Lafayette, Ind.: Purdue University, 1959).
17. A. B. Chase, "How to Make Downward Communication Work," *Personnel Journal* 49 (1970): 478–483.
18. E. Walton, "Project: Office Communications," *Administrative Management* 23 (1962): 22.
19. Ibid., pp. 22–24.
20. Level, op. cit., R. A. H. Rosen, "Foreman Role Conflict: On Expression of Contradictions in Organizational Goals," *Industrial and Labor Relations Review* 23 (1970): 541–552.
21. "Success of Chain of Command Oral Communication in a Manufacturing Management Group," *Academy of Management Journal* 11 (1968): 379–387.
22. R. G. Nichols, "Listening Is Good Business," *Management of Personnel Quarterly* 2 (1962): 4.
23. M. H. Brenner and N. B. Sigband, "Organizational Communication : An Analysis Based on Empirical Data," *Academy of Management Journal* 16 (1973): 323–324.
24. Rosen, op. cit.
25. Tompkins, "Organizational Communication: A State-of-the-Art Review." In G. Richetto, *Conference on Organizational Communication* (Huntsville, Ala.: George C. Marshall Space Flight Center, NASA, 1967), pp. 12–13.
26. S. A. Culbert and J. M. Elden, "An Anatomy of Activism for Executives," *Harvard Business Review* 48 (1970): 140.
27. Redding, op. cit., p. 391.

28. A. Walker, "1970 Survey of Business Communicators," *IABC Notebook* (February 1971): 10.
29. Level, op. cit.; Walton, op. cit.
30. D. Katz and R. L. Kahn, *The Social Psychology of Organizations* (New York: John Wiley & Sons, 1966).
31. L. I. Gilfand, "Communicate Through Your Supervisors," *Harvard Business Review* 48 (1970): 101–104.
32. G. Gemmill, "Managing Upward Communication," *Personnel Journal* 49 (1970): 107–110.
33. G. Goldhaber, *Organizational Communication* (Dubuque, Iowa: William C. Brown Company, 1979, pp. 114–116.
34. T. L. Dahle, "An Objective and Comparative Study of Five Methods for Transmitting Information to Business and Industrial Employees," *Speech Monographs* 21 (1954): 21–28.
35. K. Davis, *Human Behavior at Work*, 5th ed. (New York: McGraw-Hill Book Co., 1976), p. 386.
36. A. J. Melcher and R. Beller, "Toward a Theory of Organizational Communication: Consideration in Channel Selection," *Academy of Management Journal* 10 (1967): 39–52.
37. Ibid., p. 51.
38. G. Goldhaber, loc. cit.
39. K. Davis, op. cit., pp. 397–398.
40. C. Downs, W. Linkugel, D. M. Berg, *The Organizational Communicator* (New York: Harper & Row, 1977), pp. 27–28.
41. H. Kelly, "Communication in Experimentally Created Hierarchies," *Human Relations* 4 (1951): 39–56.
42. A. Cohen, "Upward Communication in Experimentally Created Hierarchies," *Human Relations* 11 (1958): 41–53.
43. M. Mulder, "The Power Variable in Communication Experiments," *Human Relations* 13 (1960): 241–256.
44. Katz and Kahn, op. cit., p. 245.
45. J. W. Koehler and G. Huber, "Effects of Upward Communication on Managerial Decision Making" (New Orleans, La.: International Communication Association, 1974).
46. C. J. Berhard, *The Functions of the Executive* (Cambridge, Mass.: Harvard University Press, 1938).
47. D. T. Campbell, "Systematic Error on the Part of Human Links in Communication Systems," *Information and Control* 1 (1958): 334–369.
48. A. W. Gouldner and W. Alvin, *Patterns of Industrial Bureaucracy* (London: Routledge & Kegan Paul, 1955).
49. K. H. Roberts and C. A. O'Reilly, III, "Failure in Upward Communication in Organizations: Three Possible Culprits," *Academy of Management Journal*, 17 (1974): 205–215.
50. E. Planty and W. Machever, "Upward Communication: Project in Executive Development," *Personnel* 28 (1952): 304–319.
51. International Business Machines, *Fact Book on Speak Up* (New York: IBM Publications Services Department, January 1969).
52. Yoder, *Personnel Management and Industrial Relations*, 6th ed. (Englewood Cliffs, N.J.: Prentice-Hall, 1978), p. 582.
53. E. Hardin, "Characteristics of Participants in an Employee Suggestion Plan."

M.S.U. School of Labor and Industrial Relations, Reprint Series No. 70, 1964–75; Charles Foss, "How to Administer a Suggestion System," *Management Review* 57 (August 1968): 28–30.

54. Sigband, op. cit., p. 27.
55. Ibid.
56. W. H. Read, "Upward Communication in Industrial Hierarchies," *Human Relations* 15 (1961): 1–8.
57. "How Do Your Communications Rate?" loc. cit.
58. R. Likert, *New Patterns of Managment* (New York: McGraw-Hill Book Co., 1961), p. 47.
59. S. M. Cuttip and A. H. Center, *Effective Public Relations*, 4th ed. (Englewood Cliffs, N.J.: Prentice-Hall, 1971), p. 314.
60. H. Guetzkow, "Communications in Organizations." In J. G. March, op. cit., p. 548.
61. W. H. Read, "Upward Communication in Industrial Hierarchies," *Human Relations* 15 (1962): 3–15.
62. D. Katz, "The Motivational Basis of Organizational Behavior," *Behavioral Science* 9 (1964): 131–146.
63. Tompkins, op. cit., p. 13.
64. N. R. Maier *et al.*, "Superior-Subordinate Communication: A Statistical Research Project," In *AMA Research Report* no. 52 (New York, 1961): pp. 9–30.
65. J. C. Athanassiades, "The Distortion of Upward Communication in Hierarchical Organizations," *Academy of Management Journal* 16 (1973): 224–225.
66. G. G. Sanborn, "An Analytical Study of Oral Communication Practices in a Nationwide Retail Sales Organization." Ph.D. diss. (Lafayette, Ind.: Purdue University, 1961).
67. R. L. Minter, "A Comparative Analysis of Managerial Communication in Two Divisions of a Large Manufacturing Company," Ph.D. diss. (Lafayette, Ind.: Purdue University, 1969).
68. R. D. Willits, "Company Performance and Interpersonal Relations," *Industrial Management Review* 7 (1967): 91–107.
69. Ibid., pp. 98–99.
70. Ibid., p. 101.
71. A. Vogel, "Why Don't Employees Speak Up?," *Personnel Administration* 30 (1967): 21.
72. Redding, op. cit., p. 367.
73. Ibid., p. 386.
74. J. R. Gibb, "Climate for Trust Formation," in L. P. Bradford, J. R. Gibb, and K. D. Benne, eds., *T-Group Theory and Laboratory Methods: Innovation in Re-Education* (New York: John Wiley & Sons, 1964), pp. 279–309.
75. Roberts and O'Reilly, op. cit., p. 213.
76. Kelly, loc. cit.
77. L. Festinger, "Informal Social Communication," *Psychological Review* 57 (1950): 217–282.
78. Roberts and O'Reilly, loc. cit.
79. Read, loc. cit.
80. Roberts and O'Reilly, op. cit. p. 214.
81. Davis, op. cit., p. 401
82. Downs, Linkugel, and Berg, op. cit., pp. 29–30.
83. J. Hage, M. Aiken, and C. Marrett, "Organizational Structure and Communications," *American Sociological Review* 36 (1971): 860–871.

84. G. Albaum, "Horizontal Information Flow: An Exploratory Study," *Academy of Management Journal* 7 (1964): 21–33; R. Smith, G. Richetto, and J. Zima, "Organizational Behavior: An Approach to Human Communication," In R. Budd and B. Ruben, eds., *Approaches to Human Communication* (New York: Spartan Books, 1972), pp. 269–289.

85. Katz and Kahn, op. cit., p. 244.

86. R. H. Hall, *Organizations, Structure and Process* (Englewood Cliffs, N.J.: Prentice Hall, 1972), p. 285.

87. G. M. Price, "How to Be a Better Meeting Chairman," *Harvard Business Review* 47 (1969): 98–108.

88. Katz and Kahn, loc. cit.

89. Hage, Aiken, and Marett, op. cit.

90. H. Horan, "A Communication Systems Analysis of KOB-TV," paper presented at the International Communication Association Convention, Atlanta, 1972.

91. Katz and Kahn, op. cit., p. 244.

92. H. Fayol, *General and Industrial Administration* (New York: Pittman, 1949).

93. J. R. Galbraith, *Organization Design* (Reading, Mass.: Addison-Wesley Publishing Company, 1977), Chapter 8.

5 | Message: Management

LEARNING OBJECTIVES

After reading this chapter, you should be able to
1. Explain the role of feedback in organizational communication.
2. Explain the role of listening in organizational communication.
3. Identify two types of listening.
4. Explain the qualities of feedback for which organizational employees should strive.
5. Define the grapevine and rumor in organizations.
6. Explain how one minimizes the number and severity of rumors in the grapevine.
7. Explain how the communication networks affect communication behavior.
8. Explain how the organizational climate affects communication behavior.

Communication in organizations utilizes verbal and nonverbal messages to achieve some intended response from others. Effective communication requires an understanding of the primary factors affecting the transmission and reception of messages. In the previous two chapters we have examined a number of factors that affect the reception and understanding of the message and factors that affect messages as they are transmitted vertically and horizontally within the organizational structure. In this chapter we explore several additional key elements that impact on the effectiveness of messages in the organizational environment.

Studies of organizations have revealed that the message and the response to that message are affected by problems in receiving and reacting by employees. Although the formal communication structure generally receives the most attention in any study of organizational communication, the informal structure of the organization often plays just as important a role in determining communication effectiveness. The structure of the communication networks, both formal and informal, also affects the behavior and job performance of employees. Finally, each organization has a particular climate that is affected by, and subsequently influences, the behavior of individuals in the organization. To explore these factors that impact on the effectiveness of messages, we have divided this chapter into four sections: (1) Listening and Feedback, (2) Grapevine and Rumor, (3) Communication Networks, and (4) Organizational Climates. We begin our examination with those factors affecting the reception and reaction to messages.

Feedback and Listening

"My boss never takes the time to explain what's happening around here. I see all the memos about what's going on, but they leave me more confused than ever." Do you recognize this situation?

Ideally, this employee would be able to respond to the boss and clarify the incoming messages. However, with written messages, instantaneous response from the receiver is usually missing or channels are not provided for the employee's reactions. A manager may be oblivious to the impact of a message on subordinates; the manager may not know what is happening, and only the employees may recognize that any problem exists.

When talking with an employee, however, a manager has the advantage of being able to obtain an immediate response to the message and, thus, evaluate its effectiveness. Facial expressions, questions, and replies by an employee can be used to judge understanding. Barnes states that "before a top manager can make intelligent decisions, particularly those required to instigate needed change, he must have ready access to something else which is not always so easily acquired. Before he can prescribe for what is wrong, he must know what the majority of competent people think is right."[1] The achievement of this goal requires an effective feedback system operating in the organization.

The concept of feedback originated within the field of cybernetics and refers to the capacity of a system to regulate itself. For example, if a home thermostat records a temperature that deviates from the desired temperature, a signal is fed back to the furnace to make a correction. Human communication is much more complex. As Barnlund explains, "Each person (in the relationship) must monitor his own acts to produce the words and gestures he intends, and must monitor the reactions of others to those words and gestures to see if his message prompted the reaction he sought."[2] Generally, we refer to feedback as the verbal or nonverbal response required from the individual to whom the message is directed.

Brown distinguishes between feedback involving small groups and feedback intended to assist the operation of a large organization. He calls the latter form of feedback *organizational feedback* and notes that it is less personal and threatening than feedback occurring between small groups of individuals. Both types of feedback are crucial to the successful functioning of any large organization.[3] For instance, employees need feedback from their superiors about their effectiveness on the job (small group feedback). Decisions are affected by the information the employees' receive as to whether they have succeeded or failed in achieving previous goals. One study found that individuals receiving accurate information regarding their job performance set higher goals, whereas those receiving feedback that exaggerated their errors set lower goals.[4] Managers need feedback reports about the operation of the organization to enable them to secure information upon which to base their decisions (organizational feedback).[5]

The presence of feedback in organizational groups generally increases both the time spent in discussion and the group's productivity. In addition, feedback provides group members with a more accurate view of their own self-image.[6] Employees want feedback, and the type of feedback they receive affects their subsequent job performance.[7]

Unfortunately, feedback does not always work to the advantage of an organization. Cook found that feedback can discourage as well as encourage job performance. To facilitate job performance she suggests "that information which is considered more valuable by the managers should be provided more frequently, and less essential data should be provided less frequently."[8] G. Shure, M. Rogers, I. Larsen and J. Tassone found that immediate feedback, when compared with delayed feedback, could interfere with long-range planning.[9] It is Bowman's opinion that excessive feedback can lead to a condition of "overload," which in turn induces either underreaction or overreaction to feedback messages on the part of the manager.[10] There are additional risks of too much feedback, especially from subordinates to superiors. For instance, a subordinate might inform his superior that the superior is dictatorial. This evaluation of the superior could subject the future personal relations between the superior and subordinate to intolerable strains.[11]

Nokes believed that a manager's receptivity to feedback may be related to the degree of power the manager thinks he or she possesses. "Where . . . the individual is able to control events, there is a tendency to dispense with the need for accurate information. . . . a neglect of feedback."[12] This behavior is familiar in the phenomenon of *executive isolation*. However, such isolation results from two factors occurring simultaneously: (a) the manager's resistance to potentially troublesome feedback, and (b) the subordinate's fear of transmitting upward any messages deemed likely to "upset" the boss or put the subordinate in a bad light. Any kind of feedback that is perceived to be threatening or derogatory is likely to be either neglected or distorted. Feedback in the organization works best where mutual trust exists, and therefore the emphasis should be on creating trust.[13]

Since feedback is a two-way process, it is important that the individual give as well as receive feedback. Redding proposed a way of conceptualizing the two-way character of feedback, with particular reference to managerial behavior:

1. *Feedback receptiveness*, referring to the question: to what extent does a manager open up to incoming feedback, especially from subordinates in the organization?
2. *Feedback responsiveness*, referring to the question: to what extent does a manager give feedback to messages initiated by others, especially subordinates?[14]

The problem in the organization is that the manager in many cases neglects the area of feedback responsiveness.[15]

Most American businessmen are practitioners of a structure called *high-stream coupling*; that is, department heads of a company work as a group. It is similar to feedback—permitting rapid flow of information back and forth through the management network. The feedback allows one to anticipate both internal and external changes, so that decisions can be revised and everyone can be alerted to the necessity for change.

In many organizations the network between managers and subordinates is dictated by the superiors. The managers set the time, place, and subject of discussion with subordinates. They often end up defining the meaning of words or phrases in the messages. In turn, the employees may refuse to listen, or they may listen without effective message evaluation. The employees might carry out ridiculous orders to the exact letter, as a form of "malicious obedience," or they may listen only to communications backed by the threat of possible penalty.[16]

Effective listening on the part of both superiors and subordinates may be the most crucial factor in an effective feedback process. We realize that individuals in an organization spend more time listening to messages than sending messages. However, the development of listening skills still has not received the attention that has been devoted to speaking, writing, and reading skills in organizations. And, listening is one of the weakest points of managers in oral communication.[17]

Charles M. Kelly posits listening into two categories: deliberative and empathic.[18] *Deliberative listening* is the ability to hear information, analyze it, recall it at a later time, and draw conclusions from it. The deliberative listener will first analyze what is said, and then try to understand the message source.

Most listening tests and organizational training programs are concerned with deliberative listening. *Empathic listening* occurs when a receiver participates in the feeling context of the message environment and intuitively establishes an unspoken two-way communication with the message source. If one is listening empathically, one feels what the message source is thinking or feeling, irrespective of the specific words in the message. In turn, responses convey to others that one has this knowledge. The empathic listener is equipped to be a good manager/catalyst.[19]

To become an empathic listener, no matter how inaccurate or unnecessary one considers a message, one should allow the entire message to be transmitted, heard, and answered before critically evaluating it. One should listen nonevaluatively—that is, one should try to understand the source's frame of reference and point of view to provide a basis for mutual understanding. The empathic listener will not evaluate a message until the ideas and feelings of the source have been related to the message.[20] Nonevaluative listening encourages not only more careful listening but also the presentation of more information. When a message source experiences a nonthreatening environment, he or she may have a clearer perception of what he or she is saying.[21] The development of effective listening skills is crucial to both superiors and subordinates in the organization. Basset feels that "a results-oriented personnel or training department . . . must provide expanded opportunities for managers to practice listening" and thus improve the overall level of communication within the organization.[22] Skillful listening develops the information, insight, and understanding that are indispensable in dealing with people and successfully managing an organization.

Many companies have attempted to improve the listening skills of employees by offering programmed instruction on learning.[23] Nichols lists three key elements that should be present in any listening training:[24]

1. Anticipate the source's next point—If the listener guesses correctly, learning is reinforced. If the guess is wrong the listener learns by comparison.
2. Identify supporting elements—The listener must be able to sort out facts from emotions.
3. Make summaries—The listener must be able to make summaries of the ideas communicated when the source pauses or breaks.

Davis has developed ten guides for developing effective listening habits. These guides are listed in Table 5-1.[25]

Ineffective listening is not the only detriment to effective feedback. Employees are sometimes reluctant to admit that they cannot understand a superior's message. An affirmative head nodding "Yes, sir!" does not always signify message understanding. It is, therefore, desirable to have additional means of feedback to assure that the correct message is received. Verbal responses may need to be encouraged by the source to provide a basis for evaluating receiver understanding. If the verbal message response is inconsistent with the nonverbal response, it may be necessary for the message source to repeat or reword the message.

TABLE 5-1   Ten Guides for Effective Listening

1. Stop Talking!
   You cannot listen if you are talking.
   Polonius (Hamlet): "Give every man thine ear, but few thy voice."
2. Put the talker at ease.
   Help a person feel free to talk.
   This is often called a *permissive* environment.
3. Show a talker that you want to listen.
   Look and act interested. Do not read your mail while someone talks.
   Listen to understand rather than to oppose.
4. Remove distractions.
   Don't doodle, tap, or shuffle papers.
   Will it be quieter if you shut the door?
5. Empathize with talkers.
   Try to help yourself see the other person's point of view.
6. Be patient.
   Allow plenty of time. Do not interrupt a talker.
   Don't start for the door or walk away.
7. Hold your temper.
   An angry person takes the wrong meaning from words.
8. Go easy on argument and criticism.
   This puts people on the defensive and they may "clam up" or become angry.
   Do not argue: Even if you win, you lose.
9. Ask questions.
   This encourages a talker and shows that you are listening.
   It helps to develop points further.
10. Stop talking!
    This is the first and last, because all other guides depend on it.
    You cannot do an effective listening job while you are talking.
    - Nature gave people two ears but only one tongue,
      which is a gentle hint that they should listen more than they talk.
    - Listening requires two ears,
      one for meaning and one for feeling.
    - Decision makers who do not listen
      have less information for making sound decisions.

Aronson suggests that feedback be expressed in terms of feelings, rather than in judgments or evaluations. Opinions and judgments about another person or that person's message are merely conjecture, whereas an expression of feeling is *fact*.[26] If a manager reacts to an employee's message by calling him a phony, it may be true, or it may merely be his or her personal opinion. Only the employee knows whether he or she is a phony. A manager's statement that he or she is angry with an employee's message is not a guess—it is a fact. Expressing feedback in the form of feelings provides the recipient with an indication of the source's internal states and, thereby, provides a basis for avoiding possible message misunderstanding. It should be apparent, then, that two keys to effective organizational communication—listening and feedback—are interdependent. Feedback will not mean much until the basics of listening have been mastered. Managers and employees must be able to discern the importance of each, and their interrelationship.

DeVito states that, "If speakers are to learn the effects of their messages and if they are to adapt their messages more effectively, then listeners must be trained to send these messages of feedback to speakers."[27] DeVito suggests five guidelines for training in the use of feedback by listeners: (1) feedback must be immediate, (2) feedback must be honest, (3) feedback must be directed toward the behavior that can be changed and not at the person, (4) feedback must specify the behavior or behaviors of concern, and (5) feedback must be informative.

Baird posits three related qualities of constructive feedback for which organizational employees should strive.[28]

1. Clarity—a feedback message should have only one meaning. Some messages are called *double-binds* because they tell the receiver to perform two messages and thus create problems for individuals who must decide which of the behaviors they are to perform.
2. Appropriateness—the content of the feedback message should pertain to the source's initial message. In addition, the receiver should neither overreact or underreact to the original message.
3. Positiveness—the feedback message should demonstrate a positive nonevaluative concern for the relationship with the source of the original message.

Organizations cannot continue to tolerate the costs of poor human relations or restricted productivity caused by ineffective listening. Learning a new set of listening or feedback skills can provide a substantial reward to both the organizational employee and the organization.

All organizations have formal and informal structures for communicating messages within the organization. In the next section, we examine the informal communication channel referred to most frequently as the organizational grapevine.

Grapevine and Rumor

Messages are often transmitted outside the formal communication channels of an organization. The informal communication structure is referred to as the *grapevine*. The term *grapevine* was first used during the Civil War to characterize the intelligence telephone lines that were loosely strung between trees. Since the messages were often incorrect and confusing, rumor was said to emanate from the grapevine.[29]

A middle manager of a medium-size manufacturing company was surprised when a fellow employee congratulated her on her promotion. She had received no formal announcement.

An employee was working in the morning when a colleague mentioned that the employee would be relocated in the firm's new plant. Later that afternoon he received a formal letter notifying him of the change.

In both examples, the informal communication apparatus known as the corporate grapevine was at work. The grapevine had operated quicker than the formal communication structure in the organization. Every organization has an informal communication system. The informal system may arise from the social relationships between employees and is neither required nor controlled by management. Larson and DeFleur observing the spread of information contained in a leaflet concluded that most of the social diffusion took place between friends and neighbors.[30] Similarly, Coleman, Katz, and Menzel in a study of the adoption of a new drug by physicians found that the drug was adopted first by an integrated group of doctors, then spread through social networks based on friendships, and last reached doctors through magazines and drug salesmen.[31] Erbe found that the number of interpersonal contacts and number of group memberships determined the emerging of informal communication networks.[32]

Messages passed along the grapevine are, at times, referred to as *rumors*. Davis, however, does not equate rumor and grapevine. According to Davis, rumor is only one type of communication along the grapevine—that is, messages communicated without secure standards of evidence being provided.[33] Rumors are credible to an employee because they contain some truths or half truths. Unfortunately, once a rumor is known and accepted, employees tend to distort future events to conform to the rumors.

Rumors develop, in part, because managers, supervisors, or employees perceive the formal communication structure as inadequate. When employees have difficulty either transmitting or listening to a message, they tend to look for other means to meet their perceived needs—and they look for it in rumors. Rumor is encouraged by attitudes that regard communications with superiors or subordinates suspiciously, or by the organizational policies that foster secrecy.[34] Rumors operate as an emotional safety valve for employees' frustrations and worries.[35] It allows people to "blow off steam."

Festinger developed three principles to account for rumor behavior.

1. The principle of external control—that rumors arise when important events are beyond the control of those involved in them.
2. The principle of cognitive unclarity—that rumors originate when situations are unstructured and unpredictable.
3. The principle of integrative explanation—that details tend to be distorted to conform to the dominant theme of the rumor.[36]

Schachter and Burdick suggest that rumors occur only in situations involving cognitive unclarity.[37] Their observation supports Allport and Postman's "basic law of rumor" that claims that the rumors spread as a function of the importance of the information and the ambiguity present in the situation.[38]

Rumors are not necessarily counterproductive to the operation of an organization. First, it would appear that rumors occur quite infrequently in organizations.[39] Second, most of the information carried in the grapevine is accurate. Davis reports an accuracy index of 80 to 90 percent for noncontroversial information in one industry and Marking found rumors to be 80 percent accurate.[40]

Managers who are bypassed by the grapevine should take it as a signal that their own channels of communication can be improved. For example, do they provide their employees with information when they need it? Do they talk with employees only when official business is involved, or do they talk informally with them on coffee breaks, over lunch, or at social gatherings? The grapevine provides managers with feedback from their workers. If they are not receiving this information, it may decrease the efficiency of the organization.

Bernard observed that "informal organizations are necessary to the operation of formal organizations as a means of communication. . . ."[41] Shils concludes that the effective transmission and execution of commands along the formal lines of authority can be successful only when it coincides with this system of informal groups.[42]

The grapevine helps interpret management for the employee, and provides a vehicle for translating management's formal messages into employee language by conveying information that the formal system does not wish to transmit or leaves unsaid.[43] The grapevine can be used as a constructive tool for gathering information in the organization. Management can tell the grapevine what activities certain individuals and groups are involved in, what their future plans are, and how they feel about the organizational environment and the goals and objectives of the organization.

The grapevine is often visualized as a long chain, in which A tells B who in turn passes it on to C until it reaches D. Such a pattern of message transmission maximizes the chances for error. Actually, grapevines follow several different message dissemination patterns. A tells three or four others (B, C, and D). Yet only one or two of these receivers passes on the information, and usually to more than one person. As the information becomes older and the proportion of those knowing the message gets larger, it gradually dies out.[44] Figure 5-1 illustrates the cluster chain operation of the grapevine.

MESSAGE

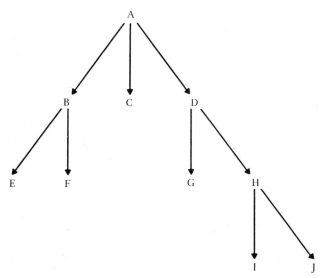

Figure 5-1. Message Dissemination along a Grapevine

Only a few individuals on the grapevine are active communicators. Davis found in his examination of two companies that only 20 and 11 percent of the individuals who knew the information actually communicated it.[45] It would appear that the situation determines who transmits the message. There is no evidence that any person or group consistently initiates a message within the informal communication channels. Any individual in the organization may become a grapevine initiator.

Messages move rapidly over the grapevine. Being flexible the grapevine can spread information faster than the formal communication system of the organization. In turn, the rapid transmission of misinformation can disrupt the organizational communication from top management down. Davis notes that in normal business situations between 75 percent and 95 percent of grapevine information is correct, even though most of the information is incomplete.[46] The 5 to 25 percent of error can be extremely important. It can produce more misunderstanding than the small percentage of error indicates. Hersey suggests controls that can minimize the number and severity of rumors passed from employee to employee over the grapevine:

1. Keep the channels of communication open. There is no substitute for good supervisor-to-subordinate communication down the line.
2. Positive and truthful presentation of facts about a topic is more effective than defensive attempts to disprove the logic of a rumor.
3. Guarding against idleness and monotony among the employees will prevent rumors.
4. Faith in the credibility and source of management's communications is another important area to develop. A company attempting to present its story accurately and convincingly must build a record of truthfulness and reliability in dealing with its employees.
5. Supervisory training programs should consider the psychology of rumors. Managers should be trained to question what anxiety or attitude prompts a rumor.
6. Our communication processes are so imperfect that it pays to analyze rumors, understand them, and take positive steps to head them off.[47]

Since the existence of a grapevine is normal in any organization, it cannot be ignored. Managers should develop methods for *working with* the grapevine. Sigband has suggested several methods, one of which is to identify the "influentials" in the informal structure of the organization. Managers consult with these individuals on issues concerning the organization and solicit their opinions and suggestions, or an employee council can be used to control the grapevine. During a council meeting, departmental representatives can question the accuracy of rumors. Some companies have "question boxes" located throughout the plant. Employees drop questions into the box and responses to these questions are posted on bulletin boards. Bulletin boards also can be used by employees to hang questions or rumors to be answered by the proper authority in the organization. Another method is to provide the employees with correct information in the company newspaper or magazine. These last two channels of communication are relatively slow in transmitting information; therefore, if it is important to correct misinformation quickly, the company might wish to use a public address system.

Finally, the IBM "Speak Up" program and Bank of America "Open Line" use a note-envelope method for controlling the grapevine. The employee writes the question on a self-sealing envelope. The envelope is forwarded by management to the proper desk and answered within twenty-four hours. Every effort is made to protect the employee's anonymity during this process.[48]

Both formal and informal channels in an organization can complement each other. Each conveys information that is suited to its needs and capabilities; together they can create effective organizational communication. Unfortunately, as has been shown, the two systems can also work at cross purposes.[49]

Several additional conclusions can be drawn about the organizational grapevine. First, the greatest spread of information occurs immediately after the information is known. Second, employees are most likely to use the grapevine when their friends and work associates are involved. Third, because grapevine messages are largely oral, it is most active in office situations that regularly bring people into contact with each other. Fourth, the organizational secretary plays a key role in the grapevine. The secretary processes correspondence of the boss, greets visitors, makes appointments, and often acts as the employer's confidante. He or she is strategically located as a communications center, and is the one most likely to initiate the information. Fifth, an organizational grapevine can be an asset or a detriment to the company. It may pass only rumors, destroy reputations, and wreck morale. But it can also be useful as a supplement to the formal channels of communication.[50] Thus, the grapevine's value is dependent upon the situational context in which it occurs.[51]

The patterns or networks that are followed by organizational personnel when transmitting a message affect their behavior and performance. In the next section, we look at communication networks.

Communication Networks

The term *communication network* is used to denote the existence of specific patterns by which messages are transmitted between three or more individuals. A number of networks exist in all organizations. Figure 5-2 illustrates the structure of four five-person communication networks. Research has indicated that the shape of the network affects the process of communication and the behavior of individuals in the network. The work of Bavelas and Barrett shows that different networks create different levels of job satisfaction, speed, and accuracy, as shown in Table 5-2.[52] The wheel-and-chain networks produce the best job performance, but they also have the lowest job satisfaction and show low flexibility to change.[53] Other studies have indicated that with more complex problems the circle is faster and leads to fewer errors than the wheel.[54] There is no one pattern for all situations. The most effective network depends on the

TABLE 5-2   Communication Networks in Work Performance

	Networks		
	Circle	*Chain*	*Wheel*
Speed of Performance	slow	fast	fast
Accuracy	poor	good	good
Emergence of Leader	none	marked	very pronounced
Job Satisfaction	very good	poor	very poor
Organization	no stable form	slow	fast
Flexibility to			
Job Change	fast	slow	slow

required speed, accuracy, leadership, organization, or flexibility that is needed in a particular organization. For example, the wheel should be used in situations requiring leadership and rapid problem solving. Management can produce the best results by using a variety of networks and media of communication in an organization.

The adaptation by group members of a particular network may in the long run lead to the same effectiveness regardless of the initial network limitations. Carzo, ... in a comparison of all-channel network, ... (any person could communicate with any other) with a chain network found that all groups eventually reached the same level of performance regardless of the structure. The results held true for both simple and complex problems.[55]

Guetzkow has identified the existence of three formal networks operating in organizations: authority, information exchange, and task expertise.[56] The authority network is defined in terms of the lines of authority or power hierarchy. The flow of messages is primarily downward, for example, a manager sending to the workers the latest company procedures to be implemented immediately. The regulative function of communication can be viewed easily through this network. The information exchange network serves the informative function of communication. Most of the messages flow upward from subordinate to superior, such as a report by workers on the implementation of new work procedures. The task expertise network "handles the communication involved in bringing the technical know-how to task performance."[57] A communication consultant who has been hired by a company to resolve a particular communication difficulty is part of this network. When utilizing outside experts, the

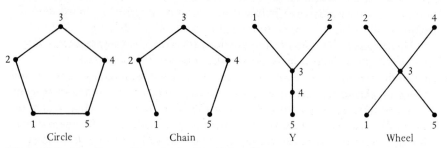

Figure 5-2. Five-Person Communication Networks

organization creates new communication networks to handle the messages. Unlike the two previously described networks, communication in the information exchange network flows freely in both vertical directions.

Reitz, in observing networks operating within a research and development laboratory, identified four crucial factors affecting the behavior of employees. First, status influences the flow of messages. High-status members communicated quite frequently with each other, but seldom socialized or discussed work-related issues with lower-status employees. Second, the social networks heavily influence the network of work-related communications. Individuals discuss their work more with friends. Third, the formal structure of the organization influences work-related communication networks. Individuals are more likely to communicate with others in their assigned work group and those who are located in close physical proximity to them. Fourth, certain individuals are used repeatedly as sources of information. These sources, called "technological gatekeepers," act as a communication link between the organization and the outside world.[58]

The effectiveness of any organization is dependent upon the management of both the formal and informal communication network channels. When the communication channels are managed correctly, one element contributes to communication integration, that is, the interconnectedness of organizational behaviors. Managers, in particular, are concerned with developing an openness within the organization. One method that promotes openness and communication integration is the establishment of an organizational climate in which growth and control can take place. In the next section, we examine organizational climates.

Organizational Climates

Ordinarily when we speak of the "climate" of a geographical region, we are referring to physical conditions that are subject to relatively direct observation. Such characteristics as temperature, humidity, prevailing winds, and rainfall can be measured against objective standards and their general effect on the life and activity of the region described without much ambiguity. On the basis of such information it can be stated with reasonable assurance that, for example, crop "A" can be grown satisfactorily in region "R," but only if the natural rainfall is supplemented with "X" amount of irrigation water annually.

The concept of "organizational climate" offers few opportunities for such objective analysis. The measurable physical working conditions are an important part of the organizational environment, of course. But in the view of most organization theorists and researchers, all such conditions taken together would not constitute the organization's climate. Rather, they would constitute one kind of *effect*, or manifestation, of the organization's climate. The climate itself is thought of as the spirit or philosophy that dominates the organization and is responsible for the relationships that exist among the individuals making up the organization. The social work climate of an organization is often an accurate reflection of its cultural history and its present personality. Just as a society has a cultural heritage, so also will an organization reflect the history of its struggles, the type of people it attracts, its internal processes, and its communication patterns through its present social climate. Not many years ago a sales manager stated that he felt that an organization had a personality just as an individual does and much of the discontent that is experienced by some organizational members is really a personality conflict between the individual and the organization.[59]

This rather elusive concept of an organizational climate may be better understood by carrying its comparison with natural climate a step further. Throughout most of its history, meteorology has been an analytical and predictive science. Its basic mission has been to acquire an understanding of the operation of weather and climate in the natural environment. Aside from fairly recent efforts at weather modification and control, the technological effect of meteorology has been to promote the development of adaptive techniques that will help society take advantage of beneficial forces and avoid destructive forces in the environment. But the forces themselves are taken for granted.

The organization, on the other hand, is an artificial environment created to achieve certain purposes. The quality of the environment, the tools used to achieve the objectives, and the way they are used all reflect the philosophy, the attitudes, and the assumptions of those who created and came to control the organization—its management. Those who study organizations and their climates, therefore, are concerned with more than the structure and processes of the organization. They are concerned also with the outlook reflected in structure and process, with the way in which it is perceived by the organization's personnel, and with the effect of these factors on organizational objectives and personal satisfaction.

The essential characteristic of an organization is neither its facilities nor its technology, but rather the relationships among its personnel. The fact that a number of people are in a particular building at a given moment does not make them an organization. What makes them an organization is their common acceptance of certain ordered patterns of interaction that in some manner link their personal objectives to the objectives of the organization. The most powerful forces at work in an organizational environment are therefore psychological rather than physical. Taken together, these forces make up the climate that is peculiar to that environment.

Whoever attempts to make an objective analysis of organizational climate will find it to be a problem fraught with ambiguities and pitfalls. The term itself is difficult to define with precision, and its most significant components are subjective. How is an objective description of "management philosophy" to be formulated? How can management "attitudes" and "assumptions" regarding employees (many of them never consciously expressed or even acknowledged) be detected, analyzed, and verified? How can a comprehensive profile be drawn of employee *perception* of management's philosophy, attitudes, and assumptions? Is such a study in reality a collection of data on something that exists independently in the organizational environment, or does it reside only in the minds of individuals? Perhaps, as Johannesson[60] speculates, it is possible that "there are potentially as many climates as there are people in the organization?" He poses the following question: "Should the effects of climate be related to personal responses such as 'job satisfaction,' or to organizational standards, such as production?"

That these difficulties and ambiguities have affected research is evident from the wide disparity of approaches and the contradictory conclusions of the studies. In the words of Hellriegel and Slocum:

> The majority of climate researchers discuss the relationship between the climate and the employees' perceptions of their jobs, organization, and the like. It remains to be demonstrated whether these internal criteria are systematically related to more objective criteria, e.g., job performance, turnover, grievances, unit costs, etc. In the future, researchers should concentrate on both external and internal criteria and how these criteria are linked together. Causal links between climate and measures of job performance, turnover, grievances, and the like should be investigated further.[61]

It goes without saying that both the sense of climate existing within an organization and the study of this climate involve complex communication processes, which are subject to all the influences that have been shown to impinge on them.

McGregor[62] states that "the all-important climate of the superior-subordinate relationship" is established by the superior "by the subtle and frequently quite unconscious manifestations of his underlying conception of management and his assumptions about people in general." These attitudes, he indicates, cannot be concealed behind even the most skillful supervisory techniques. Similarly, W. C. Schutz observed:

> What is often transmitted most accurately between people is how they feel rather than what they say. Thus, if the boss really feels his research scientist is not very important, that feeling will be communicated to the scientist much more readily than any words that pass between them.[63]

We recognize that this is often the case, but it is not easily demonstrated that it reflects a universal principle. It implies that the receivers' perceptions are infallible. Thus, if the employees felt that their work was not appreciated, it would necessarily follow that their work was not appreciated. However, employees may experience the same climate differently at different times, or different employees may perceive the same climate differently depending on seniority, age, or position in the hierarchy. Individuals can respond to the organizational climate only in terms of their perception of it, whether or not the perception is accurate. In this sense the climate of the superior-subordinate relationship is what the *subordinate* perceives it to be, and any effects of climate on personal feelings or job performance are necessarily colored by that perception.

Almost all studies emphasize the crucial role of mutual trust-distrust between superiors and subordinates in determining the quality of a particular organizational climate. G. D. Mellinger[64] emphasized the destructive role of distrust in organizational relationships, particularly its distorting effect on communication. When one suspects the sincerity or motives of another with whom one must interact, he concluded, a typical reaction is to regard the mistrusted person as a potential threat. This, in turn, encourages a stressed communication strategy that may be evasive, falsely compliant, or unnecessarily aggressive. Interestingly enough, Mellinger found evidence of a stronger inclination among superiors to conceal information in downward communication with distrusted subordinates than in the reverse situation. However, as Roberts and O'Reilly[65] found, subordinates do engage in more intensive "gate keeping" (withholding of information) in upward communication with superiors they distrust.

Read[66] discovered that strong ambition to move up in the organization ("upward-mobility aspirations") had a similar negative effect on upward communication—particularly, of potentially damaging information—not only when the subordinate distrusted his or her superior but also, to a certain extent, when the superior was trusted.

There appears to be general agreement that both upward and downward communication are significantly improved by a climate of mutual trust. Conversely, a climate of distrust inhibits accurate communication and distrusted individuals are often led into an overestimation or underestimation of their agreement with others.

Redding[67] grouped the "main components" of "the ideal managerial climate" under five headings: (1) supportiveness; (2) participative decision making; (3) trust, confidence, and credibility; (4) openness and candor; and (5) emphasis on high performance goals.

Likert[68] identifies a *supportive* climate as one that encourages and protects the individual's "sense of personal worth and importance." This contrasts with the climate of organizational defensiveness defined by Gibb[69] as being judgmental, manipulative, impersonal, superior, and rigid.[70] Likert sees supportive climates as those in which there is mutual trust and confidence; in which superiors exhibit a willingness to help subordinates, not only with job-related matters but also with personal problems; in which managers are approachable and candid about company plans, profits, and so on; and in which managers are willing to share credit for group accomplishments and recognize subordinates' ideas and abilities.

It would be virtually impossible to list all the existing variations of *participative decision making* (PDM), ranging from "pseudoparticipation," where subordinates are encouraged to believe they have a hand in decisions that are actually made without them, to unstructured "leaderless" groups with true decision-making responsibility. Tannenbaum and Schmidt[71] described PDM as a multilevel process. They defined several levels to illustrate increasing participation, beginning with a manager autocracy (zero participation), where the manager makes a decision and then *tells* the group about it. In the *sells* level, the manager goes a step further by explaining the decision and trying to enlist support for it. At the *consults* level the decision is not made until suggestions have been solicited from the group. At the *joins* level the manager joins the group and participates in decision making on an equal basis with the other members. Sadler[72] found a decided preference for the middle-ground *consults* and *sells* styles and little enthusiasm for the extremes.

Some firm conclusions can be drawn from the voluminous research material on participative decision making. Chaney[73] reported a positive correlation between job attitude and performance and the degree of participation in decision making. He reported zero improvement for individuals in the no-participation and the low-participation groups, whereas the high-participation groups exhibited an attitude and production improvement of 80 percent and 95 percent, respectively.

Significantly, Chaney found that supervisors in low-participation groups showed little interest in the group and "tended to be defensive in meetings." Chaney's conclusion was that "simply holding meetings to talk about the job will not necessarily result in the desired performance improvement." Katz and Kahn[74] observed that meetings in which true participation is discouraged can actually have a negative effect on attitude and performance.[75]

Studies of the factors affecting the efficiency of groups and the quality of their decisions emphasize the value of special training in group techniques, utilization of group resources, and encouragement of all viewpoints—minority, dissenting, and controversial.[76] Although it is not clearly established that the best decision necessarily emerges automatically when the greatest number of good ideas are considered, it is evident that a group's ability to reach a good decision is reduced by the suppression of dissenting views. Summarizing extensive studies of effectiveness of combat air crews during the Korean War, Torrance[77] found that tolerance of disagreement contributed to better decisions and stronger support for them; in fact, it could actually make "the difference between survival and failure to survive in group situations."

Katz and Kahn[78] have concluded that good decision making, particularly in complex situations, is most likely to result from a heterogeneous group where free expression is encouraged. In an examination of disastrous decision making, I. L. Janis[79] described the powerful forces that can paralyze judgment in "cohesive" groups in which dissent from group norms is equated with disloyalty. Janis coined the term *groupthink* to describe the defensive interdependence and ingroup loyalties that operate to stifle private misgivings and enforce rigid support of past decisions.

Although the value of participative decision making for both employees and organization is well established, it is impossible to demonstrate this concretely on the basis of present evidence. "Brainstorming" experiments were conducted by Taylor, Berry, and Block[80] with college students and Dunnette, Campbell, and Jaastad[81] with industrial research and advertising personnel. In both cases comparisons were made of the quantity and quality of ideas produced under brainstorming rules—the rapid-fire, uncritical production of ideas related to a particular problem. Individuals were working in isolation as well as in groups. Contrary to brainstorming theory, more and better ideas were produced in isolation than in groups in both experiments, although work in isolation did appear to be improved when it was preceded by a group session. However, there are groups or situations for which an effective participative format cannot be developed.

Participative climates emerge from a feeling of mutual trust when superiors, subordinates, and peers share a feeling of "openness" and candor. Effective communication leads to better job performance, which, in turn, results in job satisfaction. For example, Willits[82] found that "in the better performing companies, there is a freer, less guarded upward flow of ideas and opinions than in the poorer performing companies." A study by Indik, Georgopoulos, and Seashore[83] based on questionnaire responses from nearly a thousand employees of a delivery firm concluded that job performance is improved when employees believe that their frank opinions are sought and considered by management. Burke and Wilcox[84] report a similar relationship between openness and job satisfaction. A reasonable conclusion would appear to be that both job satisfaction and performance are improved by a participative climate of openness and candor, with due respect for legitimate areas of privacy where employees are assured that frank expression will not be punished.

Special Climates

A number of communication situations involving special settings and climates takes place routinely in the organizational environment. These are usually described as interviews, briefings, counseling sessions, or conferences, and their general purposes are defined as "informative" or "problem solving," although the events themselves do not always fall gracefully under one heading or another.

Ordinarily these events are initiated and planned by the individual who must achieve an objective. The planner usually determines the specific climate of the event as well. In its own limited setting this climate will take its character from the same components that make up the total climate of the organization—supportiveness, participation, trust, candor, emphasis on performance goals.[85]

The way in which the participants in an interview or conference experience the climate of the event depends upon the forethought and skill of the planner. Whether they find it easy or difficult to contribute will depend on factors such as the degree to which the participants feel consideration has been given to their own comfort and convenience, and the confidence they have in the competence and integrity of the individual conducting the session.

Sound planning for a special event involves a number of elementary steps: defining the purpose of the event, analyzing the participants, setting up the agenda, and arranging for appropriate facilities. It is obviously of critical importance to the success of any purposive event to have a clear image from the outset of what the purpose is—in the case of an interview or conference, what specific information is to be sought or communicated and what action, if any, is to be taken. In large part this will determine what items will be included in the agenda, and the demands of clarity or strategy may suggest their order. However, these considerations may be influenced by others such as the personalities who will participate, their general mood or their attitude toward the subject of the meeting, their enthusiasms or biases, and so on.

The physical setting should be thoughtfully planned for the comfort of the participants. There must be sufficient space and light. Participants must be able to see and hear the other participants clearly. Distractions must be reduced to a minimum. Only in this way will the participants be able to focus their attention on the subject of discussion in a relaxed and purposeful way.

Meetings grouped under the classification of *interviews*—usually one-to-one—are sometimes further divided into those that seek information, those that seek to persuade, and those that seek to solve problems.

Among informational interviews are the familiar *employment interview*; the *news, data,* or *opinion interview*; and the *briefing* or *instructional interview*.

The *employment interview* exhibits characteristics of more than one classification since there is a strong element of persuasion or selling in most job interviews. Principally, however, it is structured to enable each participant to obtain information, offer information, and sell himself or herself or the organization as effectively as possible. The employment interview is a crucial climate setting because it creates a first impression for prospective employees that will serve as their introduction to the climate of the entire organization.

The *news interview* is less firmly controlled by the interviewer than the other types of informational interview since the right to control the agenda appears to have been delegated, in part, to the interviewee. However, the subject of a well-planned interview has many opportunities to direct its course into desired channels, particularly if it takes place in an atmosphere of mutual trust and candor.

The *briefing interview* is almost exclusively an informational-giving session in which the individual conducting the meeting provides information on a job, assignment, or other activity. Provisions for *feedback*—comments and questions—are of considerable importance to the effectiveness of briefings.

The most common *persuasion* interview is the *sales interview*. Usually, however, the effective salesperson will turn it into a special kind of problem-solving session, in which the product represents the answer to the problem.

Some interviews generally deal with internal organizational problems only. These concern: *production, reprimands, appraisals, grievances,* and *counseling*.

In the *production* interview the supervisor will call in a subordinate to review and solve a specific problem. The procedure ordinarily is simple: the factors involved in the problem are analyzed, possible solutions are considered, and the one judged most practical is selected.

Appraisal interviews are periodic meetings in which the superior and the subordinate evaluate the latter's performance, with the intent of determining a rating that will affect the subordinate's future with the organization. An honest appraisal deals with both strong and weak points in the job performance and, needless to say, is of little value unless it takes place in a supportive climate.

The *reprimand* interview often combines elements of the production interview and the appraisal, but in a situation requiring much greater tact and control. In the proper climate of mutual respect and trust it is possible to deliver an effective reprimand in the constructive form of an appraisal that moves quickly into a problem-solving phase in which the subordinate is accepted as a full participant.

Grievance interviews deal with complaints raised by subordinates and, in the right climate, can be converted into problem-solving sessions.

Counseling interviews are themselves a product of the search for truly supportive organizational climates. Their subjects range from personal problems that subordinates bring to their superior to complaints of performance shortcomings that might otherwise be handled in reprimand or grievance interviews. Here again, everything depends on the climate.

The processes applicable to conferences and groups have been discussed in connection with participation and decision making. The conference or group objective is to bring the participants together in an atmosphere that is conducive to the fullest exchange of information, opinions, and judgments in order to solve problems and make decisions. As in all situations where people meet to communicate for a specific purpose and on a specific subject, the outcome is influenced—often to a decisive degree—by the climate in which they meet.

It is clear, therefore, that a good climate is as important to special communication situations such as interviews as it is to all other organizational processes. The atmosphere of a specific communication setting, which results from a complex of predominantly psychological factors can be strongly influenced by the care and forethought that goes into its preparation. Here, as in other events in the organizational environment, the individual contributes to the general climate by the competence, philosophy, and personal qualities reflected in the character of settings for which he or she is responsible.

REVIEW QUESTIONS

1. How does feedback affect organizational communication?
2. How can one improve one's listening skills?
3. What role is played by the grapevine in organizational communication?
4. How can one minimize the number and severity of rumors in the organization?
5. How are the levels of job satisfaction, speed, accuracy, leadership emergence, organizational ability, and flexibility affected by communication networks?
6. What role does communication play in the development of an organizational climate?

KEY TERMS AND CONCEPTS FOR REVIEW

- Grapevine
- Rumor
- Communication Networks
- Technological Gatekeepers
- Feedback
- Groupthink

- Executive Isolation
- Organizational Feedback
- Highstream Coupling
- Deliberative Listening

- Empathic Listening
- Organizational Climate
- Participative Decision Making

CASE STUDY

A faculty member at California State College requested a one-year leave of absence to complete work on a textbook. The leave was granted because it was consistent with college policy. A month later the dean of his school heard by the grapevine that the professor was teaching at a University in Florida. The action of taking a leave to teach elsewhere was not illegal, but the basis for requesting the leave originally was false. Accordingly, the vice-president for academic affairs initiated disciplinary action procedures against the professor and a letter charging unprofessional conduct was sent to the professor's home address.

The next day the faculty member called the dean, saying that he had heard that a letter was being sent to him, and that he felt a misunderstanding had taken place. He said that he thought his actions were acceptable, but if not, he would return to the college immediately. When the dean asked him how he knew of the pending disciplinary action against him, the professor said that the wife of an assistant to the vice-president had told his wife of the action.

PROBES

1. How did the administration and faculty use the grapevine?
2. After receiving the faculty member's call, what action should the dean take to control the grapevine?

Recommended Readings

Allport, G. W., and L. Postman. *The Psychology of Rumor*. New York: Holt, Rinehart and Winston, 1947.

Davis, K. *Human Behavior at Work*, 5th ed. New York: McGraw-Hill, 1977, pp. 278–289.

Keefe, F. *Listen, Management!* New York: McGraw-Hill Book Co., 1971.

Farace, R., P. Monge, and H. Russell. *Communicating and Organizing*. Reading, Mass.: Addison-Wesley Publishing Company, 1977, Chapters 8, 9, 10.

Hellrigel, D., and J. W. Slocum, Jr. "Organizational Climate: Measures, Research and Contingencies." *Academy of Management Journal* 17 (1974): 255–280.

Notes

1. J. S. Morgan, *Managing Change* (New York: McGraw-Hill Book Company, 1972), p. 211.
2. D. C. Barnlund, *Interpersonal Communication: Survey and Studies* (Boston: Houghton Mifflin, 1968), p. 230.
3. D. S. Brown, "Some Feedback on Feedback," *Adult Leadership* 14 (1967): 266–268, 251–252.
4. L. Cummings, D. Schwab, and M. Rosen, "Performance and Knowledge of Results as Determinants of Goal Setting," *Journal of Applied Psychology* 55 (1971): 526–530.
5. W. C. Redding, *Communication within the Organization* (New York: Industrial Communications Council, 1972), p. 40.
6. E. E. Smith and S. S. Knight, "Effects of Feedback on Insight and Problem Solving Efficiency in Training Groups," *Journal of Applied Psychology* 43 (1959): 209–211.
7. R. Howard and L. Berkowitz, "Reactions to the Evaluators of One's Performance," *Journal of Personality* 26 (1958): 494–507; S. Rosenberg and R. Hall, "The Effects of Different Social Feedback Conditions Upon Performance in Dyadic Teams," *Journal of Abnormal and Social Psychology* 57 (1958): 271–277.
8. D. M. Cook, "The Impact on Messages of Frequency of Feedback," *Academy of Management Journal* 11 (1968): 274.
9. G. J. Shure, M. Rogers, I. Larsen, and G. Tassone, "Group Planning and Task Effectiveness," *Sociometry* 25 (1962), 263–282.
10. E. H. Bowman, "Consistency and Optimality in Managerial Decision-Making," *Management Science* 9 (1963): 310–321.
11. Brown, op. cit., pp. 226–228, 251–252.
12. P. Nokes, "Feedback as an Exploratory Device in the Study of Certain Interpersonal and Institutional Processes," *Human Relations* 14 (1961): 381–387.
13. Brown, op. cit., p. 252.
14. W. C. Redding, "Human Communication Behavior in Complex Organizations: Some Failures Revisited," In C. E. Larson and F. E. X. Dance, eds., *Perspectives in Communication* (Milwaukee, Wis.: Speech Communication Center, University of Wisconsin-Milwaukee, 1968), p. 108.
15. Ibid., p. 59.
16. G. A. Bassett, "Three L's—Still Personal Basics, Still Neglected," *Personnel* 49 (September-October 1972): 49–55.
17. K. Davis, *Human Behavior at Work*, 5th ed. (New York: McGraw-Hill Book Company, 1977), p. 386.
18. "Empathic Listening." In R. Cathcart and L. Samovar, *Small Group Communication: A Reader* (Dubuque, Iowa: William C. Brown Company, 1974), pp. 340–348.
19. C. Duerr, *Management Kinetics* (New York: McGraw-Hill Book Company, 1971), pp. 18–19.
20. C. P. Rogers and F. J. Roethlesberger, "Barriers and Gateways in Communication," *Harvard Business Review* 30 (1952): 46–52.
21. N. B. Sigband, "Listen to What You Can't Hear," *Nation's Business* 57 (June 1969): 70–72.
22. Bassett, op. cit.
23. W. S. Wikstrom, "Lessons in Listening," *The Conference Board Record* 2 (1965).
24. R. Nichols, "Listening Is Good Business," *Management of Personnel Quarterly* 1 (1962): 8–9.

25. Davis, op. cit., p. 387.

26. E. Aronson, "The Social Animal." In Cathcart and Samovar, op. cit., pp. 325–326.

27. J. DeVito, *The Interpersonal Communication Book* (New York: Harper & Row, 1976), p. 219.

28. J. Baird, *The Dynamics of Organizational Communication* (New York: Harper & Row, 1977), pp. 75–76.

29. K. Davis, *Human Behavior at Work*, 5th ed. (New York: McGraw-HIll Book Company, 1977), p. 278.

30. O. Larson and M. DeFleur, "The Comparative Role of Children and Adults in Propaganda Diffusion," *American Sociological Review* 5 (1954): 595–602.

31. J. Coleman, F. Katz, and H. Menzel, "The Diffusion of an Innovation Among Physicians," *Sociometry* 20 (1957): 253–270.

32. W. Erbe, "Gregariousness, Group Membership and the Flow of Information," *American Journal of Sociology* 67 (1962): 502–516.

33. Davis, op. cit., p. 283.

34. D. Yoder, *Personnel Management and Industrial Relations*, 6th ed. (Englewood Cliffs, N. J.: Prentice-Hall, 1970), p. 576.

35. J. Danner, "Don't Let the Grapevine Trip You Up," *Supervisory Management* 17 (1972): 3.

36. L. Festinger, D. Cartwright, K. Barber, J. Fleischl, J. Gottsdanker, A. Keysen; and G. Leavitt, "A Study of Rumor: Its Origin and Spread," *Human Relations* 1 (1948): 464–486.

37. S. Schachter and H. Burdick, "A Field Experiment of Rumor Transmission and Distortion," *Journal of Abnormal and Social Psychology* 50 (1955): 363–371.

38. G. Allport and L. Postman, *The Psychology of Rumor* (New York: Holt, Rinehart and Winston, 1947).

39. T. Caplow, "Rumors in War," *Social Forces* 24 (1947): 298–302; K. Davis, "Management Communication and the Grapevine," *Harvard Business Review* 31 (1953): 43–49.

40. Davis, op. cit., p. 280; B. Marking, A Study of Grapevine Communication Patterns in a Manufacturing Organization, Ph.D. diss. Tempe: (Arizona State University, 1969).

41. C. Bernard, *The Functions of the Executive* (Cambridge Mass.: Harvard University Press, 1950), p. 123.

42. E. Shils, "The Study of the Primary Group," In P. Lerner and H. Lasswell, eds., *The Policy Sciences: Recent Developments in Scope and Method* (Palo Alto, Calif.: Stanford University Press, 1951), pp. 44–69.

43. K. Davis, "Care and Cultivation of the Corporate Grapevine," *Dun's Review* 102 (1973): 46.

44. Ibid.

45. Ibid.

46. Ibid.

47. R. Hersey, "Grapevine—Here to Stay but Not Beyond Control," *Personnel* 43 (1966): 62–66.

48. N. B. Sigband, *Communication for Management and Business* (Glenview, Ill.: Scott, Foresman and Co., 1976), pp. 45–46.

49. Davis, op. cit., p. 47.

50. K. Davis, "Grapevine Communication among Lower and Middle Managers," *Personnel Journal* 46 (1969), 269.

51. Danner, op. cit., p. 5.

52. A. Bavelas and D. Barrett, "An Experimental Approach to Organizational Communication," *Personnel* 28 (1951): 366–371, see J. L. Gibson, J. M. Ivancevich, and J. H. Donnelly, Jr. *Organizations: Behavior, Structure, Processes.* (Dallas, Tex.: Business Publications, 1973), p. 174.

53. H. Leavitt, "Some Effects of Certain Communication Patterns on Group Performance," *The Journal of Abnormal and Social Psychology* 47 (1951): 38–50.

54. M. E. Shaw, "Some Effects of Unequal Distribution of Information upon Group Performance in Various Communication Networks," *The Journal of Abnormal and Social Psychology* 50 (1954): 547–553; P. Mears, "Structuring Communication in a Working Group," *The Journal of Communication* 24 (1974): 71–79.

55. R. Carzo, Jr., "Some Effects of Organizational Structure on Group Effectiveness," *Administrative Science Quarterly* 8 (1963): 393–424.

56. H. Guetzkow, "Communication in Organizations," In J. March, ed. *Handbook of Organizations* (Chicago: Rand McNally & Co., 1965), pp. 543–547.

57. Ibid., p. 545.

58. H. J. Reitz, *Behavior in Organizations* (Homewood, Ill: Richard D. Irwin, 1977), pp. 361–363.

59. R. Allen, *Organizational Management Through Communication* (New York: Harper & Row, 1977), p. 71.

60. R. Johannesson, "Job Satisfaction and Perceptually Measured Organization Climate: Redundancy and Confusion." In M. W. Frey, ed., *New Developments in Management and Organization Theory.* Proceedings of the Eighth Annual Conference, Eastern Academy of Management (1971), pp. 27–37.

61. D. Hellriegel and J. W. Slocum, Jr., "Organizational Climate: Measures, Research and Contingencies," *Academy of Management Journal* 17 (1974): 277.

62. D. McGregor, *The Human Side of Enterprise* (New York: McGraw-Hill Book Company, 1960), p. 141.

63. W. C. Schutz, "Interpersonal Underworld," *Harvard Business Review*, 36 (1958): 124.

64. "Interpersonal Trust as a Factor in Communication," *Journal of Abnormal and Social Psychology* 52 (1956): 304–309.

65. K. H. Roberts and C. A. O'Reilly, "Failure in Upward Communication in Organizations: Three Possible Culprits," *Academy of Management Journal* 17 (1974): 205–215.

66. W. H. Read, "Communicating across the Power Structure," *Cost and Management* 10 (1967): 25–28.

67. W. C. Redding, *Communication within the Organization* (New York: Industrial Communications Council, 1972), pp. 139–422.

68. R. Likert, *The Human Organization: Its Management and Value* (New York: McGraw-Hill Book Company, 1967).

69. J. R. Gibb, "Defensive Communication," *Journal of Communication* 11 (1961): 141–148.

70. Blake and Mouton (1964) developed their "managerial grid" (see in Chapters 5 and 6), which plots relative degrees of concern for production versus concern for people as an alternative to the extremes described in "either-or" models of the type used by Gibb and Likert.

71. R. Tannenbaum and W. H. Schmidt, "How to Choose a Leadership Pattern," *Harvard Business Review* 36 (1958): 95–101.

72. P. J. Sadler, "Leadership Style, Confidence in Management and Job Satisfaction," *Journal of Applied Behavioral Science* 6 (1970): 3–19.

73. F. B. Chaney, "Employee Participation in Manufacturing Job Design," *Human Factors* 11 (1969): 101–106.

74. D. Katz and R. L. Kahn, *The Social Psychology of Organizations* (New York: John Wiley & Sons, Inc. 1966), pp. 239–243.

75. M. Haire, *Psychology in Management* 2d ed. (New York: McGraw-Hill Book Company, 1964) advances the idea that a superior's influence with subordinates will increase in proportion to the influence subordinates have over the superior. The importance of "reciprocity of influence," or sharing of power, the concept of participation is also stressed by L. E. Greiner, "Patterns of Organization Change," *Harvard Business Review* 45 (1967): 119–130.

76. J. Hall and M. S. Williams, "Group Dynamics Training and Improved Decision Making," *Journal of Applied Behavioral Science* 6 (1970): 39–68.

77. P. Torrance, "Function of Expressed Disagreement in Small Group Processes," *Social Forces* 35 (1957): 314–318.

78. Katz and Kahn, op. cit.

79. I. Janis, "Groupthink," *Psychology Today* (November 1971): 43–46, 74–76.

80. D. W. Taylor, P. C. Berry, and C. H. Block, "Does Group Participation When Using Brainstorming Facilitate or Inhibit Creative Thinking?" *Administrative Science Quarterly* 3 (1958): 23–47.

81. M. D. Dunnette, J. Campbell, and K. Jaastad, "The Effect of Group Participation on Brainstorming Effectiveness for Two Industrial Samples," *Journal of Applied Psychology* 47 (1963): 30–37.

82. R. D. Willits, "Company Performance and Interpersonal Relations," *Industrial Management Review* 7 (1967): 91–107.

83. B. P. Indik, B. S. Georgopoulos, and S. E. Seashore, "Superior-Subordinate Relationships and Performance," *Personnel Psychology* 14 (1971): 357–374.

84. R. J. Burke and D. S. Wilcox, "Effects of Different Patterns and Degrees of Openness in Superior-Subordinate Communication on Subordinate Job Satisfaction," *Academy of Management Journal* 12 (1969): 319–326.

85. Redding, op. cit., pp. 139–422.

PART THREE

The
Organizational
Communicator

6 | Communicator: Managerial Assumptions and Communication Behaviors

LEARNING OBJECTIVES

After reading this chapter, you should be able to
1. Define Maslow's hierarchy of needs and discuss their implications on managerial assumptions.
2. Differentiate between motivating and hygiene factors and discuss their effect on organizational personnel.
3. Describe McGregor's Theory X-Theory Y concept and the assumptions made about people.
4. Explain Likert's "Four System" approach to management theory and its communication behavior impact on organizational personnel.
5. Describe Blake and Mouton's Managerial Grid Theory and its importance in assessing managerial styles.
6. Explain Fiedler's Contingency Theory approach to management in organizations.
7. Explain the impact of managerial assumptions on communication behavior.

Any study of organizational communication and behavior must take into account the behavior of managers, leaders, and supervisors as they guide, manage, and motivate personnel toward the accomplishment of organizational goals and objectives. Organizations differ in "managerial attitudes" and in employee or personnel responses to managerial directives.

This chapter provides a brief overview of various theories or models that are descriptive of management's orientation toward employees. Some of the theories or models prescribe approaches for improving the ability of managers and organizations to motivate people; other theories merely provide schemes for assessing the quality of a particular managerial style or orientation. Each theory or model constitutes a set of assumptions concerning the nature of employee behavior under the impress of organizational roles, goals, and expectations. No matter how imprecise or incomplete they may be, the assumptions of these theories will assist us in exploring the causes and consequences of certain dispositions or tendencies in the organization.

We examine Maslow's Need-Hierarchy Theory, McGregor's Theory X and Theory Y, Herzberg's Motivator-Hygiene Theory, Likert's Participative Management Theory, Blake and Mouton's Managerial Grid Theory, and Fiedler's Situational or Contingency Theory. The six theories are representative of the major known theories, and they should provide an adequate view of different managerial perspectives.

Need-Hierarchy Theory

Maslow[1] advanced the idea of a hierarchy of human needs as a predictor and descriptor of human motivation. His theory of motivation is predicated on two assumptions. First, needs depend on what one already has. Needs that are not satisfied can influence behavior, but satisfied needs will not act as motivators. Second, needs are arranged in a hierarchy of importance. When one need is satisfied, another emerges and demands satisfaction.

Maslow postulated that some needs are qualitatively different from others; for example, the need to eat is different from the need to become president of a company. The various needs are described in a framework referred to as the *hierarchy of needs* (see Figure 6–1). According to Maslow, five general categories or levels of needs are prevalent in any organization. These needs are (1) *physiological* or survival needs, (2) *safety* or security needs, (3) *social* needs, (4) *esteem* or ego needs, and (5) *self-actualization* or self-fulfillment needs.

As shown in Figure 6–1, the five categories of needs are arranged in a hierarchy ranging from the lowest-order needs (physiological) to the highest-order (self-actualization). This hierarchy determines the priority. Specifically, Maslow suggests that behavior is always determined by the lowest-order category or level of need remaining unsatisfied. If all of a person's needs are unsatisfied at a particular time, those needs that come first in the hierarchy must be satisfied before the higher level needs, and only when the first are satisfied do the higher ones become significant. Thus, when we look for effective motivators in the

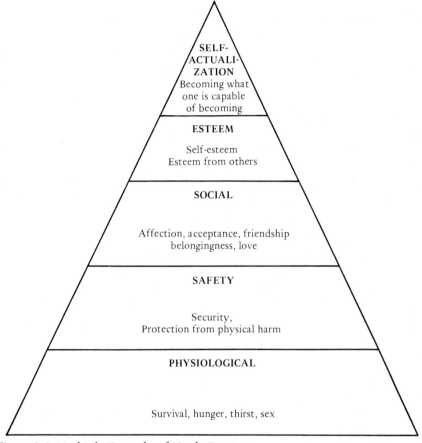

Figure 6–1 Maslow's Hierarchy of Needs Concept

organizational setting, it is necessary to recognize whether a certain motivator is directed toward satisfying a previously unsatisfied need or one that no longer exists. We now examine the five need levels:

Physiological Needs   The satisfaction of physiological needs (shelter, food, clothing) in an organization is usually associated with *money*. Most people are not interested in dollars as such but merely as a means to satisfy other needs. So it is what money can buy, not the money itself, that satisfies a person's physiological needs. To suggest that money is useful only as a satisfier of physiological needs would be shortsighted because money can play a role in the satisfaction of needs at any level. Maslow's basic premise is that food, clothing, and shelter constitute the primary needs. Because money will buy food, clothing, and shelter, it is the prime motivator. Since Maslow also held that basic physiological needs *must be satisfied* before people will become concerned about their higher needs or motivators, it can be argued that employees will be motivated to work for food, clothing, or shelter until they feel that the job has satisfied those needs. At the point of satisfaction, the employee will become concerned with the higher motivational interests on the need-hierarchy.

Safety Needs   With the physiological needs fulfilled, the next level of needs assumes importance. Basically, safety needs include protection from physical harm, ill health, economic disaster, and so on. Today the category has been broadened to encompass the quest for needs such as job security and greater financial support. For example, in the early days of labor unions the primary demands of the unions consisted of monetary needs; but in recent times more unions have demanded fringe benefits and job security from management, in addition to increases in pay.

Concern for security may play a vital role in an employee's decision to remain with or leave an organization; however, Gellerman[2] suggests that job security is not likely to be that employee's dominant motive. Conscious security needs usually play a background role, often inhibiting or restraining impulses rather than initiating outward behavior. For example, if a particular course of action, such as disregarding a rule or expressing an unpopular position, might jeopardize one's job, then security considerations may motivate a person *not* to take this course of action. Organizations can influence security needs either positively—through pension plans and insurance programs—or negatively by arousing fears of being fired, demoted, or passed over. In both cases, the effect can be to make the employee's behavior on the job too cautious and conservative.

Social Needs   Social needs are higher still in Maslow's hierarchy. They have a significant influence on the behavior of individuals only after the safety and security needs have been relatively well satisfied. They include needs for both giving and receiving love and affection; the need to accept, associate with, and be accepted by others; and the need to belong or to feel oneself a part of social groups.[3] In short, one needs to be liked and to like one's co-workers. What this means is that after people feel reasonably safe and secure financially, their next concern is how well accepted they are among their co-workers and whether or not they have friends with whom to socialize on the job.

The quest to fulfill social needs manifests itself in the formation of informal work groups within organizations. Some researchers have discovered that it was not always a need for mere fellowship that motivated a person's affiliation with an informal group. In many cases individuals were seeking affiliation because they desired to have their beliefs confirmed. People tend to seek out others who share similar beliefs. Consequently, an individual who believes the management of the organization to be inept will seek out others who may feel the same way, and soon an antimanagement clique may be formed in the organization. Management is often suspicious of informal groups that develop at work because of the potential power these groups have to influence the lowering of productivity.

Many authorities argue that some people never fulfill or overcome their third-level need for belonging and acceptance. They spend most of their time worrying about what other people think about them and how to get along with them. Although this may occur in many situations, this is not true in all cases and does not explain the behavior of all people. Some people appear to have a relatively low need to be liked by others. For them, other needs may be paramount, such as the need to be recognized as doing something really important.

Esteem Needs   The fourth level in Maslow's hierarchy consists of the esteem or ego need to be recognized for what one does. This category includes the need for respect from others; the feeling of achievement, recognition, appreciation, freedom, status, prestige, power; and, generally, a feeling of worthiness. At this level a person is motivated to work by the need for esteem itself. For example, a person may want to be known as the best manager in a manufacturing plant, or the most efficient stock clerk in a store, or the most proficient secretary in an office. According to Lawrence Steinmetz and H. Ralph Todd, when people are motivated by such ambitions, their interests are far above money and what money will buy.[4]

Self-Actualization Needs   The highest hierarchical need is for self-actualization, or self-fulfillment. Maslow defines it as the "desire to become more and more what one is, to become everything one is capable of becoming."[5] In attempting to satisfy this need an employee becomes less concerned about recognition and more concerned about the pleasure and sense of satisfaction obtained from performing a job. Obviously, as the role of the individual varies, so will the external aspects of self-actualization. In other words, whether the person is a college professor, an airline pilot, a manager, or a car-wash attendant, the drive is to be effective in the particular role. In keeping with his assumptions of a *hierarchy*, Maslow argues that the satisfaction of self-acutalization needs is possible only after the satisfaction of all other needs in the hierarchy.

We now explore the implications of the need-hierarchy theory in terms of its relevance to the management of personnel.

Management and the Need-Hierarchy Theory

Despite some criticisms, Maslow's description of a need-hierarchy is useful for pointing up some of the factors that motivate people in organizations. Most organizations succeed in satisfying lower-level needs. Salaries and fringe benefits satisfy physiological needs and security needs respectively; interactions and associations on the job provide satisfaction of social needs. However, very scant attention is given to the satisfaction of higher-level needs—esteem and self-actualization. Unsatisfied needs produce tension within the individual regardless of the level at which the need occurs. An unsatisfied physiological need can produce as much tension or disturbance as an unsatisfied self-actualization need. When an individual is unable to satisfy a particular need, *frustration* occurs. The reaction to frustration will vary from person to person and from situation to situation. Some people may manifest fairly positive or constructive behavior when faced with need-frustration; others may resort to negative or defensive behavior. Donnelly, Gibson, and Ivancevich,[6] offer a useful model to describe the reationship existing between needs and constructive-destructive behaviors; their model is shown in Figure 6–2.

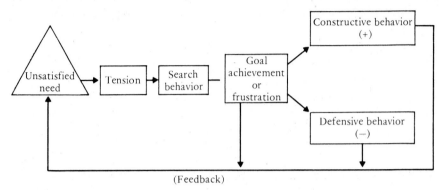

(Feedback)

Figure 6-2 Relationship between Needs and Constructive-Destructive Behaviors (Used with permission from Donnelly, Gibson, and Ivancevich, *Fundamentals of Management*, Dallas, Tex.: Business Publications Inc. 1975, p. 148.)

The diagram shows that unsatisfied needs contribute to tension within the individual motivating a search for ways of relief. It also demonstrates that if one is successful in achieving a goal, the next unsatisfied need emerges. If attempts to satisfy needs are frustrated, a person may engage in either constructive or defensive types of behavior. For example, an office secretary who is frustrated in attempts to satisfy her need for recognition on the job may steer that frustration in a *constructive* or positive direction. She may seek recognition off the job, becoming involved in civic organizations, running for office, or participating in the company bowling league. In other words, she seeks out an alternative environment that maximizes the likelihood of recognition. With this type of outlet her needs are satisfied and her job performance remains intact— at least temporarily. The organization would still be forced to reckon with her need-frustration eventually.

Sometimes, we resort to *defensive* or destructive behaviors when our needs are frustrated. These behaviors may consist of withdrawal, aggression, and substitution. Withdrawal may be physical (leaving the job), but more likely it will be internalized and manifested in apathy. Workers whose jobs provide little in the way of need satisfaction may withdraw in the form of excessive absences, lateness, or turnover. Sometimes frustration leads to aggression. In certain rare situations the frustrated employee may be aggressive toward or attack the boss. In most instances, however, the employee would be more inclined to become aggressive toward objects or other persons. Substitution takes place when an individual puts something in the place of an original object. For example, a worker who has been frustrated in attempts to get a promotion or higher status may *substitute* by trying to achieve leadership or status in an informal group whose objectives are to resist and frustrate management policies.

Maslow's Need-Hierarchy Theory is a basic, widely accepted model upon which many theories of motivation have been built. One of these is the Motivator-Hygiene Theory by Frederick Herzberg.

Motivator-Hygiene Theory

As a result of research undertaken to determine what affects employee motivation in organizations, Herzberg[7] developed the *Motivator-Hygiene Theory.* The basic assumption of this theory is that employees will be motivated to produce at high levels if they perceive that the result will satisfy their needs. Herzberg concluded that people's needs can be classsfied into categories, which are essentially independent of each other and affect behavior in different ways.

He observed that certain "critical incidents" occur daily causing members of an organization to feel pleasure or satisfaction on the job. Basically, these feelings of pleasure or satisfaction are aroused when people experience recognition for special accomplishments—when they achieve what they consider worthwhile; are proud of their responsibility; receive advancements, promotions, and pay increases—or when they enjoy their work because of the intrinsic pleasure they derive from that work.

Six factors contribute greatly to motivation and job satisfaction, but if they are not present in the organization, *this does not prove to be highly dissatisfying.* The six *motivational* factors of satisfiers are

1. Achievement
2. Recognition
3. Advancement
4. The work itself
5. The possibility of personal growth
6. Responsibility

On the other hand, certain "critical incidents" lead to feelings of unhappiness and dissatisfaction with the work itself and the results that the work provides. When people talk about the dissatisfying dimensions of jobs, they tend to mention *environmental* factors as the cause of their displeasure. Such factors mostly pertain to company policy and administration, poor working conditions, poor relationships with co-workers, lack of acceptable technical qualification in supervisors, and poor pay.

These environmental factors constitute the *maintenance* or *hygiene* factors in Herzberg's theory since they are vitally necessary for maintaining a reasonable level of satisfaction. Herzberg noted that many of these factors were perceived by managers to be the key motivators of employees but that they are, in fact, more potent as dissatisfiers when they are absent. Herzberg suggests the existence of ten maintenance, or hygiene, factors:

1. Company policy and administration
2. Technical supervision
3. Interpersonal relations with supervisor
4. Interpersonal relations with peers
5. Interpersonal relations with subordinates
6. Salary
7. Job security
8. Personal life
9. Work conditions
10. Status

TABLE 6-1   Motivation and Hygiene Factors

Hygiene Factors	Motivators
Environment	The Job Itself
Policies and administration	Achievement
Supervision	Recognition for accomplishment
Working conditions	Challenging work
Interpersonal relations	Increased responsibility
Money, status, security	Growth and development

From Paul Hersey and Kenneth H. Blanchard, *Management of Organizational Behavior* (Englewood Cliffs, N.J.: Prentice Hall, 1972), p. 47. Reprinted by permission of the publisher.

Table 6–1 lists factors that are considered dissatisfiers in the job environment and satisfiers around the job itself. As the table shows, the dissatisfiers, or hygiene factors, are significantly different from the satisfiers, or motivators. For example, Herzberg found that an employee's dissatisfaction at being paid too little or less than a co-worker was three times as intense in bitterness as the positive feelings resulting from being paid better than co-workers. In other words, while we may be tremendously upset when our pay is not large enough, we may be merely *not* upset when our pay is adequate. If we are not paid what we think we are worth, we will be very dissatisfied; if we are paid what we think we are worth, we *will not be dissatisfied, but we will not necessarily be satisfied or motivated.*

Since much of Herzberg's motivator-hygiene theory deals with the potentials for *satisfaction* and *dissatisfaction* in the organization, we now examine these potentials.

Satisfaction and Dissatisfaction

The motivator-hygiene theory suggests that job satisfaction (motivation) and dissatisfaction are not opposites. Rather, the opposite of dissatisfaction is simply the absence of dissatisfaction. This is an important distinction. As was mentioned earlier, job satisfaction and dissatisfaction appear to be caused by two entirely different sets of factors: those that influence job satisfaction and motivation are derived intrinsically from the job itself and appear to have little effect upon dissatisfaction, whereas those that influence dissatisfaction are peripheral to the job and seem to have very little effect upon satisfaction and motivation.[8]

The importance of the distinction between job satisfaction and dissatisfaction becomes clearer when the two are related to levels of performance. Figure 6–3 indicates that there is a neutral or zero point in performance levels where employees are neither dissatisfied nor satisfied with their jobs. At this point, employees simply perform at the minimal acceptable level necessary to maintain their jobs and employment.

The point, which must be reemphasized, is that job satisfaction and dissatisfaction are influenced by different factors and exert different effects upon

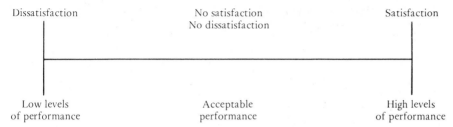

Figure 6-3. Relationship between Job Satisfaction, Dissatisfaction, and Performance

employees. One set of factors—hygiene factors—tend to affect dissatisfaction and performance below acceptable levels, whereas the second set of factors—motivators—tend to affect job satisfaction, motivation, and performance above acceptable levels. The significance of the term *hygiene* in Herzberg's theory comes from the idea of a dichotomy between *hygiene* and *motivator,* and here is where a clear-cut managerial perspective is set forth.

Motivation versus Hygiene

Herzberg argues that dissatisfying factors are basically hygienic in nature. He reasons—by way of an analogy—that a poor sewage system in a community will *cause* people to become unhealthy. But a good sewage system will not necessarily make them healthy; it will only enable them to be healthy *if all the other things necessary for a healthy community exist* such as good food, clean air, decent housing, and low noise levels.

The same principle holds, in Herzberg's view, concerning people at work in the organization. For example, a supervisor, failing to recognize the dissatisfier factors (salary, working conditions, company policy, and so on) implementing them unfairly, can indeed cause people to be very unhappy at work and, consequently, very unproductive. However, *that* supervisor could not motivate the workers to do better merely by being fair in his implementations. Using the Herzberg analogy (a poor sewage system could make you ill, but a good sewage system will not necessarily make you healthy), we can characterize the dissatisfier factors in this example as equally "hygienic" in nature—that is, if the workers are not fulfilled, they become "psychologically ill." Of course, if they *are* fulfilled, it does not ensure that the workers will be "psychologically healthy"; it merely ensures that they will not be "psychologically ill."

As Lawrence Steinmetz and H. Paul Todd[9] point out, the supervisory practices in most organizations emphasize hygienic factors. The majority of managers feel that pay, for example, which is essentially a dissatisfier, will motivate their people. If pay fails to motivate, the managers look to other, essentially dissatisfying, factors—extra vacation schedules, Christmas bonuses, more accommodating work shifts, and so on. This emphasis causes the managers to neglect the real sources of motivation on the job, which should properly be derived from the peasure of doing the job well and being recognized for it.

There is much similarity between Herzberg's framework and Maslow's hierarchy of needs. Maslow refers to needs or motives, whereas Herzberg deals

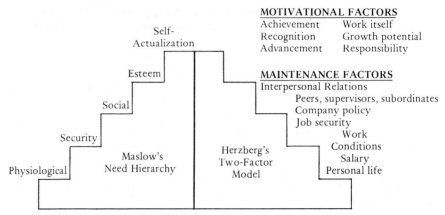

Figure 6-4. A Comparison of Maslow and Herzberg Models (From Donnelly, Gibson, and Ivancevich, *Fundamentals of Management*, p. 155)

with the goals or incentives that are necessary for satisfying these needs. Money and benefits tend to satisfy needs at the physiological and security levels; interpersonal relations and supervision are examples of hygiene factors that tend to satisfy social needs, whereas increased responsibility, challenging work, growth, and development are motivators that tend to satisfy needs at the esteem and self-actualization levels. Figure 6–4 shows the relationship between the two models.

Applications of Motivator-Hygiene Theory

Herzberg encourages management to build into the work environment an opportunity to satisfy the motivators. What we need to do, Herzberg suggests, is to *enrich* the job. Job enrichment refers to the deliberate upgrading of responsibility scope and challenge in work. Hersey and Blanchard provide the following illustration:

> An example of job enrichment may be illustrated by the experience an industrial relations superintendent had with a group of janitors. When the superintendent was transferred to a new plant, he soon found, much to his amazement, that in addition to his duties, fifteen janitors in the plant maintenance reported directly to him. There was no foreman over these men. Upon browsing through the files one day, the superintendent noticed there was a history of complaints about housekeeping around the plant. After talking to others and observing for himself, it took the superintendent little time to confirm the reports. The janitors seemed to be lazy, unreliable, and generally unmotivated.
>
> Determined to do something about the behavior of the janitors, the superintendent called a group meeting of all fifteen men. He opened the meeting by saying that he understood there were a number of housekeeping problems in the plant, but confessed that he did not know what to do about them. Since he felt they, as janitors, were experts in the housekeeping area, he asked if together they would help him solve these problems. "Does anyone have a suggestion?" he asked. There was a deadly silence.

The superintendent sat down and said nothing; the janitors said nothing. This lasted for almost twenty minutes. Finally one janitor spoke up and related a problem he was having in his area and made a suggestion. Soon others joined in, and suddenly the janitors were involved in a lively discussion while the superintendent listened and jotted down their ideas. At the conclusion of the meeting the suggestions were summarized with tacit acceptance by all, including the superintendent.

After the meeting, the superintendent referred any housekeeping problems to the janitors, individually or as a group. For example, when any cleaning equipment or material salesmen came to the plant the superintendent did not talk to them, the janitors did. In fact, the janitors were given an office where they could talk to salesmen. In addition, regular meetings continued to be held where problems were discussed.

All of this had a tremendous influence on the behavior of these men. They developed a cohesive productive team that took pride in its work. Even their appearance changed. Once a grubby lot, now they appeared at work in clean, pressed work clothes. All over the plant, people were amazed how clean and well kept everything had become. The superintendent was continually stopped by supervisors in the plant and asked, "What have you done to those lazy, good-for-nothing janitors, given them pep pills?" Even the superintendent could not believe his eyes. It was not uncommon to see one or two janitors running floor tests to see which wax or cleaner did the best job. Since they had to make all the decisions including funds for their supplies, they wanted to know which were the best. Such activities, while taking time, did not detract from their work. In fact, these men worked harder and more efficiently than ever before in their lives.[10]

This example demonstrates that even at low levels in the organization, workers can react responsibly and productively to work environments in which they are given an opportunity to grow and mature. People begin to satisfy their esteem and self-actualizing needs by participating in the planning, organizing, motivating, and controlling of their own tasks.

Theory X and Theory Y

Douglas McGregor, in *The Human Side of Enterprise*,[11] attempted to demonstrate how a supervisor's basic attitude toward employees would have a significant impact on employee job performance (see Chapter 2). He suggested that there are two basic supervisory attitudes: Some supervisors deal with personnel from the standpoint of a Theory X, some from a Theory Y orientation. Theory X assumes that workers would rather be directed than left to their own devices or initiatives; that they are not interested in assuming responsibility; that they are lazy; that they constantly seek safety and security. Inherent in this managerial philosophy is the belief that people are motivated by money, fringe benefits, and the threat of punishment. Incidentally, these assumed objectives of Theory X are essentially identical to Herzberg's hygiene factors or dissatisfiers.

Supervisors who operate under the assumptions of Theory X attempt to structure, control, and closely supervise their personnel. They believe that external control is appropriate for dealing with "unreliable, irresponsible, and immature people."

But McGregor argued that the close supervision exercised by the traditional Theory X overseer achieved less than satisfactory results in terms of employee job performance because the inividual who is so closely supervised would resist the restrictions and do only the required minimum. McGregor also felt that employees would not demonstrate any drive, initiative, or creativity toward accomplishments of organizational goals under Theory X supervisory conditions. Consequently, he suggested that management should develop practices based on a more accurate understanding of human nature and human motivation. New managerial practices should evolve from what McGregor calls Theory Y (see Table 6-2).

Managers or supervisors who deal with personnel under the terms of Theory Y do *not* usually structure, control, or closely supervise the work environment. Rather, they try to help their employees grow by subjecting them to as little external control as possible, thus allowing them to assume more and more control themselves. In this way, the workers are able to satisfy their social, esteem, and self-actualization needs. According to McGregor, supervisors under Theory Y would be more "open" in their behavior and expect employees to experience all of the enriching aspects of the job that Herzberg advocated. They basically would feel that people like work and find it as natural and rewarding as play. They would expect people to manifest drive, initiative, and diligence toward the pursuit of organizational goals, especially if these were compatible with employee goals.

TABLE 6-2   Two Sets of Assumptions about Human Nature and Human Behavior Underlying McGregor's Theory X and Theory Y

Theory X	Theory Y
1. Work is inherently distasteful to most people.	1. Work is as natural as play, if the conditions are favorable.
2. Most people are not ambitious, have little desire for responsibility, and prefer to be directed.	2. Self-control is often indispensable in achieving organizational goals.
3. Most people have little capacity for creativity in solving organizational problems.	3. The capacity for creativity in solving organizational problems is widely distributed in the population.
4. Motivation occurs only at the physiological and safety levels.	4. Motivation occurs at the social, esteem, and self-actualization levels, as well as physiological and security levels.
5. Most people must be closely controlled and often coerced to achieve organizational objectives.	5. People can be self-directed and creative at work if properly motivated.

From Paul Hersey and Kenneth H. Blanchard, *Management of Organizational Behavior* (Englewood Cliffs, N.J.: Prentice-Hall, 1972), p. 55. Reprinted by permission of the publisher.

Gerald Goldhaber has attempted to show the distinction between Theory X and Theory Y from the viewpoint of communication climates. He claims that the manager who adheres to the assumptions of Theory X will most likely employ the following communication behaviors within the organization:

1. Most messages will flow in a downward direction from the top through the rest of the line organization.
2. Decision making will be concentrated in the hands of a few people toward the top of the organization.
3. Upward communication will be limited to suggestion boxes, grapevines, and "spy systems" (employees who secretly report information about other employees to the manager).
4. Little interaction will take place with employees, and always with fear and distrust.
5. Downward communication will be limited to information messages and announcements of decisions, thus creating conditions for the grapevine to prosper as a means of supplementing the inadequate messages from above.
6. Since upward communication is almost nonexistent, decision making often will be based on partial and inaccurate information.

The net effect of these communication behaviors upon the employees will be to create an atmosphere of distrust, fear, and lack of understanding. (Employees will eventually view all communication with extreme suspicion.)

The manager who adopts Theory Y assumptions of human behavior will most likely be responsible for the following communication behaviors.

1. Messages travel up, down, and across the organization.
2. Decision making is spread throughout the entire organization. Even important decisions involve inputs from members of all levels of the line organization.
3. Since feedback is encouraged in an upward direction (management "listens"), no supplemental upward system is required.
4. Frequent, honest interaction takes place with employees in an atmosphere of confidence and trust.
5. The flow of messages downward is usually sufficient to satisfy the needs of employees.
6. Decision making is based upon messages from all levels of the organization, thus improving the accuracy and quality of the decisions.[12]

Goldhaber contends that since a Theory Y orientation is conducive to an open communication system, there would be an atmosphere of trust, mutual reciprocity, intimacy, and growth. Consequently, there would be relatively little need for coalitions, informal pressure groups, and grapevines—all of which frequently frustrate organizational goals. Employees would tend to appreciate their influence on management because of an honest, sincere acceptance of their inputs in the decision-making process. In this way, the goals of the employees are integrated with the goals of management, and Herzberg's motivator goals are met.

Participative Decision Management Theory

One of the pioneers in developing means of measuring human variables in the organization is Rensis Likert (see Chapter 2). Likert suggests that most managerial styles could be classified by means of four "systems."[13] Systems 1 and 4 are akin to McGregor's Theory X and Theory Y, respectively; Systems 2 and 3 lie somewhere between the extremes.

According to Likert, an organization can be described in terms of eight operating characteristics. They are (1) leadership, (2) motivation, (3) communication, (4) interaction, (5) decision making, (6) goal setting, (7) control, and (8) performance. The nature of each characteristic can be located on a continuum through the use of a questionnaire, which the organization's supervisors complete. The arithmetic means (averages) of each response category are calculated and plotted to produce an organizational profile.[14] The profile will describe management's attitude toward the eight operating characteristics and generally will fall under one of Likert's four systems:

- System 1-exploitive authoritative
- System 2-benevolent authoritative
- System 3-consultative
- System 4-participative

Characteristics of Likert's Four Systems

System 1   Management does not trust subordinates, who are therefore seldom involved in any aspect of the decision-making process. The bulk of the goals are set and decisions made at the top, and these are mandated down through the chain of command. Subordinates are forced to work in fear, with threats, punishments, and only occasional rewards; they lack satisfaction at the physiological and safety levels. Superior-subordinate interaction is minimal, and is generally tainted with fear and mistrust. Since all the control processes are centered in top management, an informal organization usually develops, which opposes or resists the goals of the formal organization. As previously mentioned, a System 1 orientation resembles that of McGregor's Theory X.

System 2   Management is characterized by a condescending trust in subordinates, much like that of a master toward a servant. Although the bulk of the decisions and the goals are still determined at the top, some minor decisions may be made at lower levels. Rewards and punishments are still used to motivate workers. Superior-subordinate interaction takes place in a climate of condescension on the part of superiors, and fear and caution on the part of the subordinates. The control process is still concentrated in top management, but control is usually delegated to middle and lower levels. An informal organization does develop under System 2, but it does not always resist the inductions, mandates, or directives of the formal organization.

System 3   Management has substantial but not complete confidence in subordinates. Although broad policy and general decisions are kept at the top, subordinates are permitted to make more specific decisions at lower levels. Rewards, occasional punishment, and some involvement are used to motivate workers. There is a moderate amount of superior-subordinate interaction, often with a reasonable amount of trust. Significant aspects of the control process are delegated downward, with a feeling of responsibility at both higher and lower levels. An informal organization may develop, which will either support or partially resist the goals of the organization.

System 4   Management is characterized by complete confidence in subordinates. Decision making is widely dispersed throughout the organization, and it is well integrated. Communication flows not only up and down the hierarchy but also horizontally among peers. Workers are motivated by participation and involvement in developing economic rewards, setting goals, improving methods, and appraising progress toward goals. Superior-subordinate interaction is extensive and friendly, with a high degree of trust. There is widespread responsibility for the control process, the lower units being fully involved. The formal and informal organizations are often one and the same. Thus, all forces support efforts to achieve the goals of the organization.

System 4 management is advocated by Likert and his associates. Basically, System 4 is that orientation in which managers (1) uphold the principle of supportive relationships; (2) use group methods for decision making and supervision; and (3) have high performance goals. The characteristics, when fully outlined, appear to constitute the following:

1. Leadership processes that instill confidence and trust between superiors and subordinates and vice versa. Subordinates feel free to discuss job problems with their superiors, who in turn solicit their ideas and opinions.
2. Motivational processes that develop a full range of motives through participatory methods. Attitudes are favorable toward the company and toward goals of the company.
3. Communication processes by which information flows freely throughout the organization—upward, downward, and laterally. The information is accurate and undistorted.
4. Interaction processes that are open and extensive. Both superiors and subordinates are able to affect departmental goals, methods, and activities.
5. Decision-making processes that occur at all levels of the organization through group methods.
6. Goal-setting processes that encourage group participation in setting high, yet realistic, objectives.
7. Control processes that are dispersed throughout the company, with all participants seeking information to implement self-control. The emphasis in control is problem solving, not blame setting.
8. Performance goals that are high and actively sought by superiors who also recognize the necessity for making a full commitment to developing, through training, the human resources of the company.[16]

As a result of several studies utilizing the framework of the four systems, Likert has developed a descriptive scheme showing the relationship between certain *casual* variables, *intervening* variables, and *end-result* variables.

Measuring Causal, Intervening, and End-Result Variables

Likert's major point is that managerial behavior and organizational structure (both causal variables) affect and are affected by certain intervening variables (such as motivating factors, goal performance, extent and nature of communication, and the character of the interaction-influence factors) to cause end-result variables in the areas of profits, sales, costs, and other enterprise

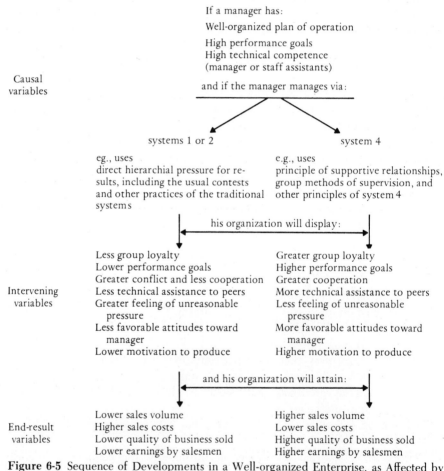

Figure 6-5 Sequence of Developments in a Well-organized Enterprise, as Affected by Use of System 2 or System 4 [From R. Likert, *Human Organization*, p. 76 (After Rensis Likert, "New Patterns in Sales Management." In Martin R. Warshaw, ed., *Changing Perspectives in Marketing Management*, Ann Arbor, Mich.: University of Michigan Bureau of Business Research, 1962. By permission of the publishers.)]

goals, such as human satisfaction. An example of the interaction of these variables is provided in Figure 6-5, in which a comparison is made between exploitive-authoritative (System 1) or benevolent-authoritative (System 2) and participative-group (System 4) managing.

Likert contends that management should analyze and study causal and intervening variables periodically to see what factors are aiding or hindering the organization's performance. The measurement and control of human variables are important, and management should seek for techniques that can improve the quality of management. The goal of every organization, as far as Likert is concerned, should be a movement toward System 4, participative decision-making orientation.

Although all of the theories discussed thus far—Maslow's Need-Hierarchy Theory; Herzberg's Motivator-Hygiene Theory; McGregor's Theory X and Y; and Likert's Four Systems Theory—do reflect various managerial assumptions concerning the nature of human behavior in the organizational setting, and although it is generally conceded that a manager's espousal of any of these theoretical orientations could influence the quality of organizational behavior and communication, many researchers have felt handicapped in attempting to pin down the variables or factors that contribute to the distinctions of each theory. For example, some researchers have been frustrated in their attempts to identify the essential qualities or attributes of *motivation* that Herzberg talks about; others have tried to study Maslow's self-actualization needs and the fulfillment thereof, with relatively little success; some have been forced to view McGregor's Theory Y stance as a colossal but unattainable ideal and have then gone on to generate their own versions of a Theory Z; still others contend that all of the necessary evidence has not (as yet) matured to completely substantiate the claims of Likert's System 4.

Out of such dissatisfaction, strong movements designed to embed certain practical realities into the study of managerial philosophies and practices began to emerge in the late 1960s and early 1970s. Two influential perspectives—Blake and Mouton's Managerial Grid Theory and Fiedler's Contingency Theory—have gained some consideration among managers.

Managerial Grid Theory

Robert Blake and Jane Mouton[17] suggest that supervisory effectiveness depends on the manager's stress of either *task accomplishment* or the *interpersonal relationships* between the worker and the manager. Even though managers may have many concerns, the authors' research indicates that concern for the employees as individuals (employee orientation) and concern for production (production orientation) are the two most important orientations affecting management styles. Their analysis of leadership styles is depicted in the well-known managerial grid of Figure 6-6.

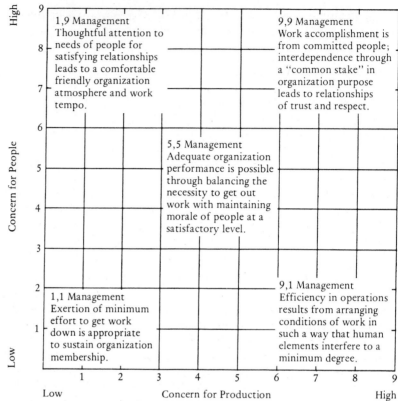

Figure 6–6   *The Managerial Grid* [From Robert R. Blake and Jane S. Mouton, "Managerial Facades," *Advanced Management Journal* (July 1966): 31.]

In the grid, the vertical axis plots the degree of concern the manager manifests for workers and the relationship they share at work. The horizontal axis plots the magnitude of the manager's concern for getting the job done. The lower left-hand corner represents the orientation of a manager who expresses a low concern for both people and production; the upper right-hand corner represents a manager who has a high concern for both people and production.

The quadrants in Blake and Mouton's Managerial Grid are descriptive of the various managerial styles that are prevalent in many organizations and are summarily referred to as: country-club leadership style; team leadership style; middle-of-the-road leadership style; impoverished leadership style; and task-centered leadership style (see Figure 6-7).

Steinmetz and Todd have furnished an excellent description of these five leadership styles:

> *Country-Club Leadership Style.* The individual who demonstrates high concern for people and low concern for production would be classed as a country-club leader. This type of leader gives thoughtful attention and devotion to the needs of people and tries to develop some kind of satisfying working relationship developing a comfortable, friendly working organization. In this particular situation the leader is more concerned about the

congeniality of the work relationship than whether or not production is accomplished. This leader wants everyone to be happy.

Task-Centered Leader. The polar opposite of the country-club leader is the task-centered leader. The task-centered leader is an individual whose main concern is efficiency of operations and getting the job done. "Results are the only thing" as far as the task-oriented leader is concerned. Any problems that get in the way of production, especially problems which have a human element to them, are only viewed as interfering with effective operations. Concern for the individuals who do the work is very small. People and machines are treated equally.

Impoverished Leader. The impoverished leader is the individual who has very low concern for both people and production. The basic attitude is one of "don't rock the boat at all." The impoverished leader can be expected to exert only a minimal effort at trying to get the work done, yet demonstrates no concern for personal relationships and the human dimensions on the job. This individual might best be characterized as both unfriendly and lazy, if he is having a good day, and grouchy and obstinate on a bad day.

Middle-of-the-Road Leadership Style. Middle of the road leadership style is the individual who has a modicom of concern for both people and production. The middle of the road supervisor usually gets acceptable organizational performance, but does so primarily by trying to balance or trade off the necessity of getting work out with the need to maintain morale among the people at an acceptable kind of level. This individual is balanced in terms of leadership style, but not overenergetic or overenthusiastic in regard to either job performance or people's satisfaction at work.

Team Leadership Style. The team leader is, of course, ideal. The team leader is a person who has both high concern for people and high concern for production. Consequently he or she can be plotted on the

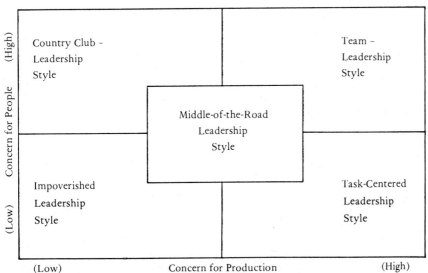

Figure 6-7. The Styles of Leadership under Terms of the Managerial Grid

managerial grid as scoring high in concern for both people and productivity. The team leader is successful at motivating achievement. People working for team leaders are committed to doing the job that needs to be done. The team leader also has the ability to get people to recognize that there is an interdependence between job satisfaction and work achievement. Thus the team leader is successful at promoting the concept that there is a need for a mutual relationship of trust and respect between the leader, his subordinates, and their respect for their job.[18]

Blake and Mouton's assumption is that the manager who is a team-oriented leader would be using the most effective style. However, in reality, it would be difficult to find a team leader for every type of job. Blake and Mouton believe that by implementing management development programs we would be able to develop that type of managerial style.

Some scholars disagree with the position taken by Blake and Mouton, citing evidence to show that some managers were very effective when they had very low concern for people, whereas other managers were very effective when they had low concern for production. In some cases, managers were effective when they had low concern for both people and production. Apparently, the effectiveness of a team-oriented style would be dependent or contingent upon the method used, the attitudes of the employees, and the situational constraints prevalent in the organization.

Following Blake and Mouton, Fiedler found some of the answers concerning the situations or contingencies in which leadership occurs.

Situational or Contingency Theory

Frederick Fiedler's contingency theory of leadership rejects the idea of a single best theory of leadership supervision.[19] Fiedler feels that it is not a matter of the best style of leadership, but rather of a leadership style that will be most effective in a particular situation. The contingency model suggests that there may be many leadership behavior styles that will be effective in any given situation.

Fiedler argues that the basic component of leadership is influence—that is, leadership is defined as a relationship in which one person tries to influence others in the performance of a common task. Consequently, Fiedler's situational assessment consists of one underlying dimension: the degree to which the leader can *influence* the members of the group. That dimension of influence is composed of three major factors: *leader-member relations, task structure, and position power.*

1. *Leader-member relations* refers to the degree of confidence the subordinates have in the leader. It entails the loyalty shown as well as the attractiveness exhibited by the leader.
2. *Task structure* refers to the degree to which the followers' jobs are routine rather than ill-structured and undefined.
3. *Position power* refers to the influence inherent in the leadership position. It

includes the rewards and punishments typically associated with the position, the leader's official authority (based on ranking in managerial hierarchy), and the support the leader receives from superiors and the overall organization.

Table 6-3 shows Fiedler's findings about the relationship among the three dimensions of leadership style for such groups as bomber crews, management groups, high school basketball teams, and foundry workers. Notice the correlation between good task performance and *directive* style under conditions 1, 2, 3, and 8, and the correlation between good task performance and *permissive style* under conditions 4 and 5. The results indicate that in specific situations one particular leadership style achieves the best results.

For example, under condition 1 the leader has excellent personal relationships with subordinates; the latter are engaged in a highly structured task with a clear-cut goal; the leader has a great deal of power and authority to accomplish the objective. This condition might prevail in a space-flight center, where a well-liked flight director is getting the crew ready for a rocket launch. The tasks to be performed by the flight director are very rigidly structured. There is no room for error or indecision, and the duties of every person on the launching team are very clearly spelled out. The flight director has total power to correct any personnel or performance problems within the launching team. Another example describes leadership under condition 5 of the table: Sam Froelich, recently graduated from college where he had taken several management courses, was put in charge of fifteen machinists on his first job in a tool company. Most of the machinists had little education past the eighth grade, but they had worked for the company for more than ten years. Some of the machinists believed that college graduates were either "wise guys" or "pencil-neck geeks"; some thought they were "good people" but "still wet behind the ears." In general, the machinists took their time deciding, and preferred to believe the worst. Because these machinists were genuine experts in their job, a formal

TABLE 6-3   Summary of Fiedler's Investigations of Leadership

| Condition | Group Situation | | | Leadership Style Correlating with Productivity |
	Leader-Member Relations	*Task Structure*	*Position Power*	
1	Good	Structured	Strong	Directive
2	Good	Structured	Weak	Directive
3	Good	Unstructured	Strong	Directive
4	Good	Unstructured	Weak	Permissive
5	Moderately poor	Structured	Strong	Permissive
6	Moderately poor	Structured	Weak	No Data
7	Moderately poor	Unstructured	Strong	No relationship found
8	Moderately poor	Unstructured	Weak	Directive

leader or manager had very little control over how the job was done. The job was structured by the experts. Thereupon, Sam Froelich concentrated on the paperwork rather than on the technical details. Thus, in accordance with condition 5 of the table, Sam Froelich *wisely* resorted to a *permissive* leadership style in a situation where the leader-member relations are moderately poor, the task is structured, and his position power is strong.

Fiedler recommends that organizations find ways and means to create situations to fit the kind of effective leadership styles described in his contingency model. Here are a few of his suggestions:

1. *Leader-member relations* could be improved by restructuring the leader's subordinates so that the group is more compatible in terms of background, education level, technical expertise, or ethnic origin. It should be noted that this would be extremely difficult in a unionized group since it may assume that this restructuring is a management plan to weaken the union.
2. *The task structure* can be modified to make it either structured or nonstructured to suit the situation. The task can be more structured by spelling out the jobs in greater detail. It can be made less structured by providing only general directions for the work that is to be accomplished. Some workers like minimum task structure whereas others want it and in detail.
3. Leader *position power* can be modified in a number of ways. A leader can be given a higher rank in the organization or more authority to do the job. A memo could then be issued indicating the change of rank or authority. In addition, a leader's reward power could be increased if the organization delegates to that leader the authority to evaluate the performance of subordinates.

Fiedler's contingency or situational model makes a unique contribution in that it does not depict a single ideal managerial behavior for every situation. For example, the high-task and high-relationship style would be appropriate only in certain situations; but in crisis-oriented organizations like the military, police, or hospital environments, the most appropriate style would probably be high-task concern and low personal relationship. The model also takes into account the leader's personality and such situational variables as the task to be completed and the behavioral characteristics of the group. Rather than insist that managers learn to be flexible and use different leadership styles, Fiedler stresses the importance of engineering jobs to fit the managers. (Other elements of effective organizational leadership are examined in Chapter 9.)

Among the six theories or models of organizational behavior discussed here, there is no single *best* theory. Each orientation has wielded an influence that lingers in every organization. The essential point is that the quality of a manager's interaction and communication with employees will be influenced largely by whatever "theory" or "model" he or she endorses.

REVIEW QUESTIONS

1. Why are Maslow's needs arranged in a "hierarchy of needs" format?
2. How can Maslow's theory be used to facilitate the accuracy of managerial assumptions and the managers' communication behaviors?
3. Distinguish between motivator and hygiene factors and their effects, respectively, on satisfaction and dissatisfaction.
4. Describe the assumptions about human nature and human behavior underlying McGregor's Theory X and Theory Y, and describe some personal experiences in which you were managed by a "Theory X" manager or by a "Theory Y" manager.
5. Using Likert's four-system theory, explain how and why certain causal and intervening variables affect end-result variables?
6. An individual whose main concern is efficiency of operations and getting the job done is what kind of leader according to Blake and Mouton? What would this individual score on the Managerial Grid?
7. What is the basic component of leadership according to Fiedler, and how does he measure this variable?
8. How does Fiedler's Contingency Theory contribute to our understanding of leadership styles in organizational communication?

KEY TERMS AND CONCEPTS FOR REVIEW

- Physiological Needs
- Safety Needs
- Social Needs
- Esteem Needs
- Self-Actualization Needs
- Motivators
- Hygiene Factors
- Environmental Factors
- Theory X
- Theory Y
- Exploitive-Authoritative
- Benevolent-Authoritative
- Consultative
- Participative
- Casual, Intervening, and End-Result Variables
- Country-Club Leadership Style
- Task-Centered Leader
- Impoverished Leader
- Middle-of-the-Road Leadership Style
- Team Leadership Style
- Influence
- Leader-Member Relations
- Task Structure
- Position Power
- Directive Style/Permissive Style

CASE STUDY

Bob Everett, an enthusiastic high school graduate in his late twenties, is an assistant manager for a major clothing store chain. He enjoys his work immensely and plans on remaining in the same organization for many years to come. Bob's immediate superior, the store manager, thinks highly of Bob's work, and views his contribution to the store's operation in a very positive way. Bob feels as though he has been ignored by his superiors because he never gets to contribute to major decisions that affect store operations. Many times when his participation in making a decision would have been very helpful, Bob's immediate superiors neglected to seek his advice. Bob is determined to become a more active participant in the decision-making process, but has been told by other assistant store managers in the organization that only managers make decisions and that assistant store managers merely implement those decisions. Bob has been feeling disheartened and demotivated lately, and is considering approaching his boss with a "let me participate in the decision-making process or I quit" ultimatum.

PROBES

1. How should Bob go about pleading his case to his immediate superior?
2. What should Bob's boss do about this matter, and how can both parties concerned be satisfied with a mutually beneficial solution?
3. What motivational factors are involved in this case?
4. What type of leadership style is Bob's boss employing?

Recomended Readings

Fossum, J. A. "The Effects of Positively and Negatively Contingent Rewards and Individual Differences on Performance, Satisfaction, and Expectations" *Academy of Management Journal* 22 (1979): 577–589.

Gould, S. "An Equity-Exchange Model of Organizational Involvement." *The Academy of Management Review* 4 (1979): 53–62.

Herzberg, F. *Work and the Nature of Man.* Cleveland: World, 1966.

McClelland, D. C. *The Achieving Society.* Princeton: Van Nostrand, 1961.

McGregor, D. *The Human Side of Enterprise.* New York: McGraw-Hill, 1960.

Miles, R. E. *Theories of Management: Implications for Organizational Behavior and Development.* New York: McGraw-Hill, 1975.

Steers, R. M. and Porter, L. W. *Motivation and Work Behavior.* New York: McGraw-Hill, 1975.

NOTES

1. A. Maslow, *Motivation and Personality* (New York: Harper & Row, 1954).
2. S. Gellerman, *Motivation and Productivity* (New York: American Management Association, 1963).
3. A. Maslow, "A Theory of Human Motivation." In Robert Sutermeister, *People and Productivity*, 2d ed. (New York: McGraw-Hill Book Company, 1969), pp. 91–92.

4. *First-Line Management: Approaching Supervision Effectively* (Dallas, Tex.: Business Publications, Inc., 1975), p. 84.

5. Maslow, op. cit., p. 82.

6. J. Donnelly, J. Gibson, and J. Ivancevich, *Fundamentals of Management: Functions, Behavior, Models* (Dallas, Tex.: Business Publications, 1975), pp. 145–418.

7. F. Herzberg, B. Mausner, and B. Snyderman, *The Motivation to Work* (New York: John Wiley & Sons, 1959); Herzberg, *Work and the Nature of Man* (New York: World Publishing Co., 1966).

8. F. Herzberg, "One More Time: How Do You Motivate Employees," *Harvard Business Review* 46 (January–February 1968): 56–57.

9. Steinmetz and Todd, op. cit., p. 88.

10. P. Hersey and K. H. Blanchard, *Management of Organizational Behavior* (Englewood Cliffs, N.J.: Prentice-Hall, Inc., 1972), pp. 58–59.

11. New York: McGraw-Hill Book Company, 1960.

12. G. Goldhaber, *Organizational Communication* (Dubuque, Iowa: William C. Brown Company, 1974), pp. 59–61.

13. R. Likert, *New Patterns of Management* (New York: McGraw-Hill Book Company, 1961); *The Human Organization* (New York: McGraw-Hill Book Company, 1967).

14. See Donnelly, Gibson, and Ivancevich, op. cit., p. 279.

15. Descriptions adapted from Hersey and Blanchard, op. cit., pp. 61–62.

16. Donnelly, Gibson, and Ivancevich, op. cit., p. 280.

17. R. Blake and J. Mouton, *The Managerial Grid* (Houston, Tex.: Gulf Publishing Company, 1964).

18. Steinmetz and Todd, op. cit., pp. 111–112.

19. F. Fiedler, *A Theory of Leadership Effectiveness* (New York: McGraw-Hill Book Company, 1967).

7 | Communicator: Personality Variables

LEARNING OBJECTIVES

After reading this chapter, you should be able to
1. Explain the characteristics of personality.
2. Define the concept labeled **personality**.
3. Describe the so-called hierarchy of needs.
4. Explain and discuss the relationship between the hierarchy of needs and personality.
5. Identify and discuss the three major determinants of personality.
6. Identify and describe the various personality types that are found in organizations.
7. Explain the nature of the six basic patterns of defense reactions.

The study of organizational behavior and communication is rather complex, for it involves phenomena that exist on many levels and are influenced by many factors. For many researchers the key to the study of organizations derives from the idea that every organization has its origin in a need to blend two basic components: persons and structure. Consequently, the nature of personality constitutes a major influence on behaviors and interactions in the organizational setting. The personality approach to the study of organizational behavior and communication may help us to understand, explain, predict, and, perhaps, control the responses that people are likely to make in various situations.

In this chapter, we discuss the nature and general characteristics of personality, the various types of personality encountered in organizational environments, the relationship between personality and defense reactions, and the association between personality and occupation.

The Characteristics of Personality

Bob Turnbull is a senior employee in a well-known accounting firm. He is thirty-six years old and has held a job as an accountant ever since graduation from business school ten years ago. He is unmarried and lives with his widowed mother in the same house in which he was born. Well liked in the community, Bob is mild mannered and treats his colleagues with considerable respect. He performs all of his work well in advance of deadlines and even helps other employees to catch up on their share of the work. The consensus at the firm is that "Turnbull is a helluva neat guy!"

"Moose" Bondrago is a good worker, but crude. He is exceptionally strong, and is perhaps the best man who has ever worked down on the loading dock. Moose rides a motorcycle, wears a black leather jacket with the word "Moose" riveted in the back. He often gets drunk, sometimes on the job (particularly on Friday afternoons), and invariably ends up challenging the other workers to fight. He professes an intense hatred for women and foremen. "Women just don't belong in places where a man must work. Too soft," he says, "too bitchy." As for the foreman, Moose believes that "one jackass has more brains in his head than twenty foremen put together."

Sally Prunella is thirtyish, a trifle plump, and a fairly good office clerk. She works for an envelope-manufacturing company, and is on the verge of being fired. According to the office manager, Naomi Saperstein, Sally has persisted in wearing "those damned short skirts" in spite of repeated warnings to "dress like a lady as all the other women do." What is more disturbing (at least to Saperstein) is the fact that Sally spends her coffee breaks sauntering through the printing area. Sally claims that she takes those walks (she calls them "constitutionals") through the plant merely to "stretch her legs." The boss contends that Sally struts through the plant to show off her legs. The whistles and catcalls of the men in the pressroom have convinced the manager that Sally delights in making a spectacle of herself. Says Naomi, "This type of exhibitionism is bad for morale!"

These simple sketches are fictitious. We concocted them simply by thinking about people we know and writing down some of their most prominent "personality" characteristics. You probably have composed similar personality sketches when describing friends, relatives, teachers, new acquaintances, your boss, and even yourself. Describing people's personalities is one of the oldest and most fascinating human pastimes, yet the formal psychological study of personality did not actually develop until this century.

There is no single definition of personality. The term *personality* comes from the Latin word *persona*, which means "mask." Thus personality has been thought of as the appearance that a person presents to the world. Personality has been defined as the totality of a person's manner or his or her general behavior pattern—that is, the sum of the person's knowledge, skills, motives, and actions. Another concept of personality consists mainly of surface characteristics, such as social skills. Even though those everyday notions of personality are less precise than the theoretical concepts of personality, each reflects something about what personality is. Therefore, instead of focusing on the fine (and often contradictory) points of a theoretical definition of personality, we combine both formal and informal thoughts about what constitutes personality in order to arrive at a definition that will adequately serve us in the discussion that follows. For our purposes, personality is the *way in which the individual relates to his or her circumstances*. It is a *combination* of the *knowledge, skills, and intentions* reflected in a person's actions as *evaluated by other people. It is that which gives order and congruence to all the different kinds of behavior in which an individual engages.*

There is wide agreement on the assumption that *personality manifests some type of energy*. For example, it could be that the employee who always feels in "tiptop shape" and is constantly on the go is a person with much energy. On the other hand, the individual who is constantly "down in the dumps" may have very little energy. Whatever the level or amount of energy, most researchers postulate that it (the energy) is located in the need system of the personality. The more important (or deeper) a need, the more potential energy it has to release. By watching people, we can infer from their behavior what need system is in action. For example, an employee cuts down on production to follow the informal shop rule of "no rate busting"; from this behavior we may infer that the employee's most important (or deepest) need—the need *in action*—is the need to belong or to be somewhat dependent upon the group.

After observing thousands of cases of people's behavior, psychologists have been able to categorize many of the needs that people in our culture seem to express. As we define these need categories, it would be wise to bear in mind that these schemes represent an individual's attempt at unifying and ordering the kinds of needs and personality exhibits.

The Structure of Needs

All human beings have certain needs that are at the heart, or the very depth, of their personality. One of the most important inner needs is the need to maintain adjustment of the self in relation to the world in which it exists. According to Argyris,[1] inner needs can be inferred as active when a person is observed being upset, expressing much emotion, or working doggedly at a task without letting up. Or if a fellow worker, much to our consternation, "blows his cool" at a suggestion, it could be that we have unwittingly activated an inner need.

For example, Joe and Harry work in the same department as quality control specialists. They are friends, and frequently exchange ideas. One morning Joe strolls over to Harry who happens to be standing at the coffee machine with two secretaries.

Joe Say Harry, I've been meaning to talk to you about some of those memos.

Harry What memos?

Joe You know what I'm talking about———the memos you've been typing up to send to the supervisor down in the die-cutting room. I don't think you're being specific enough and . . .

Harry (*backing away, his face turning red*) Who in the hell do you think you are, fella? Somebody complained to you about my memos? Eh???

Joe Shucks, Harry! I'm only trying to . . .

Harry Go and do your trying somewhere else . . . You don't try to tell me what to do. I'll write my memos any way I damned well please.

Joe Oh, hell . . . (*walks away, muttering to himself*).

What is Harry's problem? Well, we really cannot say—at least, not until we have explored the matter much further. However, we can surmise that one of the problems has to do with Joe's disturbing one of Harry's deepest inner needs—it could be a need to appear eminently capable in the eyes of significant others, in this case, two secretaries.

The outer needs are closer to the surface of the personality; little emotion is aroused if they become active. But the inner needs are more basic and vital. As Argyris puts it: Whereas the inner needs give us a cue as to what the person *is*, outer needs tells us what the person *does*.

People are never fully aware of all their needs. Some needs, usually the innermost ones, are unconscious. Thus we can ask Harry, "Why did you behave the way you did?" but he might find it impossible to answer accurately.

There is much debate concerning the number of needs that exist. Some researchers suggest at least twenty basic kinds of needs. C. P. Alderfer[2] for example, distinguishes between three classes: (1) existence needs that are related to the biological necessities of life, (2) relatedness needs that deal with relations with other people, and (3) growth needs that express personal development. Schutz[3] also suggests the dominance of three types of needs: (1) inclusion needs, (2) affection needs, and (3) control needs. Abraham Maslow,[4]

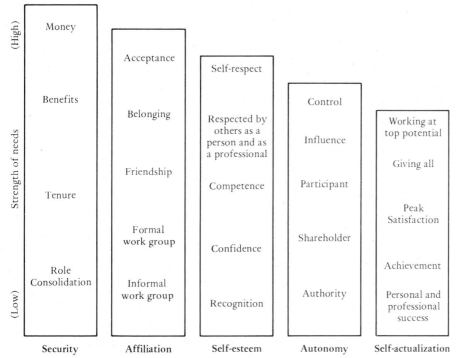

Figure 7-1 Basic Hierarchical Needs Model

in a more complex model, postulates five needs arranged in hierarchical order: (1) physiological, (2) safety, (3) love,(4) esteem, and (5) self-actualization.

We believe that the idea of a hierarchy of needs provides the most feasible framework for understanding individual differences in behavior. These differences in behavior are the characteristics that combine to form *personality*. Human or personal needs in organizations appear to fit into a hierarchy of five general types of needs. In Figure 7-1, the five types of needs are presented (1) security needs, (2) affiliation needs, (3) self-esteem needs, (4) autonomy needs, and (5) self-actualization needs. Within the framework of each need portrayed in the hierarchy, we have shown the serious concerns or drives that may be manifested as people interact or communicate with one another.

The location of a particular need in the hierarchy tells us something about its *prepotency*, predominance, strength, or driving force. The location may also give us some clue as to why a certain individual may behave so differently from those around him or her. Figure 7-1 shows that for a particular individual at a particular time, security needs are located at the top or peak of the hierarchy. In the case of another individual, the self-esteem need may have been at peak, and Figure 7-1 would have to be modified to reflect that. Returning to the model given in Figure 7-1, the need and concern for "security issues" such as money, tenure, benefits, and so on are *prepotent*. Most of the individual's behavior will be directed toward obtaining "things" or accords to satisfy the need. At times it may appear as though the individual cannot think of anything other than money, pay raises, benefits, seniority, tenure, and so on. Motivating such a person "to settle down and get off the security kick" may be a bit difficult since the need for security must be satisfied before other types of needs can act as motivators. You are not able to use appeals to self-esteem, for example, until security needs and affiliation needs are satisfied. Satisfaction throughout the hierarchy operates in a sort of domino effect, so that in order for self-actualization needs to motivate, all of the other four types of needs must be first satisfied.

The *goal* of personnel management in organizations is to get people to mature to the point of being "charged up" or motivated by *self-actualization needs*. Self-actualization is the desire to become what one is capable of becoming—such as an ideal secretary, manager, tool-and-die cutter, or foreman. At that point, the *personality* that comes across is of one who is working at top potential, giving all, enjoying peak satisfaction, achieving recognition, and enjoying personal and professional success. But, the key question is: How do we coax or entice this change in the employee's personality? One simple answer would be to create an organizational environment that allows opportunities for the satisfaction of all the other four needs along the way. Even partial success would be worthwhile.

Surrounding needs, and in most cases developing from them, are abilities. *Personality has abilities.* Abilities are the tools by which a person expresses or fulfills his or her needs. They are the communication systems for those needs. Sometimes difficulties arise because the channel between needs and abilities is not direct, or it may be distorted. In such instances, the person may interpose a set of defenses between his or her needs and abilities, which will serve to modify behavior. For example, an employee may be an excellent typist and have most of the skills necessary for the job. However, if that employee were placed in a test situation to be observed and evaluated while working, the situation would evoke defenses, which could upset the employee considerably. The tension might act to reduce the efficient expression of that person's ability, and the employee might not be considered capable.

Three primary abilities interact with each other: (1) knowing (cognitive) abilities: those we use to know our world (e.g., intelligence); (2) doing (motor) abilities: those that permit us to do things physically (e.g., working with our hands, designing, etc.); and (3) feeling abilities: those that enable us to experience the many complex feelings in life and to be sensitive to other people's feelings.

Since these abilities are interrelated and continually affect one another, it is reasonable to surmise that when so-called personality tests are administered, they will be affected by all of the person's primary abilities. A test can never be arranged to measure just one type of ability.

We see, then, that personality is a complex phenomenon. It manifests an energy that appears to emanate from the individual's need system, and it manifests certain interrelated abilities. In addition, it gives order and congruence to all the different kinds of behavior in which an individual engages.

Determinants of Personality

Three major variables, or *determinants*, influence the formation and development of personality. These variables are (1) our physiological composition, (2) primary or referent groups to which we belong or from which we take our cues for interpersonal relationships, and (3) cultural environment.

Physiological Composition

The basic tools for our survival, growth, and adjustment have been furnished us by nature. Such tools include our muscular and nervous system, glands, and mental capacity. Some people, because they are "sick on the inside," cannot avoid being "sickening" on the outside. If a person's physiological or psychological composition does indeed determine an aspect of his or her personality, it would seem fitting that we exercise tolerance, sympathy, and patience toward those who appear somewhat strange in their interactions with others. Our task as members of the organization would be to assess the motives or the causes of behavior before attempting to mete out cures for them.

The Group

The referent groups to which we belong also aid in molding our personality. These groups—for example, social clubs, local unions, political organizations, neighborhood communities, work groups—give us standards, or yardsticks, by which to chart our behavior. The groups influence the roles we play and the flair or lack of it with which we play them. It is not uncommon to visit a plant or office and observe that almost everyone walks in the same manner and wears the same kinds of clothes and hairstyles. Or, if one listens at airports to the voices on the public address system, one would get the feeling that they all sounded alike. The similarity may be attributed to the individuals' desire to conform to the "standard" of what airport personnel ought to sound like.

The Culture

Culture operates perhaps with more strength to mold personality than does the group. One may leave referent groups for a long time and, thus, get a breather from role taking, but in general one is a lifetime prisoner of one's culture. Culture "dictates" that a bank executive, a clergyman, and a company president should each project an image or personality commensurate with his or her role. Unfortunately, these roles may sometimes become so burdensome that individuals grow frustrated, disoriented, or disenfranchised. When a person fails to confirm our cultural expectations, he or she is often criticized as having a bad image or a poor personality.

Within the framework of these determinants as definitions of *personality* there is one constant—consistency. An individual will *attempt* to maintain a consistent façade in everyday interactions.

Personalities Within Organizations

The personality of an organization, in many respects, is a composite of the varied behaviors of the people within it. R. Presthus speaks of three general types of personalities in the typical bureaucratic structure.[5] At or near the top of the organizational pyramid are the "upward mobiles," who react positively to the large bureaucratic situations and succeed in it. The uncommitted majority in the organization are the "indifferents," who see their jobs as mere instruments to obtain off-work satisfactions. Then there are the "ambivalents," a small, constantly disturbed minority consisting of persons who can neither renounce their claims for status and power nor play the disciplined role needed to acquire them. Upward mobiles, indifferents, and ambivalents are only three of the different kinds of personalities that we encounter within organizations. Some of the other types are authoritarians, Machiavellians, dogmatics, high achievers, undersocials, oversocials, and adaptable-socials. We now examine each of these personality types and their relationship to organizational communication.

Personality Types

Upward Mobiles   Upward mobiles tend toward high job satisfaction and identify strongly with the organization. Frequently they receive a large share of the organizational rewards in power, income, and ego-reinforcement.
When an "upward mobile" fails, he or she is more likely to attribute the blame to personal failure rather than to system failure; the response is more likely to be, "things didn't work right because I messed up" rather than, "things didn't work right because they were out to get me!" The upward mobile is an organization man (or woman), a conformist who can act and respond without much self-analysis. This person deals with human relations as a career utility, is sensitive to feedback, and behaves accordingly. This driving type thinks strategically and will use all the ritualistic pleasantries of the organizational environment to conceal resentments.

An upward mobile person is rule- and procedure-oriented and tends to view individuals with impersonal detachment. Generally, this type of personality will place personal advancement before group acceptance and feel little sense of conflict between personal goals and group goals. Interests and aspirations are so wrapped up in the organization that the upward mobile is able to rationalize organizational claims, no matter how illogical or unreasonable those claims may be.

E. Ghiselli[6] has attempted to draw a connection between the "self-assured" manner of upward mobiles and their managerial positions. He argued that self-assurance might be a significant correlate of a manager's success only when his or her goals are selfish in seeking security and power. He found the high self-actualization scores of upward mobiles to be positively related to managerial job success indices, job security motivation, and financial rewards.

The upward mobile person dislikes to associate with losers, has great confidence in his or her decision-making ability, is bored by routine, and is challenged by risk-taking enterprises.

Indifferents   The majority of wage and salary employees fall into the category of *indifferents* who withdraw from system participation if possible. Indifferents tend to regard organizations as necessary evils—systems organized to tyrannize the "little man." They do not compete strongly for rewards, and through their lack of interest in this regard, the upward mobiles are afforded more leeway to operate or excel. Consequently, *indifferent* employees do not share in the ownership, profits, price, or ego-involvement of the organization. Since the need to work is a fact of life, how do these people survive? As we hinted earlier, a worker manifesting an indifferent personality generally seeks off-the-job satisfaction and *rejects* the values of success and power.

B. Gilmer[7] reports that many indifferents, both blue-collar and white-collar, pay lip service to mobility and transfer their expectations to their children. Theirs is a disposition that may be verbalized thus: "The only reason I work in this place is so that my kids won't have to end up like me." The indifferents expect less from the organization and tend to be less disappointed. They reject status anxiety, success striving, and self-discipline. After completing the required hours of work, they jealously regard the remaining time as private and personal—work life is separated from personal life. This person never takes work home.

Researchers have noticed—particularly in mass-production organizations—that the indifferent may depreciate the things he or she makes ("I wouldn't buy one of those cars if you paid me; they're nothing but junk!"). This type of person has become conditioned against expecting very much from the organization and does not identify strongly with it, which may be associated with the fact that the person gradually becomes immune to discipline and seeks to identify mainly with work companions. Labor economists contend that this attitude allows the small group to play a protective role and thus, through the union, shields this person from the real or imaginary threats of management.

The indifferents may have satisfactory interpersonal relations since they are not perceived as a threat by colleagues. Even in a large union indifferent workers only serve to provide numerical support for decisions made by others. For the indifferent, whether blue-collar or white-collar, there is not much difference between people, jobs, and organizations; they tend to adjust to each.

Ambivalents   Ambivalent people are described as being both creative and anxious. They usually find themselves to be marginal, with somewhat limited career chances. They are inclined neither to reject the organization's promise of success and power nor to play the required role to compete for them. Rather than being adaptive, the ambivalents are somewhat neurotic about their role in the organization. Whereas the upward mobiles like the status quo and the indifferents accept it, the ambivalents want to change it.

Ambivalents are often subjective, withdrawn, or introverted, but may attack "the system" when they are sufficiently aroused. The ambivalent celebrate theory and knowledge and have a high verbal skill. They are not system-oriented and tend to resist bureaucratic rules and procedures. Their career expectations are idealistic and often unrealistic, and they often find themselves unable to bargain effectively. Since their expectations are unrealistic, they encounter repeated frustration on the job and, in retaliation, increase the psychological distance between themselves and the organization.

The ambivalent reject authority and do not share the belief that those who attain responsible positions in management do so on the basis of talent and genuine skill. Incidentally, the ambivalent's conjecture may be defensible. Studies conducted in several companies have discovered no relationship between intelligence and aptitude, on the one hand, and rank and salary on the other.

Ambivalent people are not inclined to assume typical organizational roles and often appear to be out of step with their colleagues. They reject group-influenced values and frown on behaviors that smack of compromises with superiors. Sometimes the ambivalent may manifest a compulsive interest in a job; however, such behavior may be more indicative of a desire to appear different from colleagues than from any intrinsic value derived from the task itself. The ambivalents are not effective in practical decision making. But even though they appear generally unsuited to the quality of interaction that is essential to the operation of the organization, they are useful in one crucial regard—their criticisms generally stampede the organization into much needed change.

The three personality types described thus far—upward mobiles, indifferents, and ambivalents—are descriptive of certain general manners, behaviors, and attitudes manifested toward the organization at large. There are some other personality types that can be discussed in terms of the attitudes or dispositions of people toward actual communication or ideas within the organization. Some of these personality types are *authoritarians, Machiavellians, dogmatics, high achievers, undersocials, oversocials,* and *adaptable-socials.*

Authoritarians   In *The Authoritarian Personality* it is argued that people who had aloof, stern, and punitive fathers; whose parents administered a great deal of physical punishment; and who grew up in families organized along hierarchical lines with a feared father as the central figure, developed a particular kind of personality called *authoritarian.*[8]

A cluster of nine authoritarian character traits was considered typical of the authoritarian personality. These are

1. Conventionalism—a rigid adherence to conventional middle-class values;
2. Authoritarian submission—a submission to authority figures and an uncritical attitude toward idealized moral authorities of the in-group;
3. Hostility toward those who violate social norms—a form of authoritarian aggression—a tendency to be overready to perceive, condemn, reject, and punish people who violate conventional norms;
4. Dislike of subjectivity—an aversion to the subjective, the imaginative, the aesthetic, the tender-minded;

5. Superstition and stereotyping—beliefs in mystical determinance of the individual's fate; the disposition to think in rigid categories;
6. Preoccupation with strength, power, and toughness—concern with the dominant-submissive, strong-weak, leader-follower dimension; identification with power figures; exaggerated assertion of strength and toughness;
7. Destructive cynicism toward human nature—a rather generalized hostility— the vilification of the human;
8. Projectivity—a tendency to project unacceptable impulses—a disposition to believe that wild and dangerous and wicked things go on in the world;
9. An exaggerated concern with sex and sexual goings-on.

People's attitudes toward authority in the work situation are generally consistent even though they may have different attitudes toward other kinds of structure. The *authoritarian person* believes that it is right and proper that there should be status and power differences among individuals. This person believes "God intended" that some individuals occupy more powerful positions than others. Consequently, when authoritarians are in a position of authority and power, they tend to "bully" and shove their subordinates around. When they are in a subordinate position in the organization, they are generally quite submissive and compliant.

Authoritarians often manifest conservative attitudes, are conformist in appearance and behavior, are opposed to change, and have been found to be hostile to racial and other minority groups.

At the other extreme, one may encounter *nonauthoritarians* in an organization. These are rebellious individuals who reject the idea that there should be status and power differences among people; they reject both the superior and the subordinate ways and roles.

We believe that normalcy resides somewhere between these two extremes. It is necessary for the healthy maintenance of the organization and for the fostering of effective communication that we ensure some balance between dispositions toward extreme authoritarianism or extreme nonauthoritarianism. There should be enough acceptance of authority to implement orders, suggestions, and policies, and enough rebelliousness (or initiative) to appreciate that things are not always right merely because the boss says them.

Machiavellians   The term *Machiavellian* is derived from the name of the sixteenth-century writer, Niccolò Machiavelli. Machiavellianism refers to an amoral, manipulative attitude toward other individuals, combined with a cynical view of people's motives and their character.

According to Burgoon, Heston, and McCroskey, "not only is the high Machiavellian (high Mach) willing to manipulate others, he is more successful at it and enjoys it."[9] The Machiavellian's relative lack of emotional involvement in interpersonal relationships, his or her lack of concern for conventional outlook, make it easy for him or her to manipulate and control others. The high Mach also distrusts his or her colleagues, and has little faith in human nature. He or she tends to rate fellow workers as less interesting, less assertive, less productive, less cooperative, and less intelligent. Since the Machiavellian disdains his or her fellow workers, he or she experiences no qualms in taking advantage of them.

Christie and Geis suggest that "one consequence of the high Machs' 'cool,' cognitive, situation-specified strategy is that they never appear to be obviously manipulating, when being obvious would be a disadvantage. The high Mach is the one who gets others to help him win in such a way that, in the process, they thank him for the opportunity."[10]

Low Machs, on the other hand—i.e., low scorers on the Machiavellian scale—tend to be outsmarted on most counts by high Machs because they are so trusting of others. Low Machs tend to become overly *obsessed* with honesty, justice, courtesy, and so on, and they are largely blind to the manipulation of others. Low Machs turn out to be poor administrators; they are generally unable to detach themselves from subordinates in order to make objective, hard-nosed decisions especially when the subordinates themselves are involved.

High Machs—despite the negative connotations engendered by the definition—are usually successful at certain administrative tasks or roles. High Mach executives are very successful in organizations where relationships to organizational environments are critical. In such instances, their manipulations are directed toward people outside the organization whereas people inside the organization enjoy the trophies gained by the manipulation.

Dogmatics   Milton Rokeach[11] pioneered research into a personality state called open-mindedness (low dogmatism) and close-mindedness (high dogmatism). Rokeach defined *dogmatism* as a rigidity of beliefs and disbeliefs organized around a commitment to absolute authority. The degree of rigidity provides a framework for varying patterns of intolerance toward people and ideas.

The more dogmatic these individuals are, the more they reject any common ground between their belief system (for example, management philosophy) and their disbelief system (for example, the goals of labor). Highly dogmatic persons are often unable to see any overlap or common ground between the two systems; they look at issues in terms of black and white and overlook the vast area of gray between. Things are either right or wrong. If you argue with them, they are likely to discount your arguments as "irrelevant."

Highly dogmatic individuals tend to *narrow*—that is, they will go to great lengths to avoid ideas or people that threaten their point of view. They are careful to associate with select groups of people of similar thinking. Highly dogmatic or close-minded persons overly admire or "truckle" to powerful people they happen to like and tend to defame or unfairly criticize the authorities they do not like.

We should point out that the world does not consist of "high dogs" and "low dogs" only. We are all dogmatic to a certain degree, from time to time, or from issue to issue, depending on how ego-involved we are. We do contend, however, that extreme, chronic dogmatism creates a major problem in organizational communication, because the very basis of communication is open-mindedness, a willingness to compare and evaluate viewpoints and to accept or reject suggestions solely on the basis of merit.

Actually, all the personality variables discussed can produce disruptive friction in organizations, particularly if the persons involved are ignorant of the motivation behind manifested behaviors. We should realize that one's personality—one's expression of inner self—serves as a framework or a guide by which to make sense out of experience. All experiences are either (1) accepted and integrated with the picture one already has of the self, (2) ignored because the experiences do not make sense to the person in terms of the personality or self-concept, and (3) denied or distorted because the experience is inconsistent with the picture of the self. Since we tend to see only that which agrees with our concept of self, it is difficult for us to be truly objective. This lack of objectivity causes us to feel slighted, hurt, imposed upon, or unfairly treated. In the next section, we discuss the defense mechanisms that we use when we perceive threat to our "personal" self.

High Achievers[12]   One main characteristic of high achievers is a liking for stuations in which they are personally responsible for finding solutions to problems. They also tend to set moderate achievement goals and to take calculated risks. It seems that easy or routine problems provide very little satisfaction for high achievers, and extremely difficult problems may deprive them of the satisfaction of success.

A high achiever is generally overextended, constantly complains of overwork, encourages problems far beyond a capacity to contain or overcome them, and is most likely to be ulcer-prone.

The high achiever constantly seeks concrete and specific feedback of success. He or she thrives on figures on sales, production, costs, profits, graphs, and charts. Money can be ample incentive, but it alone does not suffice. In short, the high achiever thrives on feedback and is happy only if communicaton is frequent and rewarding.

Undersocials   Socializing and sociability are related to the *affiliation need* portrayed in Chapter 6. Undersocials deny their need for affiliation by remaining aloof from others. They are the social isolates who seldom initiate or accept interaction with others. According to Wofford, Gerloff, and Cummins, "people of the under-social type create a world of their own in which they feel secure because they unconsciously 'feel' that other people in the organization are not interested in them. In this way they need not risk the pain of rejection, but instead endure the pain of being lonely."[13]

Subordinates may be able to get by with this pattern of behavior, but the undersocial manager or supervisor has little or no chance of success. Such a manager would be viewed as a snob or as being arrogant. Effective communication would be severely curtailed, and as communication diminishes, the undersocial confirms his or her "feeling" that people in the organization are not interested in working with him or her—a sort of self-fulfilling prophecy.

Oversocials   For oversocials, the affiliation need is prepotent or dominant. The drive for satisfaction of this need often leads the oversocial type to manifest exhibitionistic behavior. They will go to great length to attract attention much to the detriment of their work accomplishment. It is no surprise that co-workers often perceive oversocials as being "goof offs," showboats, and so on.

Adaptable-socials   Whereas undersocials and oversocials represent the extremes, the *adaptable-social* represents moderation. Adaptable-socials are able to adjust their behaviors to fit the prevailing situation; they are highly affiliative when the situation dictates, and low-keyed when the opposite is called for. They like being with people but are not unduly disturbed when they are left alone. It stands to reason that adaptable socials are able to facilitate useful interaction and communication.

Inherent in our discussion of each of the ten personality types is the idea that people are "turned on" by certain things or events and "turned off" by other things or events. Whatever "turns us off" constitutes a threat to our personality. Threat produces anxiety and causes us to react defensively. Defense reactions have a great bearing on the quality of organizational communication. We now examine the question of threat and defense.

Personality and Defense Reactions

There are two ways to reduce feelings of threat to one's personality. One way would be to "change personality" to make it consistent, congruent, or compatible with whatever is causing the difficulty. If one were close-minded or highly dogmatic, one should try to become open-minded; one should accept the fact that one is wrong. Of course, this kind of admission seldom occurs. Most people adopt the second way: they defend their thinking by denial or distortion and cling to the present self-concept. This type of behavior is called a *defense reaction*. A defense reaction is a sequence of behavior in response to a threat whose goal is to maintain the present state of the self against threat.[14] The problem with defensive reactions is that although they may reduce the *awareness of threat*, they never really deal with the actual cause of the threat. Here is an example: Let us say that supervisor X is threatened because he "knows" that the boss does not think he is doing an adequate job. Let us assume also that supervisor X defended himself by placing the blame on the boss: "How on earth can I meet the quotas when *he* keeps hiring so many turkeys and goof-offs to work in my department?" It is obvious that this shifting of blame will not stop the boss from feeling the way he does about supervisor X. What is the next likely step? Supervisor X will be forced to justify his defense reaction to himself. He may do this by saying (and *believing*) that the boss is "out to get him." Each defense is a distortion, which in turn will require further justification and further defense—the supervisor, figuratively speaking, is stumbling through a tunnel of distortions taking him farther and farther away from reality.

The four most frequently threatening experiences that drive us to the adoption of defense reactions are anxiety, conflict, frustration, and failure. In such instances we may resort to one or more of the following reactions:

Aggression   Aggression refers to an attempt to hurt the person, group, or object causing the conflict. Hurt, in this regard, includes physical, social, and psychological injury.

Denial   When threatened, some people *deny* or deceive themselves into "feeling" unaware of the facts that could create one side of a conflict. There are some instances, for example, when employees apparently "do not seem to hear" instructions regarding new regulations or forthcoming changes. Under the process of *denial,* the employees do not allow what has been said to penetrate into their consciousness. Argyris points out that denial is different from deliberate pretense; pretense has to do with a person's knowing something but deciding to make believe that he or she does not.[15]

Conversion   Conversion takes place when people fear that they will not perform suitably in an unusual situation, and they *convert* that fear into some type of bodily trouble. We may recall resorting to this behavior in childhood— we did not do the homework assigned by our strict teacher; so that when morning came we complained of a severe stomach ache and were allowed to stay home. Similarly, a newly elected supervisor experiencing feelings of inadequacy may "become ill" after the first week in the job; or the foreman, afraid when summoned to the boss's office, might get a sudden illness and postpone the meeting.

Overcompensation   Frequently an employee responds to a fear of not being able to perform adequately by working so hard that he or she actually accomplishes the goal and even surpasses it. One press operator, upon joining a company, was so afraid of not making the stipulated daily rate of camera casings, he would arrive at work a full 90 minutes before start-up time so as to ensure that the stock was available and the machine in order. Even though he had made his quota by lunch-time, he would work just as furiously during the afternoon and continue through overtime. In other words, some people who believe that they are incapable of doing something try to make up for limitations and, in fact, make up too much, or *overcompensate,* for these limitations.

Rationalization   Rationalization occurs when people invent some acceptable excuse (acceptable to their own personality) to cover up a failure or an inability to accept something. Rationalization comes into play when an alibi is created for otherwise tenable behavior. For example, an employee striving for promotion, upon finding out that he or she did not receive it may respond (or rationalize) by saying to fellow workers: "I really don't know if I would have been able to undertake all that responsibility. And, anyway, I would have had to leave you guys. So I'm glad I didn't get it."

Projection   Projection is a mechanism by which we "see" in others a quality of our own—a quality that might embarrass us if we admitted to having it. For example, a "model" employee who frequently "finks" on colleagues who break company rules is actually pointing the finger as a way of denying his or her own desire to break the rules. Then there is the actual case of an individual who got into frequent trouble with the law because of his tendency to beat up those he suspected of engaging in homosexual practices. Upon psychiatric examination, it was discovered that the individual was aggressive toward homosexuals because such people "reminded" him of his own latent homosexual tendencies. Generally, the person who indulges in projection is sincere and does not consider himself or herself to be a hypocrite.

Defensive reactions make it difficult to distinguish between an individual's deep motivations and those that are superficial. In other words, the basic characteristics of an individual's personality may be hidden by defensive behavior and, consequently, may not be observed directly. What is usually seen are the methods an individual has developed to express the basic aspects of his or her personality. Only by inferring from this symptomatic defensive behavior can we assess the basic motives of an individual.

No discussion of personality and its impact on the organizational setting would be complete without examinations of the relationship between personality characteristics, job satisfaction, and role taking.

Personality and Occupational Classification

Coates and Pellegrin,[16] in a study comparing the self-perceptions of two groups of workers (50 executives and 50 supervisors), report that executives tended to rate themselves as having more initiative and energy than supervisors. Porter[17] analyzed the self-reports of 320 line workers and 463 management personnel and found that the line workers presented more of a follower's image. Ghiselli[18] concurs with the notion of a group- or occupational-level personality. It is his contention that "persons at different occupational levels perceive themselves in different ways." Each level or group has its own norms, and deviation from those norms can lead to censure not only from peers but also the other levels. Ghiselli found, in this connection, that someone in a lower-level position "who to his superior behaves like . . . a person in a higher occupation would be expected to be less favorably regarded by his superior."[19]

The basic personality or image projection of the lower levels has been characterized by Merenda and Clarke.[20] Members of the upper occupational class appear to be more aggressive and socially confident whereas those in the lower stratum appear to be more placid and submissive. In studying 208 executives and 143 supervisors of a large grocery chain, Guilford[21] found the executives as a group were more (1) sociable, (2) free from depression, (3) emotionally stable, (4) happy-go-lucky, (5) active, (6) ascendant or socially bold, (7) self-confident, (8) calm and composed, (9) objective, (10) agreeable, and (11) cooperative than were the supervisors.

Executives need to be more extroverted than workers because they interact more with people and must deal, to some extent, with personnel management. At this level extroversion can flourish and be rewarded. Meyer and Pressel[22] found a "trend . . . for better [personality] adjustment scores as the hierarchy ascends" from workers to executives.

Based on 320 male Air Force personnel, ranging from corporals to lieutenant colonels, Hetzler[23] reports that "lower status (rank) leaders favored somewhat more *directive* leadership techniques than higher-ranked leaders. Hetzler argues that differing degrees of self-confidence among the personnel at the different levels seem to account for this finding. Kipnis and Lane[24] report "findings that junior petty officers exercised less *direct* leadership and placed more reliance upon official referrals to superiors or upon placing a subordinate on report." [Note that *directive* leadership means autocratic in style, while *direct* leadership means actual leadership rather than supervision.] Having less self-confidence, lower-level personnel tend to be more autocratic and strict, not wanting to get into a situation in which their authority may be challenged.

The various levels of management and lower-level personnel have different perceptions of themselves and of other levels. However, Ghiselli warns that "the usual classification of persons as management versus line personnel may not be wholly adequate."[25] His conclusions are based on a sample of 113 top management people (president, vice-president, head of major operations), 176 middle managers (division or department heads, staff specialists), 172 lower managers (who put into effect middle-management directives), and 319 line workers—all in many different companies throughout the country. Based on intelligence, supervisory ability, initiative, and self-assurance scores, the top and middle management people as a group scored higher than did lower management and line workers as a group. This seems to indicate that a simple division between management and line workers does not invariably hold.

We agree with Ghiselli on the iron-clad forecast of personality and role occupancy, but we do find that, to some extent, personality profiles are useful in assigning personnel to organizational slots. We have devoted attention to this matter because business and industry are putting increasing emphasis on personality assessment. Sooner or later most of us will be affected by their procedures—whether we are being hired, promoted, or even fired. As a rule, the more responsible the position is, the more intensive the assessment of each candidate will be. We often find candidates for executive positions being evaluated, on the one hand, by a battery of tests structured to determine intelligence, temperament, and attitudes, and, on the other hand, by a variety of social situations (meetings, lunches, cocktail parties) stuctured to determine their (and often their wives') ability to contend with the range of possible circumstances that might arise on the job.

But it must be remembered that personality theory is still young and still developing. If we accept the proposition that people's concepts of themselves are influenced by what personality theory tells them they are, we then must conclude that their self-concepts will develop as personality theory develops. That is, new ideas, theories, and syntheses will undoubtedly continue to influence a variety of aspects of our lives—particularly life in the organization—which, in turn, will allow us new possibilities for looking at ourselves.

The study of personality should be attended or accompanied by an awareness of some of the imprecisions or errors that occur as we typecast individuals. In Chapter 3, we warned against the problems involved in "labeling." The neater, tighter, and more restricted the label, the greater is the tendency to overlook or exclude other important qualities or properties. In calling or labeling someone a Machiavellian, we unwittingly perceive that person in a very limited sense. The practical approach would be to use "personality theory" as a tool for understanding rather than ostracizing and condemning those who upset us. Before rushing in with our attempts to change "rotten" personalities, we should realize that *personality is partly a function of interpersonal relationships*. We sometimes are responsible for the way people behave; personality is not fixed. The fostering of change requires attention to the organizational environment. If we insist upon building supportive climates, we may discover that those who were once bothersome may become cooperative in the pursuit of organizational goals.

REVIEW QUESTIONS

1. What is the nature of the relationship between needs and personality?
2. What are the factors that come together to create **personality**?
3. What are the five basic kinds of needs that are featured on the so-called "hierarchy of needs?"
4. What is meant by the term, **prepotency of need**?
5. What are the three major variables that function as determinants of personality? How does each of these variables influence personality?
6. What are the various personality types that are found among members of the organization? What are some of the characteristic behaviors of each type?
7. What are the characteristics of the six basic kinds of defense reactions?

KEY TERMS AND CONCEPTS FOR REVIEW

- Personality
- Prepotency
- Self-actualization
- Upward Mobiles
- Indifferents
- Ambivalents
- Authoritarians
- Undersocials
- Oversocials
- Adaptable-socials
- Defense Reaction
- Aggression
- Denial
- Conversion

- Machiavellians
- Dogmatics
- High Achievers

- Overcompensation
- Rationalization
- Projection

CASE STUDY

Situation: You are a consultant to the manager of mechanical engineering for a large company (8,000 employees, $200 million annual sales) that manufactures industrial equipment. The manager has held this position for six months, having moved from a similar position in a much smaller company.

Manager   I just can't seem to get these guys to perform. They are all extremely competent, but they just don't seem to be willing to exert the kind of effort that we need and expect to have if this company is going to remain successful.

Consultant   What types of work do they do?

Manager   Primarily designing minor modifications to existing equipment lines to keep up with our competition and to satisfy special customer requirements.

Consultant   How do you evaluate their performance?

Manager   Mainly on whether they meet project deadlines. It's hard to evaluate the quality of their work, since most of it is fairly routine, and the designs are frequently altered later by the production engineers to facilitate production processes.

Consultant   Are they meeting their deadlines reasonably well?

Manager   No, that's the problem. What's worse is that they don't really seem too concerned about it.

Consultant   What financial rewards do you offer them?

Manager   These people are all well paid—some of the best salaries for mechanical engineers that I know of anywhere. Base pay is determined mainly on the basis of seniority, but there is also a company-wide profit-sharing plan. At the end of each year, the company distributes 10 percent of its profit after taxes to the employees. The piece of the pie that you get is in proportion to your base salary. This kind of plan was used in the company I used to work for, and it seemed to have a highly motivating effect for them. They also get good vacations, insurance plans, and all the other usual goodies. I know of no complaints about compensation.

Consultant   How about promotion possibilities?

Manager   Well, all I know is that I was brought in from the outside.

Consultant   If they are so lackadaisical, have you considered firing any of them?

Manager   Are you kidding? We need them too much, and it would be difficult and expensive to replace them. If I even threatened to fire any of them for anything short of blowing up the building, my boss would come down on me like a ton of bricks. We are so far behind on our work as it is. Besides, I'm not sure that it's really their fault entirely.

PROBES

1. Using the assumptions of the hierarchy of needs as a basis, what is your assessment of the need level(s) of these workers?
2. Why are they not motivated?
3. Is it possible for employees to adopt a sort of "group personality or mentality?" What are the variables that may influence this phenomenon? Do you surmise that a group personality or mentality has emerged in this organization?
4. Which of the personality types discussed in the chapter best characterizes the workers in this case study?
5. What should management do to correct the situation?

Recommended Readings

Altman, I., and D. Taylor. *Social Penetration: The Development of Interpersonal Relationships.* New York: Holt, Rinehart and Winston, 1973.

Blass, T. *Personality Variables in Social Behavior.* New York: Halstead Press, 1977.

Gergen, K. and D. Marlowe. *Personality and Social Behavior.* Reading, Mass.: Addison-Wesley, 1970.

Goffman, E. *Interaction Ritual.* New York: Doubleday-Anchor, 1967.

Maslow, A. *Motivation and Personality.* New York: Harper & Row, 1954.

McClelland, D. *The Achieving Society.* New York: D. Van Nostrand Company, 1961.

Notes

1. C. Argyris, *Personality and Organization* (New York: Harper & Row, 1957), p. 32.
2. C. P. Alderfer, *Existence, Relatedness and Growth: Human Needs in Organizational Settings* (New York: Free Press, 1972).
3. Wm. C. Schutz, *FIRO: A Three-Dimensional Theory of Interpersonal Behavior* (New York: Holt, Rinehart and Winston, 1958).
4. A. Maslow, *Motivation and Personality* (New York: Harper & Row, 1954).
5. R. Presthus, *The Organizational Society* (New York: Alfred A. Knopf, 1962).
6. E. Ghiselli, *The Concept of Role and Theoretical Basis for Understanding Organizations* (Bologna: University of Bologna Press, 1963).

7. B. Gilmer, *Industrial and Organizational Psychology* (New York: McGraw-Hill Book Company, 1971), p. 33.
8. T. Adorno, E. Frenkel-Brunswik, D. Levinson, and R. Sanford, *The Authoritarian Personality* (New York: Harper & Row, 1950).
9. M. Burgoon, J. Heston, and J. McCroskey, *Small Group Communication: A Functional Approach* (New York: Holt, Rinehart and Winston, 1974), p. 33.
10. R. Christie and F. Geis, *Studies in Machiavellianism* (New York: Academic Press, 1970).
11. M. Rokeach, *The Open and Closed Mind* (New York: Basic Books, 1960).
12. J. McClelland, *The Achieving Society* (New York: D. Van Nostrand Company, 1961).
13. J. Wofford, E. Gerloff, and R. Cummins, *Organizational Communication: The Keystone to Managerial Effectiveness!* (New York: McGraw Hill Book Company, 1977), pp. 99, 100.
14. R. Hogan, "A Theory of Threat and Defense," *Journal of Consulting Psychology* 16, no. 6 (December, 1952); 419.
15. Argyris, Op. cit., p. 42.
16. C. Coates and R. Pellegrin, "Executives and Supervisors: Contrasting Self-Conceptions of Each Other," *American Sociological Review* 22 (1957); 217–220.
17. L. Porter, "Differential Self-perceptions of Management Personnel and Line Workers," *Journal of Applied Psychology* 42 (1958): 105–108.
18. E. Ghiselli, "Occupational Level Measured Through Self-perception," *Personnel Psychology* 9 (1956): 169–176.
19. Ibid., p. 175.
20. P. Merenda and W. Clarke, "AVA as a Predictor of Occupational Hierarchy," *Journal of Applied Psychology* 42 (1958): 289–292.
21. J. Guilford, "Temperament Traits of Executives and Supervisors Measured by the Guilford Personality Inventories," *Journal of Applied Psychology* 36 (1952): 228–233.
22. H. Meyer and G. Pressel, "Personality Test Scores in the Management Hierarchy," *Journal of Applied Psychology* 38 (1954): 73–80.
23. S. Hetzler, "Variations in Role-playing Patterns Among Different Echelons of Bureaucratic Leaders," *American Sociological Review* 20 (1955): 700–706.
24. D. Kipnis and W. Lane, "Self-confidence and Leadership," *Journal of Applied Psychology* 46 (1962): 291–295.
25. E. Ghiselli, "Traits Differentiating Management Personnel," *Personnel Psychology* 12 (1959): 534–544.

8 Communicator: Interaction Variables

LEARNING OBJECTIVES

After reading this chapter, you should be able to

1. Explain the basis of an individual's power in an organization.
2. Explain four ways of influencing or controlling an individual in an organization.
3. List and explain five types of power.
4. Explain imbalance-reducing activities.
5. Explain the effect of status on interaction.
6. Identify and explain four functions of status.
7. Explain three orientations to the study of roles.
8. Define and explain role expectation in the organization.
9. Define and explain role conflict in the organizaton.
10. Explain how roles affect messages in the organization.

An organization derives its effectiveness and sense of order largely from the quality of human interactions prevailing within it. Although we live in an era of expanding technology and time-saving, cost-cutting organizational capabilities, we still rely on the interdependent efforts of men and women for the accomplishment of goals and objectives.

The organizational system defines all employees—from president to washroom attendant—in terms of the positions they occupy, the people to whom they are responsible, and those who are responsible to them. If we observe an organization at work, we see systems molding people into rather predictive behaviors. For example, a domineering, aggressive, doctrinaire father, upon arriving at his job, divests himself of the role of "father" to become a submissive employee.

When an employee communicates, he or she communicates within the context of that behavior-shaping system. Three major variables in the organizational system that shape behavior are *power*, *status*, and *roles*. These variables interlock to form a process whereby behaviors are exchanged or traded for the purpose of enhancing human performance. In this chapter, we examine the nature and the effects of each of these variables, and demonstrate the degree of cooperation necessary between individuals for the exercise of power, status, and roles.

The Effect of Power on Interactions

Organizational leaders—managers, supervisors, administrators, and the like—are expected to generate some measure of power in order to influence the behavior of subordinates. Some leaders use power effectively and succeed in promoting the goals and objectives of the organization; others use power ineffectively and thereby frustrate goal-accomplishment and alienate personnel. Such incompetence is widespread in organizational settings. Managerial misuse of power emanates from a misunderstanding of how power is exchanged in human interaction.

The Basis of Power

Eric Hoffer once observed that some people have the idea that power comes in cans and all that is necessary to get more power is to acquire more cans. For example, Clark Kerr[1] noted that there are more claimants for power in the colleges and universities than ever before. He contended that government spending was taking power from the boards of governors and institutional presidents, and students were also gaining in power. Thus, Kerr felt that the academic community was approaching a situation where there would be no more power left to be divided; that the entire process would then become a sort of zero-sum game—i.e., one party gets all and the other party gets none.

It is our contention that Kerr's analysis was based upon a misperception of the nature of power, because if power did "come in cans," there would surely be a limitless, inexhaustible supply of cans. Power is not a fixed, permanently allocated resource. For instance, if you get more power, it will not necessarily follow that I get less. Moreover, it is possible for persons in an organizational setting to gain more power without causing others necessarily to lose any of it—*if they know where to look*. Those who understand the nature of power and know how to maneuver their way through a system can, indeed, reach the power centers.

As more people exert power and influence in an organization, decision making often becomes slower and more complex; conflicts may arise; and bargaining and compromise will become a necessity. However, even though there will be more people in the decision-making process, the compromises and power tradeoffs made on the way to serious decisions may result in an appreciable increase in power and influence for all the people involved. More importantly, there are often many power vacuums in an organization. Consequently, many individuals can fill these power vacuums and initiate decisions and actions that lead to more power and influence for them—but not necessarily less for anyone else.

People who are not managers or administrators can also exert power, because power is not simply a hierarchical concept pertaining to formal authority or official position. For example, professors can exert tremendous informal power regarding some decisions—hiring and promoting, granting tenure, developing curricula, planning courses—because they have tools such as coercion, penalties, and rewards. The faculty as a group may even have the power to force the removal of an administrator from office. The implication is that influence and power are derived largely from personal qualities and situational factors. Although formal authority and official power are needed to ratify and implement decisions, the persons behind those decisions may have considerable influence and informal power, even if they do not have any formal authority.

What is power? Power is a quality inherent in an interaction between two or more individuals. When individuals interact to influence one another's actions, the exchange of power is involved in their interaction. As we deal with our colleagues in various formal or informal groups, we see the existence of power—in the form of our attempts to exert power or the attempts of others to alter our behavior. These operations involve an exchange of power.

The efficient functioning of any organization will occur only if the complex power or the control processes are built into that organization. Such power and control processes are commonly called *the power structure*, which is *a formalized network that gives particular individuals the right to exercise power over others*. The power structure stipulates just who should "give in" to influence attempts, and who should properly resist being influenced. The organization without a carefully defined power structure may be chaotic or anarchistic since it lacks rules for the exercising of, resistance to, and compliance with influence attempts.

Frequently, the initiating of power within organizations is entrusted to a relatively small number of persons. When power is concentrated among a minority, many capable individuals are excluded from decision-making activities and thwarted in efforts to exercise creativity and initiative. Such deprivation generally leads to unrest, apathy, or disloyalty. Thus, it is extremely important that the manager or supervisor understand the nature of power and how it should be employed in the interest of organizational growth.

Power, as a factor in human interaction, consists of three variables: resources, dependencies, and alternatives.[2]

A *resource* is something owned by someone. It can be anything from strength, money, charm, knowledge, and information to contact or influence with higherups. Whatever the resource, it allows its owner to control the environment—in terms of rewards or costs—of the people with whom he or she interacts. For example, if you possess some vital bit of information, you would be in a position to reward someone by having him or her share in that information. In that case, this person becomes information-dependent on you, and you are in a position to exert power over this person. On the other hand, should you withhold that information, you would in effect be costing discomfort or penalty to that person. In short, resources can be used to reward or to penalize.

What determines the reward- or penalty-potential of a resource is not the mere possession of it, but rather how much other people depend on it. Thus, *dependency* is another vital variable. For example, you may have a lot of influence in the engineering division of a plant and that may make you powerful over the people in that particular division; however, that kind of clout may not be transferable to the sales division. Since the sales people cannot or will not depend on you, you have no power over them. As far as the sales division is concerned, your power in the engineering division constitutes no resource at all.

Power is also a function of the availability of *alternatives*. Even though you may be dependent on a resource held by a particular person in the organization, you may choose to go instead to alternative persons. The availability of alternatives, then, would reduce the power of the person on whom you are dependent. The person who goes outside the channels is in effect making use of alternatives and, thus, reduces the power of that supervisor. Naturally, if no alternatives exist, the power of the supervisor increases.

Whether individuals in the organization tend to resist or to submit to the power inductions of their superiors will depend on the type of influence climate that is prevalent throughout the organization.

Climates for Obedience-Disobedience Relationships

Every organization, if it is to be successful, must attempt to reduce the variability of individual human acts or behaviors. People must behave in ways they would not outside the organization. They might have to wear uniforms and adopt specific styles and formalities in interpersonal relations.

How does the organization achieve this type of conformity or obedience? One method of reducing the variability of employees' behavior is to make their role requirements explicit. In order to remain employed, the individuals will submit to the organizational influence process. Cartwright[3] perceives three basic elements in this process: (1) the agent (O) exerting influence; (2) the method ($\rightarrow$) of influence; and (3) the agent (P) subjected to the influence. The influence process functions in the following manner: If O succeeds in getting P to behave in a certain way or to perform a certain task, it can be said that O has influenced P; or that O controls P; or that O has power over P.

The agent has *four* basic ways of influencing or controlling P. He or she may do it (1) *physically,* (2) through *positive* or *negative sanctions;* (3) through his or her *expertise;* or (4) by means of his or her *charisma.*

Through physical power, O could beat up P in order to influence P's behavior and to enforce compliance. However, you would hardly find the employment of such crude measures in everyday organizational practice. The exercise of power by means of the controlling of sanctions constitutes a much more subtle and normal practice.

Positive and negative sanctions refer to our ability to reward and punish. For example, O may influence P by withholding some resource that P needs. Withholding of a resource can occur only when O occupies a strategic position in the organization and is authorized to occupy that position.

O can influence P by using expertise. Thus, if O is an expert in computer technology and P is relatively ignorant in this area, O may be able to impress P's opinions, attitudes, and behaviors as far as computers are concerned.

Finally, influence may be achieved through personal magnetism or even, as Cartwright would argue, by rank in the organization. A person's rank may carry the capacity for awesome qualities and responsibilities, as in the case of the president of the United States.

We discuss the nature of the four types of influence for exercising power later in this chapter. For the moment, let us look at things from P's point of view. Remember, he or she is on the receiving end of the power induction. What causes an individual to obey orders in an organizational environment? The answer lies in the concept of authority and in the creation of a structure of authority. By *authority* we mean legitimate or positional power—that is, power recognized as appropriate in particular persons or positions.

The organization stipulates that subordinates submit to the legitimate requests of superiors. This stipulation is generally so axiomatic that it is not likely to be stated in job descriptions. An office clerk's job description may specify the procedures for sorting the mail and the times at which certain reports should be collected. However, the job description is not likely to specify: "Obey the office manager at all times as far as job-related activities are concerned." Nevertheless, the office clerk's obedience is mandatory and binding. Failure to obey or fulfil this role requirement may lead to the withholding of rewards, fines, blacklisting, censure, suspension, or outright dismissal.

It is remarkable that we *obey* the directives of our superiors so uncomplainingly. Our submission may be attributed to our cultural views about the concept of authority—views shared both by superiors and subordinates. Authority is thought either to originate at the top of the organization and pass down through the process of delegation, or to move by the consent of those being led to the top of the organization.[4]

The Top-Down Theory   Where does an administrator at a certain level in the organization get his or her authority? Generally, administrators receive authority from their superiors in the chain of command. If we were to trace the entire passage or "handing down" of authority, the journey would lead to the chief executive of the organization. This progression is characteristic of the top-down theory of authority. In a business organization, for instance, we can trace the passage of power from the executive hierarchy to the board of directors to the stockholders and, ultimately, to national law that protects the right of private property.

The top-down theory of power also is related to the legitimacy of authority. Our society views the ultimate source of authority as legitimate and is willing to accept it because of the distribution of authority throughout a system or organization.

The Consent Theory   According to this theory, authority originates from subordinates. Authority is meaningless unless subordinates in the organization *give their consent* to their superiors' exercise of it. Chester Barnard contends that since all formal organizations are founded on the consent of those governed, the administrators of these organizations should act consistently with this foundation.[5] Scott and Mitchell feel that the most efficient and economical way of gaining compliance is by voluntary, willing submission to superordination.[6]

Whatever the viewpoint, the individual exercising power must use the *type* of power that would be most beneficial for achieving the intended goals.

Types of Power

According to French and Raven,[7] there are five types of power: reward, coercive, referent, expert, and legitimate power.

1. *Reward power.* Reward power is based upon the ability to mediate rewards for others. If you can procure an increase in pay for me, or get me a promotion, or grant me a few extra dollars on my travel allowance, you would be able to exert reward power over me. Reward power may be manifested in the provision of objects, situations, and events that others may find satisfying. We should note that reward power also is determined by other individuals' *perception* of the ability or willingness of the agent—e.g., foreman, supervisor, administrator—to muster those resources.

2. *Coercive power.* Coercive power is based upon the ability to mediate punishments and penalties for others. Coercive power prevails when an employee perceives that the supervisor has the "license" to fire, withhold pay, embarrass or scold, punish by assigning very difficult, dirty, undesirable tasks, and so on. David Lawless suggests that coercive power does not go beyond the limits of the punishment that one person can mete out to another. The strength of coercive power is generally determined by the probability perceived by one person that another can or will punish. "The person may be very strong physically, for instance, but if the other thinks he will not strike him or exert physical strength against him, his physical strength will not generate power."[8]

The degree of power also will be determined by how others have observed the person use punishment or coercion in the past. The boss who has the power to use coercion but refrains from doing so, even when the situation warrants it, may be viewed as a pushover who lets others get away with murder. Eventually the directives of such a person may be ignored. On the other hand, too much coercion may cause subordinates to retaliate or to leave the supervisor's field of influence entirely.

3. *Referent power.* Referent power is based upon identification, or a "liking" relationship—when a person identifies with someone who has certain desirable qualities and wants to be like that person. Referent power can originate from many different situations. For example, a supervisor's use of reward power can be a major contributor to his or her influence and authority. As time passes, employees grow to admire the manner in which the supervisor utilizes power. Consequently, their liking for the person increases. The employees may even emulate their supervisor—by wearing the same hair style, adopting the same manner of speaking, or trying to work as hard as the boss. Referent power is, perhaps, the most extensive and effective form of influence because the "referent agent" can exercise power when not present, or even when no deliberate attempt is being made to influence.

4. *Expert power.* Expert power is based upon the belief that a powerful person has greater knowledge, skill, or information in a given area. For example, employees who observe that their boss is an expert at solving a particular type of problem, may continually go to that boss whenever that problem arises. The employees become either effect- or information-dependent on their boss. The latter's expert power comes into play when the employees are actually advised to solve a problem in a certain way. When the employees accept and value the advice, it is an indication of the expert power of the boss.

5. *Legitimate power.* Legitimate power is actual power—when one person is given the right, by agreement, to prescribe the behavior of another person. For example, if someone is older, or has seniority on the job, or has a unique title, the people may agree to *allow* that person to exercise power. In this case, power derives from the acceptance of others. This kind of power rests upon cultural values and the acceptance of a social structure in the organization.

The effectiveness of all types of power depends on the relationships of resources, dependencies, and alternatives discussed earlier. Regardless of the type of power involved, however, if subordinates do not view it as a valued resource, if their immediate destiny is not dependent on it, and if they have other alternatives, the supervisor's influence would be drastically curtailed.

What type of power is best? Scott and Mitchell offer one answer:

> We must remember that power is connected with such practices as the use of incentives or coercion to secure action toward goals. The more a superior is required to use incentives or coercion the less his subordinates have accepted the legitimacy of his authority. Naturally the most efficient and economical way of gaining compliance is by voluntary, willing submission to superordination. Coercion and incentive programs are always more costly than if people are spontaneously motivated to achieve goals which they perceive as created by legitimate authority.[9]

We should realize that power is a very costly commodity. Every usage of power represents the expending of a resource. Consequently, people who must exercise power in organizatons should be skillful at dispensing it.

The Exchange of Power: Problems of Cost and Balance

The Exchange   When we talk about the exchange of power, we are referring to agreements and/or concessions traded or transacted by both the user of power and those at whom the power is directed. The possession of reward power, for example, enables the possessor of the resource to determine the other person's profit or loss.

With referent power, the exchange is more subtle, since referent power derives its effectiveness from an individual's desire to use the behavior of another as a model. The closer that employees match the behavior of the supervisor (the behavior referent, or model), the more satisfying the relationship should be. If the employees exhibit a type of behavior that they believe the supervisor would not perform or would not like them to carry out, they would feel guilty, anxious, or perhaps dissatisfied with themselves. This would mean that the employees have suffered a loss.

In the case of legitimate power, individuals responding to the directives or the influence actually profit from adhering to the norms or standards of the organization. If they choose not to respond to that influence, they are rejecting the standards of the group and run the risk of being alienated or rejected. A similar exchange principle operates in the transaction of expert power. People allow others to influence or have power over them because of the belief that *not* accepting this may lead to a costly error. Adherence leads to success, whereas nonadherence leads to failure. Based upon calculations of a payoff, people trade obedience for expertise.

The Cost   Whenever you use power to promote organizational goals, it costs you. If you fire an employee (i.e., use coercive power), you would very likely have to hire a new employee, or you may have to explain to upper management why such drastic measures were necessary. This may, in turn, cause your boss to conclude that you really do not know how to handle workers properly. Ultimately, this means that you have used power—and are paying for it.

Let us look at cost from another standpoint. The more it costs you to use a resource, the greater the chance that you would not use it in the exchange. An example is the frustrated boss who says, "If those reports aren't done by tomorrow, I'll fire every last one of you." Obviously, the boss has a tremendous resource with which to influence these employees, but to use this influence would be too costly.

Great cost is incurred even in the use of expert power. Every time you use your resources—knowledge, information, skill, and so on—to aid others in solving a problem, you are actually training them to solve that problem. The cost to you is that, in time, they become less dependent on you. As Lawless puts it, "unless your expert power becomes referent power, it may decrease."[10]

More important than the question of cost is the question of balance. Earlier in this chapter, we suggested that power emerges from the interaction between people; power does not belong to any given individual. It is therefore reasonable to assume that each person in an interaction exercises power over the other. The individual who is intent on influencing another is dependent, to a large extent, upon the other person for the exercise of power. The two individuals are dependent on each other—one directing, the other consenting. The resolution of the directing and consenting is achieved through the process of power balancing.

The Balance and Imbalance of Power   The actual power of a person over another depends on the amount of resistance exerted against the influence attempt. Power is balanced when both individuals have equal power over each other and are, consequently, both equally dependent on each other. Conversely, power is unbalanced when either individual has more power or more dependency than the other.

Ideally, power in organizations should be balanced. Each member should be permitted to exert influence, and each should be dependent upon the resources of the other. Moreover, the maintenance of balance should be achieved by means of alternating the exercise of power, or by rotating the right to veto, or by trading the opportunity to initiate decisions.

When there is an imbalance of power in the organization—i.e., when one person tries to use power to the disadvantage of the other—much of the energy that should be expended toward task-accomplishment is spent on trying to reduce the imbalance. These imbalance-reducing activities may take the form of (1) withdrawal, (2) formation of alternative relationships, (3) coalition formation, and (4) continuous interaction.[11]

1. *Withdrawal.* The person at the disadvantage could quit or leave the environment of the person who takes the advantage. The decision depends on the potential cost. If withdrawal is less costly than hanging around and putting up with another person's dominance, one withdraws. With no one left to dominate, the agent's power is reduced.

2. *Formation of alternative relationships.* If person (A) perceived an imbalance of power existing between himself or herself and person (B), he or she could decide to forego the resources provided by B and choose, rather, to rely on the resources of an alternative person (C). The fact that an individual can interact with person C of equal or greater resources allows an employee to inhibit an employer from putting him or her at a disadvantage.

3. *Coalition formation.* Coalition formation refers to the tendency on the part of members of a power exchange or interaction to form cliques in order to resist the dominance or power attempts of individuals on whom they are forced to depend. Unionism and collective bargaining constitute an attempt by coalitions to offset imbalance.

4. *Continuous interaction.* When two people interact continuously, power tends to equalize. For example, the longer a university president associates with a special assistant, the better the latter gets to know the president, the work, and the job. This puts the special assistant in a position of being able to frustrate or facilitate the president's task.

The assistant, in time, becomes the president's major source of information. Knowing what to file and where to file it, the assistant is given the right to shield and protect the president from unnecessary or potentially damaging contacts. Ultimately, as the president grows more dependent on the special assistant, power is somewhat equalized and balance is achieved.

There are times when a president, manager, or supervisor will deliberately try to *resist* a balance of power, particularly in situations where the lines of authority must be drawn clearly and where it is necessary to maintain considerable psychological distance between roles. For example, the store manager who permits himself or herself to be totally dependent on the sales clerk may be reduced to a mere figurehead. The store manager must find new ways of maintaining prominence in the management of the organization. The basic structure of organization affords "automatic" assistance. Something like the assigning of a title—vice-president for marketing, special assistant for staff development, controller—can enforce a certain psychological distance between one role and another. Or, in some instances, territorial rights—who is permitted to eat in the company cafeteria or who may call whom by a first name—will constitute methods for avoiding total balance.

In most situations the balance of power is conducive to a healthy, effective, democratic organization. This type of climate is essential to the interaction of people possessing equal rank, role, or status. In situations where it is necessary to preserve the formal structure of authority, the organization *must* construct certain strategies for withstanding full balance of power. There are times when someone *must* make a decision, enforce a policy, or say with finality and legitimate sanction, "You are fired."

Power Strategies and Organizational Effectiveness

According to James Price,[12] there is a relationship between organizational effectiveness and control systems. Before we go much further, we should recognize that effectiveness does not specifically include individual satisfaction that is derived from organizational participation. The running of an organization should not be confused with the running of an ice cream social. The essential goal of an ice cream social is to make everybody happy. However, the primary goal of an organization is to accomplish a task; if, in the climate or the conduct of task accomplishing, we succeed in also making some or all of the employees happy—that is fine. Happiness, in this instance, is an incidental payoff. Whatever you do, you cannot guarantee that everyone will be happy.

Organizational effectiveness is achieved through a human exchange of power. According to Price, there are several techniques for exercising influence over member behavior.

1. In an organization, there should be availability of *sanctions* to reward or punish employees. In addition to the sanctions, there should be a wide range of *differing kinds* of rewards and punishments.

2. The sanction system should be *graded*. In other words, the rewards or punishments should be scaled according to the caliber of the employees' contribution or lack of same. Sometimes it will be appropriate to censure; at other times it may be necessary to demote. In some situations a raise in salary may be called for; in others, the reward might be an unscheduled promotion.

3. Organizations should be structured so that their norms, policies, and standards are enforced *uniformly and personally*.

4. A greater measure of organizational effectiveness could be achieved when organizations expend some effort in generating intense communication and messages which are geared to socializing and acculturating the employees toward the concerns and goals of the organization.

5. High levels of *vertical and horizontal communication* in the structure contribute more to organizational effectiveness than low degrees of such communication.

6. Better organizational effectiveness is achieved *if the communication* (sent through the vertical and horizontal channels) *is formal; if it contains information about job content and problems; and if it is transmitted face-to-face* between people who are directly concerned with task accomplishment.

Cohen and March[13] suggest that organizational effectiveness, control, and cultivation of power could be achieved individually in the following ways:

1. *Through willingness to spend time.* When members of the organization are willing to devote considerable time (including spare time) in meetings, on committees, developing contacts, and the like, with the aim of influencing decisions, they are likely to have an effect. They provide scarce energy resources; they may become major information sources; they are more likely to be present when something important is under consideration.

2. *Through persistence.* This can relate to time. If individuals persist, they are likely to influence the outcome and implementation of decisions.

3. *Through involvement in the critical interfaces of the system.* An interface is the point at which interrelated parts within and without the organization intersect and act upon or communicate with each other. The more relevant and significant interfaces are those in which power is a real issue, and those that commonly involve problems, if not outright conflicts. If people have a good understanding of the overall system, they are likely to be in a better position to get involved in the interfaces from which greater power and influence may be derived.

All these strategies should be guided by an understanding of what power is and what it does, remembering always that the objective is the achievement of an effective flow of authorized influence or power throughout the organization.

When we talk of *authorized influence* or *power*, we are also referring to the question of *status*. Certain individuals in an organization are given certain status positions and are allowed to wield influence of power in given circumstances. Status is a key variable in human interaction in organizations.

The Effect of Status on Interaction

Status is as important as power in the organization, because it aids in the attainment of control for the accomplishment of organizational tasks and goals. Moreover, power and status are interrelated. Status generally enhances the acceptance of power and influence. The more a person exercises power effectively, the more that person is accorded high status. Thus, it is rather difficult to separate power and status when we study their impact on human interaction in the organization.

The Components of Status

Status can be defined as *one's social rank or position in a group.* Status is the relationship between individuals that affects organizational communication, morale, and efficiency.

The components of status can be either formal or informal. Components denoting formal status may be: (1) *a person's occupation or job*, or (2) *the organizational level at which a cluster of positions or roles are located in the organization.*

Certain jobs or occupations are accorded a higher prestige or esteem level than others. For example, white-collar jobs are usually ranked higher than blue-collar ones. In a public-opinion survey, the position of highest prestige in the United States was that of Supreme Court Justice and the lowest was that of shoeshiner.[14] College professors were in eighth position, lawyers at eighteenth, policemen at fifty-fifth, garbage collectors at eighty-eighth. Within certain companies, management discovered the following status differentials: long-distance telephone operators were accorded higher job status than operators handling local calls; cooks who worked on white meat had higher status than those who worked on dark meat; cafeteria waitresses who handled fish dishes had less status than those who served beef.

The important point is that status affects the way some people respond to their jobs, and their responses to jobs and to the people holding those jobs will determine the kinds of interactions between them. The status of one's occupation depends upon the rank accorded it by one's peers *and not by management alone.* The job assigned to a person as well as the level it is in the organization are significant sources of status. The higher the organizational level, the higher is the level of prestige. But, as Edwin Flippo points out, "It would be naive to assume that there is a perfect coincidence of formal job relationships and the status accorded a person holding that formal job."[15]

The informal connotations of status are frequently derived from factors other than those directly dependent on the type of job classification held by a person. Some of the informal components of status are

- Education
- Age
- Seniority

- Race
- Religion
- Parentage
- Sex
- Competence
- Associates

The characteristics of the individual are important sources of social rank. There is a general respect in our society for the better educated and the individual who has seniority in the organization. A particular individual can possess high status even though he or she is relegated to a low-status job. If that person performs the job well, his or her skill is often recognized and respected. On the other hand, if the president of a company plods along and constantly makes mistakes and bungles the overall operation, his or her status level would be substantially reduced.

Implicit in the gaining or losing of status, is the gaining or losing of power, since it is almost impossible to separate the impact of status from that of power.

Functions of the Status Structure

The universality of status distinctions in all societies attests to their functional importance. Status structures arise in industry or other organizations for the same reason they arise in society in general. Four primary functions of status may be singled out.

1. *Social differentiation fosters social stratification.* The larger the number of positions, the greater is the probability that they will be status-ranked. Most people want to be accorded some degree of respect by others. They want to have their abilities and accomplishments recognized, and the according or granting of status constitutes tangible evidence of this respect. We also need the input of high status for our formal superiors; we view it as a requirement of a natural order. The necessity of working for and taking orders from a superior who is not respected or liked can be psychologically bruising to one's ego. A subordinate will often seek a transfer to another position, even with less pay, in order to avoid subordination to a person whom he or she cannot respect.

2. *Status structure provides additional motivational devices for management.* Positions that carry complex functions, call for extensive training, and have much authority usually are accorded greater prestige or status. The rewards constitute motivations to seek training and make necessary sacrifices to perform difficult tasks effectively.[16]

3. *Status structure facilitates the process of organizational communication.* The legitimizing function of status distinctions is closely linked to their function of facilitating organizational effectiveness and communication. In complex organizations, status distinctions facilitate the articulation of serious positions.

In addition, we receive many messages daily from people whom we do not know personally. The status *title* of the person or position helps us to evaluate the worth of the message. For example, if a written communication details an analysis of a particular electronic mechanism, we value it less when it is written by the shipping clerk than when it is written by the electronic engineer, because—presumably—the latter is a professional in the field. Thus, status structure aids the communication process by helping us to avoid message confusion. Commensurate with status of a source, we can separate out the "low consequence nonsense" from the meaningful, sound information of a system.

4. *Status distinctions help to legitimize and validate a social order, giving it a traditional justification, primarily with the use of status symbols.* In anonymous situations an employee need not question the right of an unknown person to issue orders if a symbol of authority—for example, a badge, a uniform, special equipment—is attached to the order, giving it legitimacy. In some organizations, certain people ride around on motorized carts or scooters. Here the vehicle is their badge of status and accords them the right to give orders.

It would be quite hazardous to conclude that these four functions of status structure will guarantee an effective organization. These same functions can become disrupting and lead to certain communication pathologies or dysfunctions in the organization. Unfortunately, it is easy for a status system to become so rigid, stable, and "important" that it blocks *necessary* organizational changes. When status becomes an end rather than a means, social mobility is halted, and that status system assumes a sacred character, as in a caste system.

Dealt with and managed properly, the assignment of organizational status structure aids organizational effectiveness. One should know how to acquire status in one's own organization.

The Sources of Status

Status is derived from *status systems*. As in the case with power, a person does not own status or carry it around from environment to environment. It is given by the group within the context of the status system. According to Scott and Mitchell, [17] status systems incorporate all status positions of a formal organization into an overall pattern of relationships. Every status position can be plotted on a matrix having both vertical and horizontal relationships to points representing the other status positions in the organization. [18] The horizontal status is called *functional*; the vertical status system is called *scalar*.

Functional Status System   Functional status is based upon *the job or the task* that is performed regularly in the organization. Functional status systems dictate which positions are on the same level in the organization; e.g., the vice-president of personnel could be on the same level as the vice-president of administrative coordination. This system is in *no way* predicated on the right to command others on the same level.

Scalar Status System   Scalar status carries the right to command others. Scalar status systems derive from the *vertical* structuring of job positions. In this instance, a person holds higher status and has the license to command those lower on the vertical structure. For example, a plant superintendent has higher status than an area foreman and may order the performance of certain tasks.

But even though status derives largely from a structured system, one may acquire it in other ways, particularly if the organization is not inflexible. For example, if you can provide resources that provide the greatest reward to the greatest number of people, your resources will be associated with maximum approval, and they will bring you status. However, it is essential that those resources be relatively scarce or their value would be reduced considerably.

Another way to acquire status is through investment. Seniority is a type of status resulting from the investment of time. It has no great worth of its own but is accorded a certain value by group consensus. Seniority provides certain privileges—longer vacations, higher pay, job security, choice of offices, or working hours.

Once you have reached status, a major task remains: How do you keep it? How do you publicize it? How do you keep others from encroaching upon the rights accorded to you by that status? The answers to these questions may be found in the nature and use of *status symbols*.

Status Symbols

In order to facilitate human interaction in status situations, symbols are devised and agreed upon by the claimant (the person holding status) and the audience (persons influenced by "status persons"). A status symbol is a visible, external denotation of one's social or occupational positon. The status symbol is a form of advertising and a request for deference.

According to Flippo, a stranger can enter an organization and if he or she is knowledgeable of status hierarchies, can quickly obtain a social fix through a reading of the various symbols.[19] However, we should realize that systems of symbols can vary from one company to the next. Symbols may also change with time. For example, many years ago the brass spittoon was maintained in offices to denote high status in the oil industry; fortunately, that symbol has been replaced by a water carafe on a tray. Here are a few of the more commonly found types of status symbols:

1. Job titles
2. Pay
3. Clothing
4. Size and location of desk or office
5. Location of parking spaces
6. Type of company car assigned
7. Secretaries
8. Privacy
9. Furnishings, including rugs, pictures, and tables
10. Privileges, including freedom to move about, *not* to punch a time clock, to set own working hours, and to regulate coffee breaks
11. Ceremonies of induction
12. Possessions such as a home, private automobiles, and stereo

Visible Appurtenances	Top Dogs	V.I.P.'s	Brass	No. 2's	Eager Beavers	Hoi Polloi
Brief cases	None—they ask the questions	Use backs of envelopes	Someone goes along to carry theirs	Carry their own—empty	Daily—carry their own—filled with work	Too poor to own one
Desks, office	Custom made (to order)	Executive style (to order)	Type A, "Director"	Type B, "Manager"	Cast-offs from No. 2's	Yellow Oak—or cast-offs from Eager beavers
Tables, office	Coffee tables	End tables or decorative wall tables	Matching tables, type A	Matching tables, type B	Plain work table	None—lucky to have own desk
Carpeting	Nylon—1-inch pile	Nylon—1-inch pile	Wool-twist (with pad)	Wool-twist (without pad)	Used wool pieces—sewed	Asphalt tile
Plant stands	Several—kept filled with strange exotic plants		Two—repotted whenever they take a trip	One medium-sized—repotted annually during vacation	small—repotted when plant dies	May have one in the department or bring their own from home
Vacuum water bottles	Silver	Silver	Chromium	Plain painted	Coke machine	Water fountains
Library	Private collection	Autographed or complimentary books and reports	Selected references	Impressive titles on covers	Books everywhere	Dictionary
Shoe-Shine service	Every morning at 10:00	Every morning at 10:15	Every day at 9:00 or 11:00	Every other day	Once a week	Shine their own
Parking space	Private—in front of office	In plant garage	In company garage—if enough seniority	In company properties—somewhere	On the parking lot	Anywhere they can find a space—if they can afford a car

Figure 8-1 Status Symbols (From Morris S. Viteles, "What Raises a Man's Morale," *Personnel*, published by the American Management Association, Inc. [January 1954]: 305. Reprinted by permission of the publisher.)

People in organizations strive as much for the symbols of status as for the factors that underlie status. Managers often tend to underestimate the importance of status to others. As Miller and Form argue, "Their (the managers') preoccupation with salaries, wages, and other such items makes them unaware that many dissatisfactions can be traced to their unwillingness or failure to grant status to lower-income groups."[20] For example, it may be of serious concern to a laborer that his manager respect him by calling him Mr.——.

Different types of jobs and organizational settings develop unique symbols of status. One of the most common status symbols is clothing. People who work in their street clothes generally have higher status than those who wear uniform or occupational garb. Thus, the white-collar worker is accorded higher status than the worker who must wear overalls. Of course, we can take the status symbolization of clothing too far. In fact, many people do—as was the case with the company president who repeatedly showed up at the annual beach picnic in his pin-striped suit and tie. A field study conducted in one organization reported a rather wide (and somewhat ludicrous) variation in the use of clothing as status symbols. The owner worked in a business suit and the store clerks wore no special uniform but were required to remove their coats and work in tie and shirt sleeves. The supervisor of mechanics also removed his coat, but he was required to wear a nonfunctional white smock. The mechanics wore full-length blue jumpers, and the apprentices and cleanup men (grease monkeys, as they were called to delineate their low status further) wore overalls or discarded clothing. The study reported that although the hierarchy of "uniform" was not formally spelled out, it was nonetheless scrupulously observed.

Flippo describes situations that, on the surface, may appear exaggerated, but are real nevertheless:

> Within the company, however, many of the symbols are within the control of the management, and constitutes the basis for many bloody battles. Executives have gotten down on hands and knees to measure and compare sizes of offices. Windows are counted, steps from the President's offices are paced off, secretaries are sought, parking space is fought for, and company cars are wangled.[21]

A somewhat humorous, fictionalized chart of status symbols according to organization levels is presented in Figure 8-1.

Overall, white-collar workers tend to develop many more status symbols than do blue-collar workers. One reason may be attributed to the idea that their work or the kinds of things they do may not be as distinguishable as that performed by blue-collar workers. Most of the work performed by white-collar workers is done with paper, and all paperwork looks alike to outsiders. It could be stipulated that presidents should write on executive blue and staff associates on blushing pink—but that would be ridiculous. Hence, some symbol must be employed to inform observers of the exact status of individual white-collar workers.

Status symbols are important, because they serve a number of organizational purposes:

1. *Motivation*. Status symbols act as honors or rewards for achievements. As such, they provide incentives to motivate people toward greater accomplishments.
2. *Identification*. Status symbols make it easier to determine who holds authority and performs differentiated functions. The greater the degree to which specialization of function is carried out the more important status symbols become in order to identify who does what in an organization.
3. *Dignification*. Status symbols add dignity to a position and support its authority.
4. *Stabilization*. Status symbols solidify rank, authority, and areas of functional specialization. This, in turn, facilitates the regularization of work patterns.

Do status symbols automatically guarantee that the possessor of those symbols will have power or influence commensurate with a given status situation? The answer depends on the extent of *status congruence*, or the extent to which all the characteristics and attributes of a person are greater than, equal to, or lower than the attributes of a person in a corresponding position.

Status Congruency

Status congruency occurs, for example, when a director, as compared with the assistant director, has a higher income, larger office, more experience, and better stationery. In other words, the things he or she has and receives should be congruent with his or her status.

When people's status is fairly clear, it means that they are either high or low on status resources—that is, congruent. If they are high on some and low on others, it will be difficult to ascertain whether they are superiors, colleagues, or inferiors within the hierarchy.

Some studies have shown that where status hierarchies are clear and congruent, the amount of free interchange of information, suggestions, and help is materially reduced.[22] Definitely superior persons will attempt to retain the initiative and avoid closing the social distance between themselves and others. Inferior persons are inclined to feel subservient and are restricted in their actions and comments. Only among equals is there usually a feeling of ease and relaxation that leads to mutual influence and helpfulness.[23] In short, if the status hierarchy is as rigid and stratified as the formal organization hierarchy, the former works to hinder the organization. If the status of people is not that clearly stratified, they will feel free to ask for help from their supposed inferiors and to offer suggestions to their supposed superiors.

Status congruency also implies that the higher-status person works harder or incurs more cost than the lower-status person. For example, salaried workers in the front office often work late without extra pay, whereas those in the shop will get time and a half for overtime.

The costs, investments, and rewards inherent in various status positions must be clearly observable. If too many people come to the conclusion that the organization is lacking in status congruency, rivalry and friction will result, with people and factions jockeying for their "rights." There will be the danger of diminishing organizational effectiveness.

A key question is, what effect do "status differences" have on communications? Specifically, what is the nature of communication initiated by high-status and low-status members of an organization?

Status and Communication Patterns

In general, more communications are directed toward high-status members of the organization, and the content of such messages tends to be more positive. This tendency to send a preponderance of positive or noncritical messages upward through the status hierarchy should not surprise us. Since rewards and punishments usually emanate from higher levels, it seems natural that low-status employees would be concerned with maximizing rewards and minimizing punishments through the manipulation of messages. Consequently, the bulk of the messages would tend to be positively reinforcing in nature. It is simply a matter of exchanging positive strokes for positive strokes.

Lawless contends that upward communication—i.e., communication initiated by low-status persons to high-status persons—is generally *risky* because of the possible rebuff that such communication is likely to provoke on occasion. A rebuff confirms low status or increases the social distance between the high and low positions. However, the chance for public reward from a high-status person makes the estimate of outcome a worthwhile risk under appropriate circumstances.[24]

H. Kelley[25] discovered a number of interesting effects of status upon communication: (1) low-status members communicate more task-irrelevant information than high-status members; (2) high-status persons appear to be restrained from communicating criticisms, negative attitudes, or confusions about their own jobs to those of lower status; (3) communication with high-status persons tends to serve as a *substitute* for upward locomotion on the part of low-status persons who have little or no possibility of real upward locomotion. P. Worchel[26] found that the amount of verbal aggression directed toward the agent decreases with the increasing status of the agent. This finding bears out the idea of the legitimacy or illegitimacy of certain kinds of communications. It is simply not proper to harangue people who are of higher status in the organization than we are.

Persons who are equal in status are more likely to communicate *with each other* than are persons of unequal status. However, when the status equality of people is in doubt, they are likely to avoid communicating with each other. This may be caused by a feeling that one runs the risk of confirming one's worst fear—that the other person has a higher status. This kind of hesitancy is quite common among strangers circulating at a cocktail party. We do not like to be bested or outclassed, and when in doubt, we would rather not find out.

We can now see the value and the impact of status and status symbols on human interaction in organizations. As has been pointed out, the sources of high status derive from the possession of characteristics than can provide the greatest rewards to the greatest number of people. In this regard, status is like power.

Status congruence is a goal worth striving for in that it is a manifestation of how well status symbols match up with a particular status position. When status congruence is not manifested or when it is frustrated in the organization, people tend to be dissatisfied, noncooperative, and competitive. As far as communication is concerned, we have seen that communications tend to flow upward to high-status persons and across to equal-status persons, and tend to be rather scant among persons of ambiguous status relationships.

As individuals are given particular functions and assigned to certain status positions, the social system of the organization acquires a structure in which persons assume specified *roles* to which are attached certain behavioral expectations. These roles serve to clarify and influence the patterns of organizational interaction and communication.

The Effect of Roles on Interaction

The study of roles is essential to understanding the interactional structure of any human environment. Katz and Kahn[27] consider *role* to be a key concept in any theory of organizational communication or organizational behavior. In this section, we discuss several features pertinent to the exercise and exchange of roles in the organization.

The Nature and Dimensions of Roles

Role may be studied within three orientations or approaches: sociological, psychological, or social-psychological.[28]

The sociologist sees *role* as something existing outside of the individual. In this sense, roles refer to the norms shared by members concerning the behavior of people in certain settings.[29] For example, men have different social expectations and are constrained by a different set of norms than women. Adults differ from children in the norms relevant to their roles, as do leaders from followers, generals from corporals, owners from employees, salesmen from customers, and the like. In all these instances, role is thought of as a set of social pressures that direct and support individuals in the actions they take in the organization.

This sociological view can be labeled *deterministic*. It views role as a dominant influence on behavior (see Figure 8-2).

The thesis implicit in a deterministic view is that if we understand the *content* of a role, we can predict the behavior of individuals in that role. *Role* determines behavior. Consequently, if we know the role content of "university presidency," we should be able to predict the behavior of all university presidents in the performance of their jobs.

From a *psychological* standpoint, role is viewed as "an individual's conception of the part he or she plays in an organization."[30] According to

DETERMINISTIC

```
┌─────────────────────────────┐
│            ROLE             │
│                             │
│        rights, duties,      │
│         obligations         │
└─────────────────────────────┘
              │
              │
      WHICH DETERMINE
              │
              ▼
┌─────────────────────────────┐
│                             │
│     Individual behavior     │
│                             │
│                             │
└─────────────────────────────┘
```

Figure 8-2 A Deterministic Description of the Role Concept

Gerard, "in any social situation an individual will tend to evaluate the degree to which his or her behavior has fulfilled the expectations of the role played."[31] In the psychological sense, roles refer to the variety of behaviors that are pertinent to the position a person occupies in an organization. The roles may be viewed in light of whether the behaviors are expected or enacted. The terms role-expectation and role-performance define these distinctions.

This psychological viewpoint stresses a *particularistic* character of roles (see Figure 8-3). Here the focus is on how a person perceives the particular role he or she has to play, and how the person evaluates the performance in the light of the perception.

A third approach to the study of role concept is that of the *social psychologist*. From this viewpoint, role is described in terms of the thoughts and actions of individuals, as well as the influence exerted upon individuals by certain normative, social patterns. Every unit or division within an organization has certain behavior expectations about the people who work there. Upon joining the organization, the individual must assess the organization's values and modify his or her behaviors accordingly. If an individual is impressive or resourceful enough, he or she also might be able to modify the expectations of the organization. Here, the power or influence of the individual can actually change the role expectations of the environment. Scott and Mitchell call this phenomenon *the fusion process:* it changes both the group and the individual so that their separate values may be reconciled.[32]

The social psychological stance represents a sort of *interactional* hypothesis (see Figure 8-4). The diagram portrays role as emergent at the point where the individual's values and the duties prescribed by the group converge.

It would be naive to assume that an acceptable role behavior always emerges in this convergence. Sometimes, compromise and adjustment may not

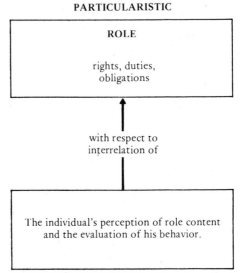

PARTICULARISTIC

Figure 8-3 A Particularistic Description of the Role Concept (Reproduced with permission from Scott and Mitchell, *Organization Theory: A Structural and Behavioral Analysis*, rev. ed. [Homewood, Ill.: Richard D. Irwin, 1972], p. 205.)

occur in the expected exchange or trade-off between the individual and the group. In that instance, role conflict is the likely result.

Whatever the point of view—be it sociological/deterministic; psychological/particularistic; or social psychological/interactional—we can see that an entire organization is, in essence, a system of interlocking or interdependent roles.

An analysis of the organization as a system of roles was made by Katz and Kahn.[33]

The Organization as a System of Roles   Organizations acquire stability and perpetuity largely because of the *relationships* that exist among the various positions, functions, and units, rather than because of the units themselves. Since the units of an organization are not linked physically in assembly-line fashion, it can be surmised that they are linked psychologically. Furthermore, since an organization consists of certain patterns of human behavior, it will continue to exist only as members' attitudes, beliefs, values, and expectations generate the desired motivation and behavior. Each behavior—in the overall pattern of organizational behavior—is caused by other behaviors. An organization will remain intact only as long as the psychological cement between the assorted roles and behaviors hold. Ultimately, the life and growth of organizations evolve out of a process in which each member learns the expectations of others and accepts and fulfills them. As Katz and Kahn put it, "There is intrinsic satisfaction in the skillful and successful meshing of our own efforts with those of others, in meeting their expectations as they meet ours, especially if the process affords the expression of valued abilities or the acquisition of new ones."[34]

INTERACTIONAL

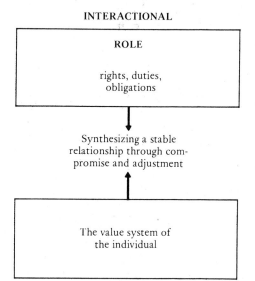

Figure 8-4 An Interactional Description of the Role Concept

The meshing of efforts with expectations and the general systemic character of interlocking roles are clearly put forth in the following excerpt:

> Consider the office of press foreman in a factory manufacturing external trim parts for automobiles. The offices most directly related to that of the press foreman might include the general foreman of the trim department and the superintendent of sheet metal operations. From these offices emanate the work assignments to the office of press foreman, and to these offices he turns for approval of work done. Also directly related to the office of press foreman might be that of the stock foreman, whose section provides sheet metal blanks for the presses, the inspector who must pass or reject completed stampings, the shipping foreman whose section receives and packages the stampings, and let us say, 14 press operators whose work the press foreman directs. Imagine the organization spread out like a vast fish net, in which each knot represents an office and each string a functional relationship between offices. If we pick up the net by seizing any office, the offices to which it is directly attached are immediately seen. Thus the office of press foreman is directly attached to 19 others—general foreman, superintendent, stock foreman, inspector, shipping foreman, and 14 press operators. These 19 offices make up the *role set* for the office of press foreman.
>
> Similarly, each member of an organization is directly associated with a relatively small number of others, usually the occupants of offices adjacent to his in the workflow structure or in the hierarchy of authority. They constitute his role set and typically include his immediate supervisor (and perhaps his supervisor's immediate superior), his subordinates, and certain members of his own or other departments with whom he must work closely. These offices are defined into his role set by virtue of the workflow, technology, and authority structure of the organization.[35]

The *role set*, to which Katz and Kahn alluded, is the "action core" of the organization. Without the fulfillment of expected role behaviors, certain dysfunctions are likely to occur. Consequently, it is necessary that each member of a particular role set understand the role expectations prevailing in his or her unit of the organization. The matter of role expectations is inherent in the larger context of role taking.

The Context of Role Taking and Role Expectation

The context of role taking consists of all the properties and characteristics of a situation in which a "role episode" or role transaction occurs. These properties and characteristics may be the structure, the mission, or the purpose of the organization itself; the personality dispositions of the people involved in the role transaction (i.e., role senders and role receivers); or even the quality or quantity of interactions already existent between the individuals involved in the role transaction. These properties, which are mainly organizational, personal, and interpersonal, interact as shown in Figure 8-5.

The role expectations entertained by all participants in a role episode are determined by (arrow 3) organizational factors (hexagon A). Such factors may be represented by the organization's technological character, size, number of status levels, growth profile, existing policies, and so on.

The personal characteristics of organizational members (circle B) refer to the values, beliefs, opinions, cognitive behaviors, insecurities, self-image, and ego-defense mechanisms that people bring to their job environments. These personality characteristics influence role episodes in many ways. First, certain traits exhibited by the employees will determine how the boss's role is played. The employees' personality may either frustrate or facilitate the necessary role enactment of the boss. Second, it is conceivable that different people will perceive or interpret the same role differently. People differ and their perceptions differ. Finally, the role behavior itself may have an effect on the actors' personality (arrow 8). The aggressive, bright individuals who are forced to submit and "cool it" every working day of their lives can, indeed, grow to be nonassertive and dull. The humane, civil, and courteous patrolman after permanent assignment to a tough, brass-knuckle type of precinct could eventually become hard-nosed and cynical toward citizens. The kindergarten teacher who continually condescends and talks down to the pupils may in time be stuck with rather childlike behaviors. In short, role behaviors if repeated often enough can be internalized so as to force one's personality to take on the characteristics of the behavior or role.

As for interpersonal factors (circle C), it can be answered that the role taken by a member of the organization will depend greatly on the quality of the rapport or interpersonal relationships existing between that member and his or her colleagues in the role set (arrow 6). That member will also interpret differently the various roles that are sent back to him or her (e.g., he or she acts a role, and receives a reciprocal role in return), based upon his or her perceptions of the interpersonal climate in the organization (arrow 7). Congratulations and censure may evoke a particular set of meanings when they come from a trustworthy source, and another set of meanings when they originate from an untrustworthy source. Finally, the behavior of the role receiver feeds back to and affects his or her interpersonal behavior with members of his or her role set (arrow 9). If the role receiver refuses to comply with or reciprocate the role sender's behavior, his or her colleagues will make some evaluation (positive or negative) concerning that refusal (arrow 2), and will also modify their liking for or attraction to him or her (arrow 9).

The three basic factors—organizational, personal, and interpersonal—constitute the major influence on the energy of role taking or role enactment in the organization. We also have alluded to the reciprocal or "tradeoff" character of role behaviors (i.e., when you enact one role behavior, someone else is influenced to respond with a complementing role behavior). One matter quite crucial to the trading of role behaviors among members of the organization is

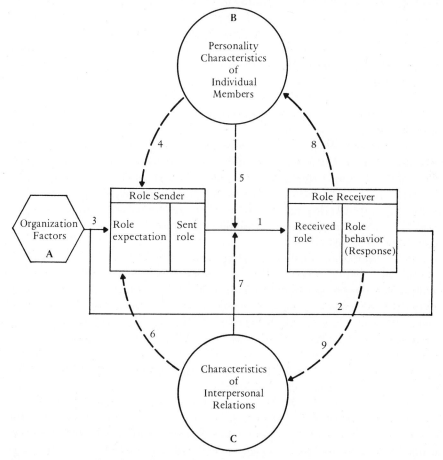

Figure 8-5 A Model of the Context of Role Taking (Adapted from D. Katz and R. Kahn, *The Social Psychology of Organizations* [New York: John Wiley & Sons, 1968], p. 187.)

that of *role expectations*. The fulfillment and denial of these expectations are key factors in the quality of human interaction.

Role Expectation   The term *role expectation* defines how a person in a certain role category is supposed to act. For example, we expect that a supervisor will express annoyance at the employee who "goofs off" on company time. It is within the supervisor's repertoire of role behaviors (we expect) to censure in such an event. The supervisor is influenced by two major sources of role expectations—the formal demands made by the organization (as in hexagon A of Figure 8-5), and the informal ones made by the various groups in the work situation. Consequently, both formal and informal expectation forces exert behavioral demands on the individual.

On the basis of these demands, the individual tries to structure the social situation and to define his or her place in it. This is the process of *role definition*, and its quality depends on the individual's value, self-image, goals, and job involvement.

The expectations that go with a role specify the particular behaviors that are relative to the occupants of other positions. Vice-president of planning specifies behaviors relative to president; assistant manager specifies behavior relative to manager. These other positions are referred to as *counterpositions*. There is no role or role taken that does not have a counterposition; there are no professors without students, no bosses without subordinates, no salespersons without customers.

Along with roles and counterpositions go certain obligations, rights, and privileges. The boss may have the *obligation* of not jeopardizing the subordinates' safety and well-being by ensuring proper working conditions, the *right* to expect job cooperation, and the *privilege* to be addressed respectfully. The subordinate, on the other hand, may have the *obligation* to report to the boss, the *right* to expect fair treatment, and the *privilege* of being groomed for a more responsible position.

Role expectations are *anticipatory* and *obligatory*. If you approach a colleague in a friendly and helpful manner about a problem, you anticipate that he or she will reciprocate and respond in as friendly and helpful a manner, that you feel that he or she is obliged to cooperate. This means that the expectations are shared between you and the other person, and that they are indeed normative in the organization. When the norms are violated, people become upset and the organizational process is disrupted.

Whatever happens—whether it be expectation-fulfillment or expectation-denial—it would appear that role expectations may influence attitudes toward the organization, but may also be influenced by existing attitudes. Lieberman's classic study demonstrates that hypothesis.[36] Lieberman was able to measure the perceptions and attitudes of employees in two appliance plants three times during a period of three years: once when all were rank and file workers; a year later when twenty-three had become foremen and thirty-five had been elected union stewards; and two years later when about half of the new foremen and stewards had reverted to nonsupervisory jobs and half had continued in their new roles.

Lieberman posed the question: "What impact does being placed in the role of foreman and the role of steward have on the role occupants? Compared to the workers who had not become foremen or stewards, Lieberman found that the new foremen had changed their attitude toward the company seeing it as a better place to work. They also had a more positive perception of top management officers and felt better about the incentive system. Compared to the workers who had not become stewards, the new stewards had become more favorably inclined toward unions in general, toward the top officers of their own union, and toward the principle of seniority rather than ability as the basis for upward mobility and wage payments.

Those foremen and stewards who subsequently returned to their original rank-and-file roles also tended to revert to the perceptions and attitudes of regular workers. Those who remained as foremen and stewards increased in their attitudes toward management and the union, respectively. Lieberman's study demonstrates that each individual in an organization acts in relation and response to the expectations of the significant members of the role set.

The question arises: "What happens to the individual who has to perform or enact two or more separate roles?" The effect of playing several roles has a number of possibilities. It is possible that nothing traumatic will occur and the individual will carry out the various roles satisfactorily; or there may be strain and the person will lose effectiveness. We now discuss the ramifications of role conflict and strain.

Role Conflict and Role Strain

Role conflict results when an individual is faced with two roles that are incompatible.[37] The person cannot meet the expectations of the two roles simultaneously, and consequently a conflict occurs between them. The severity of the conflict will depend on two factors:

1. The nature of the situation—i.e., the degree to which the roles are incompatible—and the inflexibility with which the expectations are enforced.

2. The personality of the individual, including the adjustment to the situation and the ability to ignore some of the demands of one role or the other.[38]

An individual in an organization is required to play a number of roles. For example, an administrator may find increasing demands on his or her time when placed on several decision-making committees. Obviously, all of the role expectations cannot be fulfilled—at least, not all the time. Some of the expectancies will have to be sacrificed and other members of the work environment (or those who occupy counterpositions) will feel the strain, as would the administrator. Traditionally, administrators try to ensure that role conflict does not occur, because of the consequent inefficiencies and dissatisfactions. Still, modern organizations are so complex that it is virtually impossible to eliminate all sources of role conflict.

An example of this type of conflict is the production supervisor who is hounded by the many productivity demands of his immediate boss—the vice-president in charge of production. At the same time, the people in "quality control" are also making demands of him in terms of quality standards. In most instances, these two demands are inconsistent and the foreman is faced with a quality or quantity dilemma. No matter which route he chooses, someone is likely to view him as incompetent.

In addition to role conflict between functions, there is also the problem of role conflict between the expectations of the organization and the expectations of the group. This often occurs in union shops (organization in which workers hold union membership). Where such role conflict exists, output restriction is usually a manifestation of the strain. Output restriction is a deliberate effort, informally enforced by the group, to produce below standards for fear it might be revised upward. The informal command might go like this: "Don't assemble more than 35 units per hour and don't work during your break; otherwise management will raise the production rate, and before you know it, they'll be asking us to do things on our break time. Don't be a rate buster."

Individuals coming into such a situation are faced with two sets of demands. Management wants as much output or production as possible. The group pressures the individuals to restrict or control this output. What can they do in such an instance of role conflict? They have several choices. They can join forces with the output restricters or they can be rate busters. Either way they lose. They must find another alternative. They could vacillate or try to find a niche somewhat between the two extremes. As a matter of fact, that is exactly what most of us do—we try to win something from management and something from the work group. Realistically, this matter of playing against both sides produces a constant strain of varying magnitude. If the strain is too great, it will have to be reduced. Let us see how.

Strain Reduction   Protection from role strain is often built into the organizational structure. Many organizations have negotiating committees, grievance comittees, or shop stewards to whom formal complaints can be brought.

Not allowing a person to hold more than one position simultaneously, if there is a likelihood of a clash, is a good example of a built-in strain-reduction device. Some colleges and universities allow individuals to hold the joint roles of dean and instructor simultaneously. This is far from an ideal circumstance, and faculty suspicion and blame fixing usually result.

Role conflict and role strain have been found to be related to low job satisfaction, low confidence in the organization, high job-related tension, low self-confidence, and a sense of futility.[39] Such traumas and disturbances can be costly and disruptive to organizations. Management should attempt to minimize strain and conflict when possible.

Beyond the problems of role taking, the denial and fulfillment of role expectations, and role strain, there remains one other concern—i.e., the implications of the organizational role structure for the type of communication that is likely to occur. What kind of communication is influenced by certain roles? Since the major task of the organization consists of role coordination, what must organization leaders do to ensure organizational effectiveness?

Roles and Communication

Role structure strongly influences the flow of messages within an organization. Basically, members tend to direct more messages to people they consider as playing important roles, such as administrator, president, superintendent, and the like. However, Lawless[40] points out that there is much peril in the occupancy of high roles in the organization—especially for men. It is his contention that *effective* managers are those who can maintain an optimal psychological distance from their subordinates in order to prevent personal matters from contaminating objective judgment. As managers, women are generally not as adept as men in this skill. Most women tend to be more personal than men in their response to problems; consequently, their effectiveness would be diminished in this regard. However, this appears to be a rapidly changing cultural phenomenon.

The point of peril for men in managerial roles is in their unwilliingness to show their feelings. "Grin and bear it" is, for some reason, the maxim of the male role in our society. Men have convinced themselves of the constant need to be tough, objective, unsentimental, and emotionally unexpressive. There is ample evidence that men conceal more about themselves from others (as well as from themselves) than do women. The burdens of organizational management are heavy. Borne alone, these burdens can become a menace to the manager's physical and mental health. The evidence is that men die at an earlier age than women.

Beyond the personal concern of role taking, there are several communication problems within the larger context of role coordination. An organization consists of several role positions that must be fused into an interdependent system. What does this task imply as far as communication is concerned?

Katz and Kahn[41] offer the following predictions:

1. The more activities there are contained within a role, the more likely will be the need for coordination among the activities.
2. The more interrole coordination an organization requires, the more the achievement of coordination is assigned to offices high in the organizational structure. The problem of information overload is characteristically built into the top echelons of large organizations. The incumbents (persons occupying those roles) are subject to information inputs from all over the organization, and the likelihood of information overload becomes great.
3. The greater the programming of interrole coordination, the greater is the use of organizational authority to prevent failure of role performance.

The process of role coordination constitutes one of the greatest problems in organizational communication. We believe that an understanding of the nature of roles and their impact is fundamental to the study of organizations.

REVIEW QUESTIONS

1. What is power?
2. What are five types of power?
3. How does an individual exercise influence over another individual using power?
4. What factors can contribute to informal and/or formal status?
5. What is a status symbol?
6. What is status congruency?
7. What is role expectation?
8. What are role conflict and role strain?
9. What are the effects of roles on organizational communication?
10. What are the effects of status on organizational communication?
11. What are the effects of power on organizational communication?

KEY TERMS AND CONCEPTS FOR REVIEW

- Power
- Reward Power
- Coercive Power
- Referent Power
- Expert Power
- Legitimate Power
- Status
- Status Symbol
- Status Congruency

- Fusion Process
- Roles
- Role Set
- Role Episode
- Role Definition
- Counterpositions
- Role Expectations
- Role Conflict
- Role Strain

CASE STUDY

Rentz Associates is a small construction company in California. Its primary revenue is derived from the shooting of acoustical ceilings in commercial buildings.

Robert Jones, a college student, has been employed part-time by the company for two years. Returning for work in his third year, he is assigned foreman for the second work crew. The owner, Al Rentz, reasoned that Robert had the equivalent of one full year of seniority. This action required that John Holbart, a regular employee who had been with the company nine months, be reassigned to the first crew and Paul Donaldson, a regular employee with seven months' seniority, work under Robert's supervision.

John felt that a regular employee should be in charge of all work crews. Conflicts arose when Robert and John had to work on similar projects. Paul, on the other hand, was impressed by Robert's ability to cut the normal work time in half.

PROBE

• Explain this case in terms of employee roles, status, and power.

Recommended Readings

French, J. R. P. Jr., and B. Raven. "The Bases of Social Power." In *Studies in Social Power*, D. Cartwright, ed. Ann Arbor, Mich.: The University of Michigan Press, 1959, pp. 118–149.

Baird, Jr. J.E. *The Dynamics of Organizational Communication*. New York: Harper & Row, 1977, pp. 186–203.

Bernard, C. "Functions and Pathology of Status Systems in Formal Organizations." In *Industry and Society*, W. F. Whyte, ed. New York: McGraw-Hill Book Company, 1946.

Hunt, R. "Role and Role Conflict." In *Focus on Change and the School Administrator*, H. Harty and G. Halloway, eds. Buffalo, N.Y.: Buffalo State University of New York, 1965, pp. 37–46.

Keller, R. "Role Conflict and Ambiguity: Correlates with Job Satisfaction," *Personnel Psychology* 28 (1975): 57–64.

Kipnis, K. "Does Power Corrupt?," *Journal of Personality and Social Psychology* 24 (1972): 33–41.

Kahn, R. L., et. al. *Organizational Stress: Studies in Role Conflict and Ambiguity*. New York: John Wiley & Sons, Inc., 1964, pp. 56, 99–124.

Notes

1. C. Kerr, "Governance and Functions," *Daedalus*, 1970, 99 (1): 108–121.
2. D. Katz and R. Kahn, *The Social Psychology of Organizations* (New York: John Wiley & Sons, 1968), p. 203.
3. D. Cartwright, "Influence, Leadership, Control." In James G. March, ed., *Handbook of Organizations* (Chicago: Rand McNally & Company, 1965), pp. 1–14.
4. W. Scott and T. Mitchell, *Organization Theory: A Structural and Behavioral Analysis* (Homewood, Ill.: Richard D. Irwin, 1972), p. 218.
5. C. Bernard, *The Functions of the Executive* (Cambridge, Mass.: Harvard University Press, 1939).
6. Ibid., p. 219.
7. J. French and B. Raven, "The Bases of Social Power." In D. Cartwright, ed., *Studies in Social Power* (Ann Arbor, Mich.: The University of Michigan Press, 1959), pp. 118–149.
8. D. Lawless, *Effective Management: Social Psychological Approach* (Englewood Cliffs, N.J.: Prentice-Hall, 1972), p. 234.
9. Scott and Mitchell, op. cit., p. 219.
10. Lawless, op cit. pp. 235–236.
11. R. Emerson, "Power-Dependence Relations," *American Sociological Review* 27 (1962): 31–41.
12. J. Price, *Organizational Effectiveness* (Homewood, Ill.: Irwin-Dorsey Press, 1968), chapters 5 and 6.
13. M. Cohen and J. March, *Leadership and Ambiguity: The American College President* (New York: McGraw-Hill Book Company, 1974), pp. 205–216.

14. C. Shartle, *Occupational Information*, 3d ed. (Englewood Cliffs, N.J.: Prentice-Hall, 1959), pp. 55–57.

15. E. Flippo, *Management: A Behavioral Approach* Boston: Allyn & Bacon, 1974), pp. 217–218.

16. K. Davis and W. Moore, "Some Principles of Stratification," *American Sociological Review* 9 (1945): 242–249.

17. Scott and Mitchell, op cit., p. 199.

18. C. Barnard, *Organization and Management* (Cambridge, Mass.: Harvard University Press, 1949), pp. 207–211.

19. Flippo, op. cit., p. 218.

20. D. Miller and W. Form, *Industrial Sociology: The Sociology of Work Organizations* (New York: Harper & Row, 1964), p. 482.

21. Flippo, op. cit., p. 219

22. L. Barnes, *Organizational Systems and Engineering Groups: A Comparative Study of Two Technical Groups in Industry* (Boston: Harvard Graduate School of Business Administration, 1960), chap. 4.

23. A. Strauss, "Transformations of Identity." In Warren Bennis, Kenneth Benne, and Robert Chin, eds., *The Planning of Change* (New York: Holt, Rinehart and Winston, 1961), pp. 518–558.

24. Lawless, op. cit., p. 257.

25. H. Kelley, "Communication in Experimentally Created Hierarchies," *Human Relations* 4 (1951): 39–56.

26. P. Worchel, "Cartharsis and the Relief of Hostility," *Journal of Abnormal and Social Psychology* 55 (1957): 238–243.

27. Katz and Kahn, op. cit., p. 172.

28. D. Levinson, "Role, Personality, and Social Structure in the Organizational Setting," *Journal of Abnormal and Social Psychology* (March 1959): 172.

29. Scott and Mitchell, op. cit., p. 205.

30. E. Jones and H. Gerard, *Foundations of Social Psychology* (New York: John Wiley & Sons, 1967), p. 177.

31. H. Gerard, "Some Effects of Status, Role Clarity, and Group Goal Clarity Upon the Individual's Relations to Group Processes," *Journal of Personality* 25 (1956–1957): 475.

32. Scott and Mitchell, loc. cit.

33. Katz and Kahn, op. cit., pp. 172–174.

34. Ibid., p. 173.

35. Ibid., p. 188.

36. S. Lieberman, "The Effects of Changes in Roles on the Attitudes of the Occupants," *Human Relations* 9 (1956): 385–402.

37. J. Gullahorn, "Measuring Role Conflict," *American Journal of Sociology* 61 (1956): 318–321.

38. J. Getzels and E. Guba, "Role, Role Conflict, and Effectiveness: An Empirical Study," *American Sociological Review* 18 (1954): 164–166.

39. R. Kahn, D. Wolfe, R. Quinn, J. Snoek, and R. Rosenthal, *Organizational Stress: Studies in Role Conflict and Ambiguity* (New York: John Wiley & Sons, 1964).

40. Lawless, op. cit., p. 297.

41. Katz and Kahn, loc. cit.

9 | Communicator: Leadership Effectiveness

LEARNING OBJECTIVES

After reading the chapter, you should be able to

1. Explain the trait approach to leadership.
2. Identify elements that leaders use to motivate others in organizations.
3. Explain three leadership skills needed to produce attitude and behavior modification.
4. Identify and explain three leadership styles.
5. Explain three modes of leadership attitudes.
6. Explain the role of communication in organizational leadership.
7. Explain the effect of communication networks upon leadership.

Most people would assume that without leadership no organization could achieve its goals. This assumption is generally valid, but what do we mean by the term *leadership*? Leadership, like the concept of management, means many things to many people. At times, leadership and management have been used synonymously. However, leadership is basically the ability to shape the attitudes and behaviors of others. Management, on the other hand, is the formal task of decision and command. An individual can hold a position of management and not manifest the leadership qualities by which employees are influenced successfully. Where management does not provide adequate leadership, subordinates will seek it elsewhere. If the formal organization cannot develop managers who possess the desired leadership qualities, the informal organization will attempt to supply the needed leaders.

This chapter is divided into three sections. Section one examines the role of leadership in the organization. We explore communication and leadership; the traits of leadership; the leader as motivator in the organizational situation; and leadership skills necessary for effective group performance at different levels of management. Section two investigates a wide range of factors that influence the effectiveness of the leader. We discuss leadership styles, attitudes, and behaviors, and the communication elements influencing leadership. Section three provides a verbal-pictorial model of leadership effectiveness drawn from our examination of the elements of effective leadership and our knowledge of the organizational setting.

The Role of Leadership

A manager garners the cooperation of employees through leadership. Foreman, supervisor, manager, union steward, and the collective board of directors—each has a leadership role in the organization. In fact, the potential exists for each member of the organization to exert leadership in the context of its work in either task or social areas. Individuals who are called upon to play the role of leader must seek the mobilization and utilization of fellow workers.

An executive or manager does not necessarily possess leadership qualities because of his or her particular designated position. For example, an individual may acquire or be elevated to a leadership position merely through personal inventiveness or planning. Leadership activities are directed toward getting effective work from team workers. Thus, organizational performance is related to the quality of leadership. Although competent leadership is not the only important ingredient for successful operation, it is an essential one for the organization. Effective leadership can lead to the development of an aggressive, successful organization.

Each employee is only one part of a complex organizational system. Each individual is interdependent within the system. For instance, managers are part of a decision-making subsystem of the organizational system. They are related to all levels of management and function within them; managers cannot change their methods of leadership without affecting other parts of the organization.

The employees' leadership also is affected by the leadership of their superior. Fleishman found that a foreman's attitude varied with the type of manager he served.[1] A foreman working under a supervisor who expressed positive attitudes toward him would also express positive attitudes toward his subordinates. Conversely, a foreman whose superior expressed negative attitudes toward him tended to develop similarly negative attitudes toward his subordinates. Bowers found that higher-level managers could affect leadership style by rewarding the lower-level leader with promotions and/or expressions of approval.[2] The subordinate leader, in turn, adopted the "rewarded" style of leadership, acting in accordance with the superior's expectations and his own position in the organizational structure.

There have been many definitions of leadership, but we define *leadership* in terms of the communication behavior between two or more individuals. Haiman suggested that direct leadership is an interaction process in which an individual, usually through the medium of speech, influences the behavior of others toward a particular end.[3] Leadership is a process by which an agent induces a subordinate to behave in a desired manner. It is, in most instances, a form of personal social control by means of direct or indirect interaction between leader and follower. In the organization the superior influences the subordinate to cooperate toward a goal perceived as desirable. Katz and Kahn consider "the essence of organizational leadership to be the influential increment over and above mechanical compliance with routine directions of the organization."[4] They observe that although all superiors at the same level of organization possess equal power, they do not use it with equal effectiveness to influence individuals and organization. The determining factor in the leader's success may be the proper or improper use of communication as the vehicle of persuasion. We can view effective leadership as the activity of persuading people (employees) to cooperate in the achievement of a common objective (organizational goal).

Smith equated leadership with control of the interaction process. Thus the source of interaction A, in giving a stimulus to the second participant, B, would be asserting control by interfering with B's original course of action.[5] Bass defined leadership in somewhat similar terms: "When the goal of one member, A, is that of changing another, B, or when B's change of behavior will reward A or reinforce A's behavior, A's effort to obtain the goal is leadership."[6] Both conceptualizations view leadership as an effect of communication and group action. Pigors, on the other hand, perceived leadership as a process of mutual stimulation which, by the successful interplay of individual differences, controls human energy in pursuit of a common goal.[7] Thus, leadership develops from the interaction process itself. We can look at a number of contemporary organizational theories in light of these communication orientations to leadership.

The theories of Argyris, Blake and Mouton, Likert, and McGregor view the function of leadership as modifying the organization to provide freedom for the employees to fulfill their own expectations and at the same time contribute toward the accomplishment of organizational goals.

Argyris believes that the organization will be most effective when its leadership provides the means whereby followers may make contributions to it as a function of their needs for growth and self-expression. It is the nature of organizations to structure member roles and to control performance in the interest of achieving specified objectives.

Blake and Mouton conceptualize leadership in terms of a *managerial* grid on which concern for people represents one axis and concern for production represents another axis. The leader who rates high on both develops followers committed to accomplishment of work, which leads to relationships of trust and respect. (We discuss leadership styles and managerial grid later in this chapter.)

Likert suggests that leadership is a process in which the leader must be concerned with the expectations, values, and interpersonal skills of those with whom there must be interaction. To be effective, the leader must present behaviors that are perceived by followers as supportive of their efforts and personal worth. It is the leader's influence that will further the task performance and personal welfare of employees. The leader develops group cohesiveness and employee motivation for productivity by providing freedom for decision making and the exercise of initiative.

McGregor postulated two types of organizational leadership—Theory X and Theory Y. Theory X is based on the assumption that people are passive and resistant to organizational needs. Thus, the leader must direct or motivate employees to meet these needs. Theory Y is based on the assumption that people already possess the motivation and desire for responsibility. Thus, the leader arranges organizational conditions to make possible the fulfillment of employee needs while directing the employee efforts to achieve organizational objectives.

If we examine the basic tenets of these theories, we will see that leadership is the function of interaction between leader and employee. Leadership effectiveness is viewed as the ability of the leader, through communication, to provide for the needs of the employee and the attainment of organizational objectives. Whereas the organization is by nature structured and controlled, the leader's primary task is to direct and modify followers' (employees') behaviors to conform to organizational expectations and goals.

Leadership Traits

For over seventy years researchers have attempted to identify the personality variables that would distinguish leaders from nonleaders. The personality or trait approach to leadership grew out of the assumption that leaders are born, not made. No single trait or combination of personality variables will identify the effective leader with absolute certainty. However, we will try to identify the more outstanding leadership traits.

Stogdill, in a review of leadership research, found that leaders generally surpass nonleaders in intelligence, scholarship, responsibility, participation, and socioeconomic status.[8] Geier's study of emergent leadership discovered five negative communicative traits that could hamper an individual's position of leadership in small group discussion. The traits included ignorance, nonparticipation, extreme rigidity, authoritarian behavior, and offensive verbalizations.[9]

In recent years, the trait approach to leadership has been largely abandoned. Jennings concluded that "fifty years of study have failed to produce one personality trait or set of traits that can be used to discriminate between leaders and non-leaders."[10] It has been suggested that the problem of examining traits and successfully identifying them has to do with the failure to examine a leader in relation to both group members and the situation in which the leader exerts influence.[11]

Fiedler examined one trait, *social distance*, associated with effective leadership once the individual had emerged as leader. He discovered narrow-distance leaders and wide-distance leaders. Narrow-distance leaders perceive their co-workers as similar to themselves. They tend to accept or reject co-workers on a basis other than their working ability. They cultivate social relationships with workers, do not emphasize work accomplishment, and are not effective in promoting productivity. Wide-distance leaders, on the other hand, perceive co-workers as dissimilar from themselves. They remain socially aloof and tend to reject workers with whom they cannot work. They emphasize the co-workers' task accomplishment and promote an effective level of productivity.[12]

Applbaum, Anatol, Sereno, and Bodaken suggest that effective leaders have three specific personality traits. Unlike many of the previously identified traits, these are not situation-specific.

> *Intelligence.* Persons appointed, elected, or otherwise perceived as leaders are generally of higher intelligence than the rank and file members of the group. . . .
>
> *Adjustment.* Leadership roles are probably more demanding than nonleadership roles. . . . It is likely that many manifestations of "neurotic" tendencies may interfere with leader effectiveness. . . . Thus, an individual's ability to adjust or adapt to a situation may contribute to our willingness to perceive him or her as a leader . . . leadership tends to operate most effectively when negative personality traits are absent or minimal.
>
> *Deviancy.* Leaders tend to deviate from group norms more than do other members of the group. . . . Perhaps leadership is not so much a function of deviancy as it is a function of knowing *how much* and *when* to deviate.[13]

Personality variables or traits that distinguish the effective leader from the ineffective leader are generally situation-specific. We are unable to identify a priori exactly which personality variables will produce the most effective leadership in an organization group.

Motivation and Leadership

Just as leaders are affected from above in the hierarchical system, so they, too, have a responsibility to motivate the performance of their subordinates. Employees of an organization must be induced to contribute their resources toward achievement of organizational goals. This is not always a particularly easy task in our multilithic organizations. Employees may find their jobs of little interest or challenge; their jobs may, in fact, be unpleasant or monotonous. Thus, if such jobs are to be effective, it may be necessary for the leaders to motivate the workers. As Picard put it:

> Every situation should have some minimum level of motivation for any employee, so if the worker cannot find this in the work itself, he might shop around for some other kind of motivation and find it in his relations with the foreman. As applied to our findings, [people with low job expectations] in our sample found motivations in the job and hence their demands for motivation are satisfied by the intrinsic components of the job. . . . On the other hand, [people with high job expectations] do not derive . . . enough satisfaction and motivation so that the foreman becomes the motivator.[14]

The role of motivation is to supply a personal incentive for the employees of the organization. This requires that the individuals merge their goals with those of the organization. It is a complex process involving the leader, the followers' attitudes and behaviors, the reason employees work, a variety of personnel and organizational goals, and their interrelationship. Let us examine a part of the motivational process—the tools the leader may use to motivate personnel.

Authority Managers may be followed merely because they are managers. They are influential because of their authority in the administrative hierarchy. If employees have a great respect for higher authority, they may respond almost automatically to the orders of a superior. Furthermore, the threat of penalty by the persons in authority for not abiding by their desires may stimulate the employees to greater efforts. Citing J. G. Longenecker:

> . . . there is a question as to the degree of effort that can be obtained by the use of the authoritative approach. A minimum performance might be secured in this way. At the same time, any really outstanding performance may be lacking. In other words, the individual may perform sufficiently well to avoid dismissal but lack the incentive to do an outstanding job.[15]

Authority involves the use of pressure. When the pressure becomes too strong, employees may react against it and fight back. They may become overly defensive in their communication behaviors. In the extreme we may find them feigning illness. Strauss and Sayles illustrated this behavior:

> Once we observed a group of working supervisors who had been strongly pressured to increase production under difficult circumstances with no backing from management. There were nine men regularly assigned to the day shift. One had a nervous breakdown, another had a fatal heart attack that was generally attributed to overwork and fatigue. Of the remaining seven, five had serious illness and in most cases no organic cause could be determined. All this happened during a period of twelve months. Meanwhile, the men on the night shift, where pressure was much less, had an almost perfect health record.[16]

The use of authority by the leader may engender an immediate response that is satisfactory, but pressures upon employees may lead to a deterioration of the organization.

Financial Incentives The leader may use financial reward to increase employees' output or performance. Frederick Taylor, among others, popularized a variety of individual piecework incentive plans. In the last twenty-five years there have been a number of group incentive plans—for example, the Scanlon Plan.[17] Profit sharing is a common practice in the larger industrial complexes. At the executive level a variety of stock options and bonus plans offer substantial financial reward.

There is no question that a leader can use financial reward as a tool for motivating employees. However, we must question the overall effectiveness and extent of such appeals. The results of financial reward have not been universally productive. Unofficial work quotas are often recognized by employees, with no extra production beyond a "normal" day's work. As W.F. Whyte observed:

> From my first day to my last day at the plant I was subject to warnings and predictions concerning price cuts. Pressure was the heaviest from Joe Mucha, day man on my machine, who shared my job repertoire and kept a close eye on my production. On November 14, the day after my first attained quota, Joe Mucha advised: "Don't let it go over $1.25 an hour, or the time-study men will be right down here! And don't waste time either! They watch the records like a hawk! I got ahead, so I took it easy for a couple of hours."
>
> Joe told me that I made $10.01 yesterday and warned me not to go over $1.25 an hour. He told me to figure the setups and time each operation very carefully so that I would not total over $10.25 in any one day.[18]

The manager must establish a reward system that will not lead to possible conflict, hostility, or employee satiation. If the leader uses reward as the *only* tool for inducing and sustaining employee motivation, he or she may be ineffective. In many instances, financial reward is not the primary goal of the employee and, thus, not an effective motivating agent.

Competition The leader may use competition among employees to motivate their performance. For example, a merit principle might stimulate the worker to excel in order to earn a promotion or higher pay. However, this tool is based on increased individual performance—hence, a striving for superiority. Unfortunately, excessive individual competition can be disruptive to the work group, particularly in situations needing teamwork. In addition, if competition is to be an effective tool, it requires the leaders to measure the employees' performance; it is a process generally plagued by judgmental bias and inconsistency on the evaluator's part. Perhaps that is why some organizations utilize seniority rather than merit as a basis for advancement, particularly in union plants and in the government. Although competition is limited by the organizational and human resources available to the leader, it can be quite valuable as a motivating factor. Within organizations, competition is often tied to financial incentives—that is, work groups are rewarded for high productivity, creative ideas, and the like. Direct organizational competition, however, can be considered major stimulus to economic progress.

Paternalism   A leader may motivate an employee through paternalistic benevolence; the manager-leader is "good" to employees and provides benefits to them. In return for such behaviors, the employee is expected to respond with loyalty and enthusiastic performance. The paternalistic leader expects favorable response from employees. Unfortunately, this motivational method does not consistently produce the expected results. Paternalism seems to operate in reverse, creating resentment rather than loyalty. The employees' reaction may be caused by paternalism's basic assumption that employers are superior to employees and know what is best for them; the attitude of superiority is offensive to employees and can create defensiveness in them.

Manager and employees may ultimately develop an informal understanding of desirable behavioral patterns. The superior will permit a range of behavior or standard of performance by the employees. In return, the employees will perform in a manner acceptable to the supervisor. G. Strauss quoted management he had studied as stating:

> Our policy is to live and let live. We give the foreman reasonable production. He protects us from the time-study man who tries to jack up the output rate and look the other way if we take a smoke. We look out for each other.[19]

A weakness of this approach is its failure to stimulate employee performance. It is, therefore, open to question whether this tool is an effective leadership device.[20]

We have examined several tools often employed by leaders in the organization to increase motivation. Undoubtedly, the success of a particular method calls for understanding and skill by the manager. The leader's goal is to increase the effectiveness of the work group, but increasing workers' motivation can contribute to their increased happiness and satisfaction as well as to greater organizational efficiency.

Leadership (Managerial) Skills

The goal of leadership is to control, alter, or develop behavior and attitude patterns among subordinates or fellow employees. However, there is no real agreement about specific leadership skills that must be communicated by the leader to guarantee attitude and behavior modification. On the other hand, there is agreement that technical, conceptual, and human skills do play a role in effective managerial leadership.[21] Although these skills are present at all levels of organizational management, the level of management determines which skill

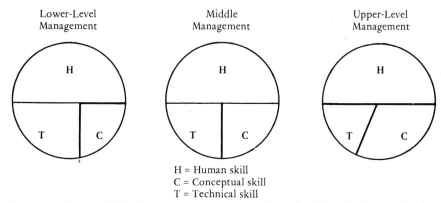

H = Human skill
C = Conceptual skill
T = Technical skill

Figure 9-1 Desired Skill Mix for Various Managerial Levels (Billy J. Hodge and Herbert J. Johnson, *Management and Organizational Behavior: A Multidimensional Approach* [New York: John Wiley & Sons, 1970], p. 263.9

is most important for the leader to communicate. For example, technical skills are crucial at lower levels, and conceptual ones are most important at the top levels of the organization. Human skills, on the other hand, are required at every level of management. Figure 9–1 illustrates the desired skill mix at three levels of management.

Human skill is the ability to weld subordinates into a cohesive unit for action as a coordinated work group. The leader must link the group members' satisfaction with organizational goals. This requires a knowledge of employee behavior and attitudes. These skills are a prerequisite to effective leadership at all levels of management.

Conceptual skill is the ability to think in abstract terms. Upper-level management must deal with actions and policies that affect the total organization and environment. Upper-level management must solve problems dealing with broad relationships rather than individual operations. They must be able to evaluate organizational policies against all relevant organizational considerations—for example, employees and production. Although conceptual skill is needed by leaders at all levels, it is crucial for the leader in upper-management level.

Technical skill is the ability to propose practical solutions to concrete organizational problems. For example, a foreman in an automobile production plant may be called upon to find a faster method for installing tires on a new car. Lower-level managers must deal with a high level of operational problems that interfere with the execution of work. Although technical skills are necessary at all levels of management, they are crucial to the effectiveness of the lower management leader.

Leadership Styles

The stylistic approach to leadership is concerned with how the leader acts toward members of the group—that is, the leader's behavior toward followers. Unlike the trait approach to leadership, the stylistic approach is concerned with what leaders do rather than the personal characteristics they possess. White and Lippitt identify three basic leadership styles:

1. Authoritarian
2. Democratic
3. Laissez-faire

Authoritarian   Many of our large American organizations are associated with authoritarian leadership. Decisions are made by leaders to the extent that political, economic, social, and other forces allow them to act as sole decision makers. While remaining personally aloof from the group, this type of leader determines group policy and dictates activities and work companions for group members, using praise and criticism to control them. Longenecker describes the case of an authoritarian leader, John H. Patterson, founder of the National Cash Register Company, and how he dealt with a department in his company that displeased him:

> . . . he abolished a cost accounting system that he considered inefficient. The erring department produced reams of statistics, but the data were too late to be of value. After fretting over the matter for some time, Patterson reached the boiling point one day, jumped up from his desk, and headed for the cost accounting department. He gave the accountants little time for reflection, walking from desk to desk and asking each employee to pick up his accounting books and to follow him. The procession carrying armloads of accounting records, headed straight for the power house, where they met the engineer in charge. "Will these furnaces burn anything except coal?" he asked. "Well, sir" said the engineer, "we've never tried anything else."
>
> Mr. Patterson then threw one of the accounting books into the fire.
>
> "That burns," he said.
>
> And with that he ordered the others to do the same with their books. In a little while all the books had gone up in smoke while the clerks stood speechless. Finally, Mr. Patterson pulled out his watch and said:
>
> "Gentlemen, it has taken just ten minutes to get rid of the Cost Department."
>
> Of course, Mr. Patterson did not mean to operate without some cost data. But, it is evident from this account, he devised little time to sampling employee thinking about system.[23]

Patterson had exercised totally autocratic controls. He had surveyed the situation and made the final decision, disregarding members of the accounting department.

Democratic   The democratic leader guides the group toward its goal. Group policy is the product of group discussion, which is encouraged by the leader. The leader will generally initiate the procedural stages for the discussion and provide technical assistance when needed. Ideally, this leader is objective and fact-minded in praise and criticism. This style of leadership works best in a committee type of organization in which the leaders' and other participants' concepts and ideas tend to merge. Subordinates are involved in the decision-making process. In the completely democratic situation the subordinates also are allowed to vote for or against the decision. In general, however, it is important for the leader to establish and maintain control over subordinates so that individual responsibility and accountability are preserved. The subordinate makes suggestions and the superior considers them when making the final decision. The organization gains from the combined knowledge of leader and follower.

Laissez-faire   Leaders of this type give complete freedom to the group and individual decisions. They supply needed information only when asked and do not take an active role in the discussion. They make no attempt to control the group members' behavior through either praise or blame. This style of leadership functions more like a tape recorder that plays back the interactions of the group. Leaders relinquish their responsibility for most decisions to their subordinates, unlike democratic leaders who retain their authority. The leadership success is dependent upon the quality of the subordinate group if this approach is to work well. It is possible that when the leader delegates decision-making power, the group may substitute personal goals for those of the organization. Consequently, whether to use this type of leadership and if so, how to select the subordinates, must be carefully considered by the organization. This style of leadership is generally limited to very special circumstances; for example, a company brainstorming session.

Different styles of leading tend to produce different kinds of communication. Some leaders constantly give orders and demand obedience, whereas others solicit suggestions and stimulate individualistic behaviors. Figure 9–2 illustrates some of the major differences in the type of communication behaviors that are characteristic of the different leadership styles. The comparison of communicative acts in each behavior category is based on four democratic, four authoritarian, and two laissez-faire leaders. About 60 percent of all authoritarian leaders' communication consists of orders, disruptive commands, and nonconstructive criticism compared with only 5 percent for the democratic and laissez-faire leaders. Major differences between democratic and laissez-faire leadership are found in three categories of communiction: guiding suggestions, extending knowledge, and stimulating guidance. The democratic leader makes more suggestions and stimulates self-guidance, whereas the laissez-faire leader spends more time giving out information when it is requested.

Lippitt and White noted that when the three styles are compared for productivity the authoritarian groups were highest in quantity, whereas democratic groups were judged better in quality.[24] Authoritarian leadership generally results in greater quantitative productivity, and democratic leadership results in higher group member morale. Shaw found that authoritarian groups made fewer errors, required fewer messages for problem solution, and required less time than nonauthoritarian groups. However, nonauthoritarian group members were much more satisfied with their groups. He also observed that it is easier to

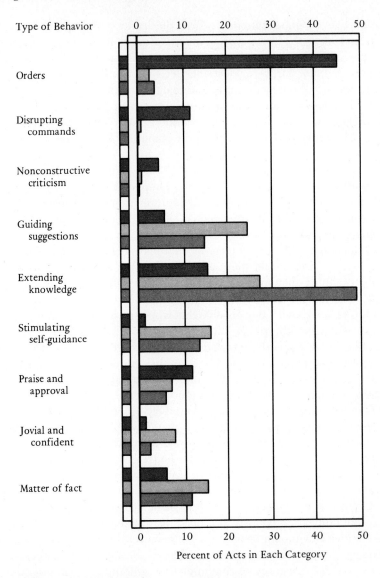

Percent of Acts in Each Category

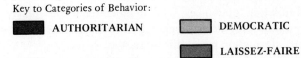

Key to Categories of Behavior:

AUTHORITARIAN   DEMOCRATIC

LAISSEZ-FAIRE

Figure 9–2 Comparison of Behavior of Average Authoritarian, Democratic, and Laissez-faire Leaders (Ralph K. White and Ronald Lippitt, *Autocracy and Democracy: An Experimental Inquiry* [New York: Harper & Row, 1960], p. 32.)

be a good autocratic leader than a good democratic leader. Shaw declares: "It is easy to issue orders, but difficult to utilize effectively the abilites of group members. If a leader doubts his ability to be an effective democratic leader, then he probably is well advised to play the autocratic role."[25] The democratic style proved to be superior in the degree of cohesiveness developed and the level of independent behavior exhibited by group members.[26]

Two other styles of leadership have been defined and studied: participatory and supervisory. Participatory leaders take part in the discussion and try to ensure an equal chance for participation to all members; they can be synonymous with democratic leaders. Supervisory leaders, on the other hand, do not take an active part in the group but merely control the activities to assure completion of the task.

Participatory leadership is more effective as a technique for influencing and even changing the opinions of group members; members, in turn, will be more satisfied with the group decision, presumably because they have been able to express their opinion.[27] Participatory leadership is most effective when the task involves nonroutine decisions, nonstandard information, and few time restrictions. It also needs an environment in which subordinates have a strong desire for independence, feel they should be involved in decision making, and are confident of their ability to work without close direction.[28] We do not mean to suggest that participatory leadership fits all organizations. In some cases, group members might become frustrated by the length of time required to reach decisions, or internal group conflicts could arise when a leader refuses to resolve differences between opposing forces.

The Institute of Social Research at the University of Michigan (ISR) has singled out two additional leadership styles directly applied in organizations—job-centered and employee-centered supervision. As the terms imply, job-centered supervision pays attention primarily to the work performed, whereas employee-centered supervision places the emphasis upon development of effective work groups.

We might ask then, is one style of leadership more effective than another? The answer will have to be multifaceted. In any situation, a group will be more effective when the members' expectations are met. When group members expect a democratic leadership style—as they do in some jobs—the democratic style is found to produce the most effective group. If the group task requires free discussion, a leader who facilitates it will be more effective. But in tasks that require mostly participation by the skilled group members, the leader who then controls the pattern of interaction will be more effective. On the other hand, in the army, and often in industry as well, group members anticipate forceful leadership from their superiors; therefore, a more authoritarian style of leadership will result in a better group. Generally, as the size of the group increases, the leadership style tends to become authoritarian. Here, the authoritarian style is the most effective, because the leader can react quickly to make needed adjustments in the group. But within a group of creative managers developing new product ideas, the most suitable leadership style would be the laissez-faire approach.

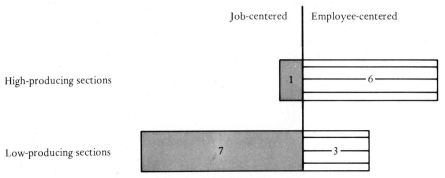

Figure 9-3 Productivity of "Employee-centered" and "Job-centered" Supervisors (From Rensis Likert, *New Patterns of Management* [New York: McGraw-Hill Book Company, 1961], p. 76.9

In 1947, the Institute for Social Research discovered significant differences in leadership of effective and ineffective organizational groups. As previously mentioned, researchers had examined two styles of leadership—job-centered and employee-centered. Figure 9–3 illustrates the relationship between these two leadership styles and productivity. Six of seven high-producing sections in one organization were directed by employee-centered supervisors, whereas seven of ten low-producing sections were directed by job-centered supervisors. These results were consistent in clerical, sales, and manufacturing areas of the organization.[29]

The ISR also investigated general versus close supervision, and found a definite correlation between general supervision and a higher level of productivity; it appears managers are more effective when they allow their subordinates greater freedom. Gellerman described three areas that influence the productivity of employee-centered supervision:

1. *Extent to which the job requires teamwork*—when employees are highly interdependent, employee-centered supervision will be more effective.
2. *Consistency of supervision behavior*—if supervision is to be employee-centered, it must be that way consistently.
3. *Personality of workers*—independent-minded employees who like to decide things for themselves respond better to employee-centered supervision than dependent personalities.[30]

The instrumental behavioral theory of leadership emphasizes the leader's role as a manager in the rational aspects of management—planning, organizing, and controlling. A leader may use a democratic or autocratic style, but the emphasis is on the task of allocating human and material resources. A considerable amount of research lends support to the belief that those who manage well are also effective leaders.[31]

The research by Likert posits the qualities of job-centered and employee-centered leadership on opposite sides of the same continuum. Some researchers have combined the participative and instrumental behavior patterns in what is sometimes called the "great man" theory. The managerial grid developed by

Blake and Mouton falls into this category of leadership behavior. The horizontal axis indicates concern for production, and the vertical axis indicates concern for people. (It should be noted that a leader's overall attitude may consist of several or all attitudes.) The managerial grid is based on the idea that the most effective leader has a concern both for people and for production (see Figure 9–4). The grid also notes leadership styles, as devised by Klos.[32] The autocrat (9,1) has the highest concern for production and lowest concern for people. The missionary (1,9) has the highest concern for people and the lowest concern for production. The deserter (1,1) represents a manager with little concern for people or production. The executive (9,9) represents an individual with the highest concern for both people and production. The compromiser (5,5) attempts to balance the concerns for people and production.[33] The two dimensions are not necessarily correlated positively or negatively. A supervisor might be considerate of employees but lack orientation toward efficient organization of work. On the other hand, the supervisor might combine a concern for both people and for production.

An important point to remember is that the managerial grid does not have final answers about leadership effectiveness. It does, however, give us a model without leadership extremes. Blake and Mouton suggest that an understanding of the grid can provide managers with the means for revising leadership practices and procedures so that they can work toward a 9,9 leadership style.[34]

Fleishman has examined two qualities of supervision labeled "consideration" and "initiating structure." Consideration involves the mutual trust and respect between superiors and subordinates. Initiating structure involves a

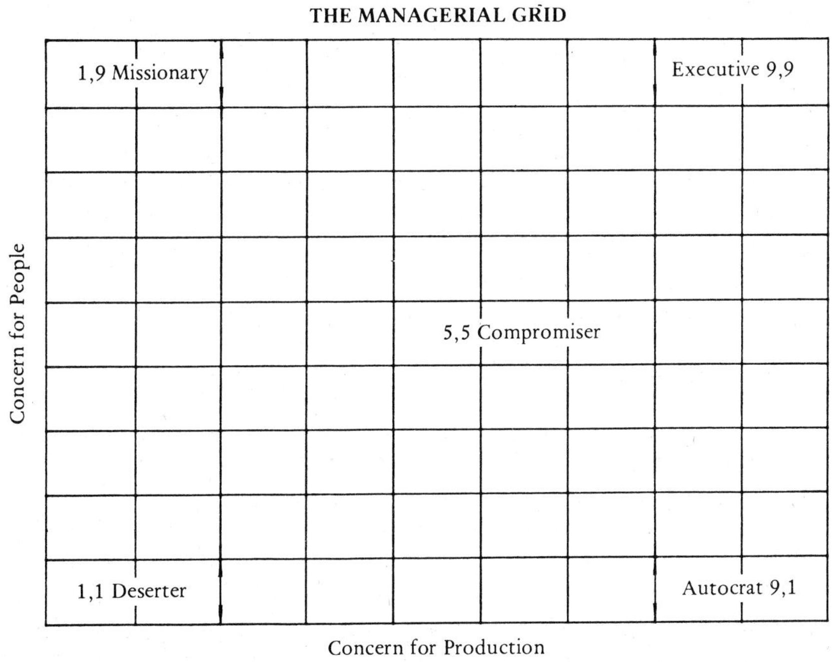

THE MANAGERIAL GRID

Concern for People (vertical axis)

- 1,9 Missionary (top left)
- Executive 9,9 (top right)
- 5,5 Compromiser (center)
- 1,1 Deserter (bottom left)
- Autocrat 9,1 (bottom right)

Concern for Production (horizontal axis)

Figure 9-4 Leadership Styles and the Managerial Grid

superior who organizes and defines the role of each employee and pushes for production. These two qualities are related to the production and person concerns portrayed on the grid. As Fleishman comments, "supervisors who emphasize one pattern at the expense of the other are apt to be less effective, but some balance between them is needed to satisfy organizational as well as individual needs."[35]

The effective manager-leader should combine a concern for people and a concern for production. We believe that there is no single "best" mix of production and person concerns and that the degree of concern should depend on the type of employee and situation the leader confronts. In sum, no one style of leadership can be considered *the most effective* for all occasions.

Leadership Attitudes

Leaders' attitudes, values, and motives all operate to influence their behavior in the group and the manner in which they attempt to modify the attitudes and behaviors of others. Leadership styles will in most cases correspond to the attitudes managers have toward their employees and their task. Miles, Porter, and Croft have grouped the theories of managerial leadership into three categories or models of leadership attitudes.[36] The three models are illustrated in Figure 9–5.

The traditional model assumes that people dislike work and will only do so when they are rewarded. This model is based on a negative attitude of the average employee's values and abilities. Only executives and top management are seen as possessing special qualities—self-direction and self-control, initiative and ingenuity, judgment and perspective, the capability of solving problems, and a sense of responsibility. The leader or manager exercises rigid control over employees; employee compliance is gained through the use of reward—primarily monetary—or by punishment, such as firing or demotion (see Chapter 2).

The human relations model assumes that both superiors and subordinates desire recognition, and they feel they are a worthwhile part of the organization. But the model continues to distinguish between superiors and subordinates. The superior initiates actions, which satisfy the needs of subordinates; the subordinates play a passive role by carrying out the supervisor's wishes. The goal of this model is to increase the morale and satisfaction of employees. However, the final goal remains the same as the traditional model—compliance with the manager's directives.

The human resources model views employees as untapped resources who possess creative abilities and the capacity for responsible, self-controlled behavior. The leader shares information with the subordinates and encourages them to participate in decision making. The purpose is to improve decision making and the efficiency of the organization. Leaders following this model will encourage subordinates to participate in decision making, and permit them to mold and modify their own jobs and exercise control over their own behavior.

Traditional model	Human Relations Model	Human Resources Model
Assumptions	*Assumptions*	*Assumptions*
1 Work is inherently distasteful to most people.	1 People want to feel useful and important	1 Work is not inherently distasteful. People want to contribute to meaningful goals which they have helped establish.
2 What they do is less important than what they earn for doing it.	2 People desire to belong and to be recognized as individuals	
3 Few want or can handle work which requires creativity, self-direction, or self-control.	3 These needs are more important than money in motivating people to work.	2 Most people can exercise far more creative, responsible self-direction and self-control than their present jobs demand.
Policies	*Policies*	*Policies*
1 The manager's basic task is to closely supervise and control his subordinates.	1 The manager's basic task is to make each worker feel useful and important.	1 The manager's basic task is to make use of his "untapped" human resources.
2 He must break tasks down into simple, repetitive, easily learned operations.	2 He should keep his subordinates informed and listen to their objections to his plans.	2 He must create an environment in which all members may contribute to the limits of their ability.
3 He must establish detailed work routines and procedures, and enforce these firmly but fairly.	3 The manager should allow his subordinates to exercise some self-direction and self-control on routine matters.	3 He must encourage full participation on important matters, continually broadening subordinate self-direction and control.
Expectations	*Expectations*	*Expectations*
1 People can tolerate work if the pay is decent and the boss is fair.	1 Sharing information with subordinates and involving them in routine decisions will satisfy their basic needs to belong and to feel important.	1 Expanding subordinate influence, self-direction, and self-control will lead to direct improvements in operating efficiency.
2 If tasks are simple enough and people are closely controlled, they will produce up to standard.	2 Satisfying these needs will improve morale and reduce resistance to formal authority: subordinates will "willingly cooperate."	2 Work satisfaction may improve as a "by-product" of subordinates making full use of their resources.

Figure 9-5 Leadership Attitudes (From R. E. Miles, L. W. Porter, and J. A. Croft, "Leadership Attitudes among Public Health Officers," *American Journal of Public Health* 56 [1966]: 1990–2005.)

The assumption is that a subordinate who exercises self-direction and self-control receives satisfaction from feelings of accomplishment that a job was well done.

The behaviors and attitudes of an organizational leader toward subordinates or fellow workers as human beings plays a role in the effectiveness of the leadership. The employees' perception of the leader's attitudes, in turn, will influence their actions in the organization. Managers who are perceived by their employees as high in understanding, consideration, and people concern will be better liked and more effective in getting the job done.[37]

Attitudes and behaviors of leaders will, in most cases, correspond to those of their own superiors. If superiors are employee-centered, then the supervisors will probably be employee-centered. The supervisors will permit the freedom to their subordinates that they themselves possess with their superiors. The effectiveness of the employee-centered approach, however, is limited by the ability of the supervisor to reward the employee for adopting the new attitude or behavior. As D. C. Pelz puts it:

> . . . the supervisory behaviors of "siding with employees" and "social climate to employees" will tend to raise employee satisfaction only if the supervisor has enough influence to make these behaviors pay off in terms of actual benefits for employees.[38]

Communication

The modes of supervisor-subordinate communication in human relations provide a basis for differentiating effective and ineffective organizational leadership. A successful foreman would have to be "communication-minded." He will be sensitive to the needs of the workers, demonstrate a concern for their welfare as well as production, and generally be a good listener.[39] A high level of employee performance seems to be related to:

1. Openness of communication channels between superiors and subordinates;
2. Subordinates' satisfaction with supervisors' supportive behavior;
3. A relatively high degree of mutual understanding of others' viewpoints and problems among those working together; and
4. A relatively high degree of local influence and autonomy on work-related matters.[40]

Redding has drawn a number of conclusions about the extent to which "good" communication characterizes effective managerial leadership:

1. The better supervisors tend to be more "communication-minded"; e.g., they enjoy talking in meetings, are able to explain instructions and policies, and enjoy conversing with subordinates.
2. The better supervisors tend to be willing, emphatic listeners; they respond understandingly to so-called "silly" questions from employees; they are approachable; they will listen to suggestions and complaints with an attitude of fair consideration and willingness to take appropriate action.

3. The better supervisors tend to "ask" or "persuade," in preference to "telling" or "demanding."
4. The better supervisors tend to be sensitive to the feelings and ego-defense needs of their subordinates; e.g., they are careful to reprimand in private rather than in public.
5. The better supervisors tend to be more open in passing along information; they are in favor of giving advance notice of impending changes and explaining the "reasons why" behind policies and regulations.[41]

The communication qualities necessary for effective leadership will vary from company to company, employee group to employee group, and employee to employee. Although this observation might lend support for a totally "situational" view of leadership effectiveness, a number of conclusions about leader behavior appear to be situationally consistent:

(a) managers should trust their subordinates to be more responsible in the performance of their jobs; (b) managers should permit subordinates to participate in the making of their own job; and (c) managers should replace much of the mechanistic structure characteristics of most institutions with organic approach to organization.[42]

The managers' willingness to allow their employees to participate in organizational decision making plays an important role in leadership effectiveness. We are referring to the engagement of individuals in the system so that they are involved in decisions that affect them.[43] Communication is a crucial element and a prerequisite for participative decision making. The allowance of "participative" decision making is a form of distribution of leadership function, or of power.

An examination of the participative practices of 109 major organizations found that there was a small decision-making echelon at the top in which participative practices were commonplace; however, the participative climate did not characterize the entire organization. The study suggested that restrictive communication practices do not occur in the upper levels of management.[44] We might view participation by individuals along a continuum from no participation to totally unrestricted participation. Tannenbaum and Schmidt developed a continuum of leadership behavior, which can be applied to the gradations in participative decision making (see Figure 9–6).

The position occupied by a particular manager or supervisor depends on a number of factors: First, the leader's own value system, which is reflected in his or her confidence of the subordinates; the leader's "tolerance for ambiguity" as opposed to the certainty of rules and procedures. Second, the behavior of subordinates, which may reflect that of the boss, grow out of the situation or come from their own values. Third, factors inherent in the immediate situation may influence managerial style; for example, a large geographically dispersed organization may need more centralized controls. Fourth, the pressure of time and the need for a decision may inhibit the degree of participation allowable. Leadership strategies will change with the needs of the particular situation. If the leader's assumptions about employee behavior grow out of a belief in

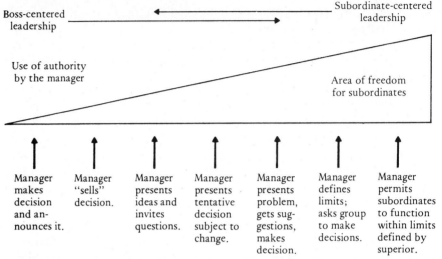

Figure 9-6 Continuum of Leadership Behavior (From Robert Tannenbaum and W. H. Schmidt, "How to Choose a Leadership Pattern," *Harvard Business Review* 36, 2 [March-April 1958]: 95–106.)

management by shared objectives, there will be flexibility to move along the scale—even using directive methods when the situation requires it, as in an emergency. Managers whose concept is one of rigid, centralized direction will restrict themselves to the left end of the continuum.

Greiner concludes that the best decisions are those in which the degree of subordinate influence is at neither end of the continuum. Shared-power approaches are to be recommended over either unilateral action or delegated authority. However, Greiner argues against the removal of expertise, information, and power from higher-level managers. Such action is not likely to produce decisions of high quality. He proposes an approach of shared power, characterized by *reciprocity of influence* between superiors and subordinates.[45] Mason Haire illuminates the concept of reciprocity of influence when he comments, "the amount of influence a superior has with his subordinates depends on the degree to which they can influence him."[46]

We suggest that directive leadership is not the most effective form in which to influence subordinates. Groups that are self-motivating, taking on more and more managerial functions, result in improved morale and production. Job attitudes and performance improvement have both been shown to be positively related to the level of participation; increased participation leads to more favorable job attitudes and production improvement.[47]

The effective leader not only permits discussion among group members but allows them to participate in the actual decision making. Unless group participation provides members with an opportunity to discuss issues of relevance to them, participative decision making will not operate successfully. The effective manager-leader is open to influence on important issues. DeCharms and Bridgeman found that productivity increased when subordinates worked under a leader who "complied with their requests"—that is, a leader who demonstrated a willingness to accept subordinate suggestions.[48] Participative decision making increases employee motivation, which, in turn, leads to both a higher level of employee effort and more frequent attempts at problem solving.

However, it is impossible to predict if participative decision making will be successful in every specific situation. It depends upon a number of situational factors, ranging from the personality of group members to the external constraints imposed by the total organization. Morse and Lorsch suggest that in the formal, controlled segments of the organization employees work best in a lightly structured environment, whereas participative approaches are likely to be more successful in less predictable situations.[49] It has also been argued that the power structure-leadership influence should match the requirements of the task. O'Brien states "it seems probable that 'power equalization' is appropriate for tasks which require a great deal of cooperation."[50]

In Fiedler's view, effective leadership grows out of situational factors, not the degree of member participation, and it is Vroom's conclusion that "the empirical evidence provides some, but not total support for beliefs in the efficacy of participative management."[51]

Leadership and Communication Networks

In Chapter 5, it was indicated that communication networks, that is, the arrangement (or pattern) of communication channels among members of a group, affect leadership. It would appear that individuals who occupy central positions in a communication network have a high probability of emerging as a leader.

The central position is located by a centrality index that was developed by Bavelas for communication networks.[53] Centrality is greatest in the wheel, and decreases with the Y, chain, and circle (see Figure 5-2). Shaw suggests that the "reasons for the centrality-leadership emergence relationship probably are availability of information and the related probability of coordinating group activities."[54] Changing the information that is available to individuals has the similar effect of changing the centrality of their position or the channels available to their position.[55] Group members with an informational advantage enter the discussion earlier, initiate more task-related communications, have their suggestions accepted more frequently, and are rated by others as contributing more to the group task.[56] Central Members, more than peripheral members of the communication network, try to change the opinion of those who disagree; however, if they fail, they tend to change more than peripheral members.[57]

Abrahamson found that in face-to-face situations, high-centrality members emerged as leaders only when no personal liability was present. It would appear that centrality is a critical dimension of leadership emergence as long as personality factors do not have an effect on the communication networks.[58]

Guetzkow found that three types of roles tend to emerge from five-person networks. A key man tended to receive information, formulate answers, and send answers. An endman sent his or her own missing information and received answers and a relayer passed on information and relayed answers. The wheel and all channel networks tended to consist of one key man and four endmen.

Some of the circle groups consisted of a key man, two relayers, and two endmen. However, two thirds of the circle groups examined had no organized structures or supporting roles. Keymen and relayers perceive the structure more accurately than endmen in all except the all-channel nets. They also transmit more messages proposing organization and nominate themselves more often for leadership roles.[59]

Cohen noted greater continuity of leadership in communication networks when individuals elected their own leaders.[60] When groups change their structure, for example, from the wheel to circle network, they tend to organize themselves in a more efficient chain system. Groups with elected leaders are retained much longer than those whose leaders are not elected. However, different leaders tend to emerge as individuals change from one communication network to another.[61]

Flexibility is the key to effective leadership. A manager must be able to use different styles and methods of management. A leader must be able to respond to a particular situation and know how to operate within it. As Tannenbaum and Schmidt observe:

> The successful leader is one who is keenly aware of those factors which are most relevant to his behavior at any given time. He accurately understands himself, the individuals and groups in which he operates, and certainly he is able to assess the present readiness of growth of his subordinates . . . the successful leader is the one who is able to behave appropriately in the light of these perceptions. If direction is in order, he is able to direct; if considerable participative freedom is called for, he is able to provide such freedom.[52]

In the previous sections we have examined personality variables, skills, motivational tools, styles, attitudes, and communication variables that contribute to effective leadership. We have introduced a multitude of ideas and concepts about the effectiveness and ineffectiveness of leadership in various situations. To place this material in a more manageable form, we now present our own model of leadership effectiveness. Remember that this is only a model, and does not indicate how to be an effective leader in every organizational situation. No model can be a complete guide.

Model of Leadership Effectiveness

This particular leadership model is designed to serve two basic functions: (1) communicative and (2) predictive. Because the leadership process is so complex and ever changing, we cannot adequately delineate its total process. The model, by fixing the process, provides a framework that allows us to isolate important elements and describe their role (communicative function). Within the framework, we also are interested in the daily leadership strategies. For example, we might want to know: How can I motivate my subordinates to increase

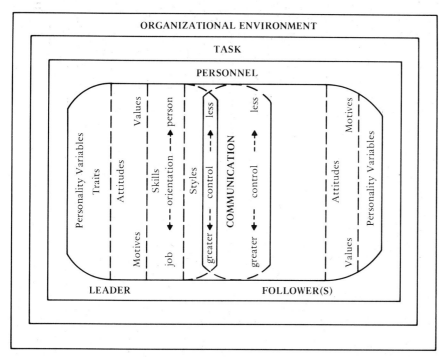

Figure 9-7 Model of Leadership Effectiveness

productivity without the use of financial rewards? Here, we would be interested in predicting what will happen so that we can make effective leadership decisions. The model will allow us to make educated guesses about the important leadership variables and how they will operate in the organization (predictive function).

As illustrated in Figure 9-7, our model of leadership effectiveness has three fundamental *external* components: the organizational environment or setting, the task, and the personnel. Each component is identified as a separate element; however, in a real situation they would overlap. Every situation forms a pattern that governs the effectiveness of the leader. Surrounding objects, the organizational climate, and the architecture all influence leadership; so, too, does the size of the room, the shape of the conference table, or the positioning of desks in an office. For example, if an organizational group without a designated leader were seated around a rectangular table, the employee seated at the head of the table would automatically be occupying a position conducive to assuming the leadership role. Another situation that is not uncommon is the sudden appointment of managers or supervisors to leadership positions. The new leaders might then find themselves unable to exert effective influence over their employees, because the latter do not want to be controlled or guided toward task achievement by someone who is designated to lead by some external authority.

The task, or purpose, of the organization is also a major influence upon leadership selection and effectiveness. For instance, a group may meet to learn of a new company hiring policy. The leader probably will be the employee who possesses a clear understanding of the company policy and is able to communicate that information to other employees. The leader must be able to meet the needs and demands of the employees. If he or she cannot provide the roles, functions, or capabilities that are necessary to facilitate accomplishment of the task, the leader's overall effectiveness will be diminished and leadership roles may be transferred to others in the organizational setting.

The third external component is personnel. Leadership and the personnel of an organization interact to provide the bases for effective or ineffective leadership. The personnel must be willing to assume leader and follower roles in order to be led effectively. Consider a company in which the lower managerial levels consist of "yes" men who are extremely eager to follow directives from higher-level management but are quite reticent to assume the leadership roles and functions necessary to supervise the employees. Such a company may be an organization with effective higher-level leadership (manager-foreman) but ineffective lower-level leadership (foreman–line-worker).

The internal core of our model consists of leader and follower(s). We look at leadership in terms of the leader's personal characteristics, behaviors, and capability as a communicator. However, leadership involves not only the overt display of certain kinds of behavior, but also the perceptions and expectations of those who are to be led (followers).

The leader component of our model consists of five basic elements: personality traits, attitudinal structures, skills, behavior styles, and communication. These elements interact to provide a basis for effective leadership and cannot be considered separate variables. Although we cannot isolate a single trait or cluster of traits for predicting successful leadership, followers may have certain perceptions about the traits a leader must possess in specific situations. For example, a manager who in the past demonstrated excellent judgment and persistence when solving a company problem may emerge as a leader because he or she can be most helpful to followers in solving new organizational problems. Effective emergent leadership appears related to the qualities of sensitivity, flexibility, and responsibility. An effective leader must be sensitive to the needs and demands of followers; must be able to change behavior to meet these needs and demands; and must show the initiative in assuming responsibility for moving followers toward their ultimate goal. The leadership traits that may provide for leader sensitivity, flexibility, and responsibility may vary from one activity to another.

Leaders' attitudes, values, and motives will all influence their behavior with followers and their effectiveness in modifying the attitudes and behaviors of the followers. A manager who believes that rigid controls over employees are necessary may be quite effective if the employees also believe that controls are necessary for accomplishing their specific task. However, if the employees believe that they should be able to mold and modify their own jobs and exercise control over their own behavior, they may react negatively to the manager's attempts at control. This would decrease the manager's effectiveness with the employees. The more consistent the leader's values, attitudes, and motives are with the follower's expectations, the more effective the leader will be.

As was suggested earlier in the chapter, technical, conceptual, and human skills all play a role in effective leadership. A leader must possess all three skills, but the specific task in which he or she is involved will dictate the skills that are needed most. In all organizational situations, however, the leader's skill in handling human relationships is crucial. For example, a manager who must work with a group of employees to increase productivity, must develop a cohesive work unit among subordinates. This requires the ability to empathize with employee problems and to resolve conflicts without alienating a section of the work force. The effective leader will master the skills necessary for the accomplishment of the organizational goal.

Leadership styles will play a dominant role in leadership effectiveness. They may correspond to the attitudes, values, and motives held by the leader, or a particular task may force a leader to use a specific style of leadership that is not otherwise consistent with his or her beliefs. The behavior of followers, communication patterns, or traits of followers also may influence a particular leadership style.

We might place the different leadership styles on a continuum of follower-behavior control. For example, the authoritarian, supervisory, or job-centered styles exercise more rigid controls over follower behaviors. On the other hand, laissez-faire leadership exercises little or no control over follower behavior. The democratic or participatory styles, although exercising a degree of control over member behavior, do permit followers to play a role in modifying their behavior and decision making. No one style of leadership will guarantee effective leadership. The effectiveness of leadership styles is ultimately determined by the situation, task, personnel, and choice of style that will enhance the accomplishment of the leader-followers' objectives.

Communication is the glue that fastens the relationship between leader and follower. The messages transmitted between them provide the vehicle for presenting the styles, attitudes, values, motives, skills, and personality variables that are possessed or demonstrated by the leader. The communication between leader-follower can be depicted on the same continuum of control. Autocratic leaders will tend to control the flow of communication between themselves and followers, whereas laissez-faire leaders will not. Will a leader be more effective when he or she has greater control over communication? This question cannot be answered in a straightforward manner. Each leader occupies a specific role in order to fulfill a specific function. If a group of employees try to solve a new problem and have little information or past experience in that area, the effective leader will exercise greater control over communication. A group of advertising copywriters, on the other hand, trying to develop a new product slogan, will be permitted greater freedom of expression by the leader. Good use of communication is determined by the situation, task, personnel, and the interrelationship of these components.

In sum, effective leadership is a situational phenomenon. The manner in which effective leadership is performed varies considerably between individuals and within organizations. The effective leader will analyze the setting, task, and personnel, and behave in a manner that will accomplish the objectives of both leader and followers.

REVIEW QUESTIONS

1. What factors can a manager utilize to motivate employees?
2. What basic managerial skills are needed to produce attitude and behavior change?
3. What are the three basic leadership styles and how do they influence leader-follower communication?
4. What qualities of good communication characterize effective organizational leadership?
5. How does centrality in a communication network influence one's potential for group leadership?

KEY TERMS AND CONCEPTS FOR REVIEW

- Leadership Traits
- Human Skill
- Conceptual Skill
- Technical Skill
- Communication-minded
- Centrality

- Social Distance
- Authoritarian
- Democratic
- Laissez-faire
- Reciprocity of Influence

CASE STUDY

Dean Exports is a large international import-export firm located in Florida. The operating board is composed of five division managers representing sales, accounting, public relations, national operations, and international operations. The board meets quarterly to set company policy and to examine existing company practices.

The last two meetings of the board have been nonproductive. Because each member is a manager of a large section of the firm, no one member wants to appear dominant in this forum. Consequently, the meetings can be characterized as mutual admiration sessions with each manager complimenting the other managers' work in the firm.

Unfortunately, the firm's most recent accounting ledger indicates a drop in profits from 10 to 5 percent over the last six months. A special meeting is called to develop methods to increase company profits for the remainder of the fiscal year.

PROBES

1. What leadership skills and styles will be needed at this meeting for the board to be successful?
2. Who do you believe will emerge as the leader of the board? Why?

Recommended Readings

Fiedler, F. *A Theory of Leadership Effectiveness*. New York: McGraw-Hill Book Company, 1967.

Geir, J. "A Trait Apprach to the Study of Leadership." *Journal of Communication* 17(1967): 316–323.

Reddin, W. *Managerial Effectiveness*. New York: McGraw-Hill Book Company, 1970.

Sargent, J. and G. Miller. "Some Differences in Certain Communication Behaviors of Autocractic and Democratic Leaders." *Journal of Communication* 21(1971): 233–252.

Stogdill, R. M. *Handbook of Leadership*. New York: The Free Press, 1974.

Tannenbaum, R., I. Weschler, and F. Massarik. *Leadership and Organization*. New York: McGraw-Hill Book Company, 1961.

Notes

1. E. A. Fleishman, "Leadership Climate, Human Relations Training and Supervisory Behavior," *Personnel Psychology* 6 (1953): 205–222.
2. D. G. Bowers, "Self-Esteem and the Diffusion of Leadership Style," *Journal of Applied Psychology* 47 (1963): 135–140.
3. F. S. Haiman, *Group Leadership and Democratic Action* (Boston: Houghton Mifflin, 1951).
4. D. Katz and R. L. Kahn, *The Social Psychology of Organizations* (New York: John Wiley & Sons, 1966).
5. M. Smith, "Control Interaction," *Journal of Social Psychology* 28 (1948): 263–273.
6. B. M. Bass, *Leadership, Psychology, and Organizational Behavior* (New York: Harper & Row, 1960).
7. P. Pigors, *Leadership or Domination* (Boston: Houghton Mifflin, 1935).
8. R. M. Stogdill, "Personal Factors Associated with Leadership," *Journal of Psychology* 25 (1948): 35–71.
9. J. Geier, "A Trait Approach to the Study of Leadership in Small Groups," *Journal of Communication* 17 (1967): 316–323.
10. E. Jennings, "The Anatomy of Leadership," *Management of Personnel Quarterly* 1 (1961): 2.
11. R. L. Applbaum, K. Anatol, K. Sereno, and E. Bodaken, *The Process of Group Communication* (Palo Alto, Calif.: Science Research Associates, 1974), p. 222.
12. F. Fiedler, "The Leader's Psychological and Group Effectiveness." In D. Cartwright and A. Zander, eds. *Group Dynamics*, 2d ed. (New York: Harper & Row, 1960).
13. Applbaum, op. cit., 224–225.
14. L. Picard, "The Effects of Personality Determinants on the Relation Between Job Content, Satisfaction and Absenteeism." Ph. D. dissertation (Boston: Harvard Business School, 1964), 6–15.
15. J. G. Longenecker, *Principles of Management and Organizational Behavior*, 2d ed. (Columbus, Ohio: Charles E. Merrill, 1969), p. 477.
16. G. Strauss and L. R. Sayles, *Personnel: The Human Problems of Management*, 3d ed. (Englewood Cliffs, N.J.: Prentice-Hall, 1967), p. 131.

17. W. F. Whyte, and M. Dalton, *Money and Motivation* (New York: Harper & Row, 1955), chap. 14.
18. Ibid., p. 23.
19. Straus, op. cit., p. 138.
20. Longenecker, op. cit., p. 482.
21. R. Katz, "Skills of an Effective Administrator," *Harvard Business Review* 33 (1955): 33–42.
22. R. White and R. Lippitt, *Autocracy and Democracy* (New York: Harper & Row, 1960).
23. Longenecker, op. cit., pp. 465–466.
24. L. Lippitt and R. White, "An Experimental Study of Leadership and Group Life." In G. E. Swanson, T. Newcomb, and E. Tartley, eds., *Readings in Social Psychology*, rev. ed. (New York: Holt, Rinehart and Winston, 1952), pp. 340–355.
25. M. E. Shaw, *Group Dynamics* (New York: McGraw-Hill Book Company, 1971), p. 274.
26. D. Gouran, "Conceptual and Methodological Approaches to the Study of Leadership," *Central States Speech Journal* 21 (1970): 217–233.
27. A. P. Hare, "Small Group Discussions with Participatory and Supervisory Leadership," *Journal of Abnormal and Social Psychology* 48 (1953): 273–275.
28. A. C. Filley, R. J. House, and S. Kerr, *Managerial Process and Organizational Behavior* (Glenview, Ill.: Scott, Foresman and Co., 1969), pp. 404–405.
29. R. Likert, *New Patterns of Management* (New York: McGraw-Hill Book Company, 1961), chap. 2.
30. S. W. Gellerman, *The Management of Human Relations* (New York: Holt, Rinehart and Winston, 1966), pp. 34-38.
31. A. L. Comrey, J. M. Pfiffner, and H. Beem, *Factors Influencing Organizational Effectiveness* (Los Angeles, Calif.: USC Bookstore, 1954): R. M. Stogdill and A. E. Coons, *Leader Behavior: Its Description and Measurement* (Columbus, Ohio: Bureau of Business Research, Ohio State University, 1957); D. Katz, N. Macobys, and N. Mourse, *Productivity, Supervision and Morale in an Office Situation* (Ann Arbor, Mich.: Survey Research Center, University of Michigan, 1950).
32. L. A. Klos, "Measure Your Leadership with the Managerial Grid," *Supervisory Management* 19 (1974): 10–47.
33. Ibid.
34. R. Blake, J. Mouton, L. B. Barnes, and L. E. Greiner, "Breakthrough in Organization Development," *Harvard Business Review* 42 (1964): 133–155.
35. E. A. Fleishman, *Studies in Personnel and Industrial Psychology* (Homewood, Ill.: The Dorsey Press, 1961), p. 313.
36. R. E. Miles, L. W. Porter, and J. A. Craft, "Leadership Attitudes among Public Health Officers," *American Journal of Public Health* 56 (1966): 1990–2005.
37. Redding, op. cit., p. 438.
38. "Influence: A Key to Effective Leadership in the First-Line Supervisor," *Personnel* 29 (1952): 209–217.
39. C. R. Walker and R. H. Guest, *The Man on the Assembly Line* (Cambridge, Mass.: Harvard University Press, 1952).
40. B. P. Indik, B. S. Georgapoulos, and S. E. Seashore, "Super-Subordinate Relationships and Performers," *Personnel Psychology* 14 (1961): 371.
41. Redding, op. cit., p. 443.
42. J. A. Lee, "Keeping Informed: Behavioral Theory vs. Reality," *Harvard Business Review* 49 (1971): 21.
43. Katz, op. cit., p. 381.

44. R. Stagner, "Corporate Decision-Making," *Journal of Applied Psychology* 53 (1969): 12.

45. L. E. Greiner, "Patterns of Organization Change," *Harvard Business Review* 45 (1967): 119–130.

46. M. Haire, *Psychology of Management*, 2d ed. (New York: McGraw-Hill Book Company, 1964), p. 202.

47. F. B. Chaney, "Employee Participation in Manufacturing Job Design," *Human Factors* 11 (1969): 104.

48. R. DeCharms and W. Bridgeman, "Leadership Compliance and Group Behavior," Technical Report 9, Contract No. 816 (11) (St. Louis, Mo.: Washington University, 1961); report in Redding, op. cit., p. 181.

49. J. J. Morse and J. W. Lorsch, "Beyond Theory Y," *Harvard Business Review* 40 (1970): 61–68.

50. G. E. O'Brien, "Leadership in Organizational Settings," *Journal of Applied Psychology* 5 (1969): 58.

51. V. Vroom, "Industrial Social Psychology." In G. Lindsey and E. Aronson, eds., *Handbook of Social Psychology*, 2d ed. (Reading, Mass.: Addison-Wesley, 1968) vol. 5, p. 228.

52. A. R. Tannenbaum and W. H. Schmidt, "How to Choose a Leadership Pattern," *Harvard Business Review* 36 (1958): 101.

53. A. Bavelas, "Communication Patterns in Task-Oriented Groups," *Journal Acoustical Society of America* 22 (1950): 725–730.

54. M. Shaw, *Group Dynamics*, 2d ed. (New York: McGraw-Hill Book Company, 1976), p. 140.

55. M. Shaw, "Some Effects of Unequal Distribution of Information Upon Group Performance in Various Communication Nets," *Journal of Abnormal and Social Psychology* 49 (1954): 547–553.

56. M. Shaw, "Some Effects of Arrangements of Information Exclusively Possessed by a Group Member Upon His Behavior in the Group," *Journal of General Psychology* 68 (1963): 71–78.

57. M. Shaw, G. Rothschild, and J. Strickland, "Decision Processes in Communication Nets," *Journal of Abnormal and Social Psychology* 54 (1957): 323–330.

58. M. Abrahamson, "Position, Personality and Leadership," *Psychological Record* 19 (1969): 113–122.

59. H. Guetzkow, "Differentiation of Roles in Task-Oriented Groups." In D. Cartwright and A. Zander, *Group Dynamics* (New York: Harper & Row, 1960).

60. A. M. Cohen, "Changing Small Group Communication Network," *Administrative Science Quarterly* 6 (1962): 443–462.

61. A. M. Cohen and W. G. Bennis, "Continuity of Leadership in Communication Networks," *Human Relations* 14 (1961): 351–367.

PART FOUR

The Organizational Environment

10 | Small Group Communication

LEARNING OBJECTIVES

After reading this chapter, you should be able to
1. Describe the nature and characteristics of small groups.
2. Explain the systemic nature of groups in the organizational setting.
3. Describe and discuss the interaction between activities, sentiments, and interactions.
4. Describe and discuss the various motives that influence people to join groups.
5. Discuss the nature and characteristics of member roles in small groups.
6. Explain the various functional roles.
7. Explain the various group maintenance roles.
8. Explain the various personal roles.
9. Discuss the impact of size, cohesiveness, and norms on group performance.
10. Discuss the sources and effects of group cohesiveness.

When the first front-wheel drive X-car recently rolled off the assembly line in General Motors' huge new assembly plant in Oklahoma City, not a single union member of the United Auto Workers (UAW) was present. General Motors (GM) would like it to remain that way. The UAW, on the other hand, is making an all-out effort to organize the 2,000 Oklahoma GM workers. Thus far, GM appears to be winning; the UAW is finding it very difficult to get the GM workers to unionize.

GM has done its best to make it hard for the union to win over the workers. Designers decorated the interior of the Oklahoma City plant in cheery colors, and company officials worked out a wage and benefits package that they claim is comparable to what is offered at GM's unionized plants elsewhere.

According to observers, GM's ace in the hole is its *group* concept. Each employee at the Oklahoma City plant is assigned to a group or team that meets regularly to discuss and vote on such issues as work assignments and overtime allotments. Each group elects a leader who, in turn, reports to the area adviser, who is similar to a foreman. Union officials, however, are enraged. One union official snorted, "Group concept area advisers! You can call it anything you like—it still smells to high heaven. All they can really vote on is where to put their lunches and how many sheets of toilet paper they get in one pull."

This chapter deals with the impact of group formation on organizational communication. The presence or absence of well-knit groups does make a difference in the quality of organization life. The situation at the Oklahoma City GM plant provides ample evidence of what can happen when management takes the initiative in forming groups and instilling them with company-oriented ideas, goals, and values. What GM did was to capitalize on human tendencies or urges to affiliate. The company's ability to form groups that were resistant to the entreaties of the UAW has to be considered as a superb victory in union-management warfare.

Our ability to influence the formation of groups that will work in our behalf and to discourage the formation of those that will work against our behalf will depend on our understanding of (1) the nature of groups and their systemic characteristics, (2) the motives that underlie the formation of groups, (3) the roles that members of groups play or fulfill, and (4) the key factors that affect group performance. We now discuss what is involved in each of these four crucial areas.

The Nature of Groups

Like people everywhere, individuals in organizations are attracted to others and seek to associate, identify, and affiliate with them. We gain positive social reinforcement from enduring face-to-face relationships with a relatively small number of individuals whom we perceive to be similar to us in some respect. Such relationships are achieved through group membership. A *group* might be defined as a unit composed of three or more individuals who come into personal, meaningful, and purposeful contact with one another on a relatively continuous basis.[1] Within work organizations, a person might be a member of two or three groups.

According to Bradford and Mial, a fully functioning group manifests the following eight characteristics:

(1) It knows why it exists; (2) it has an environment in which its work can be accomplished; (3) it has its guidelines or procedures for making decisions; (4) it has established conditions under which each member can make his or her contribution; (5) it has achieved communication between its members; (6) its members have learned to receive and give help; (7) the members have learned to cope with internal conflict; and (8) the members have learned to diagnose the group's processes and improve its functioning.[2]

Deficiency or strength in one or more of these eight characteristics usually provides a rough index of the maturity—immaturity or effectiveness—ineffectiveness of the group.

Several models have been devised for describing and analyzing small groups in the organizational setting. One of the most widely used is Homans' systems model.[3] Homans' model is useful because it (1) explains why people behave as they do in groups; (2) provides a framework for diagnosing and trouble shooting group processes within the organization; and (3) shows us how people and activities are interlocked into various systems or interdependent relationships both inside and outside the organization. Let us see how the Homans model operates.

Homans' Systems Model

Every group represents a fusion of two systems: an internal system and an external system. These two systems operate interdependently and influence the unique characteristics of the group as a whole, and the characteristics of the behaviors of each member within the group.

Internal System   The internal system is formed and developed out of the external system. Once the internal system is established, it is likely to act upon the external system as well. The basic variables comprising the internal system are activities, interactions, and sentiments.

Activities refer to such chores as taking inventories, operating a band saw, typing a report, sorting nuts and bolts, and so on.

Interactions refer to the initiation of action and the subsequent reaction between two or more individuals. The nature or quality of interactions can be determined or defined through such questions as

1. With whom do the individuals have relationships?
2. How often do the members interact?
3. How long do they interact?
4. Who initiates the interaction?

Sentiments consist of a broad category of affective states or feelings that may include the anger, happiness, or sadness that each group member experiences about both the people and the objects with which the group deals. Sentiments may also include certain deep-seated values, such as concerns for equality, freedom, and courage.

Homan suggests that *activities, interactions,* and *sentiments* coexist in an interdependent relationship; a change in any one element or variable will cause changes in the others. For example, the individual who once enjoyed working with his five-member crew comes to "believe" that his or her colleagues are low-class, crude, conniving, and selfish. Such a circumstance would represent a change in sentiment, and would naturally lead to a change in the activities and interactions within the group. The individual may absent himself or herself from work as much as is tolerable, attempt to work in isolation, withhold necessary assistance, and so on. As soon as the other group members become aware of the change, they are also likely to change their sentiments and modify their activities and interactions with the disenchanted individual. It is this action-reaction cycle that gives the group its *systemic* quality.

A few of the relations between activities, interactions, and sentiments are described in the following statements:

The more frequently persons interact with one another, the stronger their sentiments of friendship for one another are likely to be.

Persons who feel sentiments of liking for one another will express those sentiments in activities over and above the activities of the external system.

Persons who interact with one another frequently are more like one another in their activities than they are like other persons with whom they interact less frequently.[4] The rank and status of particular group members also exert some impact on the quality, range, and quantity of activities, interactions, and sentiments prevailing in the small group. Homan suggests that:

- The higher the rank of a person within a group, the more nearly his or her activities conform to the norms of the group.
- The higher a person's social rank, the wider will be the range of his or her interactions.
- A person of higher social rank than another person originates interaction for the former more often than the latter originates interaction for him or her.
- The sentiments of the leaders of a group carry greater weight than those of the followers in establishing a social ranking.[5]

External System   The second major component of Homans' model is the external system. The internal system of the group is embedded in the *external* system surrounding it. The external system represents the "givens" or circumstances that existed in the organization prior to the formation of the group, and that are likely to continue after the disbanding of the group. The "givens" in the external system may include the values and expectations of the organization, communication climate, task requirements, organizational structure, structure of work areas, and so on.

The character of a group—its solidarity, cohesiveness, productivity, energy, and longevity—can be understood and predicted through the analysis of both the internal and external systems. For example, the type of technology involved in an organization is likely to have some influence on the degree of autonomy or freedom that members may enjoy in the group. Employees working at a custom furniture factory would have greater potential for the formation of highly autonomous groups than would employees working on an automobile assembly line. The general principle is that groups functioning within a unit—or small-batch technology (e.g., custom furniture manufacturer) have more opportunities for the formation of highly autonomous groups than groups working in mass-production technology (e.g., automobile assembly plants).[6] One reasonable explanation seems to be that workers in mass-production technology are usually busier and consequently have less time for on-the-job, informal restructuring than those who work in small-batch technology. Another explanation could be that the small-batch technology allows the workers considerable control over the allocation of certain tasks among themselves such as self-selection of members, or election of a leader after initial requirements imposed by management (external system) have been met.[7]

Homans' view of the group as a component within a system—the resultant of forces in the external system coacting with variables in the internal system—tells us something about how or why groups in different settings acquire their unique characteristics. The model, however, does not deal with the question of the motives of the people who constitute the membership of the various groups. *Why do people join groups? Why does a given individual join a particular group?* Answers to these questions should give us some tools for improving organizational communication.

Motives for Joining Groups

People who have no opportunity for social contact at work tend to find their work unsatisfying. This dissatisfaction may lead to low productivity, high turnover, and absenteeism. In a textile plant, employees who worked in isolated jobs were highly dissatisfied and frequently failed to meet production standards. When the company permitted the workers to take rest periods as a group, production and satisfaction increased. Several studies have been conducted in order to discover why group activity is satisfying to the individual worker. The consensus is that membership in groups satisfies several needs, the foremost among them being the needs for *affiliation, security, self-esteem, power* or *autonomy, identity,* and *accomplishment* or *self-actualization.* You will recall the discussion in Chapter 7 of the impact of these needs on personality. We now discuss the relevance of these needs to the question of group formation.

Affiliation   People join groups because they enjoy the regular company of other people, especially those with whom they share something in common.

The experiences of these people with others indicate that they are likely to obtain friendship, friendly interaction, and acceptance by others if they are "in" with some groups. Employees in the organization are as reinforced by such things as they are outside of work. People who work long hours every day may have little opportunity for social interaction off the job. Their requirements for affiliation must be satisfied on the job, or it will not be satisfied at all.

Security   The need for security is perhaps the strongest need that we experience. This need becomes particularly acute as organizations grow in complexity. An individual who joins a large impersonal organization may experience anxiety because he or she feels that he or she must surrender a considerable amount of control over his or her behavior, and is uncertain of how the organization works and of how he or she fits into its general scheme. The insecurity created by such situations can be alleviated through group membership. Joining a group whose members have already experienced and survived the initial discomforts of organizational life is an effective means of reducing anxiety. The group can assist in solving specific problems and in protecting the individual from his or her mistakes. A new shipping clerk may not be sure how to deal with a complicated problem of returned merchandise, and a lab technician may be reluctant about asking his or her supervisor to repeat instructions and yet may need clarification in order to avoid ruining a crucial test. In each case, the employee is likely to turn to co-workers for assistance because, for most employees, this is the preferred source of help. As Peter Blau points out, new and inexperienced employees consistently prefer to get assistance from their fellow employees rather than from their managers. Moreover, fellow employees are likely to encourage the information seeking because so much prestige is gained thereby.[8]

Esteem   Self-esteem can be increased through group membership. One can gain a boost in one's self-esteem by becoming a member of a high-status group. It is both extrinsically and intrinsically rewarding to be perceived as belonging to the "in" crowd. We usually find much reinforcement from association with high-status or prestigious people.

     The close relationships that we develop through being in the group provide us with opportunities for recognition and praise that are not available outside the group. There is the opportunity for greater visibility in the small group, and an increase in self-esteem appears to be a function of that visibility. We usually receive positive reinforcement whenever we express opinions and views that are similar to those held by the group. The group provides us with an atmosphere in which we feel secure in the expression of ideas—we may gripe and complain about the job, the pay, the boss without fear of censure, contradiction, or reprisal.

Power   According to the common maxim, "There is strength in numbers." In our society, it appears that the individual upon joining a group is able to acquire more benefits or considerations than he or she would when trying to achieve them on his or her own. Student groups, organized as a means of gaining and exercising some control over their fate in the college environment, have been very successful in changing curricula, academic regulations, and the like. Although the value of some of the changes may be challenged, the key point to consider is that students, through group membership, were able to influence more change in a decade than was seen in the fifty previous years. In organizations, similar advantages of power and influence are derived from unionization. Collectively, workers enjoy much greater power than they do as individuals. A union is usually characterized as a formal group, but even in informal groups, an individual is inclined to be secure in the notion that the group will protect him or her from being crushed by the surrounding bureaucracy, and will be his or her advocate in a crisis.

Group membership also provides us with the opportunity to exercise power over others. The chances of becoming a leader in one or several of the small groups to which we belong are greater than our chances of becoming a leader in the larger organization. The advantage in the small group situation is that such a leader can avoid the responsibilities that usually go with formal positions of power.

Identity   Most of the information that we receive concerning ourselves comes from those around us. We do not see ourselves directly, but only as reflected in the actions and reactions of those with whom we interact. We "know" that we are funny if people laugh at our jokes; we "know" that we are important if people always appear willing to listen to what we say. The answer to the question "Who am I?" will be supplied by the group.

As members of the group, we can get more information for two reasons. First, our experiences with other members give us confidence in interpreting their reactions—we generally know when they are "leveling" with us. Second, the group members' experience and familiarity with us gives them a better basis for evaluating our personality and behavior.

Accomplishment   Most individuals realize that tasks are made easier through cooperative effort, and that it may take more than one person to accomplish a particular task. So, they join groups. Several people may form a group to share knowledge about a common problem. They may need to pool their abilities, tools, contacts, or power to accomplish an objective. Our confidence in relying on group interaction to improve the chances for accomplishment appears to be supported by findings that:

1. Group interaction provides for a greater sum total of knowledge and information—i.e., groups know more than individuals.
2. Group interaction provides for a greater number of approaches to a problem through the sharing of insights.

We see, then, that group membership offers a pathway to the satisfaction of our needs for affiliation, security, self-esteem, power, identity, and accomplishment. Since a satisfied employee tends to be a productive employee, management may find it worthwhile to provide leeway for small groups to emerge spontaneously rather than to outlaw them. Although some groups can be disruptive, experience shows that most groups do facilitate the achievement of organizational goals.[8] The impact of small groups on the overall character of the organization may be largely determined by the types of general and specific roles that are "played out" by people in those groups.

Members' Roles in Small Groups

After membership has been acquired and the group has stabilized as a functioning entity, individuals tend to adopt various roles. The two main categories are *functional roles* and *personal roles*.

Functional Roles

Functional roles are those generalized, nonpersonal roles that are assumed by one or more individuals with the intent to enhance task performance and group maintenance. *Task roles* are geared toward the completion of assigned tasks whereas *maintenance roles* are geared toward the satisfaction of the social-emotional needs of group members. Those who fulfill task roles gain satisfaction as productivity increases; those who fulfill maintenance roles gain satisfaction as collegiality increases. Both roles are essential to the maturity of the group. Goldhaber points out that "groups which fail to take into account the social emotional needs of its members often find that these needs subtly complicate task interactions."[9]

Benne and Sheats [10] provide a useful description of a few behaviors that are typical of *task roles* and *maintenance roles*. These include

Group Task Roles

- Initiator: defines problem, contributes ideas and suggestions, proposes solutions or decisions, offers new ideas.
- Information Seeker: asks for clarification, promotes participation by others, solicits facts and evidence.
- Energizer: prods members to action.
- Orienter: keeps group on track, guides discussion.
- Secretary: keeps track of group progress, remembers past actions.

Group Maintenance Roles

- Encourager: provides support, praise, acceptance for others.
- Harmonizer: resolves conflict, reduces tension.
- Comedian: provides humor, relaxes others.
- Gatekeeper: controls communication channels, promotes evenness of participation.
- Follower: accepts ideas of others, goes along with group movement.

In addition to the functional roles that facilitate group productivity and group maintenance, certain roles are unique to the individual. We refer to these roles as *personal* or idiosyncratic roles.

Personal Roles

Figure 10.1 represents a framework in which personal or idiosyncratic roles may be described. One aspect of personal roles involves the degree of commitment to tasks that are assigned to the group (task-relevant behavior); the other aspect involves the degree of commitment to the feelings and well-being of the other members of the group (socially relevant behavior). By dichotomizing and cross-classifying the task-relevant behaviors and the socially relevant behaviors, we are able to describe the general characteristics of five personal or idiosyncratic roles. The five *personal* roles are team players, task compulsives, conciliators, misfits, and average participants.

Team players are those who, in the estimation of other group members, rate highly on socially relevant and task-relevant behaviors. They are generally the most active and dedicated of all the people in the group, and are open, honest, and accommodating in their involvements. Their ability to be calm, cool, methodical, and resourceful even in crises is impressive. Team players are skillful at dealing with others on a personal level, and are usually instrumental in fostering supportive communication climates. Though outstanding, they are not pushy or condescending. Unlike most group members, team players are able to achieve balance between the task-relevant and socially relevant endeavors of organizational life.

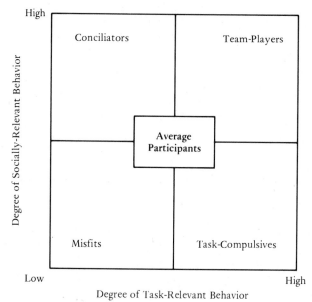

Figure 10.1 Roles of Individuals in Groups

Task compulsives are the "workaholics" of the small group; they appear to be always "under pressure." They have very little patience for attending to social problems, and prefer to avoid personal involvement. Task compulsives are interested in group membership largely because of the support that the group affords for the satisfaction of security needs and accomplishment needs. They are relatively withdrawn, quiet, and nontalkative, except when called upon to discuss a particular task, when they will elaborate at length. About one such task compulsive, other members were heard to remark often: "Gomer is not much for socializing, but ask him about the job and you couldn't get him to shut up!"

Conciliators are those who are adept at nurturing the group and holding it together. They perform what are known as group-maintenance behaviors. As can be seen in Fig. 10–1, conciliators are highly attuned to the social needs of the group but exhibit relatively low concern for task accomplishment. Production is usually sacrificed or deemphasized in favor of social relations and fellowship. A group comprised of conciliators would produce rather little. On the other hand, the presence of conciliators in addition to team players, task compulsives, and the like makes for a well-balanced group. Conciliators are most instrumental in heightening the group's potential for satisfying affiliation needs.

Misfits are those who join groups but remain uncommitted and disinterested concerning group activities. They are basically self-centered and are not the least bit interested in the group's welfare. Misfits generally interfere with the progress of the group by being consistently negative in their responses, and by attacking other members in an effort to promote their own status. They withdraw from discussion by refusing to participate, by engaging in irrelevant conversations, by daydreaming, and the like. All in all, misfits are disruptive; they create problems for those who are committed to promoting group goals.

Average participants share some of the characteristics of the other four types. Some average individuals are that way by temperament; others are that way by design or strategy. In either case, the behaviors of the average participants are strictly middle-of-the-road, and would seem to be characteristic of most individuals. Although "stars," conciliators, and even task compulsives may be called upon to lead the group, those who habitually hold to the *average* role are not usually appointed to leadership unless the group perceives it to be tactically sound to do so.

These findings concerning the five types of roles that are usually played out in groups—team players, task compulsives, conciliators, misfits, and average participants—have several implications for supervisors and managers. First, it is not likely that all individuals can or will play the identical role in groups. Second, the framework constitutes a useful diagnostic tool for trouble-shooting. We may discover, for example, that a group is "oversupplied" with misfits, task compulsives, or conciliators. That discovery, in itself, may provide a clue as to why the group might be counterproductive because *domination by any of these three roles invariably leads to ineffectiveness.* The idea is to find a group in which a preponderance of members are able to occupy team-player roles. In this case, the total group behavior would be attuned toward the drive for self-actualization. Such groups are propelled by what we call high productive momentum. Members are willing to work at top potential because such activity is intrinsically and extrinsically satisfying to them; they are "turned on" by achievement and they perceive themselves as being personally and professionally successful because of who they are and what they do. Third, managers and supervisors may use this framework to gain self-insight about their own behaviors in work groups.

The roles that members play in the small group constitute just one set of factors that influence the quality of interaction and group performance. Other factors such as group size, group cohesiveness, and group norms also influence the quality of interaction and character of the group, as well as group performance.

Factors Affecting Group Performance

The situation that was described in the General Motors versus the United Auto Workers standoff is a good indication of what can happen when managers of organizations understand the factors that affect group performance. The key factors are *size*, *cohesiveness*, and *group norms*. We discuss the impact of these factors in this section.

Group Size

The most visible aspect of a group's structure is the number of persons comprising its active membership. When a group increases or decreases in size, various properties or aspects of the group change. These changes can be so disruptive that group members are often concerned about how rapidly their group should grow, whether a group that has grown too large should be broken down into smaller units, and what effects changes in size will have upon the individual members and the group's productivity.

A considerable amount of research on the effects of a group size has been conducted, and excellent reviews of the research have been provided by Willens,[11] Porter and Lawler,[12] Indik,[13] and Thomas and Fink.[14] According to this research, a number of changes occur in groups and in their performance as they increase in size from three members up to twenty members. As group size increases beyond seven members, it becomes proportionately more difficult for the members to engage in interaction with all of the other members at one time. At that point, a smaller proportion of persons become central to the organization, makes decisions for it, and communicates to the total membership. Some of the results of studies point out that as group size increases:

1. Greater demands are made on the leader and the leader is more differentiated from the membership at large;

2. The group's tolerance of direction by the leader is greater and the proceedings are more centralized;

3. The active members dominate the interaction within the group to a greater degree;

4. The ordinary members inhibit their participation more, and hence the group's discussion is less exploratory and adventurous;

5. The group atmosphere is less intimate, the actions are more anonymous, and generally, the members as a whole are less satisfied;

6. It takes longer to get to nonverifiable (judgmental) decisions;

7. More subgroups form within the membership, and the rules and procedures of the group become more formalized.[15]

The implication is that a smaller proportion of group members keep in touch with one another as an organization grows; there are too many persons for complete communication to occur among them, and many members do not know one another. Complaints about poor communication are thus more often heard in larger groups than in smaller ones. Consensus or agreement is harder to develop; factions, cliques, or splits within the group are more likely to occur; and there tends to be less satisfaction with administrative decisions.

These findings suggest that managers can influence the character and quality of group performance by controlling group size. Hellreigel and Slocum[16] recommend that groups that are engaged in intensive problem-solving tasks be kept to a maximum of seven members. Keeping group size to about seven or fewer members may be a necessary condition, but it is certainly not a *sufficient* condition for establishing effective group problem solving. The manager might break a large group (twenty or more members) into smaller groups to facilitate the processing and analysis of task-related information by all members. The larger group might then be used by the manager to confirm one of the subgroups, or some combination of the subgroups' decisions. Furthermore, a manager who is leading a large group needs to recognize that there is likely to be several subgroups within it, each having its own informal leaders.

The large group structure may be efficient when the primary purpose of the group session is to begin to communicate or reinforce new policies, procedures, plans, and the like. With an adequate opportunity for questions from the members, the objective "to inform" may well be satisfied.

In sum, the manager's behavior will need to be substantially different in small-group than large-group sessions. With the latter, a more guiding and structured approach is usually desired and necessary.

Group Cohesiveness

One characteristic that has a great influence on the behaviors of group members is *cohesiveness*, which is defined as the extent to which group members are attracted to one another and to "the group" as a whole. Cohesiveness is also viewed as the result of the sum of the forces acting on the members to remain in the group. Group cohesiveness should be thought of as a relative quality, a matter of degree, rather than as an absolute attribute. The degree or amount of cohesiveness in a particular group is generally estimated through such characteristics as group pride, solidarity, loyalty, team spirit, and teamwork.

The success or effectiveness of a group is largely dependent on its cohesiveness or internal strength. Cohesiveness contributes to the stabilization of values and expected behaviors or norms. If these values or norms do not develop, group members may not be motivated to cooperate with one another.

Cohesiveness is both a cause and a consequence. As a *cause*, it may facilitate or frustrate the accomplishing of group goals. As a *consequence*, cohesiveness may be created or strengthened by the sharing of teamwork or concentrated effort.

Sources of Cohesiveness

Cohesiveness in groups can be affected by the following factors:

- Communication
- Isolation
- Group size
- Interpersonal attraction
- Threat or pressure
- Homogeneity
- Stability
- Status of the group
- Cooperation
- Severity of initiation

Let us examine the nature of the impact of each of these factors.

Communication　　For groups to form, people must be able to communicate with one another. Through communication, their similarities and common interests are developed, their values and standards are established, and joint action is initiated. Groups in which members can communicate easily with one another are more likely to be cohesive. Internal group unity can be thwarted in such areas as noisy mills, long assembly lines, or even quiet offices where "gossiping" is frowned upon and there is no privacy for conversation.[17]

Isolation　　Physical isolation from other groups tends to build cohesiveness. For example, the mining industry has demonstrated, in a number of lengthy strikes, that workers who are isolated from the larger community will stick together more stubbornly than those who are socially integrated with it. The difference between spirited, enthusiastic student associations on rural, isolated college campuses and the generally apathetic, "lowly involved" ones on urban campuses may also be attributed to the relationship between isolation and cohesiveness.

According to Webber,[18] even simple physical boundaries on a group may be essential for cohesion. He suggests that cohesion will be low if a group cannot identify its members and clearly differentiate itself from other groups. In long assembly lines, it is often difficult to identify and distinguish among the various groups. Some offices are so large and lacking in clearly defined boundaries—with several hundred clerical and supervisory personnel working together—that it is difficult for cohesive groups to emerge.

Group Size   The effects of group size on cohesiveness are fairly predictable. As group size increases, cohesiveness tends to decrease. This relationship is evident in the recently cited example of the large office building. As the number of people in a given unit increases, it is more difficult for a given member to interact with or to be aware of all the members. The more members, the more likely the differences in backgrounds and attitudes among the members.

As group size increases, it is also more difficult to get the group to agree on common goals and activities, and expressions of disagreement and dissatisfaction increase. Moreover, as group size increases, the need for tighter organization and division of labor also increases, and this places certain restrictions on intergroup communication and leads to a decrease in common activities. Perhaps the most significant effect of group size on cohesiveness is that, as group size increases, a group tends to break up into smaller groups and cliques. The fundamental principle is that small group size is conducive to cohesiveness; an overwhelming increase in size is generally detrimental to cohesiveness.

Interpersonal Attraction   Cohesiveness grows out of the attraction of the members for each other. Groups whose members have many opportunities to interact, groups with high status, groups whose members have similar backgrounds and similar attitudes, successful groups, and groups with successful members—all tend to have greater cohesiveness than groups without these characteristics.

Threat or Outside Pressure   Since people tend to "herd together" or affiliate under stress, frequent and continuous outside pressure from management may produce high cohesion. Under conditions of threat or outside pressure, horizontal and peer communications tend to increase, whereas vertical communications decrease. Common fate and mutual dependence quickly transform strangers into a strong group of people who are united in their desire to survive. Personal differences are minimized when threatened by a common danger—or a tough supervisor. Moreover, the cohesion may persist even though the threat ceases to exist. This phenomenon is exemplified in the activities and sentiments of a group of World War II veterans who served in the armored division of the U.S. Army. During the war, that division took a heavy, disastrous pounding from the German forces in the Battle of the Bulge. Today—almost four decades later—these veterans still publish a newsletter, meet frequently, hold annual conventions, and maintain friendships. The fact that the "men of the 11th" do not all belong to similar socioeconomic orientations has not really diminished the cohesion or group strength that was built during the stress of battle.

In the organization, a tough management policy or attitude toward employees or personnel may influence or encourage the formation of strong informal groups as a protective and retaliatory device. On the other hand, the sophisticated and "manipulative" manager who systematically promotes internal competition, transfers people, and prevents communication will hinder the development of group cohesion.

Homogeneity   In school, on the job, or at play, people of similar backgrounds, tastes, and aspirations tend to stick together. One of the most cohesive groups we observed was composed entirely of an ethnic group of Lithuanians at an automobile manufacturing plant. These workers held stable values, were more solicitous of each other's needs, lunched together in their own "little corner," fraternized off-the-job, controlled production rates, were unanimous in their demands, and were generally successful in getting both the union and management to respond to them.

Groups whose members have different interests and backgrounds are often less effective in promoting their interests. For example, student associations that are comprised of several cultural interest groups are seldom successful in presenting a unified appeal to university and college administrations. The same may be true for work groups comprised of people with wide disparities in pay, work groups containing both male and female members, groups comprised of faculty and staff, and so on. Such groups often foster conflicting cliques that hinder common action.

Stability   Organizations in which the employee turnover rate is high among all levels of employment seldom foster group cohesiveness. Stable membership contributes to higher cohesiveness as members get to know each other and learn the values and expectations of the group.

Status of the Group   People generally prefer to belong to and identify with high-status groups and are more likely to feel loyalty toward a high-status group than a low-status one. The characteristics that lead us to perceive a group as being high in status are quite similar to those that lead us to view some people as being of high status. These characteristics are special skills, influence in organization matters, preferential treatment in working conditions and location, control over functions and decisions, responsibility and autonomy, and opportunities for promotion into more desired functions and roles.

There is some question as to whether status itself is the cause of high cohesiveness. Some would argue that the high cohesion is attributed to *factors that confer status*—for example, seniority, autonomy, and self-supervision. However, most researchers agree that high-status groups tend to reflect higher cohesiveness.

Cooperation   Tasks that promote cooperation between workers can lead to increased cohesiveness. Working together in the pursuit of common goals exerts a unifying effect on members. Evidence even shows that the mere existence of clear, well-defined, and feasible goals can of itself lead to increases in group cohesiveness. In a study conducted by Raven and Rietsema,[19] the subjects were members of groups whose task was to produce and assemble toy houses. Some subjects were clearly informed as to the goal (assembly of houses) and the means to that goal. Other subjects were given only vague references to a goal and how it would be accomplished. Subjects who were given clear goals liked the task more, felt closer to the group, and showed greater concern for their own and the group's performance.

Severity of Initiation   The more difficult it is to gain admission to a group, the more cohesive the group becomes. The difficulty in gaining admission could be enforced in various ways. In some fraternities, for example, the initiation rituals are organized to be rather severe and long-lasting. Some social and athletic clubs insist upon elaborate screening procedures and high standards for membership.

Colleges and universities that require high grade point averages and test scores for admission, and companies that require excellent college grades, superior recommendations, and prior success for hiring, usually acquire a certain status and prestige that somehow rubs off on the students who attend these colleges and the employees of these companies. As a result, the attraction of the group, here the college or company, is increased. This same effect can be achieved by making the group members believe that they are uniquely qualified, specially chosen, and part of an elite.

Thus far, we have discussed ten factors that contribute to group cohesiveness. These factors are communication, isolation, group size, interpersonal attraction, threat or pressure, homogeneity, stability, status, cooperation, and severity of initiation. Once the cohesiveness of a particular group begins to increase, certain effects are likely to be manifested. We now explore the nature of these effects in the next section.

Effects of Cohesiveness

Cohesiveness exerts a major impact on the behaviors of members in the group. The most important effect of cohesiveness on group members is observed in changes in *communication activities* and in *task performance*. We now discuss these changes separately.

Effects of Cohesiveness on Communication Activities

As group cohesiveness increases, there tends to be

1. An increase in members' willingness to initiate and receive communication.
2. An increase in the exchange of favorable evaluations.
3. An increase in the expression of hostility toward nonmembers or outsiders.
4. An increase in the pressure to conform to group standards and norms.

The following is a brief explanation of what is involved in the changes in these four areas of communication activities.

1. Increase in Communication   Communication has been found to be both a cause and a consequence of cohesiveness—i.e., the more group members communicate with one another, the more cohesive the group becomes, and the more cohesive the group becomes, the more the members communicate with one another. Members of cohesive groups communicate with one another more than do members of noncohesive groups. This communication provides positive social reinforcement, as members share information about their attitudes, goals, and intentions.

2. Increase in Favorable Evaluations   Members of cohesive groups usually perceive each other and their groups more favorably than do members of less cohesive groups. According to Yalom,[20] the increased communication characteristics of cohesive groups can be an important factor in the development of self-concept and self-esteem largely because so much information about one's self is communicated by others.

Unfortunately, there are instances when the positive evaluations about one's self, the group, and the task may be highly exaggerated. This exaggeration would eventually lead to perceptual distortions and to problems in the relationships between the groups that must coexist in the same organization.

3. Increase in Expression of Hostility   Members of cohesive groups tend to express more hostility than do members of less cohesive groups. This hostility is usually directed toward nonmembers, since cohesiveness increases a member's identification with his or her group and tends to produce discrimination toward nonmembers as outsiders. In an experimental study conducted by Dion, highly cohesive groups were more cooperative with fellow members than with nonmembers and they evaluated their fellow members more highly.[21]

4. Increase in Pressure to Conform   Cohesive groups are highly attractive to their members. Over a period of time, members of cohesive groups grow to like and appreciate one another and to perceive themselves as similar. That perception of similarity may be exaggerated; nevertheless, the perception is what really matters. The mutual attraction and perceptions of similarity eventually lead members to depend on the group for satisfaction. This dependency, in turn, leads members to become highly susceptible to influence.

As was pointed out earlier, a great deal of the communication in cohesive groups concerns the sharing of information about attitudes, goals, intentions, and so on. It is through this type of communication that the cohesive group is able to enforce conformity. Studies have shown that cohesive groups increase their communication toward a member who is deviating from commonly held values, attitudes, or norms in an attempt to bring the "deviant" back into line. If the deviant persists in his or her deviation, the group may lose its patience and cease its pursuit altogether. At times, this tactic is more effective in reducing

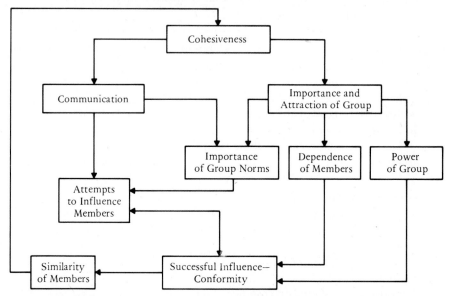

Figure 10-2 Relationships Between Cohesiveness and Conformity in a Group (From H. Joseph Reitz, *Behavior in Organizations* [Homewood, Ill: Richard D. Irwin, 1977], p. 331).

deviance than an increase in communication. The deviant may, in fact, be reinforced by being in the spotlight of attention, but may find rejection utterly punitive and undesirable.

Figure 10–2 shows how cohesiveness, communication, and conformity are related.

The model begins at the point at which cohesiveness increases the importance and attractiveness of the group for the members. This increases the dependence of the members on the group. The group's attraction gives it power over members; the members' dependence makes them more susceptible to group influence. Power, dependence, and communication increase the influence exerted by the group. The successful influence reinforces the members, increasing their attempts to influence each other. Successful influence reduces deviance, thereby increasing similarity. As similarity and communication increase, cohesiveness also increases.

Effects of Cohesiveness on Task Performance

Because highly cohesive groups consist of individuals who are motivated to be together, there is a tendency to expect effective group performance in all instances. Unfortunately, this outlook is not supported by research evidence. As the cohesiveness of a work group increases, the level of conformity to group norms also increases and these norms may sometimes be inconsistent with those of the organization. The group pressures to conform are more intense in the

		Congruency With Organizational Goals	
		Low	High
Degree of Group Cohesiveness	Low	Individualistic behavior. Low identification with the group, and low identification with organizational objectives. Low productivity.	Individualistic behavior. Relatively little dependency on the group. Relatively little pressure to conform. High productivity.
	High	Disruptive, group-oriented behavior. High identification with the group. Little regard for organizational goals and objectives. Low productivity.	Positive organization-oriented group behavior. High esprit de corps. High productivity.

Figure 10-3 The Relationship between Group Cohesiveness and Agreement with Organizational Goals and Group Performance

cohesive group. A member who attempts to defy the group jeopardizes his or her position and status in the cohesive unit.[22]

The importance of group cohesiveness was indicated in a study conducted by the Tavistock Institute in Great Britain.[23] The British coal mining industry had introduced many drastic changes in mining equipment and procedures. Before new technologies were installed, miners worked together as teams. The group of miners dug out the coal, loaded it into cars, and moved it to a station where it was taken from the mine. The task, physical proximity, and awareness of constant danger had welded the miners into a hard-working, cohesive unit.

The new technology upset and disrupted the groups of miners. Sophisticated equipment now performed a few of the tasks previously done by the miners and the miners were no longer required to work together in groups or teams. As a consequence, they lost many of their opportunities for on-the-job socializing. Without the support of the highly cohesive groups, and with the increase in physical distance between them, the miners began to slow down their production.

The concept of cohesiveness is important to an understanding of groups in organizations. The degree of cohesiveness in a group may exert positive or negative effects depending upon how congruent the group goals are with those of the formal organization. Figure 10-3, shows four possible effects.

Figure 10-3 indicates that if cohesiveness is high and if the group's goal or outlook is congruent with the organization's goals, the group's behavior will be positive as viewed from management's standpoint. There will be a relatively high level of esprit de corps, teamwork, and productivity. On the other hand, if the group is highly cohesive but harbors goals that are not congruent or consistent with those of the organization, the group's behavior will be perceived by management as being somewhat disruptive. Workers in a "union shop" tend to be "lumped together" in this category by management, in whose view "the employees want everything for themselves but they don't want to do anything for the company."

Figure 10-3 also indicates that if a group is low in cohesiveness and the members have goals that are not in agreement with those of management, the results will probably be negative from management's standpoint although the behavior will be more individualistic than group-oriented. We can also see the possible existence of a group that is low in cohesiveness in which the members' goals agree with those of the formal organization. In this case, the results will generally be positive yet more on an individual basis than on a group basis.[24]

Overall, the model depicted in Figure 10-3 implies that high-cohesive groups with high-productivity standards are generally the most productive, and high-cohesive groups with low-productivity standards are the least productive. It is reasonable to conclude that *cohesiveness alone does not determine productivity; it only increases the determination of the group to achieve its goals or standards*, which may or may not be congruent with those of the organization. What cohesiveness does affect is the variance of performance.

Managerial actions can have a significant impact on group cohesiveness. For example, a reward system based on group productivity may tend to facilitate cohesiveness, whereas one based on individual output may reduce it. Trouble begins to brew, however, if members view the individual reward system as a "divide and conquer" strategy. Distrust of management is the most likely consequence, and the cohesiveness of the group could well increase. Unfortunately for the management, the resultant cohesiveness would be utilized by the group to withstand management directives and to impose limits on individuals and group productivity.

Norms

Norms are ideals or standards that exist in the minds of group members. They are decisions or rules indicating what group members should do under specific circumstances. Individuals may hold norms independent of their membership in a group, as well as accept norms that have emerged as a result of the interaction between members and the situation in which they find themselves. Group norms exist when three criteria have been met.[25]

First, standards exist about appropriate behavior for individuals as group members. For example, a work group may share norms as to the amount of output that is appropriate. Second, there must be a relatively high degree of agreement among members concerning compliance with the norms. Third, the members need to be aware that the group not only supports the norms but is also willing and able to enforce adherence toward the norms. Norms are reinforced and supported by punishments following violations of the norms and rewards following compliance with them.

The group's ability to enforce norms is dependent, in part, upon the intensity of rewards and punishments and the probability that these will be forthcoming in the event of a violation of, or adherence to, the norms. For example, a member who values the group might still violate its norms if he or she believes that there is very little chance of being caught. The intensity variable reflects the meaning of the group to the individual. If the individual does not value the reward or punishment dispensed by the group, there may be very little motivation for this individual to adhere to the norms of the group. An example is the management-trainee who is assigned to work, for a short duration, as a regular assembly-line operator. The idea is that a manager should get to know every facet of the company's operation. The management-trainee may find the work group to be antagonistic toward management, and that a prevailing norm is to keep production at the minimum possible level. The trainee may well be able to reject the norm since he or she does not care about maintaining an enduring dependence on the work group. The work group may threaten, harass, and cajole the trainee to little or no avail.

If the individual in this case were a new assembly-line worker, rather than a management-trainee, would he or she have the similar option of exceeding the rate set by the group? That is not likely. Here the *intensity* factor of rewards and punishments really matters. In the face of threats, harassments, or curtailment of resources and materials needed for doing the job, the new employee would eventually conform.

In summary, norms are ideas about what people think behavior ought to be under specific circumstances. Within cohesive work groups, norms often specify the range of acceptable performance. Depending upon the group's attitude toward the organization and management, these norms may specify restrictions on the quality or quantity of output or may be neutral, if not supportive, about high output.

Groups constitute the very nerve center of an organization. They exist because of man's natural tendency to seek out similar others. Once groups are formed, they can become supportive or disruptive as far as organizational objectives are concerned. The direction that groups take therefore may be largely influenced by the creative, skillful, and knowledgeable manager, leader, or supervisor. With an understanding of the nature of groups, the motives that drive workers to join groups, the various roles that people play in groups, and the factors that affect group performance, we should be able to ensure that the groups that exist in the work place will help us in furthering the mission of our organizations.

REVIEW QUESTIONS

1. What are the characteristics of a fully functioning group?
2. What are the characteristics that give a group its systemic quality?
3. What is the relationship between activities, sentiments, and interaction in small group communication?

4. Why do people join groups? What are the various motives?
5. What are the two main types of functional roles, and name the kinds of behavior that are performed under each?
6. What are the five personal roles that are generally played by group members?
7. How does group size affect group performance?
8. How does cohesiveness affect group performance?
9. How do group norms affect group performance?
10. What are the sources of cohesiveness?
11. What are the effects of cohesiveness?
12. How does cohesiveness affect conformity?

KEY TERMS AND CONCEPTS FOR REVIEW

- Group
- Systems
- Activities
- Interactions
- Sentiments
- Internal System
- External System

- Functional Roles
- Group Maintenance Roles
- Personal Roles
- Size
- Cohesiveness
- Norms
- Conformity

CASE STUDY

Last year, Bubba Johnson was chosen to be the supervisor of a newly formed maintenance crew for the Snap Dragon Drill Company. This crew was formed to maintain what was called "highly sophisticated, expensive, and sensitive electronic equipment."

Bubba's crew was given the responsibility for minimizing the downtime and maintenance costs for the very expensive machinery. The crew was promised a bonus if the goal were achieved.

Bubba was an extremely capable "mechanic," and some members of the crew boasted that he was "the smartest troubleshooter at Snap Dragon, and perhaps in the whole country." They claimed that anyone who had to work with Bubba would "really have to know his stuff." In any event, management chose five other maintenance-technicians, and entrusted them to Bubba Johnson for training.

Each of the five technicians chosen was assigned to work with a specific type of equipment. Bubba worked to train them in the construction, operation, and maintenance of the equipment. The crew really seemed to enjoy its work with the machinery "that only a few people in the nation could repair." After eight months, the program had reduced downtime by 40 percent and cut maintenance costs by 25 percent.

Management was so pleased with the performance record that management gave the crew a free hand to shut down equipment for preventive maintenance any time they wished. The other employees generally cooperated with the crew, and thanked them for the "fantastic job" that they performed.

PROBES

1. What were some of the factors that might account for the high cohesiveness of Bubba's crew?
2. Explain how Homans' ideas about the relationship between activities, sentiments, and interactions appear to be at work in this group.
3. What are some of the factors in the external system that impinge upon the maintenance crew with positive effects?

Recommended Readings

Applbaum, R., E. Bodaken, K. Sereno, and K. Anatol. *The Process of Group Communication*. 2d Ed. Chicago, Ill.: Science Research Associates, 1979.

Baird, J. and S. Weinberg. *Communication: The Essence of Group Synergy*. Dubuque, Iowa: William C. Brown Company, 1977.

Cathcart, R. and L. Samovar. *Small Group Communication: A Reader*. Dubuque, Iowa: William C. Brown Company, 1974.

Zander, A. *Groups at Work*. San Francisco: Jossey-Bass, Publishers, 1977.

Notes

1. T. M. Mills, *The Sociology of Small Groups* (Englewood Cliffs, N. J.: Prentice-Hall, 1967), p.2.
2. L. P. Bradford and D. Mial, "When Is a Group?" *Educational Leadership* 21 (1963): 147–151.
3. G. C. Homans, *Social Behavior: Its Elementary Forms* (New York: Harcourt, Brace & Co., 1961).
4. G. C. Homans, *The Human Group* (New York: Harcourt, Brace & Co., 1950).
5. *Ibid.*, pp. 141, 145, 181.
6. G. I. Susman, "Automation, Alienation and Work-Group Autonomy," *Human Relations* 25(1972):171–180.
7. R. Mayo, *The Human Problems of an Industrial Civilization* (Boston: Graduate School of Business Administration, Harvard University, 1946).
8. P. Blau, "Patterns of Interactions Among a Group of Officials in a Government Agency," *Human Relations* 7 (1954): 337–348.
9. G. Goldhaber, *Organizational Communication*, 2nd Ed. (Dubuque, Iowa: William C. Brown Company 1979), p. 238.
10. K. Benne and P. Sheats, "Functional Roles of Group Members," *Journal of Social Issues* 4, no. 2 (1948): 41.

11. E. P. Willems, "Review of Research." In R. Barker and P. Gump, eds., *Big School, Small School* (Stanford, Calif.: Stanford University Press, 1964).

12. L. Porter and E. Lawler, "Properties of Organization Structure in Relation to Job Attitudes and Job Behavior," *Psychological Bulletin* 64, (1965):23–51.

13. B. Indik, "Some Effects of Organization Size on Member Attitudes and Behavior," *Human Relations* 16 (1963): 369–384.

14. E. Thomas and C. Fink, "Effects of Group Size," *Psychological Bulletin* 60 (1963): 371–384.

15. B. Berelson and G. Steiner, *Human Behavior: An Inventory of Scientific Findings* (New York: Harcourt, Brace and World, Inc., 1964), p. 358.

16. D. Hellriegel and J. W. Slocum, *Management: A Contingency Approach* (Reading, Mass.: Addison-Wesley Publishing Co., 1974), p. 377.

17. Robert Blauner found that the assembly line increases worker desire for informal groups while simultaneously restricting the chance of their actually developing. *Alienation and Freedom* (Chicago: University of Chicago Press, 1964). Also see M. Krain, "Communication as a Process of Dyadic Organization and Development," *The Journal of Communication* 23 (December 1973): 392–408.

18. R. Webber, *Management: Basic Elements of Managing Organizations* (Homewood, Ill.: Richard D. Irwin, 1979), p. 105.

19. B. H. Raven and Jan Rietsema, "The Effects of Varied Clarity of Group Goal and Group Path upon the Individual and His Relationship to His Group," *Human Relations* 10 (1957): 29–45.

20. I. D. Yalom, *The Theory and Practice of Group Psychotherapy* (New York: Basic Books, 1970), p. 38.

21. K. L. Dion, "Cohesivenes as a Determinant of Ingroup-Outgroup Bias," *Journal of Personality and Social Psychology* 28 (1973): 163–171.

22. A. J. Lott and B. E. Lott, "Group Cohesiveness as Interpersonal Attraction: A Review of Relationships with Antecedent and Consequent Variables," *Psychological Bulletin* 57 (October 1965): 259–309.

23. E. L. Trist and K. W. Bamforth, "Some Social and Psychological Consequences of the Longwall Method of Coal Getting," *Human Relations* 4 (February 1951): 3–38. For other important research on group cohesiveness see S. E. Seashore, *Group Cohesiveness in the Industrial Work Group* (Ann Arbor: University of Michigan, Institute for Social Research, 1954) and S. M. Klein, *Workers under Stress: The Impact of Work Pressure on Group Cohesion* (Lexington: The University of Kentucky Press, 1971).

24. The general idea for the figure came from J. L. Gibson, J. Ivancevich, and J. Donnelly, *Organizations: Behavior, Structure, Processes* (Dallas, Tex.: Business Publications, 1979), p. 149.

25. A. G. Athos and R. E. Coffey, *Behavior in Organizations: A Multidimensional View* (Englewood Cliffs, N.J.: Prentice-Hall, 1968), pp. 97–98.

11 | Decision Making: Process and Strategy

LEARNING OBJECTIVES

After reading this chapter, you should be able to
1. Describe the decision-making process, the elements that are involved, and the sequential pattern of steps that must be utilized in making both programmed and nonprogrammed decisions.
2. Explain and give examples of the Reactive Problem Identification Model, Pro-active Problem Identification Model, and Decision-Making Model.
3. Identify the major concepts and value of the Normative Model (Vroom-Yetton decision tree), and the PERT Model of administrative decision making.
4. Identify and analyze the many variables that affect the decision-making process, and their effect on organizational outcomes.

If any single task can be said to influence a manager's role, it is the responsibility for making decisions. For example, Simon suggests that "decision-making is synonymous with management."[1] The concept of "decision" implies making a selection from among available alternatives. A situation in which only one course of action is possible does not offer an opportunity for decision. In order for a valid decision to be made, the opportunity to choose between acting and not acting must exist.

According to Peter Drucker:

> A decision is a judgment. It is a choice between alternatives. It is rarely a choice between right and wrong. It is at best a choice between "almost right" and "probably wrong"—but much more often a choice between two courses of action neither of which is probably more nearly right than the other.[2]

The contemporary concept of management decision making goes beyond making a choice among alternatives, however. The decision-making process includes corporate functions that rely heavily on decisions, such as planning, goal setting, and task assignment, as well as functions that contribute to or flow from decisions, such as information gathering and evaluation, implementing, feedback, and the like.

It is customary and feasible to consider decision making under two or more headings, one dealing with the abstract process of decision making, and others with factors that influence, enhance, or limit the process. Although we touch upon a number of decision-making factors, we focus on two principle subjects in this chapter: the decision-making *process* and decision-making *strategy*.

The Decision-Making Process

The term *process* is generally used to denote a series of related operations that are collectively aimed at producing a particular effect. An individual who propels through water by a methodical cycle of body motions may be said to engage in the process of swimming. Depending on the prevailing conditions and skill, purpose, and inclination, the individual may employ one or a combination of styles, and perform efficiently or inefficiently. Regardless of these variables, the individual is still engaged in the general process of swimming as long as a series of purposeful operations are performed whose effect keeps that person afloat and moving in a selected direction.

Implicit in the term *process* is the assumption that the activity to which it is applied can be described as a cycle of operations subject to definition and analysis. Consequently, nearly all discussions of the *decision-making process* include a list of "steps" that should be followed in decision making. For instance:

1. Define and limit the problem
2. Analyze the problem

3. Establish criteria or standards by which solutions will be evaluated
4. Explore alternative solutions
5. Select the most effective solution
6. Implement the solution

In describing the elements of the decision-making process, Peter Drucker differentiates between problems that are unique (processed as exceptional cases) and those that are "generic" (processed according to principles applicable to all problems of the same nature). Drucker asserts that the "effective decision-maker always assumes initially that the problem is generic."[3] That is, you search for the "core of the real problem," assuming that it is *not* an exceptional case, but a situation that can be handled by the normal decision-making process.

Drucker's remaining elements suggest that you be specific about what you want to achieve; focusing on "what is right" rather than "what is acceptable"; activating the decision; and the development of a feedback system.[4]

A representative schematic model, without the implementation steps, reflects the same general progression:

1. Information input
2. Analysis
3. Performance measures
4. Model
5. Strategies
6. Prediction of outcomes
7. Choice criteria
8. Resolution[5]

Underlying each description is the assumption that decision making is a consistent process made up of rational operations, which can be analyzed and mastered.

Programmed and Nonprogrammed Decisions

Computer science has provided us with terminology and models for a number of insights into decision making, such as the simple but valuable distinction between *programmed* and *nonprogrammed* decisions. *Programmed decisions* means those sufficiently familiar and repetitious to be handled by routine procedures; *nonprogrammed decisions* are considered novel, complex, or otherwise puzzling enough to require the decision maker to break new ground.

The distinction between programmed and nonprogrammed decision making is obviously at extreme ends of the spectrum. A cashier who is required to add sales tax on each item rung up might calculate the tax on each item individually, memorize the tax increment for each price range, refer to a printed schedule, or punch a key commanding the register to calculate the tax automatically. But in any case the procedure, once established, is routine and unvarying. On the other hand, decisions involved in entering a new market area or acquiring a subsidiary would not normally be subject to routine, programmed procedures.

Most management decision making falls somewhere between the extremes, combining programmed and unprogrammed operations. One of the characteristics of an effective decision maker, in fact, appears to be the ability to distinguish between problems for which existing procedures are appropriate and those for which new ground must be broken. It is ineffective and inefficient to deal with an exceptional problem as though it were routine, or a generic problem as though it were an exceptional case.

The distinction between programmed and nonprogrammed decisions is not the same as the distinction Drucker draws between "generic" and "unique" problems.[6] Just as the exceptional or unique situation cannot be processed according to established procedures, neither can it in most cases serve as a model for future situations. An exceptional event is either an unrecognized generic event or a new type of event likely to occur in the future. A plant forced to close down temporarily because it was struck by a meteorite might justifiably be considered a unique disaster for which no routine procedure exists and for which none need be devised. If the disruption resulted from an unprecedented level of air pollution in the locality, the event might well be viewed as an emerging generic problem that probably will occur again. Generic problems, according to Drucker, can only be solved by a decision which "establishes a rule, a principle."[7]

Using this definition, all programmed decisions and all but the extremely rare exceptions among unprogrammed decisions deal with generic problems. As noted previously, programmed decisions are the familiar, simple ones that have been reduced to a routine; unprogrammed decisions deal with unfamiliar, complex, or infrequent problems for which it is impractical to establish standard procedures.

Although most individuals would probably find it difficult to explain exactly how they make a decision, it is possible to observe that effective decision makers do follow procedures. Because real-life processes fail to exhibit the neatness and balance implied by models, we may not perceive these procedures in everyday decision making. The models suggest a series of operations of equal importance performed from beginning to end. But in difficult decision-making situations the most noticeable activity is often an irritable threshing. This action may actually occur somewhere in the middle of the decision-making process, with the earlier steps being taken for granted. Some steps may be ignored altogether, whereas others are receiving disproportionate attention. Alternatives may be sharply defined or remain clouded and uncertain. The consequences of one course as against another can only be visualized imperfectly. Data may continue to trickle in right up to the moment of decision—and after. Irrelevant considerations and personal biases are likely to influence the outcome.

No matter how obscured or distorted decision making may be in practice, there is a necessary underlying order to the procedure by which a decision is made. This procedure consists of at least three parts:

1. Recognizing a desired objective
2. Considering the obstacles to achieving it
3. Selecting a way to overcome the obstacles

These are the procedures that the human mind appears to resort to automatically in problem-solving situations. It is reflected in psychological terms in the three types of thinking described by J. P. Guilford[8] as:

1. Cognition—recognition of information
2. Production—use of information or, in some cases, use to generate new information. Production may be divergent or convergent:
   a. Divergent Production—thinking that goes off in different directions during searching
   b. Convergent Production—thinking that focuses on achieving one right answer
3. Evaluation—determination of outcome, whether what was produced or conceptualized is suitable, correct, or adequate

Thus, the thousands of operations of which the human mind is capable (except for memory, which Guilford treats as a separate subject) can be categorized into four basic capabilities: ability to seize upon significant data, to make judgments, and to find relationships by searching either outward from a subject, or inward from related data to its organized principle.

Regardless of the variations in terminology and methods of subdividing the process, there is a consensus that the entire decision-making process requires performance of the operations described in the following sections.

The Decision-Making Approach

Problem Definition   Peter Drucker suggests that "the only people who have developed a systematic and standardized approach to decision-making are the Japanese."[9] He states that one of the distinguishing elements of the Japanese method is that they ". . . do not focus on giving an answer. They focus on defining the question."[10] An accurate definition of the problem at the beginning will save time, energy, and aggravation throughout the process. This is the time to ask all the questions to which the answers may seem self-evident. Is there really a problem? Is it a problem or a symptom? Whose problem is it? What would happen if nothing were done? What situation would have to be achieved for the problem to be solved? Are there any advantages to leaving things as they are? Will attempts to solve the problem create undesirable effects in other areas, and if so, how can these effects be limited?

In the initial stage it should be determined whether the problem is an isolated phenomenon or part of a pattern. If you discover a piece of electrical equipment that has begun to perform erratically, you may diagnose the problem as equipment failure. But if, on checking with other departments, you uncover an inordinate number of similar malfunctions throughout the plant, you will certainly want to investigate the possibility that you have an entirely different kind of problem, such as an unstable or overtaxed power supply.

Constructing Guidelines   In this stage the limits and requirements that will govern the process are established. How much time and money is the organization willing to commit to the solution of this particular problem? To what existing policies must the solution conform? What expectations must the solution satisfy in order to be considered successful? What criteria should be applied in choosing between solutions of equivalent promise?

Identifying Alternatives   This stage will be greatly simplified if the groundwork has been carefully laid in the preceding stages. One important alternative—that of doing nothing—should have been eliminated, tentatively at least, in the course of defining the problem. Although no promising alternative should be ignored, many possibilities will obviously rate no more than cursory consideration, and the guidelines set in the previous stage will undoubtedly eliminate many others that are in conflict with existing policy or exceed cost limitations.[11] If the work of these early stages is conscientiously done, the final list of acceptable alternatives will be relatively short and confined to practical solutions that merit serious consideration.

Evaluating Alternatives   In this stage, all pertinent and verifiable information relating to the various alternatives is reviewed. The significant alternatives are compared and contrasted. An attempt is made to project the probable effect of each alternative if it were put into effect.

March and Simon[12] propose that alternatives be evaluated in relationship to expected outcomes. They suggest the following typology:

1. A "good" alternative is one that is viable. It is better than expected and is likely to produce a positive outcome for the decision maker.
2. A "bland" alternative is one that is unlikely to produce either a positive or negative outcome.
3. A "mixed" alternative is one that has a high probability of producing both positively and negatively valued outcomes.
4. A "poor" alternative is one that is likely to produce a negative outcome.
5. An alternative is "uncertain" if the degree of probability regarding its outcome cannot be identified.

Selecting "Best" Alternative   Drucker points to the importance of choosing the best solution on the basis of "what is 'right,' and not on 'what is acceptable.'" He suggests that you focus on the solution that will fully satisfy the specifications *before* attention is given to the compromises, adaptations, and concessions needed to make the decision acceptable.[13] Deciding among the alternatives available—the actual selection of a course of action—is compared with the guidelines set forth earlier in the process.

Implementation and Modification   Implementation is the process by which the decision is put into effect. It involves the authorization of the required changes as well as gaining acceptance from those people the decision affects: informing and sometimes persuading the people who must know, defining what action should be taken, and explaining when and how the decision is to be carried out. A feedback system is necessary to monitor results and to verify and evaluate the outcomes of the decision. You may need to revise, adjust, or even reactivate the entire decision-making process.[14]

Decision-Making Models

Behavioral Models

Carter[15] provides a useful comparison between a behavioral theory proposed by Cyert and March[16] and the actual process of corporate decision making.

Cyert and March portrayed organizational activities as a reflection of the shifting relationships among uneasy "coalitions" of individuals who share corporate power unequally among themselves. In the Cyert-March view, decision making is concerned with three basic factors: *goals* (i.e., what the organizational objectives should be),[17] *expectations* (what consequences may flow from organizational actions), and *choice* (what the action should be). They attribute the erratic performance of the decision-making function to four characteristic features of the process:

1. *Quasi-resolution of conflict.* Internal conflict is kept below the flash point by such devices as limited departmental autonomy. Emphasis is placed on subunits and subunit goals. Everyone is accommodated and no one feels completely neglected, settling for minimal rather than optimal standards.
2. *Uncertainty avoidance.* A deliberate strategy for not fulfilling the function of long-range planning by living as close to the moment as possible—responding with temporary solutions to problems rather than to anticipate them.
3. *Problemistic search.* A quest for a solution that is triggered by an occurrence of a problem for which a solution is sought. New solutions are sought that resemble as closely as possible the procedures that have not worked. The search ends the instant it turns up a solution of minimum acceptability. Search information is often unreliable because of communication distortions that emerge in an atmosphere of unresolved conflict.
4. *Organizational learning.* An adaptation process where adjustments are made by an assessment of past performance, expectations, and past performance of competitive organizations.[18]

Carter undertook to evaluate the Cyert-March theory on the basis of a three-month field study of six investment and acquisition decisions made by a young, rapidly growing, high-technology company.[19] The company's president was an ambitious, aggressive business-school graduate who was committed to a plan for doubling company earnings annually for the next six years. The company employed a number of highly skilled technicians, with personal and career interest in designing and developing advanced computer equipment.

Technical as well as financial decisions were included in the study. The president's policy was to seek advice and suggestions but to retain firm personal control over final decisions. Each of the six decisions was consistent with the company's current mission and future plans. It also offered substantial profit possibilities, though with varying degrees of assurance. The decisions were made fairly quickly, considering their scope and the uncertainty and risk involved.

In general, Carter found that the decision-making process was considerably more "centralized" in the hands of the president when financial questions were involved—possibly because the president trusted his own expertise in such matters more than that of his associates or because of the fateful nature of these decisions.[20] The president was the initiator and mover in these cases.

The process leading to the technical decisions was set in motion by either the president or a staff member. Although the president remained the ultimate authority, he relied heavily on his staff for information and advice in making technical decisions. In fact, there was considerable evidence that the rigor with which a proposal was screened was related to the standing of its sponsor—that is, the more an individual was respected, the less additional support his suggestions required.

One intriguing relationship—which, Carter suggests, may explain why organizations do not always use the same standards in judging projects—was found to exist between uncertainty and organizational goals. In view of his observation that the company tended to employ a greater number of criteria (goals) in evaluating projects in conditions of uncertainty, Carter hypothesized that organizations manipulate goals as a means of adjusting to uncertainty levels.[21] For example, the organization studied began with a single criterion against which all proposals were to be judged: the financial growth of the company. Secondary company objectives were added as criteria, however, in the case of certain attractive technical proposals with uncertain prospects of making a strong financial contribution. These proposals were considered in terms of their probable contributions to company prestige and standing in the industry, to new products and services, and to similar secondary criteria. In one case a profitable project was approved partially because of its anticipated impact on morale, since it would engage and challenge the technical staff's highest skills and demonstrate that their ability was appreciated and would be encouraged and developed by the company.

An additional phenomenon suggested by the study was termed the "Pollyanna-Nietzsche effect."[22] A psychological state combining optimism with a sense of invulnerability, the P-N concept implies that all participants in a decision have become convinced not only that the decision is the right one but also that their expectations for it are certain to be realized. The effect is to convert uncertainty into a motivating force by creating the conviction that any failure to realize goals is the result of substandard effort.

Carter asserted on the basis of this study that "alterations were needed in the Cyert-March theory."[23] In the Cyert-March behavioral model the "coalition" operates as a sort of corporate senate that formulates expectations and then translates them into actions. Expectations and actions reflect the current balance between unrest and apathy in the coalition.[24] But in the Carter study the bulk of coalition-type activity takes place as "bilateral bargaining" between two individuals or two groups of people. The participation of many different organizational levels and groups in the decision-making process has an effect on the kinds of decisions made.[25]

Carter suggests that in the Cyert-March organization search occurs as a reaction to a pressing problem. In his perspective, however, search is a response to corporate strategy. Also, in the Cyert-March organization, people respond to uncertainty by restricting their vision to the events of the moment; in the Carter organization, people respond to uncertainty by expanding their agenda of goals.[26]

Information and Decision-Making Model

Thomas P. Ference supplied useful clarification of the interdependencies of organization communication systems and decision processes. He integrated a series of general propositions—some well established in the literature and some original—with a model of the communications function in a problem-solving mode.[27]

The choice and interpretation of decision information, Ference suggests, depends on its relevance, whereas the information processing depends on the individual doing the processing, his or her relationship to his or her sources, and the nature of the information itself.[28] Information that ultimately will play a part in determining the kinds of decisions made is shaped, to some degree, by the personal and professional characteristics of the people who handle the information, and by their role as subordinate, peer, or superior to the individual supplying the information.

Several general propositions govern this process: When interpreted data are communicated, they usually will *not* be accompanied by documentation. More credibility will be accorded information supplied by a source who is (a) inside the organization, (b) in a high position, and (c) familiar as a source of information. Information will be tailored to fit the sender's perceptions of the recipients' needs. The sender's professional function will influence the editing more than his or her personal motivation.

Information needed in decision making is subject to some bargaining, time lags, and the observance of "rules of contact."[29] That is, to obtain information usually requires negotiation; there are often difficulties in obtaining reliable data; both the formal and informal "protocol" unique to organizational environments must be respected.

When information is acquired, it is evaluated in relationship to its consistency with other information at hand, along with its source. This process, also, is subject to certain peculiarities. For example, Ference's propositions reveal that "the later information is acquired in the problem-solving process, the greater the chance it will be rejected" (particularly if it conflicts with information acquired earlier) or even when it is "totally accepted."[30] Also, the more credible or powerful the source, "the less likely it is that the information it provides will be rejected" under any circumstances.[31]

Decision Making: Problem Identification Models

As discussed earlier, perhaps the most difficult task in decision making is to identify the "real" problem. According to Koehler, a major barrier to organizational effectiveness is the inability of members to identify problems that directly affect organizational outcomes.[32] He suggests that productivity is directly affected because members waste time by continuously reacting to symptoms of problems rather than to the problems themselves. Problems, Koehler maintains, emerge from unanticipated events that affect organizational goals negatively, *or* from anticipated obstacles that have a negative effect on desired outcomes. He proposes a reactive problem-identification system for identifying the "real" problem in unanticipated difficulties, and a pro-active system for identifying anticipated problems.[33]

Reactive Problem Identification Model

This model (Figure 11-1) prescribes intervention between an unanticipated negative reaction and problem identification by submitting your reaction to a five-step process. That is, you refrain from concluding that you have identified a problem when you merely perceive a situation that you feel has a negative effect upon you and/or your organization. Instead, you intervene in your thinking process by subjecting your reaction to the following analysis: First, define what you expected to occur; second, describe what actually occurred; third, identify the effect of what occurred on personal and/or organizational goals; fourth, identify the negative effects if any; and finally, define the cause of this effect. This final definition describes the real problem.

For example, a few years ago organizations had not anticipated a stylistic change in the length of men's hair. Management first became aware that a problem existed when some of the male employees began to show up at work wearing "unconventional" hairstyles. Management had expected conformity to a certain standard of appearance and individuals suddenly put in an appearance who did not conform to it. Management expectations were not met. It was assumed that long hair on men somehow interfered with the achievement of organizational goals. Management reactively defined the problem as "long-haired men are not acceptable; what shall we do about them in our ranks?"

Solutions were offered from all quarters. Some organizations embarked on campaigns of ridicule and harassment that were designed to embarrass the deviant members. Others were more forthright and fired the nonconformists. Neither solution was particularly effective. A more effective course might have been to apply the process demonstrated in the model: when a difficulty or unanticipated behavior is detected; intervene immediately in the automatic reaction process. Rather than leaping from the assumption that the new hairstyle represented a problem to proposed solutions, you intervened by defining what you expected (in this case, that everybody would conform to the short-hair standard), as contrasted to what actually occurred ('A' showed up for work with his hair down to his shoulders).

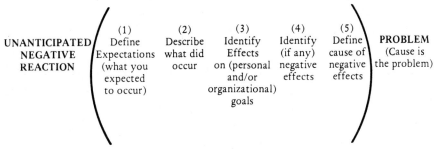

Figure 11-1 From J. W. Koehler, *Decision-Making in Administration* (Irvine, Calif.: Center for Organization Research and Development, 1975).

What was the effect of the unanticipated behavior on personal and organizational goals (Step 3)? (Was there a drop in productivity? A safety or health problem? Did A's appearance disrupt his work or that of others? Was there evidence of actual effect on organizational goals?)

You now identify the most likely negative effect (if any). If none can be found, there is no real problem. If there is no evidence that A's behavior is producing a negative effect, the "problem" can be disregarded. However, if Organization X comes to a different conclusion (that the presence of long-haired men in the firm damages its public image, an important organizational asset), the conclusion might be that "the presence of men with shoulder-length hair will have a disastrous effect on organizational goals." The next step would, therefore, be to identify the cause (a disgruntled employee? radical agitators?). Whatever is identified as the cause is the real problem: For example, "We have no policy forbidding men to wear long hair" or "We can't reverse the trend toward new life styles."

An important element in Koehler's approach is his contention that organizations waste uncounted hours making decisions about "problems" that do not interfere with organizational productivity or outcomes. The key to his reactive system is the decision to *intervene* between your perception of an event you fear will interfere with achievement of organizational goals and your reaction.

Pro-Active Problem Identification Model

Effective organization managers spend considerable time trying to anticipate obstacles that may prevent their units from attaining goals. Rather than waiting for problems and then reacting, they try to predict occurrences that will have negative effects on organizational outcomes. Koehler's model for identifying anticipated problems is different from the one he proposes for defining unanticipated problems. He suggests that each time you identify a specific goal, you subject the goal to the pro-active problem identification model (see Figure 11-2). It represents a form of intervention between goal setting and action taken to reach the goal.

PRO-ACTIVE IDENTIFICATION MODEL

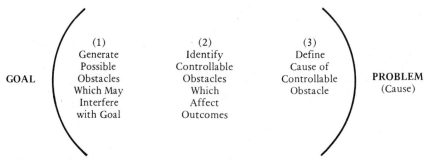

GOAL

(1)
Generate
Possible
Obstacles
Which May
Interfere
with Goal

(2)
Identify
Controllable
Obstacles
Which
Affect
Outcomes

(3)
Define
Cause of
Controllable
Obstacle

PROBLEM
(Cause)

Figure 11-2 From J. W. Koehler, *Decision-Making in Administration* (Irvine, Calif.: Center for Organization Research and Development, 1975).

The purpose of this model is to identify in advance problems that may require a decision. The process requires that, having identified a goal, you intervene by (1) generating possible obstacles that could prevent you or your unit from achieving the goal; (2) identifying obstacles you can do something about; and (3) defining the cause of each controllable obstacle. The cause of the obstacle is the real problem that you submit to decision-making analysis.

If, for example, a father has a goal that his child graduate from college, he should attempt to anticipate from the outset what events must take place if the goal is to be realized. He will want to identify potential problems as early as possible in order to make decisions that will enable him to forestall them. Rather than waiting for the problems to identify themselves, he attempts to identify them in advance and prepare for their emergence.

Part of the father's goal planning, therefore, would be the generation of a list of obstacles that could prevent him from achieving the goal. The list might contain such items as resistance from the child, an incapacitating physical handicap, poor grades or poor performance on entrance exams, financial problems, and so on. His second step would be to identify the controllable obstacles—lack of motivation, poor preparation, financial problems, and the like. He would then undertake to define the cause of each obstacle in turn. If, for example, the cause of a potential financial obstacle is defined as "no savings plan," then the problem would appear as: How do I save money for my child's college education? This problem is then subjected to the decision-making model that follows.

Decision-Making Model

Once a problem has been identified, Koehler offers a typical decision-making process (see Figure 11-3), except that it provides for a unique feedback loop for further exploration in situations where an apparently "best" solution proves inadequate upon evaluation. (The loop consists of a continuous recycling of Steps 3, 4, and 5, discarding one possible solution after another until a workable one is found.)

In the example given, a potential problem was defined as a lack of adequate

DECISION-MAKING MODEL

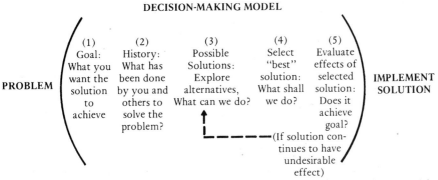

Figure 11-3 From J. W. Koehler, *Decision-Making in Administration* (Irvine, Calif.: Center for Organization Research and Development, 1975).

funds. The goal is now narrowed from "child will graduate from college" to "save X amount for child's college education." The father would then examine methods others have used to solve this problem, explore available savings plans, and select the apparently best plan. He would then project the consequences of this plan—does it mean giving up the family's annual vacation, driving the automobile a little longer before trading it in, or possibly giving up vital interests? If the price of this solution is unacceptably high, the father may conclude that the goal is impractical, or he may continue to loop back to Step 3 for an exploration of alternate solutions.

Normative Model

Vroom and Yetton developed a decision-making system in which specific rules can be applied to determine when, how, and if participation is demanded by subordinates in a decision situation.[34] They began with the development of a descriptive model *describing* what the "best" managers do. Then they developed a normative model *prescribing* what the "best" managers should do when making decisions in organizations.

The objective of their system is not to solve problems directly but rather to set forth a procedure for matching the decision-making behavior of managers with the demands of the situation, specifically when the situation involves subordinates. As is evident from Figure 11.4, what is principally involved in their normative model is the degree to which a particular situation requires the participation of subordinates in order to achieve the "best" solution, coupled with the support required actually to solve the problem.

One advantage of the Vroom-Yetton normative model is that it simplifies the choice of leadership styles. Managerial style selections emerge from the process of making and implementing a decision. Styles emerge from the managers' responses to the questions that appear at the top of the figure, rather than in some predetermining leadership style as suggested by Lewin, Lippitt, and White,[35] Maier,[36] Heller,[37] and Likert.[38]

To employ the normative model (sometimes referred to as the Vroom-Yetton decision tree) you begin with the question designated "A." You answer the question in relation to the specific situation requiring a decision. Depending on your answer (*yes* or *no*), you follow the line representing your response. If, for example, you were to answer "yes" to question "A," you would proceed to box "B" to ask and answer question "B." You continue the process until you have reached the end of a "branch." When you have reached the end of a branch, it will reveal a number that designates the type of problem. For example, if your branch ended with 7, you would find the matching number at the bottom of the figure, which would indicate that the solutions to your problem will be found under G:GLL for group problems or I:GL for individual problems. At that point you would turn to Figure 11-4 to find what you should do. It would tell you to "share the problem with subordinates as a group . . ." or to "share the problem with your subordinate, and together you analyze the problem and arrive at a mutually agreeable solution."

In order to better understand this model, insert yourself into the following situation and complete the guidelines provided.

A. Is there a quality requirement such that one solution is likely to be more rational than another?
B. Do I have sufficient info to make a high quality decision?
C. Is the problem structured?
D. Is acceptance of decision by subordinates critical to effective implementation?
E. If I were to make the decision by myself, is it reasonably certain that it would be accepted by my subordinates?
F. Do subordinates share the organizational goals to be attained in solving this problem?
G. Is conflict among subordinates likely in preferred solutions? (This question is irrelevant to individual problems.)
H. Do subordinates have sufficient info to make a high quality decision?

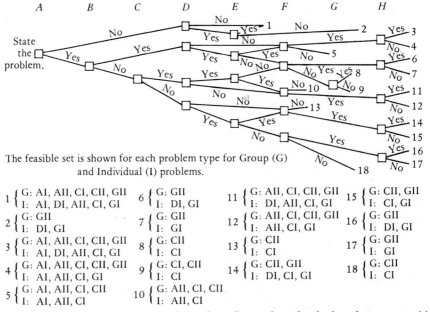

The feasible set is shown for each problem type for Group (G) and Individual (I) problems.

1 { G: AI, AII, CI, CII, GII / I: AI, DI, AII, CI, GI

2 { G: GII / I: DI, GI

3 { G: AI, AII, CI, CII, GII / I: AI, DI, AII, CI, GI

4 { G: AI, AII, CI, CII, GII / I: AI, AII, CI, GI

5 { G: AI, AII, CI, CII / I: AI, AII, CI

6 { G: GII / I: DI, GI

7 { G: GII / I: GI

8 { G: CII / I: CI

9 { G: CI, CII / I: CI

10 { G: AII, CI, CII / I: AII, CI

11 { G: AII, CI, CII, GII / I: DI, AII, CI, GI

12 { G: AII, CI, CII, GII / I: AII, CI, GI

13 { G: CII / I: CI

14 { G: CII, GII / I: DI, CI, GI

15 { G: CII, GII / I: CI, GI

16 { G: GII / I: DI, GI

17 { G: GII / I: GI

18 { G: CII / I: CI

Figure 11-4 Decision-Process Flow Chart for Both Individual and Group Problems (From Vroom and Yetton, *Leadership and Decision-Making*, p. 194.)

You are the production manager of a large pharmaceutical company.. The firm you work for has recently installed a new ordering system by which individual drugstores may request merchandise from your store. As efficient and timesaving as these new machines were expected to be, they are proving to be very troublesome. Not only have costs risen instead of being reduced, the amount of ordering by individual stores has dropped off, shipments have decreased, and employees are dissatisfied with their new work load.

A quick survey indicates that nothing is wrong with the machines themselves. Your immediate subordinates feel that the cause of the problem lies in several areas. Some feel that the machines are too complicated, and others say that they resent the new system after having used the old methods succesfully for over twenty years. It quickly becomes evident that this issue is causing considerable consternation among employees and could escalate into a problem of major proportions.

Your telephone rings. It is your immediate supervisor expressing concern that money and profits are being lost somewhere down the line. After some discussion, you both agree to take steps to rectify the situation. Following the Vroom-Yetton Normative Model of discussion making you would, first, state the problem. (Begin at the left side of Figure 11-4). As the production manager you must first answer the question under the Letter A: "Is there a quality requirement such that one solution is likely to be more rational than another?" In other words, is the quality of the decision of some importance? Because this hypothetical example will ultimately affect the productivity of your company and eventually the profits, your answer would be "yes." Placing your finger on the first box on the left-hand side of the figure and tracing the appropriate path on the branch of the model labeled "yes" you would come to another box located under Question B: "Do I have sufficient information to make a high-quality decision?" The answer in this case would have to be "No" because as indicated by your subordinates' comments, you cannot yet be sure of the cause of your crisis. Again tracing the appropriate path, your finger comes to rest under Question C: "Is the problem structured?" As of yet, the problem lacks structure so that your answer would again be "No." Following the model progressively, you come to Question D: "Is the acceptance of the decision by subordinates critical to effective implementation?" Based on your knowledge of the mixed reactions to the new system of ordering, your answer to this question would be "yes," the subordinates' acceptance of the solution is necessary. Tracking the path to the next question, "E," you would then ask yourself, "if I were to make the decision by myself, is it reasonably certain that it would be accepted by my subordinates?"

For this same reasons, your answer to this question would most probably be "No." This answer would then lead you to Question F: "Do subordinates share the organizational goals to be obtained in solving this problem?" In other words, would the employees have the same motivation for choosing one outcome over another as the company? Because the solution of this problem would ultimately lead to more productivity and an eventual increase in wages, the answer to Question F would be "yes." Answering "yes" to question F would lead to the final question, H: "Do subordinates have sufficient information to make a high-quality decision?" Finally, because the employees are the ones who are most involved with the system, and because they are experiencing the problem firsthand, the answer would be "yes."

Group Problems	Individual Problems
AI. You solve the problem or make the decision yourself, using information available to you at the time.	AI. You solve the problem or make the decision by yourself, using information available to you at the time.
AII. You obtain the necessary information from your subordinates, then decide the solution to the problem yourself. You may or may not tell your subordinates what the problem is in getting the information from them. The role played by your subordinates in making the decision is clearly one of providing the necessary information to you, rather than generating or evaluating alternative solutions.	AII. You obtain the necessary information ation from your subordinate, then decide on the solution to the problem yourself. You may or may not tell the subordinate what the problem is in getting the information from him. His role in making the decision is clearly one of providing the necessary information to you, rather than generating or evaluating alternative solutions.
CI. You share the problem with the relevant subordinates individually, getting their ideas and suggestions without bringing them together as a group. Then *you* make the decision, which may or may not reflect your subordinates' influence.	CI. You share the problem with your subordinate, getting his ideas and suggestions. Then you make a decision, which may or may not reflect his influence.
CII. You share the problem with your subordinates as a group, obtaining their collective ideas and suggestions. Then you make the decision, which may or may not reflect your subordinates' influence.	GI. You share the problem with your subordinate, and together you analyze the problem and arrive at a mutually agreeable solution.
GII. You share the problem with your subordinates as a group. Together you generate and evaluate alternatives and attempt to reach agreement (consensus) on a solution. Your role is much like that of chairman. You do not try to influence the group to adopt "your" solution, and you are willing to accept and implement any solution which has the support of the entire group.	DI. You delegate the problem to your subordinate, providing him with any relevant information that you possess, but giving him responsibility for solving the problem by himself. You may or may not request him to tell you what solution he has reached.

Figure 11-5   Decision Methods for Group and Individual Problems (From Victor H. Vroom and Philip W. Yetton, *Leadership and Decision-Making* [Pittsburgh: University of Pittsburgh Press, 1973], p. 13.)

TABLE 11-1   Vroom-Yetton Problem-Solving Rules (Individual and Group)*

1. *The leader information rule.*   If the quality of the decision is important, and the leader does not possess enough information or expertise to solve the problem by himself, then AI is eliminated from the feasible set.

2. *The subordinate information rule (applicable to individual problems only).*   If the quality of the decision is important, and the subordinates(s) is (are) not likely to pursue organizatin goals in his (their) efforts to solve this problem, then GII, DI, and GI are eliminated from the feasible set.

4a. *The unstructured problem rule: group.*   When the quality of the decision is important, if the leader lacks the necessary information or expertise to solve the problem by himself and if the problem is unstructured, the method of solving th problem should provide for interaction among subordinates likely to possess relevant information. Accordingly AI, AII, and CI are eliminated from the feasible set.

4b. *The unstructured problem rule: individual.*   In decisions in which quality is important, if the leader lacks the necessary information to solve the problem by himself and if the problem is unstructured, the method of solving the problem should permit the subordinate to generate solutions and in so doing provide information concerning all aspects of the problem. Accordingly AI and AII are eliminated from the feasible set.

5. *The acceptance rule.*   If the acceptance of the decusion by the subordinate(s) is critical to effective implementation and if it is not certain than an autocratic decision will be accepted, AI and AII are eliminated from the feasible set.

6. *The conflict rule (applicable to group problems only).*   If the acceptance of the decision is critical, an autocratic decision is not certain to be accepted, and disagreement among subordinates in methods of attaining the organizational goal is likely, the methods used in solving the problem should enable those in disagreement to resolve their differences with full knowledge of the problem. Accordingly, under these conditions AI, AII, and CI, which permit no interaction among subordinates and therefore provide no opportunity for those in conflict to resolve their differences, are eliminated from the feasible set. Their use runs the risk of leaving some of the subordinates with less than the needed commitment to the final decision.

7. *The fairness rule.*   If the quality of the decision is unimportant, but acceptance of the decision is critical and not certain to result from an autocratic decision, it is important that the decision process used generate the needed acceptance. In group problems, the decision process used should permit the subordinates to interact with one another and negotiate over the fair method of resolving any differences with full responsibility on them for determining what is fair and equitable. In individual problems, the decision-making process should provide for the affected subordinate to be at least a full and equal partner. Accordingly, under these circumstances AI, AII, CI, and CII are eliminated from the feasible set.

8. *The acceptance priority rule.*   If acceptance is critical, not certain to result from an autocratic decision, and if (the) subordinate(s) is (are) motivated to pursue the organizational goals represented in th problem, then methods which provide equal partnership in the decision-making process can provide greater acceptance without risking decision quality. Accordingly AI, AII, CI, and CII are eliminated from the feasible set.

---

* These rules apply to the model in Figure 11-5. (From Vroom and Yetton, pp. 218–220.)

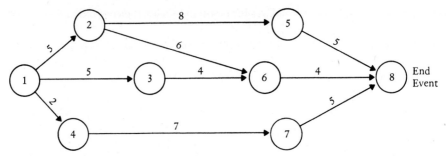

Figure 11-6 Simplified PERT Network

Having begun at the left-hand side of the chart and working systematically across to the right-hand side, the final question would have led you to the number sixteen. Looking below to the number sixteen in the included feasible sets, we find that several choices are inclusive in this set. Because our hypothetical example is a group problem, however, only one solution is applicable: G II. Turning now to Figure 11-5, we find that G II instructs us to:

> Share the problem with your subordinates as a group. Together you generate and evaluate alternatives and attempt to reach agreement (consensus) on a solution. Your role is much like that of a chairman. You do not try to influence the group to adopt 'your' solution, and you are willing to accept and implement any solution which has the support of the entire group.

This model, although first seeming to be mechanical, is based on the consummate experience of over 500 managers surveyed by Vroom and Yetton during their initial research. As artificial as this model may first appear, the hypothetical example given actually happened to a large Florida pharmaceutical company and was handled in just the same style as indicated by the Vroom-Yetton Model.

Figure 11–5 describes the behaviors prescribed for processing both group and individual problems. The letter "G" refers to group problems, "I" refers to individual problems, and "D" refers to delegation to subordinate(s). You will note that each problem type usually provides a number of management-style options. Your final selection will be determined by the feasibility of each option—that is, its applicability to your situation.

The Vroom-Yetton model also lists specific rules (see Table 11–1). The rules are intended "... to protect both the quality and acceptance of the decision."[39] Three of these rules protect decision quality and four protect decision acceptance. Rule eight is applicable only to the individual problems.[40]

PERT Model

Many people became familiar with the acronym PERT (Program Evaluation and Review Technique) because of the enthusiastic reception given this technique by the defense and space industry after it was credited with reducing the completion schedule of the Polaris Weapon Systems Project by many months. Understanding of the program is less widespread.

Basically, PERT is an administrative tool used in planning, scheduling, and controlling complex projects. It is often associated in practice with intricate mathematical and statistical analyses, but its underlying principles are relatively simple.

PERT deals with a project in terms of *events* (a specified accomplishment at a particular moment) and *activities* (operations requiring time and resources that carry the project from one event to the next). Three crucial PERT concepts are *interdependence* (every project can be reduced to a finite number of individual events, *all* of which must take place in order to complete the project); *sequence* (events must be scheduled in a rational order so the "successor" events will not be undertaken before all of their "predecessor" events are completed); and *time* (the time consumed in each activity must be integrated into an overall schedule that is keyed to the project completion date).

A PERT *network* is a diagram of all the project events and activities, the relationship among them, and the time required for completion of each activity. Events are usually symbolized by circles; activities are lines, with arrows leading from predecessor events to their successors; and time (in weeks or decimal fractions of weeks) is entered above the activity lines. Figure 11–6 depicts a simple PERT network.

Events 2, 3, and 4 in the figure are all dependent on the completion of event 1 and the performance of the activities represented by the lines connecting them to event 1. Events 2, 3, and 4, however, are independent of each other; that is, 1–2, 1–3, and 1–4 are "parallel" activities, whereas 1–3 and 3–6 are "series" activities. The importance of this distinction is that parallel activities may be carried on concurrently, whereas series activities must be performed consecutively. Thus, the time required to complete a group of parallel activities is that of the longest single activity, but the time required to complete a series of activities is the *sum* of their *combined* time requirements.

This distinction accounts for one of the most powerful analytical tools associated with PERT—the Critical Path Method or CPM. In the network illustrated in Figure 11–6, four serially linked chains, or paths, lead to end event 8: (a) 1–2–5–8, (b) 1–2–6–8, (c) 1–3–6–8, and (d) 1–4–7–8. The total time required for completion of path (a) is eighteen weeks, path (b) fifteen weeks, path (c) thirteen weeks, and path (d) fourteen weeks.

Obviously, if work goes forward on all paths simultaneously, the total project cannot be completed in less time than it takes to complete the longest path—in this case path (a), eighteen weeks. Path (a) is therefore designated the *critical path*. The critical path activities may constitute no more than 10 percent to 20 percent of the total, but they control the schedule for the whole project time (unless delays on a noncritical path exceed the difference, or "slack time," between its requirements and those of the critical path).

Special precautions are necessary to maintain the critical path schedule. If the completion date must be advanced, activities along the critical path must be examined and shortcuts, overtime, and commitment of additional resources reallocated.

REVIEW QUESTIONS

1. What does "process" mean in decision making?
2. Differentiate between programmed and nonprogrammed decisions.
3. Discuss March and Simon's typology of possible alternatives and relate those alternatives to particular decisions that you have made recently.
4. What are the five major steps in Koehler's Reactive Problem Identification Model?
5. Why should organization managers spend a considerable amount of their time trying to anticipate obstacles that may prevent their units from attaining their goals rather than waiting until an obstacle impedes such progress?
6. What kinds of problems would best be solved by using the Pro-Active Problem Identification Model?
7. What is the unique feature of Koehler's Decision-Making Model, and why is this feature so important in the decision-making process?
8. Discuss the Normative Model process of decision making and briefly list the advantages and disadvantages of utilizing this process in the organizational setting.
9. What is meant by the Critical Path Method (CPM) in the PERT Model of decision making?
10. What are the three crucial PERT concepts suggested in the book, and discuss their relevance to the PERT process of decision making?

KEY TERMS AND CONCEPTS FOR REVIEW

- Decision Making
- Decision-Making Process
- Decision-Making Strategy
- Unique Problems
- Generic Problems
- Programmed Decisions
- Nonprogrammed Decisions
- Cognition, Production, and Evaluation in Decision Making
- Problem Definition
- Constructive Guidelines
- Alternatives
- Goals in Decision Making
- Expectations of Decision
- Choice of Alternatives
- Centralized Decision Making
- Polyanna-Nietzsche Effect
- Reactive Problem Identification Model
- Pro-Active Problem Identification Model
- Decision-Making Model
- Vroom-Yetton Normative Model
- Decision-Making Tree
- PERT Model of Administrative Decision Making
- Events and Activities in the PERT Model
- Interdependence
- Critical Path
- PERT Network

CASE STUDY

Joan Peri, a woman in her early twenties, recently accepted a position as an accountant in one of the major national accounting firms. Within a week after she began working there, her immediate superior strongly suggested that she buy a new car because it would be in the best interests of the company's image of an "only the best" firm. Joan has saved enough money to consider her superior's request, but she had planned to spend her savings on a trip to Florida. Joan enjoys her job very much, and feels that she might very well dedicate a number of years of service to this firm. One of her philosophies is that everyone should stand up for his or her own rights.

PROBES

1. What should Joan do?
2. Joan is an "upward mobile" in the firm. What should she do?
3. Joan resents other people telling her what to do, and has been characterized as an "ambivalent" in the past. What should she do?

Recommended Readings

Gerwin, D., and F.D. Tuggle. "Modeling Organizational Decisions Using the Human Problem Solving Paradigm." *The Academy of Management Review* 3 (1978): 762-773.

Gifford, W.U., H.R. Bobbitt, and J.W. Slocum. "Message Chracteristics and Perceptions of Uncertainty by Organizational Decision Makers," *Academy of Management Journal* 22 (1979): 458-481.

Harrison, E. *The Managerial Decision-Making Process*. Boston: Houghton Mifflin Company, 1975.

Jackson, K.R. *The Art of Solving Problems*. New York: St. Martin's Press, 1975.

MacCrimmon, K.R. "Managerial Decision Making." In W. McGuire (Ed.) *Contemporary Management*. Englewood Cliffs, N.J.: Prentice-Hall, 1973.

Newell, A., and H.A. Simon. *Human Problem Solving*. Englewood Cliffs, N.J.: Prentice-Hall, 1972.

Van de Ven, A.H. "Group Decision Making and Effectiveness: An Experimental Study," *Organization and Administration Science* 5 (1974): 1-110.

Vroom, V.H., and P.W. Yetton. "Leadership and Decision-Making: Basic Considerations Underlying the Normative Model," In W.R. Nord (Ed.) *Concepts and Controversy in Organizational Behavior*, 2nd ed., Pacific Palisades, Calif.: Goodyear Publishing Co., 1976, pp. 626-643.

Notes

1. H. A. Simon, *The New Science Management Decision* (New York: Harper & Row, 1969), p. 1.
2. P. F. Drucker, *The Effective Executive* (New York: Harper & Row, 1966), p. 143.
3. Ibid., p. 128.
4. Ibid., pp. 123-138.
5. S. Eilon, "What Is a Decision?," *Management Science* 16 (December 1969): B-173.
6. Drucker, op. cit., p. 123.
7. Ibid.
8. J. P. Guilford, *Personality* (New York: McGraw-Hill Book Company, 1959), p. 360.
9. P. Drucker, *Management: Task, Responsibilities, Practices* (New York: Harper & Row, 1974), p. 465.
10. Ibid., p. 470.
11. Peter Drucker (Ibid., p. 470) applauds the Japanese because they "bring out dissenting opinions; because there is no discussion of the answer until there is consensus, a wide variety of opinions and approach is being explored." Also, "the focus is on alternatives rather than on the right solution. The process further brings out at what level and by whom a certain decision should be made. And finally, it eliminates selling a decision. It builds effective execution into the decision-making process."
12. J. G. March and H. A. Simon, *Organizations* (New York: John Wiley & Sons, 1958), p. 114.
13. Drucker, *The Effective Executive*, pp. 134–136.
14. E. F. Harrison, *The Managerial Decision Making Process* (Boston: Houghton Mifflin, 1975), p. 39.
15. E. E. Carter, "The Behavorial Theory of the Firm and Top-Level Corporate Decision," *Administrative Science Quarterly* 16, no. 4 (December 1971): 413–428.
16. R. M. Cyert and J. G. March, *A Behavioral Theory of the Firm* (Englewood Cliffs, N.J.: Prentice-Hall, 1963).
17. Five principal goals of organizations are named: *production, sales, inventory, market share,* and *profit.*
18. Carter, op. cit., pp. 413–416.
19. Ibid.
20. Ibid., pp. 420–421.
21. Ibid., p. 423.
22. Ibid., pp. 426–427.
23. Ibid., p. 427.
24. Ibid., p. 421.
25. Ibid.
26. Ibid., pp. 423–424.
27. T. P. Ference, "Organizational Communications Systems and the Decision Process," *Management Sciences* 12, no. 2 (October 1970): B83–B96. Ference's article provides an extensive analysis, but only selected propositions are cited. The reader is encouraged to read the original source.
28. Ibid., p. B-84.
29. Ibid., p. B-92.
30. Ibid., p. B-93.
31. Ibid.

32. J. W. Koehler, *The Corporation Game* (New York: Macmillan Publishing Company, 1975), pp. 131–145.

33. J. W. Koehler, *Decision Making in Organizations* (Irvine, Calif.: Center for Organization Research and Development, 1975).

34. V. H. Vroom and P. W. Yetton, *Leadership and Decision-Making* (Pittsburgh, Pa.: University of Pittsburgh Press, 1973).

35. K. Lewin, R. Lippitt, and R. K. White, "Patterns of Aggressive Behavior in Experimentally Created Social Climates," *Journal of Social Psychology* 10 (1939): 271–299.

36. N. R. F. Maier, *Psychology in Industry*, 2d ed. (Boston: Houghton Mifflin, 1955).

37. F. A. Heller, *Managerial Decision Making* (London: Tavistock Publications, 1971).

38. R. Likert, *The Human Organization* (New York: McGraw-Hill Book Company, 1967).

39. Vroom and Yetton, op. cit., p. 32.

40. Ibid., pp. 218–220.

12 | Conflict and Communication

LEARNING OBJECTIVES

After reading this chapter, you should be able to
1. Describe the conditions that lead to the emergence of conflict.
2. Discuss the various stages through which conflict develops in organizations.
3. Describe the four types of conflict situations that confront individuals.
4. Demonstrate how conflict may be beneficial to an organization.
5. Discuss the various factors or variables that affect the emergence and duration of conflict.
6. Explain the nature and characteristics of win-lose, lose-lose, and win-win conflict resolution strategies.
7. Discuss the various personal styles that individuals manifest in conflict situations.

Mac Stewart and Vince Ruocco were supervisors at a paper products company. Mac was the supervisor of the maintenance department and Vince was the supervisor of production. Both men were called into the office of vice-president Bill Peters because Bill was "tired of the guerrilla warfare that has been going on between the two departments for the past three months." As the meeting began, Bill Peters stated, "In all of my years of running this company, I had never known what a jackass looked like until I had to deal with you two 'critters'."

The vice-president was obviously and justifiably upset. For the past three months, the maintenance and production departments were deadlocked concerning concessions that each should make so that the work of each department could proceed smoothly. Mac and his maintenance crew contended that they were being paid to repair and maintain equipment and not to lift and haul the cartons that prevented easy access to the equipment. Vince and his production crew argued that they were doing their best to keep up productivity, that the cartons had to be stacked somewhere, and that the maintenance crew thought that they were so special that everyone had to cater to them.

The result of this standoff was that the maintenance crew refused to work on machines that were blocked by cartons, and breakdowns were disrupting the production schedule. Vice-president Peters screaming that he was "fed up to here" (making a slashing gesture on his forehead) "with you yo-yo's", had called for a meeting with Mac and Vince to solve the problem.

For many years it was regarded as a point of both pride and strategy for organizations to deny the existence of conflict in the ranks. When the existence of conflict could not be denied, it was attributed to the temporary effects of forces that were out of step with, or hostile to, the spirit of the organization. Managers proved their worth by their ability to knock heads together, get rid of troublemakers, and restore corporate serenity.

The attention paid to the nature and role of conflict had as its pragmatic objective the development of methods for anticipating and suppressing it. This surveillance gradually evolved into the contemporary study of conflict processes as a natural, inevitable, and, under certain circumstances, beneficial part of the organization. But to regard conflict as a potentially healthy process requires a considerably more detailed examination of the meaning and function of the activity we identify as *conflict*.

The potential for conflict exists when two units depend upon a common pool of scarce organizational resources, such as physical space, equipment, manpower, operating funds, capital funds, central staff resources, and centralized services (e.g., typing, shipping, and drafting). If the two units have interdependent tasks, the competition between them for scarce resources will tend to decrease interunit problem solving and coordination. Also, if competition for scarce resources is not mediated by some third unit, and the two competing units must agree on the allocation of these resources, they will come into direct conflict. It is the purpose of this chapter to discuss the various phases through which conflict progresses, the nature of various conflict situations, the sources of the effects of conflict, factors that induce conflict in organizations, and strategies for resolving conflict.

Conflict: Definition and Analysis

Any term in common usage acquires a range of definitions, only one or two of which may be applicable to a particular set of circumstances. Thus, the word *conflict* may with equal accuracy describe an armed struggle between nations or the influence of private interests upon the public duty of an elected official.

Any number of definitions have been advanced to narrow the scope of the word so it can be applied with some precision in specific circumstances. Beck, for example, provides a concise definition of conflict as it applies to confrontation politics: "Conflict, in contrast to *disagreements*, *debates*, and *games*, is a form of competition in which the parties involved seek to destroy or eliminate each other as they function from strong, emotive, and abstract positions."[1]

This definition reflects a sense of the potential violence in the situation that produced it (1970 student-police confrontations). This is a prospect that is present in certain extreme forms of organizational conflict, such as highly charged labor-management clashes. Beck's definition also suggests an absolutism that is more likely to be characteristic of the emotional state of the participants than of any real-life resolution. Usually neither side is able to "destroy or eliminate" the other, and the two continue to coexist, though often in an altered relationship. As Beck's definition indicates, the elimination of the opposition is what the parties "seek," not necessarily what they expect.

Beck cites Rapoport's definition of conflict as a "fight,"[2] and Boulding's less muscular description: "a situation of competition in which the parties *are aware* of the incompatibility of potential future positions and in which each party *wishes* to occupy a position that is incompatible with the *wishes* of the other."[3] Beck distinguishes the various levels of discord he has identified with the following illustration:

> For example, two college professors may discover an opposite viewpoint on a question over a cup of coffee (*disagreement*); pursue it into an active verbal controversy before others (*debate*); extend it into a serious legal maneuver within the university in competition for power (*game*); and eventually escalate it into a violent power struggle as each party, through fair means or foul, seeks to destroy the other in order to gain sole occupancy of the behavioral space (*conflict*).[4]

In the conventional organization, conflict is usually viewed as a somewhat broader phenomenon than this, embracing the levels that Beck and Rapoport identify as "conflict," "debate," and "game," as well as some aspects of "disagreement," with the prospects for constructive results largely confined to the debate and game levels. This point is underscored by Laughlin and Kedzic, who distinguish between "unnatural" conflict, in which the intent or the effect is to destroy your opponent, and "natural" conflict which is aimed at or permits the emergence of more effective participants.[5]

Another important factor for the productive resolution of conflict is the degree to which it involves real issues, as opposed to clashes of personality. Walton regards "interpersonal conflict" neither as good nor a matter of bad but as a process that "may be exhilarating or debilitating, which may lead to creative ideas and change or to cautious, protective behavior." However, Walton draws a fundamental line between those conflicts that relate to "substantive issues," such as the way the organization is run, and "antagonisms" arising from "personal or emotional differences."[6]

A related, though not identical, distinction may be made between the participants' perceptions of the conflict and its reality. Not only may an individual or group misunderstand or misinterpret an act or an event but the tensions of preconflict and conflict situations may exercise a distorting influence on the perceptions of the participants.[7]

In order to achieve a sharp focus concerning events that prevail in a typical conflict situation, one should be aware of the various phases through which conflict passes—from its origin to its resolution and beyond. Conflict does not usually appear suddenly. It passes through a series of progressive stages as tension builds. These stages of development are as follows:

1. Latent conflict—At this stage the basic conditions for potential conflict exist but have not yet been recognized.
2. Perceived conflict—The cause of the conflict is recognized by one or both of the participants.
3. Felt conflict—Tension is beginning to build between participants, although no real struggle has yet begun.
4. Manifest conflict—The struggle is under way, and the behavior of the participants makes the existence of the conflict apparent to others who are not directly involved.
5. Conflict aftermath— The conflict has been ended by resolution or suppression. This establishes new conditions that will lead either to more effective cooperation or to a new conflict that may be more severe than the first.[8]

Conflict does not necessarily pass through all of these stages. Furthermore, each participant in a conflict may not be at the same stage. One participant could be at the manifest stage of conflict while the other participant is at the perceived stage.

Conflict Situations

Although it is convenient and traditional to treat conflicts as straightforward expressions of the differences they purport to indicate, it is a common observation that the stated issues are not always the real ones. Personality and status conflicts, for example, frequently masquerade as differences over substantive matters or principles. Deutsch has given the name *manifest conflict* to the surface controversy, and *underlying conflict* to its deeper cause.[9] This distinction serves as a valuable reminder that the apparent conflict may be no more than a facade.

Maslow, focusing on the internalized conflict experienced by the individual, identifies four conflict situations: "sheer choice," "multiple means," "multiple goals," and "catastrophic conflict."

Sheer choice represents a blind decision—one that must be made in the absence of guiding information or principles.

Multiple means situations are characterized by two or more alternatives that appear to be equally desirable.

Multiple goals situations offer mutually exclusive goals of apparent equal desirability.

Catastrophic conflict involves a single, undesirable course—such as a financial situation in which there is no alternative to bankruptcy.[10]

Dollard, Doob, Miller, Mower, and Sears,[11] whose "frustration-aggression" hypothesis states that aggressive behavior is always associated with the persistent frustration of goal-directed efforts and vice versa, offers, according to Kelly, a similar classification of conflicts in terms of individual responses: "approach-approach" (equivalent to Maslow's "multiple goals"), "approach-avoidance" (in which the choice involves a weighing of positive and negative affects), and "avoidance-avoidance" (in which all alternatives are negative or threatening).[12]

Conflict Sources

The "simplistic" view of conflict, in the definition offered by Kelly, finds the cause of organizational controversy in "personal idiosyncrasies," and it is attributed to "troublemakers," "boat rockers," "prima donnas," "misfits," and so on.

In the more "realistic" view, Kelly suggests, "the causes of conflict are to be found in the structural factors which determine the total situation." These causes appear at four levels: the *individual* (as a result of individual frustration and aggression), the *group* (because of differences in value systems and uneven satisfaction of individual needs), the *organization* (as a result of unequal sharing of power and rewards between levels and between functions), and *society* (because of inequities between classes and ethnic groups).[13]

If the source of conflict is in the situation structure rather than in individual idiosyncrasies, it is apparent that there are many potential sources—the organizational structure, policies, decisions, practices, the reward and promotion system, company politics, the distribution of space and equipment, favoritism, discrimination, comfort and safety provisions, the distribution of authority and responsibility, how and by whom decisions are made, and innumerable others.

House suggested that since large contemporary organizations are so complex, it is virtually impossible to eliminate role conflict entirely. But his research indicated that although "role conflict" does tend to create dissatisfaction and reduce effectiveness, its negative effect varies with individual personalities. People who are acutely conscious of role conflict or who have a low tolerance for stress and pressure are more likely to experience serious negative effects.[14]

Perhaps the most poignant examples of the negative effect of role conflict during the past decade are the American servicemen and draft evaders who were unable to reconcile the conflicting authorities of state and conscience.

In many cases the potential for individual and group conflict is a built-in feature of the organizational structure. It grows inexorably as the company develops vertical and horizontal dimensions, dividing tasks and assigning responsibilities. In a manufacturing firm, the functions of control, accounting, planning, design, acquisition of material, production, and product sales are allotted to separate departmental teams, each of which exists in a state of perpetual dependence and warfare with one or more of the other teams.

At budget time, each department is obliged to exaggerate its own needs and accomplishments at the expense of others. Throughout the year, the sales department is under constant pressure to move greater quantities of products. In order to do so, salesmen exaggerate the product's capabilities and press for the limit in inducements, discounts, and delivery schedules. The pressure then shifts to the line organization to get the raw materials into the plant to make good on the salesmen's promises. Production demands immediate materials, plans, and manpower in order to meet the performance and schedule requirements to which it has been committed. Purchasing snarls at production for its impatience and at sales for its failure to take into account vendor lead-time requirements. Design chimes in with the complaint that the performance specifications are impossible. Accounting adds that the special inducements and discounts, coupled with the cost of design changes and overtime to meet the promised delivery schedule, will seriously affect the profit margin unless production costs can be cut. Production bellows that the hotheads in the plant are already agitating for a wildcat strike, and where will the delivery schedule be if *that* happens? Meanwhile, from somewhere "Up There," the chairman of the board has written a congratulatory note to the sales manager on the department's record-breaking quarter, suggesting that it would be most gratifying to see the record broken again in *this* quarter. And so it goes.

The ready-made resentments are often even more severe, if less obviously displayed, in the vertical structure of the departments. The various department heads can at least battle out their differences as peers, a privilege that is denied their departmental subordinates. The uneven distribution of power and responsibility, along with the potential for real or imagined inequities in distributing the work load, allotting praise and blame, and expediting raises and promotions, makes the chain of command a hotbed of conflict.

The conflict potential is heightened if supervisors overtly take advantage of their positions; if they play favorites, discriminate, or withhold reward and praise. Leadership style can be equally conflict-producing. Day and Hamblin compared the effects of "close" supervision and of a negative, insulting, "punitive" style on teams simulating complex assembly work under laboratory conditions.[15] Workers who were constantly instructed and watched responded with lowered production and increased manifestations of aggressive feelings, which they, in turn, took out on their co-workers. Workers who were subjected to punitive supervision responded with significantly lowered production and increased aggressive feelings directed at the supervisor.

The broadening technological base of modern industry has proved to be a fertile arena of conflict. As companies must rely more and more on costly, highly specialized departments, whose contributions are often difficult to assess and predict, clashes inevitably develop between the "technical" and "management" sections over priorities and the allotment of resources.

Such conflict is likely to play a dynamic role in corporate development. The focus of decision shifts from *whether* to support a technical operation to *which* operations offer the greatest promise, and in what priority. Rather than battle "management" for an adequate budget, contending groups of specialists compete for available resources. The groups in the forward fringe of a promising new technology will then make a place for themselves at the expense of older specialties, which have settled down or become "routinized." As this conflict posture suggests, the emphasis falls increasingly on the planned development of new products and processes in large, technology-based organizations.

As it becomes necessary to project this process further and further, and to plan for longer periods ahead, the possibility of disagreement grows accordingly. In the present, the competing groups differ in their emphasis. But they also anticipate the future in a different way, tending to project an exaggerated vindication of their own point of view.

In this atmosphere the various technical groups in a large organization do not clash with "management" but with each other, as each group seeks the largest possible allotment of resources for its own projects. All technical employees become advocates, in a sense, for their own department's point of view and antagonists of the viewpoint of competing groups.

From the foregoing, it is apparent that some degree of conflict is natural and unavoidable in all organizations. It is also evident that the rigid suppression of conflict, or its unmanaged and unrestrained expression, may be equally destructive. Accepted as part of the natural process by which an organization grows, adapts, and maintains its internal equilibrium, it can be a positive factor in the life of the organization.

What are some of the functions of conflict within an organizational system? Conflict—through its testing of interpersonal relationships—generates new norms and subsystems in the organization. Sulfrin points to the effects of union pressure "goading management into technical improvement and increased capital investment."[16] Conflict within and between bureaucratic structures provides the means for avoiding the ossification and ritualism that threatens such structures. To use physiological analogy, we could say that conflict may prevent the hardening of the organizational arteries. Conflict, though seemingly dysfunctional or disruptive, may actually have important functional consequences. By attacking and overcoming the resistance to innovation and change that seems to be a kind of occupational psychosis, which constantly threatens people who manage an organization, conflict can keep the systems from becoming stifled by deadening routine.

The central point here is that conflict is, potentially, of personal and social value in the organizational setting. It prevents stagnation, it stimulates interest and curiosity, and it is the medium through which problems can be aired and solutions arrived at. Rigid organizational systems or bureaucratic structures that suppress the "reality" of conflict may unintentionally provoke the emergence of more violent forms of conflict. Flexible organizational structures, which allow an open and direct expression of conflict and adjust to the resultant shifting balance of power, are less likely to be disrupted or damaged permanently. Thus, when conflict is properly harnessed, it may be beneficial, but when it goes unnoticed or when it is suppressed, it may be detrimental. The final outcome of the conflict may depend on the facility for *conflict resolution* provided by an organization. This issue is discussed later in the chapter. We now look into the question of the effects of conflict. It should be no surprise to learn that conflict can be considered in terms of a few of its constructive effects.

Effects of Conflict

The effects of conflict or a conflict episode may be good (constructive), bad (destructive), or both. It is largely a question of how the particular participants view the situation. However, the results of conflict must also be evaluated from the organization's point of view. For example, in a struggle between two employees to gain a much preferred, prestigious assignment, the winner will generally feel that the conflict was most worthwhile, whereas the loser will probably reach the opposite conclusion. How the organization is affected may, however, be the most important consideration in the long run. If the conflict leads to the better employee's gaining the assignment, the effect will be seen as good or constructive from the organization's point of view. At the same time, there may be several bad or destructive effects that counteract the good effects. The productivity of the company may have suffered during the conflict. The loser, an otherwise efficient employee, may resign or decide to work with only minimum allowable efficiency. The contest may have caused other employees to choose sides and some to end up jubilant and others morose.

These destructive effects of conflict are generally obvious. The constructive effects may be more subtle or imperceptible or difficult to detect initially. It is important that supervisors, leaders, managers, employees, and organization members sharpen their ability to recognize constructive effects and to weigh their benefits against the costs. The following is a summary of some of the useful effects of conflict:

1. Conflict energizes people. Even if not all of the resulting activity is constructive, it at least wakes people up and gets them moving.
2. A functional or strategic conflict usually involves a search for a resolution of the underlying issue. In resolving the conflict, needed changes in the organizational system may be discovered and implemented.
3. Conflict is a form of communication, and the resolution of conflict may open up new and lasting channels.
4. Conflict often provides an outlet for pent-up tensions resulting in catharsis. With the air cleared, the participants can again concentrate on their primary responsibilities.
5. Conflict may actually be an educational experience in that the participants may become more aware and more understanding of their opponents' functions and the problems with which they must cope.[17]

There are times when the encouragement of conflict may serve the objectives of the organization rather well. That kind of conflict is usually defined as *functional* or *strategic* conflict. On the other hand, there is often an urgent need to bring a particular conflict to some kind of end or resolution. The next section provides a discussion of the issues that are involved in *conflict resolution.*

Conflict Resolution

It was pointed out earlier that conflict is a natural consequence of human interaction in organizations. The fact that one organization may be healthier and more efficient than another may be attributable to the willingness and the speed with which conflict is resolved. As we talk about conflict resolution, we should be mindful of (1) the variables or factors that affect the course of conflict; and (2) the methods of conflict resolution.

Factors Influencing Conflict

When we identify certain points of conflict in interpersonal relationships or in interstructural relationships, it is useful to know something about the various factors or variables that affect both the emergence and the duration of that conflict. Deutsch suggests that our responses, in managing the resolution of conflict, be guided by the following:

(1) *The general characteristics of the parties in the conflict.* We should try to assess their values and motivations; their aims and objectives; their physical, intellectual, and social resources for continuing or resolving conflict; their beliefs about conflict—i.e., do they perceive conflict as natural and beneficial or as sinister and inevitably harmful? We should also try to understand their impressions, ideas, or opinions about strategy and tactics.

(2) *The relationship existing between parties in the conflict prior to the manifestation of the conflict.* In this instance we would be concerned with the attitudes, beliefs, and expectations that the individuals maintain in their interpersonal orientations. Of significance, also, is the perception that the individuals have concerning the attitudes about each other. Obviously, if you believe that the other party (or parties) in the conflict situation holds negative attitudes toward you, the nature, duration, and resolution of the conflict would be affected differently than in circumstances where you felt that the other parties were favorably disposed toward you.

(3) *The nature of the issue giving rise to the conflict.* Here we are concerned with the *scope* of the conflict—i.e., how many people are involved; what are the various facets of the issue that must be settled before the conflict is resolved; if the items of conflict are resolved in a particular fashion, what new conflicts are likely to develop. Very often management settles an organizational labor-management conflict in a particular unit with salary hikes and boosted

benefits, only to discover that other units, which previously perceived no conflict, are now stampeded into conflict because of the resultant salary and benefit discrepancy.

Another aspect of the issue concerns the matter of *rigidity*. People can be flexible in their responses to certain issues; but on others they will be totally rigid. The flexibility or rigidity manifested by the people involved will definitely affect the intensity of organizational conflict. For example, one large midwestern manufacturing agency almost collapsed because of a conflict between line and staff about the use of the company cafeteria. The line workers deemed it well within the terms of their civil and company rights to eat wherever they chose; the staff viewed that as a gross violation of "cultural norms." Consequently, they became embroiled in a sort of "class struggle" that almost spelled doom for the company.

We should also take the *periodicity* of the conflict into account. Some conflicts are seasonal, or only occur periodically. For example, many companies are confronted with conflicts about contract issues every year; many other companies encounter this type of conflict only every two or three years. The periodicity of the issue may provide us with certain patterns of behavior allowing for predictability of outcomes. This, in turn, will provide us with clues for generating effective strategies.

(4) *The social environment within which the conflict occurs.* Some organizational environments facilitate conflict resolution, whereas others frustrate it. The key concerns here are represented by the facilities and the restraints, the encouragements and the deterrents that the environment provides with regard to the different strategies and tactics of waging or resolving conflict. A decal manufacturing company in New York, for example, maintained such a managerially punitive environment that conflict was totally suppressed. However, the basic problem was that certain orientations, procedures, and regulations in the company would surely contribute to the arousal and manifestation of conflict. Layoff notices were usually given a day in advance, employees were forced to work overtime against their wishes, salary schedules were administered haphazardly, and there were remarkable discrepancies between the pay of men who worked at printing presses and those who worked on silk-screen presses. There was the need for the venting of discontent, but management encouraged no gripes or arbitration. After a considerable length of time the employees resorted to sabotage and vandalism, culminating in physical assaults and serious injury to three supervisors. Thus, it is obvious that the social norms and the institutional forms for regulating conflict are crucial to the nature and course of conflict.

(5) *The interest of the parties in the nature of the payoff.* When the gains to be derived in a conflict struggle are relatively small, we may not be willing to devote as much energy as we would in cases where the payoff could be substantial. Sometimes the payoff may be inherent in the conflict itself. That is, the ability to fight and flex the collective muscle could be sufficiently satisfying to certain members of an organization. Sometimes workers feel that they have to "stand up to management, or else they'll just take us for granted!" To

management that type of conflict may appear pointless, but to workers it is sufficient gain that management was forced into dealing with them.

(6) *The strategies and tactics employed by the parties in the conflict.* Strategy and tactics grow out of the assessments made concerning the resources or power, or lack thereof, that members bring to the situation. Every strategy is geared to enhancing one's personal utility or resource, and the diminishing of the other person's use of his or her resource. These tactics may include employment of positive and negative incentives, such as promises and rewards, threats and punishments, or freedom of choice—coercion, the openness and sincerity of communication and sharing of information, the degree of commitment, the types of motives appealed to, and so on.

(7) *The consequences of the conflict to each of the participants and to other interested parties.* Organizational change inevitably occurs during and after the duration of conflict. Both the individual and the organization itself are affected by the gains or losses that are related to the issue in conflict, and also by the strain and tension—no matter how minor—that emerge in the conflict situation. There is concern for the kinds of precedents established in terms of either the course of the conflict or the resolution of it, as well as for the internal changes that occur in the participants because of their involvement. For example, some of us may be inclined to alter the intensity or length of conflict if we perceived potential detriment to the physical or emotional well-being of another, or we might back off entirely if we perceived that prolonged conflict might impair a person's ability to perform a particular task beneficial to both of us.

Another consequence may be calculated on the basis of the long-term effects on the relationship between the parties involved. As we contemplate or approach conflict, a vital question could be: What effects would the payoff have on ongoing relationships, and would it turn out to be worthwhile over the long haul? In many instances in which employees contemplate an initial identification with a particular union, the question of a disruption of prior relationships looms large in importance. The aims and objectives of unions and those of management are usually in conflict. Some employees may be inclined to avoid upsetting a relationship that they view as being rather benevolent; by resisting the overtures of the union, they are in effect either avoiding conflict or postponing it. Of course, by refusing to upset the organization they may run the risk of upsetting the union. In this case conflict occurs, but the venue or locale of the battle is shifted. Finally, employees may be very much concerned with the reputations they are likely to gain through their participation in conflict. This concern is related to the one involving reluctance about upsetting the status quo. If one runs the risk of damaging one's reputation, one may be inclined to decrease the intensity or the duration of conflict. Conversely, the person who perceives the likelihood of enhancement of reputation or credibility in the eyes of peers or some other significant audience will tend to revel in and promote conflict.

In addition to the factors that influence the course of conflict, various *symptoms* may provide some clues concerning the quality of conflict and the likelihood of its resolution. Conflict may consist of *two* different qualities—one type may be cooperative, the other may be competitive. It is generally accepted that the parties in conflict are more likely to reach an agreement if their cooperative interests are stronger than their competitive interests in relationship to each other.[19] An awareness of the emergence or continuation of either a cooperative or a competitive state may assist us in making whatever adjustments are necessary to mediating beneficial outcomes. A few symptoms are generally manifested in *interpersonal communication, perception, attitudes toward one another,* and *task orientation.* Interpersonal responses pertinent to each of these four items would differ in either the cooperative or the competitive process.

Interpersonal Communication   A *cooperative* process is indicated by open lines of communication that furnish relevant information between organizational members. Faced with the inevitability of conflict, the members calculate that cooperation would be more practical than competition, and that communicating openly and honestly is better than not communicating. Each person is therefore interested in informing others as well as in being informed.

As far as communication is concerned, a *competitive* process is marked by either a conspicuous lack of communication or altogether misleading communication. Additionally, a great deal of spying or infiltration may be attempted in order to gain the upper hand over the other contesting party. The basic need for information still exists, but the difference here is that people would be more interested in information getting than information giving.

Perception   When a cooperative process prevails in response to conflict, individuals tend to look for similarities or common interests. They are able to see themselves as realistically sharing a common fate and being mutually dependent on each other for the maximizing of gains and minimizing of losses. Above all, in a cooperative process, individuals would be more willing to *minimize* the differences brought to the situation.

In a competitive process people tend to recognize differences (e.g., values, orientations, goals, concerns), but they may be inclined to exaggerate the importance of those differences. It is somewhat akin to an "I'm okay; you're not okay" outlook concerning the other party. Some commentators argue that competition does indeed produce a stronger bias toward "genuinely" misperceiving the others' neutral or conciliatory actions as antagonistic than the bias induced by cooperation to perceive the others' actions as friendly or helpful. Apparently, then, when competition prevails amidst conflict, the opposing parties would find themselves in a sort of "damned-if-I-do-and-damned-if-I-don't" dilemma.

Attitudes Toward One Another   A cooperative process should encourage a trusting, friendly attitude. That attitude would be characterized by accurate and well-informed cognitions, good or positive feelings, and a willingness to act supportively in response to needs or requests arising from the conflict.

A competitive process breeds hostile or negative attitudes, which in turn facilitates the desire to exploit the needs of the other person and respond negatively to the requests that emerge.

Task Orientation   When members are in a cooperative orientation, there will be a greater willingness to define the terms of conflict, in the realization that a resolution will occur only as individuals collaborate in the pursuit of solutions. Cooperation also aids members in recognizing the legitimacy, or the "rights," of each others' interests; it stimulates all parties to utilize power, influence, and talents conjointly. In fact, since the goal is to cooperate, the members of the organization would simultaneously enhance their own personal power, for each person is ultimately dependent on the resources of others to "iron things out."

Under the influence of competition, members tend to feel that any type of resolution would have to be biased in favor of one side or the other. This is tantamount to an "I will win, but you must lose" situation. Mutual gains or losses are not calculated in the analysis. Consequently, the enhancing of one's own power and the diminishing of the other person's power become the key concerns in the strategy. When individuals become hell-bent on nullifying the power or influence of others, they are in effect signifying that the concerns of others are not as legitimate as theirs. Before long the problem agenda expands, and issues that were once irrelevant now come into focus. The conflict then escalates into an all-out testing of principles rather than the resolution of a single issue. According to Deutsch, "the expansion of the conflict increases its motivational significance to the participants and intensifies their emotional involvement in it. These, in turn, may make a limited defeat less acceptable or more humiliating."[20]

At this point in the conflict, something must be done. Neither the ends of the individuals nor the organization's will be served by further delay. The following five options or alternatives are now available:

1. Withdrawal of one or more of the participants.
2. Smoothing the conflict and pretending that it does not exist.
3. Compromise for the sake of ending the conflict.
4. Forcing the conflict to a conclusion by third-party intervention.
5. Confrontation between the participants in an effort to solve the underlying problem.

Only the last method, confrontation for problem solving, will yield the permanent and constructive results than an organization should seek to obtain from its inevitable conflicts. Even so, the confrontation must be planned and guided. Mere confrontation is not the answer as we see in our description of the three strategies that are usually followed with varying results.

Strategies of Conflict Resolution

The various methods for dealing with conflict-confrontation may be grouped according to their likely outcomes. These outcomes may be called *win-lose, lose-lose,* and *win-win.*[21]

Win-Lose Strategies

One type of win-lose strategy is manifested in the typical exercise of raw authority. When a supervisor says, "Damn it, you do it as I tell you because I am the boss," he or she is exercising legitimate power bestowed upon him by the organization. If conflict arises in an organization, such authority permits the supervisor to reward or punish those who work under his or her control, and it is conceivable that the conflict may be curbed or suppressed. However, as we see later, this type of conflict resolution may not work out to the mutual satisfaction of everyone. In fact, there may be no conflict resolution but merely conflict postponement. A *second* type of win-lose strategy is that which utilizes mental or physical coercion to force compliance toward a particular way of doing things, as in the case of a supervisor who threatens an individual or entire group with dismissal if they dare to disagree with an existing orientation. A *third* win-lose strategy involves a failure to respond. For example, in a company sales conference dealing with a problem of reduced sales in some territories Sam says, "I think we ought to reorganize the territory among salesmen." If no one responds, in effect, his idea falls flat. He loses and everyone wins. Given several experiences of this sort, Sam may withdraw from further discussion, thereby avoiding the path of losing.

A *fourth* win-lose strategy employs majority rule. The democratic ethic is centered around voting on issues. In addition, there is empirical evidence that the majority is more often correct than the minority. Yet there are ways to achieve good decisions without creating a losing group through voting. Voting seems to be a suitable strategic operation when a group meets together over a period of time; members sometimes vote on the winning side and sometimes on the losing side, and the alternatives voted upon are reasonably acceptable to all. However, when a minority continually loses and when such losses are viewed as personal defeats, then majority rule can be quite destructive.

A *fifth* win-lose strategy employs minority rule. There are two common examples of this approach. The first example of minority rule is a situation in which the chairman of a meeting says, "I think we have enough work to warrant meeting at the same time next week; what do you think?" If there is no response, the chairman manipulates silence into support for his own position, saying, "since no one disagrees, we'll have a meeting next week." We would not be surprised if the subsequent meeting were poorly attended. The second example of minority rule is the scene in which an issue is "railroaded" through a meeting by only a few supporters. That is, if three people in a group of nine agree to support a proposal prior to the meeting, the strength of their agreement may intimidate the majority at the actual meeting. For instance, member A might say, "I propose that we do thus and so." Supporting members B and C then might vocalize their strong support of the issue. But member D may say, "I haven't heard this proposal before, but there is something about it that bothers me and I'm not sure that I like it." Then members A, B, and C may say to D, "Well, you're a little thick-headed," or "You don't seem to understand why this is a good method," or "You're obstructing progress." At this point other group members, not wanting to be similarly embarrassed or put down, may remain silent; and without further dissent the minority position may emerge as the official position of the group.

Lose-Lose Strategies

This strategy is designated lose-lose or *stalemate* because neither faction in conflict will accomplish its total objectives. At best, each may get only a part of what is desired. According to Filley, the lose-lose strategy is based on the assumption that half a loaf is better than none. A constant reliance on this type of "half-a-loaf" expectation could lead to a further escalation of conflict. For example, if one faction believes that, at best, the only gains to be expected from management would be half of what was requested, it may decide that the only way to get a "sizable" half would be to ask for an exorbitant whole. In other words, "I need $500; however, I believe that my boss will give me only $250; consequently, in order to come close to what is needed, I'll ask him for $1000. In that way I may get the $500." So we would start with an unreasonable first demand and end up with a frustrated response on the part of management. Very soon the entire negotiation will lose touch with the reality of the circumstances.

A second lose-lose strategy involves side payments. In essence, one who offers a side payment means, "I will bribe you to take a losing position." Organizations use side payments extensively and at great cost, paying individuals extra income to do disagreeable tasks; thereby both sides are partial losers.

A third lose-lose strategy calls for submitting an issue to a neutral third party. Thus, when two department managers ask their common superior to decide an issue about which they are in conflict, they avoid confrontation and problem solving in favor of a process that they hope will yield at least some benefit to each. Similarly, when two parties in a labor dispute submit the issue to arbitration, they do so in the hope that their individual positions will be enhanced to some degree. When a third party resolves a dispute totally in favor of one disputant, this method may be viewed as all or nothing. Arbitrators, however, frequently resolve issues at some middle ground between the positions held by disputants. Although it is to the advantage of the arbitrator as well as the disputants, to have both sides gain at least something from the conflict resolution, the outcomes are rarely satisfactory to both sides.

A fourth lose-lose strategy involves the practice of resorting to rules—either those established on an ad hoc basis to resolve the issue, or those already in existence. For example, when an employee asks for a day off (for some "good" reason) and the supervisor utilizes a rule as a basis for rejecting the request, problem solving or conflict resolution is not achieved. Rules are simply a way to avoid confrontation.

Notice that win-lose as well as lose-lose strategies are based on disagreements about means—my way versus your way; Alternative A versus Alternative B. For instance, sales and production managers often argue about whether additional funds should be given to the sales department to enhance marketing or to the production department to improve manufacturing techniques. The end goal—increased profitability—is typically not kept in focus during such discussions. The parties argue about means for solving the problem as each views it, rather than agree upon a common definition of an ultimate objective.

In summary, the win-lose as well as the lose-lose strategies share certain characteristics:

1. There is a clear we-they distinction between the parties, rather than a we-versus-the-problem orientation.
2. Energies are directed toward the other party in an atmosphere of total victory or total defeat.
3. Each party sees the issue only from its own point of view, rather than defining the problem in terms of mutual needs.
4. The emphasis in the process is upon the attainment of a solution, rather than upon a definition of goals, values, or motives to be attained with the solution.
5. Conflicts are personalized rather than depersonalized via an objective focus on facts and issues.
6. There is no differentiation of conflict-resolving activities from other group processes, nor is there a planned sequence of those activities.
7. The parties are conflict-oriented, emphasizing the immediate disagreement, rather than relationship-oriented, emphasizing the long-term effect of their differences and how they are resolved.[23]

Win-Win Strategies

The set of *win-win* strategies is predicated on the assumption that (1) problem-solving methods are positively related to effective conflict management, and that (2) problem solving is more likely when parties are perceived by each other as having the power to fight but the preference to cooperate.

Two types of win-win strategies are *consensus* decision making, and *integrative* decision making. They are called *win-win* methods because they attempt to meet the needs of both parties.

Consensus decisions occur when a group of two or more individuals reach a decision which is not unacceptable to anyone. In striving to reach consensus decisions, all participants must focus on defeating the problem rather than each other. They should avoid voting or trading; they should use facts rather than force to solve problems, and they should take the view that conflict is often beneficial.

The second win-win method is *integrative* decision making, which involves a joint identification of the needs and values of both parties, a thorough search

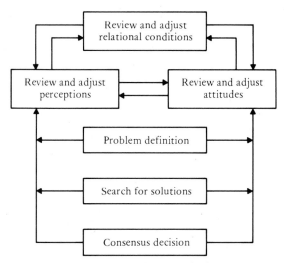

Figure 12-1 The Integrative Decision-Making Method

for alternatives, and the selection of the best alternative. The integrative decision making involves the following steps:

1. Reviewing and adjusting relational conditions
2. Reviewing and adjusting perceptions
3. Reviewing and adjusting attitudes
4. Defining the problem
5. Searching for solutions
6. Deciding by consensus[24]

Figure 12-1 demonstrates how each of the six steps fits into the overall integrative decision-making process. Let us see how the process works.

Review and Adjustment of Relational Conditions

In this first step, there should be an attempt to review the actual conditions that are related to the disagreement itself and to the conditions surrounding the disagreement. Sometimes, one may discover that the conflict could be resolved by merely adjusting an antecedent condition that led to the conflict. For example, the management of a factory that employed a sizable amount of personnel was faced with constant complaints of violations of working conditions. The employees contended that the morning and afternoon fifteen-minute break periods were not sufficient for them to visit the rest rooms, purchase coffee, and so on. The employees had a legitimate gripe, considering the number of individuals who had to share limited facilities in the space of fifteen minutes. Management, however, was adamant about not extending the break period. The conflict was resolved when management resorted to a staggered break plan—i.e., the machinists would break at 9:30, the diecutters at 9:45, and maintenance personnel at 10:00.

In addition, we should try to adjust the process of group interaction in a manner that promotes cooperation and reduces the likelihood of conflict. The following represent a few vital considerations:

- Spatial arrangements that provide a clear separation into two subgroups may be changed to avoid a we-they distinction.
- Large groups with nine or more people often break into subgroups and make balanced discussion difficult; group size may be adjusted to five or seven people.
- Group leaders who impose their own content may be changed to leaders who control the process of discussion according to problem-solving processes.
- Information that has been hoarded or distorted for the advantage of some group members may be shared with all members.
- Opportunities may be provided to deal with problems as they occur rather than holding them for discussion at a later date.[25]

Review and Adjustment of Perceptions

In this step, we attempt to test the "reality" of our perceptions. We should get ourselves and other participants to ask, "Are we viewing the situation accurately?" "Are we really hearing what we think we are hearing?" Our perception of the problem usually plays a major role in helping us to shift from win-lose, lose-lose attitudes to the more desirable win-win posture. An example would be the employees at a cement factory who threatened a work stoppage when the factory owner issued an order that said "No more union leaflets distributed in the factory." Both sides—management and labor—were faced with the conflict of whether to allow the union leaflets or not. When perceptions were adjusted to fit "reality," the problem was deescalated to a question of "how to allow the union leaflets to be distributed without violating the factory's authorized work schedule." In this case, it is no longer a question of who wins and who loses, but rather how can we both manage to win.

Review and Adjustment of Attitudes

Our attitudes serve as filters or screens through which we process information. Our attitudes are partly responsible for the distortions and faulty judgments that we often make. To achieve effective conflict resolution, we should attempt to identify our attitudes and feelings concerning the total conflict situation before problem definition and later steps take place. In this venture, there should be an effort to encourage trust, mutuality of interest, and cooperation.

Problem Definition

The integrative decision-making method works best when the values or goals of all the parties are clearly identified. Although the goals may be different, each party must be led to accept the expressed goals of the other. Furthermore, the problem should not be considered solved until the solution is acceptable to both parties or sides.

As one commentator correctly observes, "most conflicts are arguments about two *solutions.*"[26] If you say to a colleague, "Let's stack the boxes on the left side of the truck" and he or she says, "I want to stack the boxes on the right side," you are both disagreeing about two solutions; you are not really identifying the goals that you are mutually seeking. The proper posture would be for both of you to identify and express what you hope to gain with the solution and then combine the two needs. You may both conclude that it is more efficient to load the truck directly by having one person work on the truck and the other lift the boxes directly, thereby eliminating the extra step of stacking.

Alternative Generation

Try to gather as many solutions as possible without judgment or evaluation. The emphasis, at this stage, should be on the *quantity* of ideas rather than on the *quality* of ideas. There are many techniques for doing this, including brainstorming, discussion groups, surveys, suggestion boxes, and so on.

Evaluation and Consensus Decision

In this final step, all of the possible solutions should be evaluated. Strive to arrive at an agreement that is acceptable to all parties concerned. As a rule, consensus decisions will usually result in better solutions than individual decisions. An added value is that consensus decisions influence a better understanding of, and commitment to, an agreement.

Although we have argued for the superiority of win-win strategies over the other two strategies, you should not be surprised to discover that many people and organizations are committed to dealing with conflict via win-lose and lose-lose methods. A significant result of this is that most conflict situations are merely postponed rather than resolved. Perhaps, we should try to find out why there is the tendency to resort to methods that lead to failure. An examination of various personal styles of conflict behavior should prove helpful.

Personal Style in Conflict Behavior

We all have our own personal "response habits" and tendencies when we are faced with conflict. Some of us maintain habits that facilitate conflict resolution; others of us maintain habits that work against conflict resolution. For the latter, the goal should be to eradicate the bad response habits and cultivate good ones.

Our personal style in dealing with conflict situations may be determined by our concerns along two dimensions. The first dimension deals with the extent to which we are willing to assert or express ourselves in the pursuit of our own goals, needs, and values. The second dimension deals with the extent to which we are willing to assert or express ourselves in assisting others and in cooperating with them in the fulfillment of their needs. The *first* dimension is *self-oriented;* The second dimension is *relationship-oriented.* Figure 12-2 portrays the two

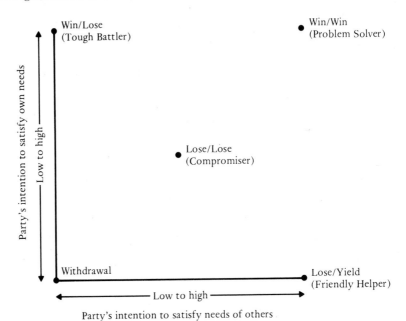

Figure 12-2 Personal Styles in Conflict Behavior. From A. Filley, R. House, and S. Kerr, *Managerial Process and Organizational Behavior* (Glenview, Ill.: Scott, Foresman and Co., 1976), p. 168.

dimensions and four of the personal styles that result from a blending of response habits.

As Figure 12-2 indicates, there are some individuals who go to extremes in assertions to seek their own goals while ignoring the needs of others. This type of behavior inevitably leads to attempts to defeat and wipe out the other party—a confirmed win-lose strategist. Then, there is the other extreme whereby some individuals are terribly nonassertive with respect to their own needs and are inclined to "bend over backward" to accommodate or appease other people. This type of individual generally takes a beating in negotiations (lose-yield).

The four basic personal styles are "Tough Battler," "Friendly Helper," "Problem Solver," and "Compromiser." We can imagine what happens when, for example, a Tough Battler meets a Friendly Helper, a Problem Solver meets

TABLE 12-1 Outcomes in Combinations of Personal Styles in Conflict-Negotiation

	Tough Battler	Friendly Helper	Problem Solver
Tough Battler	Stalemate 80%	Battler wins 90%	Battler wins over 50%
Friendly Helper	X	Stalemate 80%	Problem Solver wins
Problem Solver	X	X	Quick agreement

Source: A Filley, R. House, and S. Kerr, *Managerial Process and Organizational Behavior* (Glenview, Ill.: Scott, Foresman and Co., 1976), p. 169.

a Tough Battler, and so on. Table 12-1 provides a breakdown of the likely results when certain kinds of confrontation occur.[27]

Battlers often find themselves in a stalemate with other battlers. They win when engaging a Friendly Helper, and win over half the time with a Problem Solver. Friendly Helpers engage in stalemates with other Friendly Helpers largely because both parties become excessively concerned with yielding and conceding. Also, confronted by Problem Solvers, a Friendly Helper will generally yield. From Table 12-1, it appears that negotiations proceed well when Problem Solvers meet. They are usually capable of working out confrontations with each other through integrative decision making. Win-win outcomes generally result.

Beyond the concern about conflict resolution strategies and personal style, the leaders and managers of organizations have a responsibility to set up a healthy climate for the management of conflict. At the outset, it was suggested that some conflict is beneficial to organizations. What is needed is sound management of the so-called *conflict interface* How should conflict be managed in the organization? We take up this question in the final section of this chapter.

A Model for Conflict Management

Richard Walton and John Dutton have devised a model, as shown in Figure 12-3, for managing conflict in organizations. In the model, the conflict situation is viewed from two perspectives—the manager's as an intervening force, and the perspective of higher-level managers.

The management of the conflict interface is based on monitoring the behavior of all participants as the conflict develops. The manager's or leader's duty is not to resolve conflict arbitrarily but to act as a referee and advisor as participants are encouraged to reach an acceptable solution.

In order to be a useful, effective referee or counselor, one should be aware of six ground rules for verbal confrontation:

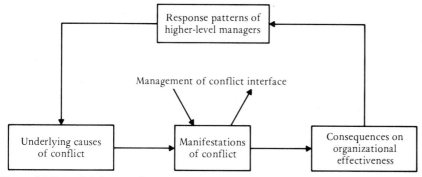

Figure 12-3 Model for Conflict Management. From Richard E. Walton and John M. Dutton, "The Management of Interdepartmental Conflict: A Model and Review," *Administrative Science Quarterly* 14, no. 1 (March 1969): 74.

1. Review past actions and clarify the issues before the confrontation begins.
2. Communicate freely; do not hold back grievances.
3. Do not surprise the opponent with a confrontation for which he or she is not prepared.
4. Do not attack the opponent's sensitive spots that have nothing to do with the issues of the conflict.
5. Keep to specific issues; do not argue aimlessly.
6. Maintain the intensity of the confrontation but ensure that all participants say all that they want to say. If the basic issues have been resolved at this point, agree on what steps will be taken next toward reaching a solution.[27]

A good role for the leader or manager is to help the participants understand why the conflict exists, what the realistic goals are, and what underlying issues ought to be considered or resolved. Help could also be given in obtaining information that may be necessary in order for them to reach a solution. Sometimes, assistance may be given in regulating the frequency of contacts between the participants. The most important contribution is to keep them working toward a true resolution of the conflict.

REVIEW QUESTIONS

1. When does conflict potential exist in an organization?
2. How would you define conflict?
3. What are the various stages through which conflict builds and develops?
4. What are the four conflict situations that may confront members of an organization?
5. How may conflict serve to improve an organization?
6. What are the various factors or variables that affect both the emergence and duration of conflict?
7. What are the characteristics of a win-lose strategy for conflict resolution?
8. What are the five win-lose strategies commonly used in conflict resolution?
9. What are the characteristics of a lose-lose strategy?
10. What are the four lose-lose strategies commonly used in conflict resolution?
11. What are the characteristics that are commonly shared by win-lose and lose-lose strategies?
12. What are the two assumptions on which win-win strategies are based?
13. What are the two common types of win-win strategies for conflict resolution?
14. What are the six steps involved in integrative decision making?
15. How is an attempt at conflict resolution affected by each of the various personal styles?
16. What are the six ground rules for verbal confrontation that should be followed by an effective referee or counselor in conflict resolution?

KEY TERMS AND CONCEPTS FOR REVIEW

- Conflict
- Latent Conflict
- Perceived Conflict
- Felt Conflict
- Manifest Conflict
- Conflict Aftermath

- Conflict Sources
- Win-Lose Strategy
- Lose-Lose Strategy
- Win-Win Strategy
- Integrative Decision Making
- Consensus Decision

CASE STUDY

The manager of an engineering department was concerned about the low productivity of an engineering section. The engineers themselves complained about the time they had to spend with marketing personnel in solving routine quotation problems. Marketing relied on the engineers for sales engineering assistance; individual marketing men consulted the engineers whenever they felt it necessary. These contacts included person-to-person discussions, written inquiries, and phone calls.

The engineering manager issued a ruling that all marketing men should log in and out of the engineering section by signing a register. The stated purpose of the log was to measure the amount of time that marketing employees spent in the engineering section.

When the first marketing man entered the engineering department after the order, he was advised by the engineering secretary to sign the log. The advice was ignored and the individual went to contact an engineer in the accustomed manner. The engineer refused to talk with the marketing man unless the register was signed. Superiors were brought in and an argument ensued, but the marketing man refused to sign and stomped away.

In the next few days some of the marketing people signed the register but many refused. The engineering manager went to the marketing manager and demanded that all marketing men sign the register, since the new policy would not work without complete cooperation. Each of the holdouts consented to sign when they were ordered to do so by their superior, but actually they ceased consulting the engineers.

The relations between the marketing and engineering departments were further strained when individual engineers placed signs on their desks advising the marketing men to sign the register. A previously healthy communication flow between the departments came to a screeching halt. Engineers sometimes contacted marketing men for specialized information, but the marketing department rebelled against the engineers by becoming very uncooperative. Engineering, in reaction to hostile marketing actions, would not advise salesmen when special customers were delayed because of errors in ordering instructions. Several of the marketing men refused to request information from engineering. Naturally, company objectives suffered when salesmen advised their customers that they would not quote on products requiring engineering assistance. Refusal to quote enabled the marketing men to avoid the engineering section but orders were lost in the process.

In talking to a sales manager who refused to sign the register, it was discovered that he objected to the principle of the new arrangement. "Why should I sign? Why can't the engineering secretary log marketing personnel in and out if it is so important? She doesn't do a day's work anyhow! If the manager of engineering had come to the marketing department and talked it over—O.K., I would have cooperated. Not now."

PROBES

1. Identify and discuss the various factors or variables that contributed to a change in interaction patterns.
2. What are the sources of conflict in this case study?
3. Using the integrative decision-making format, plan a strategy for resolving the conflict in this situation.
4. What are some of the beneficial aspects that are likely to emerge from this conflict situation?

Recommended Readings

Doolittle, R. *Orientations to Communication and Conflict*. In *Modcom*, eds. R. Applbaum and R. Hart. Chicago: Science Research Associates, 1976.

Filley, A. *Interpersonal Conflict Resolution*. Glenview, Ill.: Scott, Foresman and Co., 1975.

Jandt, F. *Conflict Resolution Through Communication*. New York: Harper & Row, 1973.

Mack, R. and R. Snyder. "The Analysis of Social Conflict: Toward an Overview and Synthesis." *Journal of Conflict Resolution* 1 (1957): 212–248.

Notes

1. D. E. Beck, "Communication through Confrontation: A Case Study in Intergroup Conflict Reduction." Paper presented at International Communication Association, Phoenix, Arizona, April 22–24, 1971.
2. A Rapoport, *Fights, Games, and Debates* (Ann Arbor: University of Michigan Press, 1960).
3. K. E. Boulding, *Conflict and Defense* (New York: Harper & Row, 1962), p. 5.
4. Ibid., p. 4.
5. T. C. Laughlin and D. P. Kedzic, "Role of Conflict," *Best's Review* 72 (May 1971): 96.

6. R. E. Walton, "Theory of Conflict in Laterial Organizational Relationships." In *Operational Research and the Social Sciences*, ed. J. R. Lawrence (London: Tavistock Publications, 1966), pp. 410–414.

7. M. Sherif, "Superordinate Goals in the Reduction of Intergroup Conflict," *American Journal of Sociology* 63 (1958): 349-358.

8. L. R. Pondy, "Organizational Conflict: Concepts and Models." In J. M. Thomas and W. G. Bennis, eds., *Management of Change and Conflict* (Middlesex, England: Penguin, 1972), pp. 360–366.

9. M. Deutsch, "Conflicts: Productive and Destructive," *Journal of Social Issues* 25 (1969):7–42.

10. A. H. Maslow, "Conflict, Frustration, and the Theory of Threat." In J. K. Zawodny, ed., *Man and International Relations* (San Francisco: Chandler, 1966), pp. 166–169.

11. J. Dollard, L. Doob, N. Miller, O. Mower, and R. Sears, *Frustration and Aggression* (New Haven, Conn.: Yale University Press, 1939).

12. Maslow, Op. cit., pp. 508–509.

13. J. Kelly, *Organizational Behavior* (Homewood, Ill.: Richard D. Irwin, Inc., and Dorsey Press, 1969), p.500–505.

14. R. J. House, "Role Conflict and Multiple Authority in Complex Organizations," *California Management Review* 12, no. 4 (Summer 1970): 53–60.

15. R. C. Day and R. L. Hamblin, "Some Effects of Close and Punitive Supervision," *American Journal of Sociology* 69 (1964): 499–510.

16. S. Sulfrin, *Union Wages and Labor's Earnings* (Syracuse, N.Y.: Syracuse University Press, 1951).

17. J. Templeton, "For Corporate Vigor, Plan a Fight Today," *Sales Management*, 102, no. 13 (June 15, 1969): 32–36.

18. M. Deutsch, "Conflict and Its Resolution." In C. Smith, ed. *Conflict Resolution Contributions of the Behavioral Sciences* (Notre Dame, Ind.: University of Notre Dame Press, 1971), pp. 37–40.

19. M. Deutsch and R. Krauss, "Studies of Interpersonal Bargaining," *Journal of Conflict Resolution* 6 (1962): 52–76.

20. M. Deutsch, "Conflict and Its Resolution", p. 40.

21. A. Filley, *Interpersonal Conflict Resolution* (Glenview, Ill.: Scott, Foresman and Co., 1975), pp. 21–34.

22. Filley, Op. cit., p. 23.

23. Ibid., p. 25

24. A. Filley, R. House, and S. Kerr, *Managerial Process and Organizational Behavior* (Glenview, Ill.: Scott, Foresman and Co., 1976), p. 171.

25. Ibid., p. 171.

26. Ibid., p. 173.

27. Henry Assael, "Constructive Role of Interorganizational Conflict," *Administrative Science Quarterly* (December 1969): 573–582; Richard E. Walton, "Third-Party Roles in Interdepartmental Conflict," *Industrial Relations*, 7, no. 14 (October 1967): 29–43.

13 | Organizational Development

LEARNING OBJECTIVES

After reading this chapter, you should be able to

1. Describe the role of change in organizational settings and discuss some typical attitudes toward change.
2. Identify the significant characteristics of organizational development as synthesized from the various scholarly definitions provided.
3. Describe Beckhard's ten characteristics of organizational effectiveness.
4. Discuss the role of intervention in organizational development.
5. Identify and explain organizational development intervention techniques.
6. Detail the application of the ICA audit to the process of organizational development.
7. Understand and explain the role of the "communication consultant."
8. Conceptualize the impact of development strategies on overall communication training within the organization.

"We shall find it increasingly difficult to understand our personal and public problems without making use of the future as an intellectual tool."[1] This is the way Alvin Toffler succinctly described the challenge of change in the modern world. Once, an understanding of the past was thought to be the surest tool for coping with the present and preparing for the future. Now the future comes upon us at such a rapid rate that it is no longer effective simply for us to react to events as they occur. The individual or institution that hopes to survive, let alone prosper, is required to anticipate coming events, to be "pre-active"— or "proactive," as it is commonly called. This requires a coherent image of the future.

Although the pace and cumulative impact of change are creating new problems for planners, there is nothing new about the process of change. Change has always been a major source of the threats and hopes felt by individuals and organizations. The footnotes of history are crowded with the wreckage and near-wreckage of organizations that attempted to ignore or stop change—the now-defunct typewriter company that rejected the idea of an electric carriage return because it would require expensive retooling; the dairy interests who lobbied through Congress a bill to forbid the upstart margarine industry from comparing its product to butter by name, only to have butter dismissed airily as "the other spread" in a massive advertising campaign by the margerine interests; and the American automobile industry that almost waited too long to recognize the irresistible trend to small, safe, nonpolluting, and fuel-efficient vehicles.

A principal cause (and product) of the accelerating process of change that transforms our world almost while we watch is our enormously improved communication system. Whereas it once took months or years for news of an important event to spread from one continent to another, and sometimes decades for the impact of the event to be felt, today's news spreads in seconds, with its impact often only minutes behind. Moreover, the domino effect of a major event can often be felt in areas remote from its original point of impact.

If granted one wish, most successful organizations would probably wish for a halt to change, so that they could go on forever selling the same product to the same customers without having to make changes in established design or tooling or procedures. Failing this, they would probably ask for control over the process of change and, if that too were denied them, organizations would ask for the ability to anticipate change and turn it to their advantage.

This last wish brings us within the realm of possibility. Many modern organizations are working out procedures for accepting and coping with change rather than fighting it. The objective is to create a flexible, responsive organism that accepts change as a normal and inevitable part of the flow of events, and makes change a positive factor in planning and growth. The process is sometimes referred to as *planned change*, or *organizational development*.

Organizational Development

One analyst describes organizational development as "a response to change, a complex educational strategy intended to change the beliefs, attitudes, values, and structure of organizations so that they can better adapt to new technologies, markets, and challenges, and the dizzying rate of change itself."[2]

Another observer sees organizational development as a strategy which is "(1) planned, (2) organization-wide, (3) managed from the top, to (4) increase organization effectiveness and health through (5) planned intervention in the organization processes, using behavioral science knowledge."[3]

A third analyst describes this process as "a long-range effort to improve an organization's problem-solving capabilities and its ability to cope with changes in its external environment with the help of external or internal behavioral science consultants, or change agents as they are sometimes called."[4]

After reviewing a number of definitions such as these, Raia summarizes: "The emphasis of organizational development, then, is on planned change and is generally directed toward improving system effectiveness. In addition to learning new ways of dealing with complex internal and external relationships, the organization also learns to view change as a natural rather than an extraordinary phenomenon."[5]

Rush offers a more comprehensive definition of organizational development as ". . . a planned, managed, systematic process to change the culture, systems, and behavior of an organization in order to improve the organization's effectiveness in solving its problems and achieving its objective."[6]

We can thus identify the following significant characteristics of planned change or organizational development:

1. It is a managed, systematic, organization-wide process involving the basic philosophy and structure of the organization.
2. It makes use of consultants, or change agents, who are skilled in behavioral science.
3. Its objective is to improve the organization's effectiveness and problem-solving capabilities as a part of a broader competence in dealing with change in the external environment.

As these definitions suggest, organizational development is a complex, far-ranging process. We examine some of the more important facets of this process in the remainder of this chapter.

Organizational Effectiveness

Traditionally, organizational effectiveness is measured according to some complex formula that takes into account profits, efficiency, productivity, growth, morale, turnover, absenteeism, satisfaction, safety, and a host of similar variables. Certainly these values provide a measure of something significant, but they fall far short of measuring effectiveness for the purposes of organizational development. Such an evaluation requires a different set of measurements, which assesses such factors as (1) the climate of trust in the organization, (2) the openness of communication, (3) the openness of problem solving, (4) the degree of commitment to organizational goals, (5) the extent to which conflict centers on ideas rather than on personalities, (6) the intensity of personal involvement in organizational objectives, (7) the level of encouragement and support, and similar components of the psychological atmosphere of the organization.

From the organizational development standpoint, the healthy, effective organization will score high on both types of variables and, more important, will be more successful in dealing with change and the future than one with a lower score. From this standpoint, a healthy organization is one that reflects an open and trusting atmosphere, with freely flowing communication, procedures for confronting rather than avoiding conflict, and a willingness to share responsibility and authority, coupled with expectations of excellence in performance.

Beckhard describes an effective organization in terms of ten characteristics:

1. The total organization, the significant subparts, and individuals, manage their work against *goals* and *plans* for achievement of these goals.
2. Form follows function (the problem, or task, or project, determines how the human resources are organized).
3. Decisions are made by and near the sources of information regardless of where these sources are located on the organization chart.
4. The reward system is such that managers and supervisors are rewarded (and punished) comparably for: short-term profit or production performance, growth and development of their subordinates, creating a viable working group.
5. Communication laterally and vertically is *relatively* undistorted. People are generally open and confronting. They share all the relevant facts including feelings.
6. There is a minimum amount of inappropriate win/lose activities between individuals and groups. Constant effort exists at all levels to treat conflict and conflict situations as *problems* subject to problem-solving methods.
7. There is high "conflict" (clash of ideas) about tasks and projects, and relatively little energy spent in clashing over *interpersonal* difficulties because they have been generally worked through.
8. The organization and its parts see themselves as interacting with each other *and* with a *larger* environment. The organization is an "open system."
9. There is a shared value, and management strategy to support it, of trying to help each person (or unit) in the organization maintain his (or its) integrity and uniqueness in an interdependent environment.
10. The organization and its members operate in an "action-research" way. General practice is to build in *feedback mechanisms* so that individuals and groups can learn from their own experience.[7]

Intervention

In addition to the concept of organizational health already described, organizational development literature has provided another concept called *intervention*.

A number of definitions of intervention have been provided, of which the following is perhaps representative: "Organizational development interventions are sets of structured activities in which selected organizational units (target groups or individuals) engage with a task or a sequence of tasks where the task goals are related directly or indirectly to organizational improvement. Interventions constitute the action thrust of organization development. They 'make things happen' and are 'what's happening.'"[8]

As its name implies, intervention is a deliberate interference with an ongoing process with the intent to alter and improve that process. As anyone who has tried it can testify, this procedure can unleash highly dynamic forces. People in general tend to develop strong proprietary feelings for the familiar, and to resent and resist interruptions and changes, seemingly determined to underscore the impatient comment of Maurice Maeterlinck that "Every progressive spirit is opposed by a thousand men appointed to guard the past." Maeterlinck called this tendency "the immense dead-weight that nature drags along."

In a more analytical tone, Kurt Lewin has described the two counterbalancing forces of drive and restraint that he observes in organizations. Driving forces, according to Lewin, are those that move in the direction of change, whereas restraining forces are those that resist change. Ideally, these forces function to maintain a balance between the chaos of change that comes too rapidly and the stagnation of change that is too slow.

According to Lewin, a managed, permanent change in an organization is a three-step process. In the first, or "unfreezing," step, the forces opposing change are identified and neutralized. Only then is it feasible to take the second, "moving" step in the direction of the desired change. When this has been accomplished, it is then necessary to "refreeze" the organization with regulations and procedures that consolidate the new configuration.[9]

As this analysis implies, the difficulty is not encountered in developing a new organizational format, but in effecting the necessary changes in human behavior to make the new format effective. This is the reason for the emphasis on behavioral psychology in organizational development, as well as for the reliance of this process on communication-oriented intervention techniques. Some of these intervention devices—survey feedback, team building, T-groups, the managerial grid, transactional analysis, planning and goal setting, training (including communication effectiveness training), organizational mirroring, and process consultation—are described in the paragraphs that follow.

Intervention Techniques

Survey Feedback   This technique involves the use of a questionnaire, which is usually anonymous, to determine the organization members' perceptions of their environment. Generally the questionnaire is designed to elicit the respondents' subjective attitudes regarding the organizational climate, decision-making processes, departmental cooperation, reward system, receptivity to suggestions, leadership support, goal consensus and clarity, communication adequacy, work flow coordination, job satisfaction, morale, and the like.[10]

As a rule, the information generated by the questionnaire is summarized and distributed among the participants as a basis for group discussion. The makeup of the discussion group offers a key to the difference between it and many other similar groups. As an organizational development group, its objective is not simply enlightenment, but enlightened action. Consequently, the group does not necessarily include all those who filled out questionnaires— only those with the authority to implement the positive changes indicated by the group's analysis.

This exclusiveness of the discussion group can emerge as one of the strengths of the survey. Much of the most significant information may come from lower-echelon personnel, who may be encouraged to express their feelings with greater candor under the double protection of anonymity and exemption from the analytical process. The survey thus serves as a means of facilitating the upward flow of information and of circumventing the bureaucratic barriers to communication in general.

Team Building   "Team building at its best begins with an understanding of organizational systems, the interaction of groups within the organization, and the interpersonal dynamics at play among individuals within groups."[11]

One of the most dramatic effects of accelerating change has been the exposure of the weakness of the traditional autocratic organizational structure at the point at which it was often supposed to be strongest—the area of decisive response. The image of a high-discipline army of employees dominated by a single general with the authority to make decisions and the power to command unquestioning compliance with those decisions becomes increasingly less realistic as organizations grow in size and complexity. No single individual can be equally expert in all phases of a large modern organization. The professional bureaucracy that is required to manage such an operation takes on a strength of its own, and tends to offer increasing resistance to autocratic decisions. Even lower-echelon personnel resent exclusion from the information-sharing and decision-making processes. Autocratic organizations tend to become inflexibly set in their ways, and pressure to share authority and responsibility may range from mutiny in the ranks to stockholder revolt.

Team building is the organizational development technique for creating a structure to handle shared authority and responsibility effectively. It is a process designed to enable individuals to work together with a sense of unity.

According to Harley, "team development is based on the assumption that any group is strengthened and enabled to work more efficiently if its members continually confront such questions as "Under what conditions can we best learn the information and skills required in order to be an effective working unit? How can this collection of individuals learn to work together most effectively as a team? How can we communicate with one another to make team decisions? What conditions, norms, assumptions, areas of inadequate information impede our performance?"[12]

The workshop is the traditional arena for effective team development. Lehner, one of the more successful workshop developers, describes five major phases in the workshop process.

In the *initiating* phase, Lehner utilizes appropriate techniques to promote a comfortable atmosphere of openness, trust, and idea sharing, and to establish his role of making things happen, facilitating interaction and the production of information, and eventually offering guidance.

In the second, *team diagnostic*, phase, the participants are asked to (a) list positive or negative factors perceived as influencing the individual or team effectiveness or level of satisfaction, (b) evaluate their personal level of openness on a scale of 1 to 5, and (c) list the opportunities perceived for increasing individual and team effectiveness, both in the workshop and in the organization.

The third phase, which Lehner calls *team perscriptive*, focuses on solving problems and making changes to increase effectiveness and satisfaction. The participants work with a five-step problem-solving model to develop an answer to the question "How might I help to increase the effectiveness of our staff meetings?"

The fourth, *team implementation*, phase deals with converting options to action items, using options selected and tested in an earlier phase, determining which option to implement; who does what, when, with whom, for what expected payoff, and under what provisions for follow-up and monitoring.

The final Lehner phase is *team assessment*. Here the group identifies the criteria that might be used to evaluate the effectiveness of staff meetings.[13]

Harley describes a six-point team-development process:

1. Problems are solicited from the participants, usually by individual interview.
2. The group selects a problem for priority work and planning.
3. Information is shared, anonymously if necessary, until a climate of trust is established in which participants feel comfortable commenting openly.
4. Plans and commitments for on-the-job implementation are worked out by the group.
5. Cooperation of subordinates is obtained, if required.
6. The implementation is reviewed and any required changes are made or new alternatives are selected and evaluated.[14]

Team building is a unique communication-oriented intervention process that many organizations have used with extraordinarily good results.

T-Groups "A T-group is an unstructured, agendaless group session for about ten to twelve members and a professional 'trainer' who acts as catalyst and facilitator for the group. The data for discussion are the data provided by the interaction of the group members as they strive to create a viable society for themselves. Actions, reactions, interactions, and the concommitment feelings accompanying all of these are the data for the group.''[15]

T-group, laboratory training, and sensitivity training are all different names for essentially the same process. The objective of this process is to improve the development of a keener awareness of oneself and one's relationships with others.

T-group sessions typically are fairly intense, sometimes running continuously for three or four days, sometimes meeting periodically over a period of a few weeks. These sessions employ a variety of techniques to help the individual clarify his or her values, and to gain greater insight into his or her reactions, emotions, and relationships. Feedback is used extensively to sharpen the individual's awareness of how he or she is perceived by others.

The technique is not without its critics. Some feel that it is not especially effective, whereas others feel that it is manipulative and risks negative effects, such as the loss of self-confidence, if it is badly handled or imposed on individuals who do not respond in the expected way. There can be considerable pressure to surrender one's autonomy to the group and to share problems that the individual may not feel ready to share.

At the same time, the T-group is a quite familiar technique in the organizational development field, where it is generally regarded as an effective, nonthreatening intervention procedure when handled competently.

The Managerial Grid   As noted in earlier chapters, the managerial grid was invented by Blake and Mouton[16] for improving the structure and performance of large organizations. As an intervention technique, it is a massive project occupying four or five years as it systematically applies the six phases into which it is divided.

In the initial, *orientation* phase, the participants thoroughly diagnose their personal management styles and the organizational environment, using questionnaires and other assessment tools.

In the *teamwork development* phase, the participants describe how they would like to operate, analyze the obstacles, define objectives, and set up a realistic schedule for their achievement.

In the *intergroup development* phase, the participants develop a model of the desired relationships, exchange group images, identify the barriers to the desired relationships, and develop their action plan.

In the fourth, *strategic* phase the participants design an ideal model of the organization as it should be, and develop overall strategies, objectives, and policy structure.

In the *implementation* phase, the strategic model is compared to the existing organization, and specific changes to be effected are identified and defined.

In the final phase, called the *systematic critique*, the intervention program and its progress are evaluated for weaknesses and explored for ways to reinforce and consolidate the positive changes that have been made.[17]

Throughout, the managerial grid is employed to measure progress.

Transactional Analysis   Similar to T-group in objective, but drastically different in approach, is the intervention technique called *transactional analysis*, that was popularized by Eric Berne in his 1964 best-seller *Games People Play.*[18]

The general concept of transactional analysis is that we interact with others in one of three specific ego states: parent, adult, or child.

As a parent, we are the guardians of tradition and critics of behavior, and our interaction is loaded with judgmental and coercive terms such as "good," "bad," "always," "ought," and "should." In our adult role, we are objective and understanding, offering orderly processes and effective decision making. In the child state, we are spontaneous, self-centered, and dependent, with behavior patterns that may be carefree, adventurous, angry, frightened, or difficult by turns.

Our roles may change from situation to situation, sometimes within the same interaction. Interactions may be crossed, parallel, or ulterior; and complementary or noncomplementary. When the lines of communication are parallel and complementary, the participants interact and accept each other in an adult/adult, parent/parent, or child/child transaction. The lines become crossed and noncomplementary when one participant is in a parent/child mode and the other responds in a parent/parent mode. In such interactions, one party is communicating as a parent to a child, but the other is responding, not as a child but as a parent. Misunderstandings and disagreements are almost certain to occur in such transactions.

Ulterior transactions are those marked by manipulative devices.

Transactions are also marked by the quality of the "strokes" the participants may exchange. Positive strokes are those characterized by friendliness, admiration, praise, or respect; negative strokes are critical or hostile.

Another contribution of transactional analysis is its characterization of the "o.k." stance, ranging through the full list of possible combinations from a healthy, optimistic assumption, "I'm o.k., you're o.k.," to the depressed and denigrating "I'm not o.k., you're not o.k."[19]

Planning and Goal Setting   In the sense in which the term is used here, planning and goal setting focuses on the individual's relationship to the organization and to other individuals. Although it includes consideration of the organization as it might be and as it is, and how it might be changed and improved, this intervention concentrates on helping individuals to understand themselves and their aspirations.[20]

Planning and goal setting encourages the individual to define his or her career objectives and life objectives, and to assess personal strengths, weaknesses, and potentials. In relationship to the organization, the individual is encouraged to develop personal techniques for avoiding unnecessary conflict, resolving unavoidable conflict, and improving understanding and effectiveness in team interactions.

Training   Training, as an organizational development intervention, is concerned with training people in specific skills and activities in the organizational framework, such as interpersonal communication competence, leadership, performance appraisal, decision making, problem solving, conflict resolution, and other capabilities that contribute to improved organizational performance.

Although training may consist of instruction in performing a specific operation more effectively, as an organizational development process it focuses on the broader communication and interpersonal skills that are designed to improve the way human beings relate to each other in the organization environment.

Organizational Mirroring   One of the most striking differences between the traditional autocratic, vertical organization and the modern organization is the way in which the organizational divisions relate to each other. The older structure was joined at the top. If you wished to communicate with your counterpart in another department, you were expected to "go through channels," which carried your message to the top of your department, transferred it to the top of his or her department, and eventually carried it back down to him or her. The structure was designed to prevent direct interfacing between parallel divisions.

Although modern organizations rely increasingly on interdepartmental teams and task forces that must cooperate across the old vertical divisions, the old parochial psychology still crops up in interdepartmental suspicions and hostilities that interfere with the ability to interface.

Organizational mirroring is an intervention technique for improving teamwork between different groups in the organization, which ordinarily involves three or more teams from different divisions that are having difficulty interfacing. The procedure is to bring the groups together under the auspices of the "host group" that is experiencing the greatest difficulty. The other groups are invited to "mirror"—that is, to express how they perceive—the host group, and to suggest the changes required for them to interface effectively with the group.

The groups are then encouraged to work together to develop action plans for improving their cooperation.

Process Consultation.   Process consultation is an intervention process that is unique to organizational development, in which a skilled consultant, either from inside or from outside the organization, assists a department or unit in becoming more effective. One authority describes the unique characteristic of this type of consultation in the following words: "Where the standard consultant is more concerned about passing on his knowledge, the process consultant is concerned about passing on his skills and values."[21]

The process consultant, in other words, does not analyze the department's problem and propose a solution. The process consultant helps the department develop its own problem-solving capabilities.

The process conslutant is a resource person whose skill consists in facilitating the diagnosis and analysis of organizational problems. His or her function is not to provide an answer to the specific problem at hand but to facilitate the development of a climate for effective communication; provide feedback; raise questions; and encourage the development of the group's ability to define, diagnose, and correct its own malfunctions. In this capacity, the consultant may set up the agenda, referee interactions, provide unbiased feedback, and suggest procedures—anything, in fact, that may help the group to discover its own problem-solving ability.

Improving Communication

It is a common, but serious, error to assume that good communication results from some single talent or skill, such as oratorical ability. Communication—particularly interorganizational communication—is a dynamic, multifaceted interaction, of which such high-visibility components as verbal expression are only contributing parts. Oral and written verbal expression are obviously important means of transmitting meanings, but so are the nonverbal forms—gestures, facial expression, body language—and the semiverbal forms—tone, inflection, pitch, volume, context, and the like.

These make up only half of the communication process—the sender, or transmitter, half. The other half consists of all of the elements involved in receiving and interpreting the message transmitted.

But this still is not the complete communication picture. Medium, format, and setting are also of enormous importance in effective communication. Otherwise excellent communication efforts can be defeated by the use of a letter rather than a personal exchange; a large meeting where a small meeting would be more appropriate; or a large meeting held in a cramped, underventilated room.

For the most effective communication, all of the elements must be not only individually effective but in harmony with each other. To cite an obvious example, you may be doing an excellent verbal job of expressing your appreciation for one employee, while granting a significant raise to a second. In the absence of any clear justification for the different treatment, the first employee can be expected to conclude that he or she is getting contradictory messages from you.

Because of its complexity and virtually limitless possibilities, organizational communication can almost always be improved, sometimes dramatically. One of the most effective organizational development tools for identifying the "soft" areas in a communication system is the ICA audit.

ICA Audit

Like a financial audit, a communication audit is an objective procedure for determining the health and effectiveness of a communication system. Developed by the International Communication Association, the ICA audit has been described as ". . . a research procedure which assesses the effectiveness of the organizational communication system according to a set of standards."[22] The product of the audit is a comprehensive picture of the organization's total communication activity during a specific period of time.[23]

The ICA audit employs the five basic tools described in the following paragraphs.

1. *The mini-audit questionnaire.* Designed to measure general communication activity, this 122-item survey includes 12 demographic questions and up to 34 questions tailored to the individual system being audited. In addition to factual data, the respondents provide their personal perceptions and evaluation of the system, as well as their concept of how an ideal system would operate.

2. *The exploratory interview.* Many individual and group interviews are conducted to fill in the details of the system and individual perceptions of and responses to it.

3. *The network analysis.* This is a computer-analyzed survey of the information flow designed to identify formal and informal communication links, flow-control "gatekeeping" functions, and other factors affecting the movement of communications in the organization.

4. *The communication diary.* This is a log of individual phone calls, meetings, memos, conferences, and conversations, usually maintained over a one-week period, as a measure of communication volume.

5. *Expert observation.* Specialists trained in communication analysis verify and expand the collected data by direct observation.

When completed, all of the audit data is fed into a central computer where it is analyzed independently and in comparison with data from all other audited organizations and arranged in a format for evaluation and action.

Communication Consultant

As a rule, effective communication analysis and system engineering cannot be carried out satisfactorily without the help of a trained communication expert who may be either an outside consultant or a member of the organization with special training. Like the heating engineer in the time-honored story who, after correcting a faulty furnace by hitting it with a hammer, presented a bill for $1,000 ($5 for hitting—$995 for know where to hit), the communication consultant's chief value lies in knowing what to look for, where to look for it, and what to do about it.

The communication analyst will look not only at the upward, downward, and lateral communication channels but also at all of the areas likely to furnish clues to communication malfunctions—-management styles, interpersonal relationships, decision-making and problem-solving procedures, complaints, grievances, turnover and absenteeism statistics, motivation devices, discipline, raise and promotion policies, and so on. If there is a glaring communication problem, the chances are that this problem will affect most or all of these areas and many others as well. If the source of the problem is not readily apparent, it will probably become apparent long before such a broad exploration is completed.

One observer has described communication consultation as a nine-step procedure: (1) exploration, to determine the nature of the problem; (2) agreement, on the need for action and the performance to be expected from each of the parties; (3) diagnosis, to pinpoint and describe the problem; (4)

data analysis —gathering and interpreting the evidence; (5) implementation of a proposed solution; (6) evaluation of the effect of the proposed solution; (7) final report, summarizing orally or in writing the problem, procedure, solution, and evaluation; (8) termination of agreement, identifying and, if possible, resolving any misunderstandings and tying off loose ends; and (9) feedback, for perspective on what was accomplished.[24]

Communication Training

In emphasizing the need for expertise in conducting an analysis of organizational communication, there was no intention to suggest that communication training should be restricted to a few specialists. On the contrary, everything said in this chapter supports the idea that every member of a communication network is a positive or negative contributor to its effectiveness, and that every participant should be regarded as a change agent in improving the system.

To the fullest extent practicable, every member of the organization should be considered a candidate for some appropriate level of training in communication skills. The format may range from simple, one-session classes and seminars to full academic courses of study, depending on circumstances, subject, and depth of exploration. The variety of forms of training is almost limitless. Classes are often conducted in-house by especially capable or trained members of the organization or by experts called in from outside. The classes may take place in a conference room or lunchroom, in an auditorium or a corner of the shop, in an adult education classroom, at a college, or at a private institution.

Careful consideration needs to be given to the subject matter to be included in any communication-training program. The tendency in planning such a program for the first time is to think of communication training only in terms of "public speaking" types of classes. Although such training is undeniably valuable, it may actually be less valuable to the organization than a simple conference on how the organization's communication system is supposed to work and how it ties into a particular department. A given employee may benefit far more from a description of the flow of paperwork through the system than from a session on vocabulary building.

Decision making, conflict resolution, problem solving, conference leadership, tips on how to participate in a group discussion, how to write an effective memo—all of these and many other subjects will suggest themselves to the resourceful training planner faced with the task of improving a specific communication system in a given organization. In many cases, the subjects do not require highly formal or extensive treatment—sometimes a single, informal, one-topic session will prove to be sufficient—but the sessions always have to be planned carefully.

Even the experienced training-program planner often neglects an important communications area that has been touched on only briefly—the role of the receiver in determining the meaning of the message received. No communication training program can be complete without some time being spent on the art of *listening*, which can be interpreted to mean all of the functions involved in receiving any kind of message. Under this topic it is appropriate to take up the whole problem of subjective filtering, and how personal preconceptions, biases, and attitudes affect our interpretation of what we hear and read. This topic provides a natural introduction to the value of feedback as a means of verification that the listener is actually hearing what the speaker intends to transmit.

The all-pervading nature of communication in organizational activity can hardly be overemphasized. Whether it is regarded as a dependent variable—a goal in itself or as an instrumental variable—a subject for analysis as a gauge of organizational health or effectiveness, communication is an integral part of all activities that involve two or more individuals.

For this reason, communication training is one of the most powerful and effective of the intervention techniques employed in organizational development, as well as one of the most sensitive barometers of organizational health. The responsibility for planning a comprehensive communication training program is among the most challenging and absorbing assignments that organizational development offers.

The task begins with the data provided by the audit or a similar analysis, which is virtually a blueprint of the organization's strengths and weaknesses and, at the same time, a projection of the desired ideal. Working from this basic information, the planner usually begins to discover the same elemental communication problems repeated in trouble spot after trouble spot. When these problems are broken down into the classes of skills required to solve them, a program of training can be drawn up for the organization as a whole.

Communication training intervention often proves to be the key to the problem of organizational development.

REVIEW QUESTIONS

1. Discuss the impact of change on the organizational setting and some typical responses to it.
2. How does communication affect change and vice versa? Discuss the role of communication in this change process.
3. Provide a contrast of the different definitions of organizational development with an overall synthesis of some common characteristics.
4. Distinguish between the traditional approaches to organizational effectiveness and the ten characteristics provided by Beckhard.
5. What is the process of intervention in regard to organizational development?
6. What is the survey feedback instrument generally designed to do?
7. What are the various phases of team building? How do Lehner and Harley describe the development process?
8. Describe the goal of the "T-Group" and some criticisms of this process.

9. How does the Blake-Mouton managerial grid function? What are its phases?
10. How are transactional analysis and the technique of planning and goal setting similar? How are they different?
11. Which intervention technique is organizational mirroring similar to? In what ways does it differ from this technique.
12. Delineate the difference(s) between a "process consultant" and the more general "communication consultant."
13. How does the ICA audit function? What is it designed to indicate?

KEY TERMS AND CONCEPTS FOR REVIEW

- Coherent Image of the Future
- Organizational Development
- Organizational Effectiveness
- Intervention
- Unfreezing and Refreezing
- Survey Feedback
- Decisive Response
- Team Development
- Initiating Phase
- Team Diagnostic Phase
- Team Prescriptive Phase
- Team Assessment Phase
- T-Groups
- Managerial Grid
- Orientation Phase
- Teamwork Development Phase

- Intergroup Development Phase
- Strategic Phase
- Implementation Phase
- Systematic critique Phase
- Transactional Analysis
- Parent/Adult/Child
- Strokes
- Planning and Goal Setting
- Organizational Mirroring
- Process Consultation
- ICA Audit
- Mini-audit Questionnaire
- Exploratory Interview
- Network Analysis
- Communication Diary
- Communication Consultation

CASE STUDY

Allied Industrial, a large manufacturing concern providing piece parts to other smaller companies, is experiencing a significant drop in productivity. Within the company, several departments are inexorably linked to one another in the production process. The managers of these individual departments are all responsible to an overall production manager whose job it is to keep up productivity. In addition, the production manager is not well liked.

PROBES

Assume that you are a communications consultant. The president of Allied Industrial has contacted you to intervene in his company. However, because of his devotion to Eric Berne, the president insists that you use a transactional approach to the problem.

1. Of the various techniques described in this chapter, do you agree with the president's choice?
2. Why or why not?
3. What other intervention techniques might you use?
4. Which techniques would best suit this situation? Describe the reasons for your ultimate choice.

Recommended Readings

Argyris, C. *Intervention Theory and Method: A Behavioral Science View*. Reading, Mass: Addison-Wesley, 1970.

Bennis, W. G. *Organizational Development: Its Nature, Origins and Prospects*. Reading, Mass: Additon Wesley, 1969.

Dyer, W. G. *Team Building: Issues and Alternatives*. Reading, Mass: Addison-Wesley, 1978.

French, W. L. and C. H. Bell. *Organization Development*. (2nd Edition) New York: Prentice Hall, Inc., 1978.

Luthans, F. "An Organizational Behavior Modifications Approach to Organizational Development," *Organization and Administrative Science*, Spring, 1976, pp 47–53.

Schein, V. E. and L. E. Greiner. "Can Organization Development be Fine Tuned to Bureaucracies," *Organizational Dynamics*, 5 (1977): 48–61.

Zaltman, G. and R. Duncan. *Strategies for Planned Change*. New York: John Wiley and Sons, 1977.

Notes

1. A. Toffler, *Future Shock* (New York: Random House, 1970), p. 4.
2. W. G. Bennis, *Organizational Development: Its Nature, Origins, and Prospects* (Reading, Mass.: Addison-Wesley Publishing Company, 1969), p. 2.
3. R. Beckhard, *Organizational Development, Strategies and Models* (Reading, Mass.: Addison-Wesley Publishing Company, 1969), p. 9.
4. W. French, "Organizational Development: Objectives, Assumptions, and Strategies," *California Management Review* 2 (1969): 23.
5. A. Raia, "Organizational Development: Some Issues and Challenges," *California Management Review* 14 (1972): 14.
6. H. M. F. Rush, *Organizational Development: A Reconnaissance* (New York: The Conference Board, 1973), preface.
7. Beckhard, op. cit., pp. 10–11.
8. W. L. French and C. H. Bell, Jr., *Organizational Development: Behavioral Science Interventions for Organization Improvement* (Englewood Cliffs, N.J., Prentice Hall, 1973), p. 99.
9. K. Lewin, "Group Decision and Social Change." In *Readings in Social Psychology*, T. Newcomb and E. L. Hartley, eds. (New York: Holt, Rinehart and Winston, 1947), pp. 340–344.

10. For an excellent review of this technique, see French and Bell, op. cit. pp. 130–133.
11. W. I. Gordon and R. J. Hawe, *Team Dynamics in Developing Organizations* (Dubuque, Iowa: Kendall-Hunt Publishing Company, 1977), p. 1.
12. K. Harley, "Team Development," *Personnel Journal* (1971): 439.
13. G. F. Lehner, "Team Development Trainer's Workshop," *Public Administration Review* (1974).
14. Harley, op. cit., p. 442.
15. French and Bell, op. cit., p. 142.
16. R. R. Blake and J. S. Mouton, *Building a Dynamic Corporation Through Grid Organization Development* (Reading, Mass.: Addison-Wesley Publishing Company, 1969).
17. R. R. Blake and J. S. Mouton, "An Overview of the Grid," *Training and Development Journal* 29 (1975): 29–36.
18. E. Berne *Games People Play* (New York: Grove Press, 1964).
19. T. Harris, *I'm OK You're OK* (New York: Harper & Row, 1967).
20. A. P. Raia, *Managing by Objectives* (Glenview, Ill.: Scott, Foresman and Company, 1974), pp. 10–27.
21. E. Schein, *Process Consultation: Its Role in Organization Development* (Reading, Mass.: Addison-Wesley Publishing Company, 1969), p. 135.
22. ICA Audit, International Communication Association, ICA Headquarters Office, Balcones Research Center, 10,100 Burnet Road, Austin, Texas.
23. G. M. Goldhaber, *Organizational Communication*, 2d. ed. (Dubuque, Iowa: William C. Brown Company Publishers, 1979).
24. J. W. Koehler, "The Role of the Communication Consultant." Paper presented at the American Business Communication Association, Atlanta, GA, 1978.

Glossary

activities Tasks performed by a member of the group

adaptable socials Individuals who are capable of moderate, normal behaviors in terms of communicating and interacting with others

aggression Behavior intended to hurt or destroy a source of threat or one's ego

allness Fallacy caused by communicator's belief or attitude that he or she knows everything or can say everything about a particular issue

ambivalents Individuals who are simultaneously attracted toward and repulsed from the goals and objectives of the organization

authoritarians Individuals who rigidly adhere to conventional middle-class values and have an exaggerated concern with such values; are overly submissive toward their kind of authority; are quick to condemn and reject people who violate conventional values

channel Means by which the message is transmitted to the receiver

chronemics Meanings intended by and attached to attitudes regarding time

coercive power Ability to mediate punishments or penalties for others

cohesiveness The extent to which group members are attracted to one another and to the group as a whole

communication consultant One who observes the process of an organization and attempts to provide an analysis of the strengths and weaknesses of the process

communication networks Patterns by which messages are transmitted between three or more individuals

communication style A specialized set of interpersonal behaviors that are used in a given situation

conceptual skill Ability to think in abstract terms

conflict A situation of competition in which the parties are aware of the incompatibility of potential future positions and in which each party wishes to occupy a position that is incompatible with the wishes of the other

conversion The interpersonal process whereby fear of a particular situation or event is converted into complaints of a physical ailment

decoding Translating the message received into an interpretable format by the receiver

defense reaction A sequence of behavior in response to a threat whose goal is to maintain the present state of the self against threat

defensive climate An environment created by the tendency to initiate messages that threaten the comfort and well-being of members of the organization

deliberative listening Ability to hear information, analyze it, recall it at a later time, and draw conclusions from it

denial The process whereby an individual subconsciously "tunes out" or ignores a threatening circumstance

dogmatics High dogmatics are extremely closed-minded; low dogmatics are extremely open-minded

downward communication Transmitting messages downward from superiors to subordinates

economic man A theoretical acquisitor driven by fear of hunger and hope of material reward

empathic listening Receiver participates in the feeling context of the message environment

employee-centered Management approach that concentrates on building a healthy relationship with individual employees and among the work group

encoding Translating information or ideas into words, signs, or symbols

esteem needs Fourth level in Maslow's hierarchy consists of esteem or ego need to be recognized for what one does

executive isolation Individual dispenses with feedback and need for accurate information

expert power Based upon the belief that a person has greater knowledge, skill, or information in a given area

external system The "givens" or circumstances existing in an organization prior to the formation of the group

feedback Response of the receiver to a source's message

feedback loop The cycle over which meanings and messages are shared as a sender initiates the message and the receiver acknowledges receipt and understanding of that message

functional position Refers to the specialized positions outside the direct chain of command

fusion process Power of influence of the individual changing the role expectations of the environment

gatekeeping To block or withhold information

generic problems Problems that are processed according to principles applicable to all problems of the same nature

grapevine Informal communication apparatus in the organization

group A unit composed of three or more individuals who come into personal, meaningful, and purposeful contact with one another on a relatively continuous basis

groupthink Defensive interdependence and in-group loyalties that operate to stifle private misgivings and enforce rigid support of past decisions

hierarchy of needs Five general categories or levels of needs prevalent in an organization

high achievers Individuals who thrive in situations in which they are personally responsible for finding solutions to problems

highstream coupling High-level managers of a company work as a group

horizontal communication Messages between individuals on the same hierarchical level

human skill Ability to weld subordinates into a cohesive unit for action as a coordinated work group

ideation Creating an idea or choosing a piece of information to communicate

indifferents Individuals who regard organizations as systems that inevitably tyrannize workers

inference-observation confusion Resultant of the tendency to treat subjective judgments (inferences) as if they were similar to "real" facts or objective reality

informative communication functions Operates to give information regarding the personnel and organizational operations

integrative communication functions Operate to give the organization unity and cohesion

interactions The initiation of action and the subsequent reaction between two or more individuals

internal system Interrelationship of activities, interactions, and sentiments in a group

interpersonal competence Used to describe interpersonal relationships marked by honesty and openness as against hostility and defensiveness

intervention Interruption of the normal or standard organizational process with the ultimate goal of improving the effectiveness of the organization

intervention techniques Methods used to improve organizational effectiveness, e.g., survey feedback, ICA audit, managerial grid

job-centered Management appproach that focuses on technical and operational details

job enrichment Deliberate upgrading of responsibility, scope, and challenge in work

kinesics Impact of body motion including gestures and movements of the body and posture; one area of nonverbal communication

language A map of ideas conceived or initiated by communicators

legitimate power Right is given, by agreement, to prescribe the behavior of another person

line position Direct chain-of-command posts in authority from the peak to the base of the authority pyramid

lose-lose strategies Strategies based on the maxim that "half a loaf is better than none"; strategies involve compromise, side-payments, arbitration, and resorts to rules.

machiavellians Individuals who habitually manipulate others in order to achieve their own ends

manifest conflict The surface controversy of observable aspects of a conflict situation

maintenance roles Roles that cater to the satisfaction of the social-emotional needs of group members

message The product of a source's ideas and feelings translated (encoded) into a set of symbols

message overload Input of messages that exceeds the employees' ability to process them efficiently

nonprogrammed decisions Decisions that are considered novel, complex, or puzzling enough to require the decision maker to break new ground

nonverbal message Information transmitted through such nonlinguistic means as proxemics, body movement, facial expressions, eye contact, vocalizations, and chronemics

norms Ideals or standards that exist in the minds of group members

open and closed systems Systems are open or closed depending on the degree of interaction permitted across its boundaries within its environment

open communication The probability that an individual will attempt to share accurately his or her feelings, views, and intentions with another on matters pertinent to organizational objectives

organization A structured system of relationships that coordinates the efforts of a group of people toward the achievement of specific objectives

organizational development A managed, systematic, organization-wide process with the objective of improving the organization's effectiveness and problem-solving capabilities in dealing with change

organizational effectiveness A measurement of the ultimate outcomes and impacts (positive or negative) of significant organizational behaviors

organizational feedback Feedback intended to assist the operation of a large organization

overcompensation Making up for limitations or feelings of inadequacy by overacting or overworking

oversocials Individuals who are excessively motivated to initiate and accept interaction with others

participative decision making Individuals participate in the organizational decision making process

personality Way in which the individual relates to his or her circumstances

personal roles Roles that are habitual and unique to the individual

persuasive communication functions Operate to influence the behavior of organizational personnel

physiological needs Lowest ordered need in Maslow's hierarchy; category of primary needs including food, clothing, and shelter

pollyanna-nietzche effect All participants in a decision become convinced not only that their decisions are the right ones but also that their expectations for the decision are certain to be realized

power structure A formalized network that gives particular individuals the right to exercise power over others

prepotency Predominance, strength, or driving force of a particular need

process Series of related operations collectively aimed at producing a particular effect

programmed decisions Standardized decisions that can be carried out without separate evaluation and decision each time

projection Distortion of the perception of one's own personality so as to put or "project" disturbing negative impulses into others; projection may sometimes cause the individual to behave aggressively toward others

proxemics Meanings intended by and attached to the utilization of personal space and physical environment

rabble hypothesis Each individual pursues self-interest to the exclusion of all other motivation

rationalization Invention of excuses or reasons to account for involvement in or with a troubling circumstance

reciprocity of influence Amount of influence a superior has with his or her subordinates depends on the degree to which they can influence him or her

referent power Identification with someone who has certain desirable qualities and wants to be like that person

regulative communication functions Operate to control and coordinate activities of the organization

reward power Ability to mediate rewards for others

role Norms shared by members concerning the behavior of people in certain settings; an individual's conception of the part that he or she plays in an organization; thoughts and actions of individuals

role conflict When an individual is faced with two roles that are incompatible

role expectation How a person in a certain role category is supposed to act

rumors Messages communicated without secure standards of evidence

safety needs Second level of Maslow's hierarchy includes protection from physical harm, ill health, and economic disaster

self-actualization needs Highest level in Maslow's hierarchy consists of the need for self-actualization or self-fulfillment

semantic information distance Difference in understanding and/or information between groups in an organization

sentiments Broad category of affective states or feelings

serial transmission effect Loss of information and meaning that occurs as a message travels or is transmitted by several individuals at different levels or points in an organization

social needs Third level in Maslow's hierarchy includes the need for giving and receiving love and affection; need to accept, associate with, and be accepted by others; and the need to belong or feel oneself a part of social groups

source Individual or group attempting to communicate with another individual or group

staff position Agents of the line of functional authority to which they are attached

status One's social rank or position in a group

status congruency When the things the individual in the organization has and receives are commensurate with his or her status

status symbol Visible, external denotation of one's social or occupational position

supportive climate Environment created by the tendency to initiate messages that are non-threatening

task roles Roles that facilitate the completion of assigned tasks

technical skill Ability to propose practical solutions to concrete organizational problems

technological gatekeeper Individuals used repeatedly as sources of technical information

underlying conflict Deeper cause and the psychological environment of a conflict situation

unique problems Problems that are processed as exceptional cases

upward mobiles An "organization" person; a person who strongly identifies with an organization and is willing to conform to the extreme

upward communication Transmitting messages upward from subordinates to superiors

verbal message Information transmitted through such linguistic means as words or word labels

visual interaction Eye contact established by communicators during face-to-face interaction

vocalization Cues transmitted by the voice through vocal tone, stress, length of hesitation, and pauses

win-lose strategies Use of dominance through power and authority, majority rule, and railroading as methods for reducing conflict

win-win strategies Use of consensus and integrative decision making as modes for resolving conflict

Selected Bibliography

Alderfer, C. P. *Existence, Relatedness, and Growth: Human Needs in Organizational Settings*. New York: Free Press, 1972.

Allen, R. *Organizational Management Through Communication*. New York: Harper & Row, 1977.

Applbaum, R. L., K. W. E. Anatol, E. Hays, O. Jensen, J. Mandel, and R. Porter. *Fundamental Concepts in Human Communication*. San Francisco: Canfield Press, 1973.

———*The Process of Group Communication*. 2d Ed. Palo Alto, Calif.: Science Research Associates, 1979.

Argyris, C. *Integrating the Individual and the Organization*. New York: John Wiley & Sons, 1964.

———*Interpersonal Competence and Organizational Effectiveness*. Homewood, Ill.: Dorsey, 1962.

———"Management Information Systems: The Challenge to Rationality." *Management Science*, 17 (1971): 275–292.

———*Personality and Organization*. New York: Harper & Row, 1957.

Athos, A. G., and R. E. Coffey. *Behavior in Organizations: A Multidimensional View*. Englewood Cliffs, N. J.: Prentice-Hall, 1968.

Back, K. W. "Influence through Social Communication." *Journal of Abnormal and Social Psychology* 46 (1951): 190–207.

Baird, J. *The Dynamics of Organizational Communication*. New York: Harper & Row, 1977.

Barnard, C. *The Functions of the Executive*. Cambridge, Mass.: Harvard University Press, 1938.

Barnlund, D. C., ed. *Interpersonal Communication: Survey and Studies*. Boston: Houghton Mifflin, 1968.

Bass, B. M. *Leadership, Psychology and Organizational Behavior*. New York: Harper & Row, 1960.

Beckhard, R. *Organizational Development, Strategies and Models*. Reading, Mass: Addison-Wesley Publishing Company, 1969.

Bennis, W. G. *Organizational Development: Its Nature, Origins, and Prospects*. Reading, Mass.: Addison-Wesley Publishing Company, 1969.

Berelson, B., and Steiner, G. *Human Behavior: An Inventory of Scientific Findings*. New York: Harcourt, Brace and World, 1964.

Blake, R. R., and J. S. Mouton. *Building a Dynamic Corporation Through Grid Organization Development*. Reading, Mass.: Addison-Wesley Publishing Company, 1969.

——— and ———. "The Fifth Achievement." *Journal of Applied Behavioral Science* 6 (1970): 413–426.

———. *The Managerial Grid*. Houston, Tex.: Gulf Publishing Company, 1964.

Blau, P. M., and W. R. Scott. *Formal Organizations*. San Francisco: Chandler, 1962.

Blauner, R. *Alienation and Freedom*. Chicago: University of Chicago Press, 1964.

Bormann, E. G., S. Howell, R. Nichols, and G. L. Shapiro. *Interpersonal Communication in the Modern Organization*. Englewood Cliffs, N.J.: Prentice-Hall, 1969.

Boulding, K. E. *Conflicts and Defense*. New York: Harper & Row, 1962.

Burgoon, M., J. Heston, and J. McCroskey. *Small Group Communication: A Functional Approach*. New York: Holt, Rinehart and Winston, 1974.

Burke, R. J., and D. S. Wilcox. "Effects of Different Patterns and Degree of Openness in Superior-Subordinate Communication on Subordinate Satisfaction." *Academy of Management Journal* 12 (1969): 319–326.

Campbell, D. T., et al. *Managerial Behavior, Performance, and Effectiveness.* New York: McGraw-Hill, 1970.

Carter, R., ed. *Communication in Organizations: A Guide to Information Sources.* Detroit: Gale Research Company, 1972.

Chase, A. B. "How to Make Downward Communication Work." *Personnel Journal* 49 (1970): 478–483.

Child, J. "Organizational Structure, Environment and Performance—The Role of Strategic Choice." *Sociology* 6 (1972):1–22.

Christie, R., and F. Geis. *Studies in Machiavellianism.* New York: Academic Press, 1970.

Coch, L., and J. R. French. "Overcoming Resistance to Change." *Human Relations* 1 (1948): 512–532.

Cohen, M., and J. March. *Leadership and Ambiguity: The American College President.* New York: McGraw-Hill Book Company, 1974.

Cook, D. M. "The Impact on Messages of Frequency of Feedback." *Academy of Management Journal* 11 (1946): 263–278.

Cyert, R. M., and J. G. March. *A Behavioral Theory of the Firm,* Englewood Cliffs, N. J.: Prentice-Hall, 1963.

Dance, F. E. X. "The Concept of Communication." *Journal of Communication* 20 (1970): 201–210.

Davis, J. "Success of Chain-of-Command Oral Communication in Manufacturing Management Group." *Academy of Management Journal* 11 (1968): 379–387.

Davis, K. *Human Behavior at Work.* 5th ed. New York: McGraw-Hill Book Company, 1977.

Deutsch, M. "Conflicts: Productive and Destructive." *Journal of Social Issues* 25 (1969): 7–42.

DeVito, J. *The Interpersonal Communication Book.* New York: Harper & Row, 1976.

_____*Communicology: An Introduction to the Study of Communication.* New York: Harper & Row, 1978.

DeWhrist, H. D. "Influence of Perceived Infomation-sharing Norms on Communication Channel Utilization." *Academy of Management Journal* 14 (1971): 305–315.

Downs, C., W. Linkugel, and D. M. Berg. *The Organizational Communicator.* New York; Harper & Row, 1977. Chapter 2.

Drucker, P. F. *The Effective Executive.* New York: Harper & Row, 1966.

_____*Technology, Management and Society.* New York: Harper & Row, 1970.

_____*Management: Tasks, Responsibilities, Practaces:* New York: Harper & Row, 1974.

_____*The Practice of Management* New York: Harper & Row, 1954.

Dubin, R. *The World of Work.* Englewood Cliffs, N. J.: Prentice-Hall, 1958.

Dunnette, M., J. Campbell, and M. Hakel. "Factors Contributing to Job Satisfaction and Job Dissatisfaction in Six Occupational Groups." *Organizational Behavior and Human Performance* 2 (1967): 143–174.

Eilon, S. "Taxonomy of Communication," *Administrative Science Quarterly* 14 (1968), 266–288.

Etzioni, A. *Modern Organizations.* Englewood Cliffs, N. J.: Prentice-Hall, 1964.

Falcione, R. L. "Credibility: Qualifier of Subordinate Participation." *The Journal of Business Communication* 11 (1974): 43–54.

Farris, G. F., and F. G. Lim. "Effects of Performance on Leadership, Cohesiveness, Influence, Satisfaction, and Subsequent Performance." *Journal of Applied Psychology* 53 (1969): 490–497.

Ference, T. P. "Organizational Communication Systems and the Decision Process." *Management Sciences* 12 (1970): B83-B96.

Fiedler, F. E. *A Theory of Leadership Effectiveness.* New York: McGraw-Hill, 1967.

_____ and M. M. Chemers, *Leadership and Effective Management.* Glenview, Ill.: Scott, Foresman, 1974.

Filley, A. C. *Interpersonal Conflict Resolution.* Glenview, Ill.: Scott, Foresman, 1975.

Filley, A. C., R. House, and S. Kerr. *Managerial Process and Organizational Behavior.* Glenview, Ill.: Scott, Foresman and Co., 1976.

Fisher, B. A. *Perspectives on Human Communication.* New York: MacMillan Publishing Co., 1978.

Flippo, E. *Management: A Behavioral Approach.* Boston: Allyn & Bacon, 1974.

French, W. L., and C. H. Bell, Jr. *Organizational Development: Behavioral Science Interventions for Organization Improvement.* Englewood Cliffs, N. J.: Prentice-Hall, 1973.

Ghiselli, E. *The Concept of Role and Theoretical Basis for Understanding Organizations.* Bologna: University of Bologna Press, 1963.

Gibb, J. "Defensive Communication." *Journal of Communication* 11 (1961):141–148.

Gibson, J. L., J. Ivancevich, and J. H. Donnelly, Jr. *Organizations: Behavior, Structure, Processes.* Dallas, Tex.: Business Publications, 1979.

Gilmer, B. *Industrial and Organizational Psychology.* New York: McGraw-Hill Book Company, 1971.

Goldhaber, G. M. *Organizational Communication.* 2nd Ed. Dubuque, Iowa: William C. Brown Company, 1979.

Gordon, W. I., and R. J. Hawe. *Team Dynamics in Developing Organizations.* Dubuque, Iowa: Kendall-Hunt Publishing Company, 1977.

Greenwald, A. G. "Behavior Change Following a Persuasive Communication." *Journal of Personality* 33 (1965): 370–391.

Guetzkow, H. "Communication in Organization." In J. G. March, ed., *Handbook of Organizations.* Chicago: Rand McNally, 1965.

Hage, J. *Communication and Organizational Control.* New York: John Wiley & Sons, 1974.

_____M. Aiken, and C. Marrett. "Organization Structure and Communications." *American Sociological Review* 36 (1971): 860–871.

Hall, R. H. *Organizations: Structure and Process:* Englewood Cliffs, N. J.: Prentice-Hall, 1972.

Halpin, A. *Theory and Research in Administration.* New York: MacMillan Publishing Co., 1966.

Haney, W. *Communication and Organizational Behavior: Text and Cases,* rev. ed. Homewood, Ill.: Richard D. Irwin, 1973.

Harvey, J. B., and C. R. Boettger. "Improving Communication within a Managerial Workgroup." *Applied Behavioral Science* 7 (1971): 164–179.

Hellriegel, D., and J. W. Slocum. "Organizational Climate: Measures, Research and Contingencies." *Academy of Management Journal* 2 (1974): 255–280.

_____ and _____ *Management: A Contingency Approach.* Reading, Mass.: Addison-Wesley Publishing Company, 1974.

Herzberg, F. *Work and the Nature of Man.* New York: World, 1966.

Homans, G. C. *Social Behavior: Its Elementary Forms.* New York: Harcourt, Brace & Co., 1961.

_____ *The Human Group.* New York: Harcourt, Brace & Co., 1950.

House, R. J. "Role Conflict and Multiple Authority in Complex Organizations." *California Management Review* 12(1970): 53–60.

Huse, E., and J. Bowditch. *Behavior in Organization*. Reading, Mass.: Addison-Wesley Publishing Company, 1973.

Huseman, R. C., C. M. Logue, and D. L. Freshley, eds., *Readings in Interpersonal and Organizational Communication*, 2d. ed. Boston: Holbrook, 1973.

Indik, B. P., B. S. Georgopoulos, and S. E. Seashore. "Superior-Subordinate Relationships and Performance." *Personnel Psychology* 1 (1971): 357–374.

Jackson, J. "The Organization and Its Communication Problem." *Advanced Management* 24 (1959): 17–20.

Jacobsen, E., and S. Seashore. "Communication Practices in Complex Organizations." *Journal of Social Issues* 7 (1951): 28–40.

Jacobson, W. D. *Power and Interpersonal Relations*. Belmont, Calif.: Wadsworth, 1972.

Kast, F. E., and J. E. Rosezweig. *Organization and Management: A Systems Approach*. New York: McGraw-Hill, 1970.

Katz, D., and R. Kahn. *The Social Psychology of Organizations*. New York: John Wiley & Sons, 1966.

Kelly, H. H. "Communication in Experimentally Created Hierarchies." *Human Relations* 4 (1951): 39–56.

Kelly, J. "Make Conflict Work for You." *Harvard Business Review* 48 (July–August 1970): 103–113.

_____*Organizational Behavior*. Homewood, Ill.: Irwin-Dorsey, 1969.

Kerman, J. B., and R. Mojena. "Information Utilization and Personality." *The Journal of Communication* 23 (1973): 315–327.

Klemmer, E. T., and F. W. Snyder. "Measurement of Time Spent Communicating." *The Journal of Communication* 22 (1972):142–158.

Knapp, M. "A Taxonomic Approach to Organizational Communication." *Journal of Business Communication* 7 (1969): 37–46.

_____ "Public Speaking Training Program in American Business and Industrial Organizations." *Speech Teacher* 18 (1969): 129–134.

_____, and J. McCroskey. "Communication Research and the American Labor Union." *The Journal of Communication*. 8 (1968): 160–172.

Krain, M. "Communication as a Process of Dyadic Organization and Development." *The Journal of Communication* 23 (1973): 392–408.

Lawler, E. E. "Job Attitudes and Employee Motivation: Theory, Research, and Practice." *Personnel Psychology* 23 (1970): 223–237.

_____ *Motivation in Work Organizations*. Belmont, Calif.: Wadsworth, 1973.

_____, L. W. Porter, and A. Tanenbaum. "Managers' Attitudes toward Interaction Episodes." *Journal of Applied Psychology* 52 (1968): 432–439.

Lawless, D. *Effective Management: Social Psychological Approach*. Englewood Cliffs, N. J.: Prentice-Hall, 1972.

Lawrence, P. R., and J. W. Lorsch. *Organization and Environment*. Cambridge, Mass.: Harvard University Press, 1967.

Leavitt, H. J. *Managerial Psychology*, 3d ed. Chicago: University of Chicago Press, 1972.

Lesikar, R. *Business Communication*. Homewood, Ill.: Richard D. Irwin, 1972.

Levinson, H. "Management by Whose Objectives?" *Harvard Business Review* 48 (1970): 125–234.

Lewis, P. V. *Organizational Communication: The Essence of Effective Management*. Columbus, Ohio: Grid, Inc., 1975.

Likert, R. *The Human Organization: Its Management and Value*. New York: McGraw-Hill Book Company, 1967.

_____*New Patterns of Management*. New York: McGrawHill Book Company, 1961.

McClelland, J. *The Achieving Society*. Princeton, N. J.: Van Nostrand, 1961.

McCroskey, J. C., and L. R. Wheeless. *Introduction to Human Communication*. Boston: Allyn and Bacon, 1976.

March, J. G., and H. A. Simon. *Organizations*. New York: John Wiley & Sons, 1958.

_____*Handbook of Organizations*. Chicago: Rand McNally & Co., 1965.

Margulies, N., and J. Wallace. *Organizational Change: Techniques and Applications*. Glenview, Ill.: Scott, Foresman, 1973.

Marrow, A. J., D. G. Bowers, and S. E. Seashore. *Management by Participation*. New York: Harper & Row, 1967.

Maslow, A. *Motivation and Personality*. New York: Harper & Row, 1954.

Mayo, R. *The Human Problems of an Industrial Civilization*. Boston: Graduate School of Business Administration, Harvard University, 1946.

Miles, R. E. *Theories of Management: Implications for Organizational Behavior and Development*. New York: McGraw-Hill Book Company, 1975.

Miller, D., and W. Form. *Industrial Sociology: The Sociology of Work Organizations*. New York: Harper & Row, 1964.

Mills, T. M. *The Sociology of Small Groups*. Englewood Cliffs, N.J.: Prentice-Hall, 1967.

Morgan, J. S. *Managing Change*. New York: McGraw-Hill Book Company, 1972.

Myers M. S. *Every Employee a Manager*. New York: McGraw-Hill Book Company, 1970.

Odiorne, G. S. "An Application of the Communication Audit," *Personnel Psychology* 7 (1954): 235–243.

Perrow, C. *Complex Organizations: A Critical Essay*. Glenview, Ill.: Scott, Foresman, 1972.

Pondy, L. R. "Organizational Conflict: Concepts and Models." *Administrative Science Quarterly* 12 (1967): 296–320.

Porter, L. W. "A Study of Perceived Need Satisfaction in Bottom and Middle Management Jobs." *Journal of Applied Psychology* 45 (1961): 1–10.

_____. "Job Attitudes in Management: Perceived Deficiencies in Need Fulfillment as a Function of Job Level," *Journal of Applied Psychology* 46 (1962): 375–384.

_____"Job Attitudes in Management: Perceived Deficiencies in Need Fulfillment as a Function of Size of Company." *Journal of Applied Psychology* 47 (1963): 386–397.

_____and E. E. Lawler. "The Effects of Tall and Flat Organization Structures on Managerial Job Satisfaction." *Personnel Psychology* 17 (1964): 135–148.

_____, E. E. Lawler, and J. R. Hackman. *Behavior in Organizations*. New York: McGraw-Hill Book Company, 1975.

_____ and K. H. Roberts, "Communication in Organizations." In D. Dunnette ed., *Handbook of Industrial and Organizational Psychology*. Chicago: Rand McNally, 1976.

Praetus, R. *The Organizational Society*. New York: Alfred A. Knopf, 1962.

Price, J. *Organizational Effectiveness*. Homewood, Ill.: Irwin-Dorsey Press, 1968.

Raia, A. P. *Managing by Objectives*. Glenview, Ill.: Scott, Foresman and Company, 1969.

Rapoport, A. *Fights, Games and Debates*. Ann Arbor: University of Michigan Press, 1960.

Read, W. H. "Communicating across the Power Structure." *Cost and Management* (June 1967): 25–28.

_____"Upward Communication within Industrial Hierarchies." *Human Relations* 15 (1962): 3–15.

Redding, W. C. *Communication within the Organization*. New York: Industrial Communication Council, 1972.

_____and G. A. Sanborn, eds. *Business and Industrial Communication: A Source Book*. New York: Harper & Row, 1964.

Reitz, H. J. *Behavior in Organizations.* Homewood, Ill.: Richard D. Irwin, 1977.

Ritti, R. R., and F. H. Gouldner. "Professional Pluralism in an Industrial Organization." *Management Science* 16 (1969): B233–246.

Roberts, K. H., and C. A. O'Reilly. "Failure in Upward Communication in Organizations: Three Possible Culprits." *Academy of Management Journal* 17 (1974): 205–215.

Ross, J. E. *Management by Information System.* Englewood Cliffs, N.J.: Prentice-Hall, 1970.

Rudolph, E. E. "Informal Human Communication Systems in a Large Organization." *Journal of Applied Communications Research* 1 (1973): 7–23.

Rush, H. M. F. *Organizational Development: A Reconnaissance.* New York: The Conference Board, 1973.

Russell, G. H., and K. Black. *Human Behavior in Business.* Englewood Cliffs, N.J.: Prentice-Hall, 1972.

Sarbin, T. T., and V. L. Allen. "Increasing Participation in a Natural Group Setting: A Preliminary Report." *The Psychological Record* 18 (1968): 1–7.

Schein, E. H. "The Individual, the Organization, and the Career: A Conceptual Scheme." *Journal of Applied Behavioral Science* 7 (1971): 401–426.

_____*Organizational Psychology,* 2d ed. Englewood Cliffs, N.J.: Prentice-Hall, 1970.

_____*Process Consultation: Its Role in Organization Development.* Reading, Mass.: Addison-Wesley Publishing Company, 1969.

Schneider, A. E., W. C. Donaghy and P. J. Newman. *Organizational Communication.* New York: McGraw-Hill Book Company, 1975.

Schneider, B. "Organizational Climate: Individual Preferences and Organizational Realities." *Journal of Applied Psychology* 56 (1972): 211–217.

_____and C. J. Bartlett. "Individual Differences and Organizational Climate: I. The Research Plan and Questionnaire Development." *Personnel Psychology* 21 (1968): 323–333.

Scholz W "Communication Networks." In L. Berkowitz, ed. *Advances in Experimental Social Psychology,* vol. 1. New York: Academic Press, 1964.

Scott, W., and T. Mitchell, *Organizational Theory, A Structural and Behavioral Analysis.* Homewood, Ill.: Richard D. Irwin, 1972.

Seashore, S. E., and D. G. Bowers. "Durability of Organizational Change." *American Psychologist* 25 (1970) 227–233.

Sedwick, R. C. *Interaction: Interpersonal Relationships in Organizations.* Englewood Cliffs, N.J.: Prentice-Hall, 1974.

Selznick, P. *Leadership in Administration.* Evanston, Ill.: Row, Peterson, 1957.

Shull, F., A. Delbecq, and L. Cummings. *Organizational Decision Making.* New York: McGraw-Hill, 1970.

Sigband, N. B. *Communication for Management and Business.* Glenview, Ill.: Scott, Foresman, 1969, 1976.

Simon H. A. *Administrative Behavior,* 2d ed. New York: Macmillan 1957.

_____. *The New Science of Management Decision.* New York: Harper & Row, 1960.

Skinner, B. F. *About Behaviorism.* New York: Alfred A. Knopf, 1974.

Smith, R. L., G. M. Richetto, and J. P. Zima. "Organizational Behavior: An Approach to Human Communication." In R. Budd and B. Ruben, *Approaches to Human Communication.* New York: Spartan Books, 1972, pp. 269–389.

Starbuck, W. H. "Organizational Growth and Development." In J. G. March, ed. *Handbook of Organizations.* Chicago: Rand McNally, 1965.

Steers, R. M., and L. W. Porter, eds. *Motivation and Work Behavior.* New York: McGraw-Hill Book Company, 1975.

Stine, D., and D. Skarzenski, "Priorities for the Business Communication Classroom: A Survey of Business and Academe," *The Journal of Business Communication* 16 (1979): 15–30.

Stogdill, R. M. *Individual Behavior and Group Achievement.* New York: Oxford University Press, 1959.

———. "Personal Factors Associated with Leadership." *Journal of Psychology* 25: 35–71.

———. "The Structure of Organizational Behavior." *Multivariate Behavioral Research* 2 (1967): 47–61.

Sutton, H., and L. W. Porter. "A Study of the Grapevine in a Governmental Organization." *Personnel Psychology* 21 (1968): 223–230.

Swanson, D. L. and J. G. Delia. *The Nature of Human Communication.* Palo Alto, Calif.: SRA, 1976.

Svetlik, B., E. Prien, and G. Barrett. "Relationships between Job Difficulty, Employee's Attitude toward His Job, and Supervisory Ratings of the Employee Effectiveness." *Journal of Applied Psychology* 48 (1964): 320–324.

Taguiri, R., and G. H. Litwin. *Organizational Climate: Explorations of a Concept.* Cambridge, Mass.: Harvard University Press, 1968.

Tannenbaum, R., and S. Davis. "Values, Man and Organizations." In W. Schmidt, ed. *Organizational Frontiers and Human Values.* Belmont, Calif.: Wadsworth, 1970, pp. 124–149.

———, and W. Schmidt. "How to Choose a Leadership Pattern." *Harvard Business Review* 36 (1958): 95–101.

Taylor, F. W. *The Principles of Scientific Management.* New York: Harper & Row, 1911.

———. *Shop Management.* New York: Harper & Row, 1911.

Thayer, L. *Communication and Communication Systems.* Homewood, Ill.: Richard C. Irwin, 1968.

———"Communication and Organizational Theory." In F. E. X. Dance, ed., *Human Communication Theory.* New York: Holt, Rinehart and Winston, 1967.

Thompson, A. A. "Employee Participation in Decision Making: The TVA Experience." *Public Personnel Review* 18 (1967): 82–88.

Tortoriello, T., S. Blatt, and S. DeWine. *Communication in the Organization: An Applied Approach.* New York: McGraw-Hill Book Company, 1978.

Tosi, H. "A Re-examination of Personality as a Determinant of the Effects of Participation." *Personnel Psychology* 23 (1970): 91–99.

———, ed. *Theories of Organization.* Chicago: St. Clair Press, 1975.

———, and W. Hamner, eds. *Organizational Behavior and Management: A Contingency Approach.* Chicago, St. Clair Press, 1974.

Turner, A. N., and G. F. Lombard. *Interpersonal Behavior and Administration.* New York: Free Press, 1969.

Valenzi, E., and I. R. Andrews. "Individual Differences in the Decision Process of Employment Interviewers." *Journal of Applied Psychology* 58 (1973): 49–53.

Vardaman, G., and C. Halterman. *Managerial Control through Communication: Systems for Organizational Diagnosis and Design.* New York: John Wiley & Sons, 1968.

———, and P. Vardaman. *Communication in Modern Organizations.* New York: John Wiley & Sons, 1973.

Vroom, V. H. "Leadership." In M. D. Dunnette, ed., *Handbook of Industrial and Organizational Psychology.* Chicago: Rand McNally, 1976.

———, *Work and Motivation.* New York: John Wiley & Sons, 1964.

———, L. D. Grant, and T. S. Cotton. "The Consequences of Social Interaction in

Group Problem Solving," *Organizational Behavior and Human Performance* 4 (1969): 77–95.

———, and P. W. Yetton. *Leadership and Decision Making.* Pittsburgh: University of Pittsburgh Press, 1973.

Walton, E. "Motivation to Communicate." *Personnel Administration* 25 (1962): 17–19.

Walton, R. E. *Interpersonal Peace Making: Confrontations and Third-Party Consultation.* Reading, Mass.: Addison-Wesley, 1969.

Wanous, J. P. "Effects of a Realistic Job Preview on Job Acceptance, Job Attitudes, and Job Survival." *Journal of Applied Psychology* (1973): 327–332.

Watson, J. B. *Behaviorism.* Chicago: University of Chicago Press, 1930.

Webber, R. *Management: Basic Elements of Managing Organizations.* Homewood, Ill.: Richard D. Irwin, 1979.

Weick, K. E. *The Social Psychology of Organizing.* Reading, Mass.: Addison-Wesley Publishing Company, 1969.

Wells, W. *Communication in Business.* Belmont, Calif.: Wadsworth, 1968.

White, B. F., and L. B. Barnes. "Power Networks in the Appraisal Process." *Harvard Business Review* 49 (1971): 101–109.

Whyte, W. H. *The Organization Man.* New York: Doubleday, 1956.

Wofford, J. C., E. Gerloff, and R. Cummons. *Organizational Communication: The Keystone to Managerial Effectiveness.* New York: McGraw-Hill Book Company, 1977.

Woodward, J. *Industirial Organization: Theory and Practice.* London: Oxford University Press, 1965.

Yalom, I. D. *The Theory and Practice of Group Psychotherapy.* New York: Basic Books, 1970.

Yoder, D. *Personnel Management and Industrial Relations,* 6th ed. Englewood Cliffs, N.J.: Prentice-Hall, 1970.

Yukl, G. "Toward a Behavioral Theory of Leadership." *Organizational Behavior and Human Performance* 6 (1971): 414–440.

———, and K. Wexley. *Readings in Organizational and Industrial Psychology.* London: Oxford University Press, 1971.

Zajonc, R. B., and S. M. Sales. "Social Facilitation of Dominant and Subordinate Responses." *Journal of Experimental Social Psychology* 2 (1966): 160–168.

Zand, D. E. "Trust and Managerial Problem Solving." *Administrative Science Quarterly* 17 (1972): 229–239

Zelko, H. P. *The Business Conference: Leadership and Participation.* New York: McGraw-Hill Book Company, 1969.

———. *Successful Conference and Discussion Techniques.* New York: McGraw Hill Book Company, 1957.

———, and F. E. X. Dance. *Business and Professional Speech Communication,* 2nd ed. New York: Holt, Rinehart and Winston, 1978.

Index